Sports Marketing

To my family! You remain a tireless source of joy and you have an amazing tolerance for my reclusiveness when deadlines loom. I love you all!
JD

To Matt, Mom, Dad, and Mike. Thanks for following me around the world and back in all of my pursuits! I wouldn't be anywhere near where I am today without your love, support, and jabs.
JZH

# Sports Marketing

## Creating Long Term Value

John A. Davis
*SP Jain School of Global Management, Singapore-Dubai-Sydney*

Jessica Zutz Hilbert
*University of Oregon, USA*

**Edward Elgar**
Cheltenham, UK • Northampton, MA, USA

Published by
Edward Elgar Publishing Limited
The Lypiatts
15 Lansdown Road
Cheltenham
Glos GL50 2JA
UK

Edward Elgar Publishing, Inc.
William Pratt House
9 Dewey Court
Northampton
Massachusetts 01060
USA


A catalogue record for this book
is available from the British Library


Library of Congress Control Number: 2013938963

ISBN  978 1 84844 841 4 (cased)
ISBN  978 1 78254 819 5 (paperback)
ISBN  978 1 78254 927 7 (eBook)

Typeset by Servis Filmsetting Ltd, Stockport, Cheshire
Printed and bound in Great Britain by T.J. International Ltd, Padstow

# Contents in brief

# Full contents

# About the authors

## John A. Davis

John Davis's career spans both the academic and business worlds. He is the Dean, Global MBA and Masters of Global Business and Professor of Marketing at SP Jain School of Global Management Dubai/Singapore/Sydney. He is the author of several acclaimed marketing books: Measuring Marketing: 110+ Key Metrics Every Marketer Needs (2nd edition ©2013; 1st edition ©2006); The Olympic Games Effect (2nd edition ©2012; 1st edition ©2008); Competitive Success: How Branding Adds Value (©2010); Magic Numbers for Sales Management (©2007); and Magic Numbers for Consumer Marketing (©2005). He is a contributing author to Fast Track to Success-Marketing (©2009). He has received several teaching awards: the 2012 BAC Teaching Award from University of Oregon; the 2010 'Best Professor of Marketing' award in 2010 from Asia's Best B-School Awards; the 'Most Inspiring/Distinguished Teacher' award (2007); and Dean's Teaching Honors every year from 2004-2009 from Singapore Management University. John's prior positions were: Interim Department Coordinator, Lundquist College of Business-University of Oregon; Department Chair and Professor of Marketing at Emerson College; Professor of Marketing Practice and Director of the Center for Marketing Excellence at Singapore Management University. He is a visiting professor at the International Olympic Academy in Olympia, Greece, and has also taught at University of Washington, UC Davis and Stanford University, and in partner programs with faculty from University of Chicago, INSEAD, Emory, Munich Business School, and the European Business School. In business, he has won awards as the leader of global marketing organizations for Fortune 500 companies and two companies he founded with private investor groups, including Brand New View (www.brandnewview.com), where he remains chairman. John has spoken at conferences around the world, from Tokyo to Cairo to San Francisco to Shanghai, including TEDx, and has been interviewed by global media, including: the BBC, MSNBC, CNBC, ChannelNewsAsia, Bloomberg, and NPR. He received his M.B.A. from Columbia University and his B.A. from Stanford University.

John and his amazing wife Barb have three terrific children: Katie, Chris and Bridget. They have 4 pets: Milo, Grinner (both are dogs, although

Grinner fancies herself as Commander of the Universe while Milo is happy supporting her delusions of grandeur), Printer Mo and Zola (the latter two are cats that find endless amusement playing with a simple feather attached to a stick, to the extreme annoyance of Grinner).

## Jessica Zutz Hilbert

Jessica Zutz Hilbert was born in Wilmington, Delaware. After attending Stanford University where she earned a B.A. in Communication and played varsity field hockey and softball, she spent several years in hospitality management in Los Angeles, California. A recipient of a Pacific-10 Conference Post Graduate scholarship, she is pursuing concurrent Juris Doctorate and Master of Business Administration degrees at the University of Oregon where she has studied business law and sports business at the Warsaw Sports Marketing Center. During her time at the University of Oregon, she co-founded an artisan ketchup company called Red Duck Ketchup. With her husband Matt and daughter, she lives in Eugene, Oregon where she enjoys playing soccer, ice hockey, and softball as well as cooking, baking and wine and beer tasting.

# Acknowledgments

This book and its emphasis on global sports marketing would not be possible without the energetic support of the editorial and publishing team at Edward Elgar Publishing. This project was first conceived when Alex Pettifer, Editorial Director at Edward Elgar Publishing, and John Davis met in Singapore to discuss books related to sports. Both agreed that sports texts to date offered useful foundational knowledge about traditional marketing practices as applied to sports, but that crucial discussions about the globalization of business and sports were either not fully explored or were missing entirely. This book is the result of those early discussions.

As this book developed, Jessica Zutz Hilbert joined the project, initially to conduct additional supporting research. Her contributions quickly evolved and included the numerous case studies and examples discussed throughout this book. She evolved from first-rate researcher to co-author on the strength and quality of her work. In addition, she has also been pursuing dual graduate degrees in business and law at University of Oregon while also serving as a teaching assistant for a course on Olympic Sports Marketing. Jessica has also been on an award-winning entrepreneurship team in the consumer foods business, and she and her husband, Matt, have co-founded a ski and snowboard company called Deviation. Needless to say, she is a tireless and talented professional whose mark on the world will be significant.

While this book began several years ago when John Davis was Professor of Marketing Practice at Singapore Management University, it was completed while he was on the faculty at the Lundquist College of Business at the University of Oregon. The Lundquist College of Business offers excellent undergraduate and graduate degree programs with an option to concentrate in sports business through its Warsaw Sports Marketing Center, recognized as the top sports business program in the United States and designed to help students prepare for careers in the sports industry. There are several core Lundquist faculty members whose work is inspiring, including: Lynn Kahle, the Ehrman Giustina Professor of Marketing, who has been a consistent source of support and whose academic research in consumer behavior and sports marketing has been at the top of the field for many years; David Boush, the Gerald B. Bashaw Professor, Senior Associate

Dean for Administration; T. Bettina Cornwell, the Edwin E. & June Woldt
Cone Professor of Marketing, Director of Research for the Warsaw Sports
Marketing Center; Dennis Howard, the Philip H. Knight Professor of
Business, Emeritus; and Bob Madrigal, Associate Professor of Marketing.
All are terrific colleagues whose dedication to new insights in marketing is
unwavering. After completing this book, John returned as Dean – Global
MBA and Masters of Global Business, and Professor of Marketing at the
SP Jain School of Global Management Dubai/Singapore/Sydney, ranked in
the top 100 business schools worldwide by the *Financial Times*, and recognized for its innovative approach to the study of global business. There are
additional people from academia around the world whose lifetime of work
remains an important and motivating force:

- Dr. Kostas Georgiadis, Dean of the International Olympic Academy in
  Olympia, Greece and Vice Rector of the University of Peloponnese;
- Dr. Benoit Seguin, School of Human Kinetics at the University of Ottawa
  and Supervising Faculty at the International Olympic Academy;
- Dr. Glenn Hubbard, Dean and Russell L. Carson Professor of Finance
  and Economics, Columbia Business School at Columbia University in
  the City of New York;
- Richard H. Burton, David B. Falk Professor of Sport Management, David
  B. Falk College of Sport and Human Dynamics, Syracuse University;
- Dr. Dae Ryun Chang, Professor of Marketing/International Business,
  Yonsei School of Business, Yonsei University;
- David Montgomery, former Dean of the Lee Kong Chian School of
  Business at Singapore Management University and the Sebastian S.
  Kresge Professor of Marketing (Emeritus) at Stanford Business School;
- Dr. Jin Han, Professor of Marketing at Singapore Management
  University;
- Nitish Jain, President of S P Jain School of Global Management;
- Dr. Bernd Schmitt, Robert D. Calkins Professor of International Business
  at Columbia Business School;
- Dr. Jean-Claude Larreche, Alfred H. Heineken Chair at INSEAD and
  Founder/CEO of StratX;
- Dr. Janis Andersen, former Dean-School of Communication at Emerson
  College;
- Dr. George Foster, the Konosuke Matsushita Professor of Management,
  Stanford Graduate School of Business.

There are far more industry leaders whose expertise and insights have been
instrumental in understanding the role of businesses in fostering a successful sports industry than can be adequately listed here. Key among them are:

David Haigh, Founder/CEO of Brand Finance; Zach Nelson, President and CEO of NetSuite; David Maddocks, former Chief Marketing Officer of Converse; Steve Leonard, President of EMC Asia Pacific/Japan; Kevin Gould, Regional President for Asia Pacific of ACE Life Insurance; and Brad Gebhard, former CEO USA of Hi-Tec. To those not listed, your efforts are deeply appreciated and have not gone unnoticed!

Most of all, we would like to thank our respective families, whose support has been necessary to maintaining our collective sanity.

# Introduction

## Why this book?

Sports marketing has become a significant academic field of study at the same time that it has also become an important strategic tool for companies seeking to enhance their brand reputations and value. Over the past ten to 15 years several good text books about sports marketing have been published, offering a highly structured approach to the field that borrows heavily from traditional, non-sports marketing. Most of these works have emphasized sports in the United States, with some references to international sports such as football (soccer) and, particularly, the FIFA World Cup. We owe a debt of gratitude to these authors for developing a superb foundation for the study of sports marketing. John Davis's own research on sports marketing and Olympic Games (*The Olympic Games Effect*, 2012, John Wiley & Sons) revealed important insights into why companies sponsor the Olympics, how the Olympic Games have built one of the world's most successful sports brands, and why fans follow the Olympics. The combination of these findings reinforced our excitement that the timing is right for a sports marketing book with a truly global orientation.

This book grabs the proverbial baton from that first leg of foundation-building sports marketing books and accelerates quickly toward a more global, action-oriented perspective. In this book we focus on understanding sports marketing activities that are likely to produce successful results in different international markets. We developed over 20 new case studies specifically designed to illuminate the challenges associated with international sports marketing issues, while also showing the connection to important marketing tools. Furthermore, we emphasize the important role brand building plays in developing value for sports marketing's many stakeholders, including fans, athletes, owners and leagues. We believe this approach reflects the rapidly globalized business world in which companies are seeking ways to connect directly and authentically with fans in those markets.

## How this book is organized

The book takes you through a comprehensive review of the sports business, providing fundamental information marketers use to guide their conceptual, analytical and sports marketing implementation plans. The first six chapters are designed to provide a broad, strategic overview of sports and sports marketing around the world, including leagues, sports histories and legacies, the allure of sports for companies and fans alike, and the types of measures marketers can use to help evaluate their sports marketing efforts.

## Chapter 1  Sports marketing value chain

This chapter discusses sports marketing in the context of well-known leagues and sports events, the five Ps of marketing, the cycle of value in sports, and the sports value chain. Students will also learn about the valuations of the world's leading sports clubs/teams. The end of chapter case studies are: Case Study 1, about NASCAR (the National Association for Stock Car Auto Racing) and the challenges this sport faces as it works toward increasing fan interest; Case Study 2, about Oklahoma City Thunder of the NBA (National Basketball Association), which was formerly located in Seattle, Washington and known as the Seattle SuperSonics. The case presents students with important questions related to fan loyalty, city identity, and a team's brand reputation.

## Chapter 2  The sports marketing context

Chapter 2 compares and contrasts sports business with non-sports industries, to help students understand both the similarities and differences in these two business worlds. A discussion follows about league structure and competition models, explaining the ways professional sports leagues in different countries allocate revenues. Students are then introduced to brand planning and brand value frameworks, which help identify where reputation and values can be effectively leveraged. The end of chapter case studies are: Case Study 1, about the Australian Football League and its efforts to grow abroad, asking students to consider how international expansion might affect a sport's national identity; Case Study 2, about the New York Red Bulls and its initiatives to build an identity, both for the club and for Red Bull.

## Chapter 3  Sports histories and sports fans

Discusses important historical antecedents of different sports around the world and how fans have come to appreciate the unique qualities of each. A discussion about fan segmentation ensues, using classic marketing approaches to customer identification. A follow on discussion about three customer layers: intense enthusiasts, shared enthusiasts, and casual enthusiasts shows students how identifying fan needs can uncover a wealth of useful findings that will help companies fine-tune their customer-oriented sports marketing activities. The end of the chapter case study is: The Monaco Grand Prix, its importance in the world of F1 racing, and its impact on local citizens and fans.

## Chapter 4    Fans – delivering value through deep relationships

This chapter continues the discussion about fans in Chapter 3, emphasizing the importance of developing deep, profitable relationships. We show why sports are appealing to fans, helping sports marketers understand their motivations more clearly so that sports marketing activities can be planned accordingly. The end of chapter case study is: A look at the fans of the National Hockey League's Vancouver Canucks, offering a cautionary tale about the risks to a sport's reputation, when fan violence grows.

## Chapter 5    Association benefits of sports marketing

Chapter 5 the benefits, and risks, companies realize when they use sports as an important part of their marketing investment. Companies use sports marketing partly to develop an association with their sport of choice in the minds of that sport's followers, thereby hopefully helping the marketplace view the company in a more favorable light. In addition, the options available to companies considering sports marketing as a growth strategy are reviewed, with examples of companies employing each of the market growth choices. The end of chapter case study is: Tiger Woods and the 2009 scandal resulting from his personal life travails. Students will weigh the impact of the scandal on sponsors, including the impact to the company's image when negative issues arise.

## Chapter 6    Sports marketing measures

This chapter discusses select measures that sports marketers can use to determine the success or failure of their strategic sports marketing activities. The end of the chapter case study is: Visa and its sponsorship of the Olympic Games, which provides useful guidance about the merits of mega-sports events sponsorships and the longevity of such investments.

Chapters 7–8 are designed to help sports marketers in their understanding of the ways to develop action plans guided by their company's overall vision and unique points of distinction. This includes an exploration of the new five Ps of sports marketing, as well as insights about the sources of sports marketing revenues.

## Chapter 7    *Sports marketing strategy and activation planning*

Chapter 7 expands on a key aspect of the brand planning discussion from Chapter 2: how sports marketing engenders and reinforces a company's unique identity. Numerous examples are used to highlight how companies have used sports to enhance their reputation and the factors that affected senior management decision-making relative to the sports marketing investment. The end of chapter case study is: Tsingtao beer's use of sports to craft a distinctive reputation and corporate identity, illustrating how sports have offered the company an important channel for defining its strategic goals and developing a distinctive identity.

## Chapter 8    *The sports marketing fusion*

This chapter is an analysis of the sports marketing fusion, which describes an update to the five Ps marketing framework introduced in Chapter 1. We show the linkages between the traditional marketing framework and the five Ps of the sports marketing fusion, which describes how marketers can more directly relate sports to their firm's overall business direction. This also helps students understand the differences between a premium and non-premium image, which is a vital distinction for both companies and sports entities. The end of chapter case study is: BP (British Petroleum) and its sustainability efforts in the wake of its disastrous 2010 Gulf oil spill, and the company's attempts to repair its image using sports marketing.

Chapters 9–11 will help students understand about the key variables that both directly and indirectly impact a company's, and sports entity's reputation. This analysis includes a brand 'audit', designed to inspire marketers to fully identify and understand the factors that shape their organization's reputation. This sequence of chapters concludes with a discussion about the various organizational roles required in successful brand planning.

## Chapter 9    *Sports marketing touchpoints and customer journeys*

Chapter 9 shows how to identify the innumerable qualities and characteristics that, in aggregate, define the market's understanding of a sports marketer's company and/or a sports entity. Students will learn how to identify brand 'touchpoints' that are instrumental in fostering a quality, long-term reputation. Similarly, students will also learn how sports marketers can plan their interactions with customers in ways that lead to long-term, profitable loyalty. The end of chapter case studies are: Case 1, about Manchester United and the club's various brand touchpoints, the combination of which has helped produce the world's most valuable sports club; Case 2, about Penn State University and its plans to repair its reputation following a 2011 sex scandal involving a college football coach and teenage boys. Students will be able to use the touchpoints analysis from the chapter to create a map of Penn State's brand strengths and weaknesses.

## Chapter 10  Sports marketing – leadership and organizations

This chapter helps explain the important responsibilities management takes on in supporting sports marketing investments. While every company is different, there are several marketing-specific functions that have direct influence on the success of sports marketing and brand planning activities. The end of chapter case studies are: Case 1, about the NFL's work to broaden its appeal in China, illustrating the importance of management outreach for a major professional sports league; Case 2, concerning Mark Cuban, owner of the Dallas Mavericks basketball team in the NBA, and his role in influencing the direction of his sports organization.

Chapters 11–15 discuss tactical activities in both traditional and non-traditional marketing and media. Included are discussions about broadcast and print advertising, social/digital media, sources of revenues, sponsorship and event management, and licensing/merchandising.

## Chapter 11  Traditional advertising

Chapter 11 explains the different traditional advertising options available to sports marketers, describing the attributes of each and showing how they work. The end of chapter case study is: Pepsi and Pakistani Cricket, and the company's use of broadcast media to position itself to the larger Pakistani market, comprised of intense and passionate cricket fans.

## Chapter 12  Social and digital advertising

This chapter provides insights about social and digital advertising, showing marketers about these tools and their application in a sports context. Chapters 11 and 12 work well together to illustrate the wide range of advertising options available to sports marketers. The end of chapter case studies are: Case 1, about Adidas and its 2010 FIFA activation program. This includes Nike's ambush marketing activities and its potential impact on adidas's strategy; Case 2, describing the social media tactics of the Portland Timbers of MLS (Major League Soccer). The Timbers are reputed to have the most passionate fans in the MLS and their use of social media has been an important factor.

## Chapter 13    *Sports marketing revenues*

In this chapter we discuss the sources of revenues for different sports around the world. Students will gain a great appreciation for the sheer size and scale of the money involved in various global sports. The end of chapter case studies are: Case 1, about the San Francisco Giants of MLB (Major League Baseball) and their dynamic ticket pricing practices as a major contributor to the team's overall revenues; Case 2, about the Chinese Basketball Association (CBA) and its efforts to build a credible league modeled in part on the success of the NBA. Students will find that the emergence of the CBA poses interesting questions about how the league can develop a sustainable revenue model.

## Chapter 14    *Sponsorship and event management*

Chapter 14 focuses on sponsorships and event management activities. Sponsorships and event management are explored at the individual athlete, team venue, and governing body levels. The end of chapter case studies are: Case 1, about Matthias Steiner, a gold medal winning Olympic weightlifter from Germany, and the appeal of his story to sponsors; Case 2, discussing the relationship between the toy brand Hot Wheels and the X Games, and the potential impact to the company from this relationship.

## Chapter 15    *Licensing and merchandising*

The final chapter discusses licensing and merchandising, providing marketers with insights about how to develop a licensing plan, with numerous examples of the benefits to different sports from having a robust licensing and merchandising program. The end of chapter case study is: Ralph Lauren's golf merchandising activities, asking whether golf, or Ralph Lauren, or both, are too traditional to allow for innovative fashion.

A concerted effort to use examples from around the world distinguishes this book and provides students with the latest insights from sports marketing. We believe that having a global perspective about sports marketing will help readers understand the dynamic nature of sports today and apply the principles within to their own needs.

*John A. Davis*
*Jessica Zutz Hilbert*

**1**

# Sports marketing value chain: roles and interdependencies

 **CHAPTER OVERVIEW**

This chapter introduces the sports industry overall, defines sports marketing, and describes the key elements that are common across the world's many distinctive sports, providing students with a solid foundation from which the in-depth study of sports marketing in subsequent chapters will be more rewarding.

## 1.1 Size and influence

From humble beginnings nearly a century ago, the global sports industry has grown significantly to an estimated $480 billion to $620 billion in total size,[1] although a few sources say it is even larger – closer to $750 billion.[2] While estimates vary, it is clear that sports, and sports marketing in particular, are substantial economic and cultural forces.

As an industry, sport creates many of the most innovative products and services around the world. The influence of sports extends well beyond products and services. The language of sports is universal – fans and athletes understand their favorite sports and the rules of play. The idea that sports are meant to be played fairly, albeit competitively, is also widely understood. These commonalities cross cultural and language boundaries. Sports metaphors are common in business as well, with management often referring to the importance of being on a 'good team', with everyone following the same 'playbook', developing strategies designed to help the firm 'win', and building distinctive reputations along the way.

Developing recognizable distinction includes associating companies with other prestigious organizations and events. Major sports, such as football, rugby, basketball, auto racing, and cricket have fans numbering in the hundreds of millions. Major sports events, such as the Olympic Games, World Cup Football, and Formula 1, generate significant global audiences that also attract substantial corporate financial investment. Major global sports events can confer important and memorable association benefits, casting a positive glow across those people and organizations associated with the sport. Perhaps more than any other industry, sport fosters extraordinary fan (customer) loyalty, making sports marketing a particularly seductive and attractive investment for companies around the world seeking to enhance their credibility while also reaching a sizable, devoted audience. Unlike conventional marketing activities, like advertising and promotions, that are planned and scripted, sports events are inherently unpredictable. Fans, athletes, teams, and companies do not know outcomes. Despite even the most formidable track records of success, one cannot know for certain whether past sport performances will continue or whether expectations will be upended. This very unpredictability separates sports from almost all other corporate marketing activities. Indeed, many business managers find this prospect of uncertainty distinctly uncomfortable and consequently shy away from using sports as a marketing platform. Yet sports fans follow sports partly because outcomes are not guaranteed. Fans have an emotional attachment to their favorite teams and athletes, irrespective (mostly) of their recent performances. If sports were scripted then they would lose credibility, spontaneity would be lost, and they would be no different than a conventional company-directed ad campaign. Given the credibility of sports as a trusted industry, the growth of social media and two-way communications between customers and companies, and growing skepticism of conventional advertising, sports marketing's emergence as an important part of a company's overall marketing efforts is understandable.

## 1.2 Most popular sports and events

Casual observers are most familiar with the athletes, teams, and events associated with the world's leading sports bodies. The most popular include:

- *The Olympic Games.* The Games alternate every two years from Summer to Winter Games, with four years between each Summer Olympics and four years between each Winter Olympics. Over 200 nations and territories compete in the Summer Olympics, with more than 10 500 athletes competing in 28 sports and more than 300 events; and 82 nations compete in the Winter Olympics, with over 2500 athletes competing in seven sports and 82 events. In 2010 the International Olympic Committee (IOC) introduced the Youth Olympic Games (YOG), designed for participants between ages 14 and 18. The YOG also include

Summer and Winter Games on alternating schedules. Over 2 billion people watch the YOG, 3 billion watch the Winter Olympic Games, and 4 billion+ watch the Summer Olympic Games. For the 2009–12 Quadrennial period (comprising the 2010 Vancouver Olympics and the 2012 London Olympics), broadcast revenues were $3.914 billion and TOP program sponsorship revenues were $957 million.[3]

- *FIFA (the Federation of International Football Associations)* comprises 208 member football (soccer) clubs from around the world. The World Cup is FIFA's championship, held in a different city every four years. In 2010 the FIFA World Cup was held in South Africa, and in 2014 it will be held in Rio de Janeiro. Thirty-two national teams from around the world compete in each FIFA World Cup tournament. More than 3 billion people around the world watch the FIFA World Cup. Statistics from all World Cup matches indicate a cumulative audience of approximately 27 billion. $1.072 billion in marketing rights (sponsorships) and $2.408 billion in TV rights revenues were generated in 2010.[4]

- *International Cricket Council (ICC)*. ICC has 19 teams (nations) competing, culminating every four years in the ICC Cricket World Cup. In 2011 Sri Lanka, India, and Bangladesh hosted the World Cup, won by India. The Cricket World Cup is the third most popular event in the world after the FIFA World Cup and the Summer Olympics, with more than 2.2 billion viewers in 200 countries. $500 million in sponsorship rights and $1.1 billion in television rights for the 2011 and 2015 World Cups were sold.[5]

- *The Premier League* (more commonly called English Premier League and also by its title sponsor's name, Barclay's Premier League) comprises the top 20 member football (soccer) clubs in that season. The bottom three clubs at the end of each season move to a lower division called the Football League Championship (FLC), replaced by the top two teams from the FLC plus the best team from teams ranked 3–6 resulting from a play-off. More than 600 million people watch the Premier League each season, making it the most watched football (soccer) league in the world. TV revenues currently average more than $1.7 billion per year. Barclay's spent $127 million as title sponsor for the 2009–13 period, and the Premier League generates over $3 billion in annual revenue, the highest among the world's football (soccer) leagues.[6]

- *F1* (known more formally as Formula 1) is the world's premier auto racing league. F1 consists of 20 races (in 2012) across the world. There are 12 teams that compete each season for two world championships: the drivers' championship and the constructors' championship (each team designs and builds its own chassis within certain guidelines, which allows for engineering ingenuity across teams), and each team is required to have two cars in each race, and are allowed to use up to four drivers during the season. Both the drivers' and constructors' championships are determined based on points awarded to the top ten finishers, from 25 points for the winner to one point for tenth place. F1 has a global television audience of approximately 600 million people per race. Global TV broadcast revenues are $450 million (this figure is lower compared to the Olympics and FIFA World Cup partly because there is little interest from the US market, which is ordinarily among the top TV viewing markets for sports), and global sponsorship revenues are $887 million.[7]

- *The Commonwealth Games* are similar to the Olympics in many ways, with a wide variety of sports (21), Winter and Summer versions, and a Commonwealth Youth Games. However, the Commonwealth Games offer several sports not found in the Olympics, including lawn bowling, squash, ten-pin bowling, rugby sevens, cricket, and billiards. These sports are unique to the countries that comprise the British Commonwealth, which contains 54 members (when territories and Crown dependencies are included, then more than 70 teams participate in the Commonwealth Games). The number of viewers is between 16 and 30 million. Approximately $81 million in sponsorship revenues were generated in the last Games, along with $54 million in TV broadcast rights.[8]

- *The Indian Premier League (IPL)* plays a form of cricket called Twenty20, which is played in the span of three to four hours (versus the longer one- and five-day test matches of traditional cricket). Launched in 2008 the IPL has enjoyed rapid growth and success, with nine teams located throughout India. The TV fan base is estimated at over 200 million. A ten-year TV broadcast deal worth $1.74 billion was signed with Sony Entertainment Television in 2008. From 2008 to 2012 DLF Group was the league's title sponsor, paying $50 million for the rights. Estimates for additional sponsorship deals range from $50 to $60 million.[9]

- *The International Rugby Board (IRB)* oversees a global league comprising 98 member teams and 20 associate members. Similar to the FIFA World Cup, the Olympics, and ICC World Cup Cricket schedules, the Rugby World Cup is held every four years. Over 4 billion television viewers watch the Rugby World Cup. During the 2011 Rugby World Cup, total revenues were estimated to be $220 million, of which sponsorship revenues were approximately $130 million. TV revenues were not reported.[10]

- *PGA (Professional Golfers' Association)*. The PGA is responsible for 45 events in 45 weeks, however it is not responsible for any of golf's four majors (Masters, British Open, US Open, PGA Championship). The PGA runs three golf tours: the PGA Tour; Champions Tour (for golfers aged 50 and over); and the Web.com Tour (a developmental for pro-spective PGA players). There are approximately 175 million viewers who watch the PGA Tour during each season.[11] Sponsorship revenues are approximately $461 million[12] and TV revenues are approximately $600 million.[13]

- *National Football League (NFL).* The NFL has 32 teams across the United States. US football is not like FIFA football (soccer). Instead, the ball is similar in shape to a rugby ball, but more tapered at the ends, and players use their hands to throw and catch the ball. Feet are used only for special kicks called point after touchdowns (PATs), field goals, and punts. Players also wear protective equipment to protect their heads and upper bodies due to the extreme contact required to play the sport successfully. The top two teams play each other in the Super Bowl game, which has become a mega-sports event and media spectacle over the years. Four networks broadcast NFL games each year (CBS, NBC, Fox, and ESPN), providing a combined $20.4 billion in revenue. The TV audience averages over 20 million viewers per game during the season and the domestic Super Bowl TV audience is over 100 million viewers. Sponsorship revenue averages over $800 million per year.[14]

- *Major League Baseball (MLB).* MLB has 30 teams in North America – 29 in the USA and one in Canada, divided into two leagues: the National and American. The top team from each of the two leagues plays in the season-ending best-of-seven championship called The World Series. Broadcast TV revenues from ESPN, Fox, and Turner average $711 million per season, cable revenues are over $900 million, and local TV revenues are projected to exceed $1.5 billion by 2015.[15] The total TV viewership is estimated at over 114 million households (note that baseball counts households, and not individual viewers). Sponsorship revenues were $548 million in 2010.[16]

- *National Hockey League (NHL).* The NHL is a North American league with 30 teams, 23 of which are in the USA and seven are Canadian. The top eight teams in the league's two conferences, Eastern and Western, play in the Stanley Cup play-offs, with the final two teams (one from each conference) playing a best-of-seven game series to determine the Stanley Cup champions. NHL sponsorship revenues were $327 million in 2010. In 2011, the NHL signed a ten-year broadcast agreement with NBC valued at $2 billion.[17] During the 2011–12 season, an average of 332 000 viewers watched each televised NHL regular season game, and nearly 3 million people watched the Stanley Cup Finals between the Los Angeles Kings and the New Jersey Devils, won by Los Angeles.

- *National Basketball Association (NBA).* The NBA has 30 teams, 29 in the USA and one in Canada, playing in two conferences: Eastern and

Western. After the play-offs, the top two teams play a best-of-seven game series called the NBA Finals. The NBA made $536 million in sponsorship revenues in 2010. The TV revenues are $930 million per year, through 2015 when a new deal will presumably be negotiated. In 2011–12, an average of 391 000 viewers watched each televised NBA regular season game. An average of 16 million fans watched each of the five games of the 2012 NBA finals between Miami Heat and Oklahoma City Thunder, won by Miami.[18]

- *NASCAR (National Association for Stock Car Auto Racing)*. There are 36 auto races during the NASCAR season. An average of 6.5 million viewers watched NASCAR across the three TV networks: FOX, TNT, and ESPN/ABC. NASCAR has an eight-year TV contract through 2014 that produces $4.48 billion in revenue.[19] Sponsorship revenues are approximately 11 percent of total revenues ($3 billion in 2012), equivalent to $330 million.[20]

There are three important, and obvious, points one should understand about each of these sports. First, there is significant variety in the types of sports and the associated fan base; second, the number of fans and viewers is enormous – far larger than almost any other target audience for non-sports offerings; and third, the cumulative sponsorship commitments to each of these sports are enormous and growing. In other words, companies around the world are increasingly using sports as a vital part of their marketing strategy. These three points have a direct impact on the design, development, and implementation of sports marketing plans, as we will see throughout this book.

## 1.3 How the sports industry creates value

The sports industry creates value in five areas:

- *events* (live events, gate revenues, concessions);
- *content* (specialized, packaged content for digital, broadcast, print distribution);
- *properties* (leagues/tours/federations, teams, players);
- *rights management* (owners and agents that structure media, identity, licensing, merchandising, sponsorship, and marketing rights);
- *sporting goods* (footwear, apparel, hard goods, accessories).

### Events

This refers to live events and associated revenues from gate (ticket) receipts and concession sales. Live events examples include:

- Mega-sports events (Olympics, World Cup, F1). These are the world's largest sports events, with global fan bases in the billions.
- Transnational sports events (UEFA [Union of European Football Associations], Rugby World Cup, World Cup Cricket). These events are typically regional, with global fan bases in the high several hundred million to low billions.
- National sports events (Super Bowl, World Series, NBA Championships, Stanley Cup). These sports tend to attract fans from within a single country, or a limited number of countries. The fan base is in the high tens of millions to low hundred million.
- University sports events (NCAA [National Collegiate Athletic Association], March Madness, bowl games). These sports events comprise collegiate amateur athletes. The fan base is also in the high tens of millions to low hundred million.

## Content

Content describes the news, information, and data related to sports that are consumed by people everywhere via traditional and digital media. Events, teams, athletes, leagues from around the world produce a steady stream of new content everyday, derived from athletic competitions, sports-related business activities, and even entertainment/lifestyle news from the lives of the world's athletes. In turn, this content can be enhanced by tailoring and packaging it to specific audiences to maximize the value of the information.

## Properties

Properties are the legally protected and/or owned sports entities managed by rights owners (individuals or organizations with the legal authority, ownership, and responsibility to manage the properties). These properties include leagues/tours/federations, teams, and players.

## Rights management

Modern sports generate revenues from multiple sources beyond gate revenues, including marketing (particularly licensing and merchandising activities) and media rights. Rights owners develop and implement the media, identity, licensing, merchandising, sponsorship, and marketing rights deals on behalf of their properties directly, or they retain sports agents/consultancies that structure the rights deals for them.

## Sporting goods

Sporting goods describes the manufacturer of sports-related footwear, apparel, hard goods (sport balls, racquets, protective equipment, masks, helmets etc.), and accessories (hats, bags, gloves, watches, sunglasses etc.).

# 1.4 Understanding sports marketing

Sports marketing describes the value-creating activities of those organizations that use sports-related entities (athletes, teams, coaches, leagues) to increase interest in and sales of the offerings listed below:

## Products, participation and events

These include:

- sports-specific products (such as athletic shoes);
- sports-specific services (such as online ticket sales);
- non-sports offerings (such as financial services);
- public participation in sports (such as grassroots activities designed to inspire increased participation in community sports programs, youth and adult leagues, regular fitness programs);
- events (games and matches), mega-sports events (Olympics, FIFA World Cup), leagues (Premier League, National Basketball Association).

Each of the value-creating sports areas relies on the five sports marketing mix elements shown in Figure 1.1 to attract and retain profitable customers. These five elements are updated from the classic marketing mix known as the four Ps (product, price, place, promotion). The marketing mix is still the foundation of most marketing activities, whether in sports or any other industry, but the techniques and technologies have changed, including the rapid rise of digital media and marketing, providing marketers with a wider range of tools they can use to attract and retain customers and grow their brand value.

## People

The addition of people to the marketing mix recognizes the simple fact that all products and services are ultimately designed for a particular person or group of people. Furthermore, people are required to conceptualize innovative ways to appeal to target customers and then commercialize these ideas into profitable economic gain. In the sports industry, significant effort is put

**Figure 1.1** The five sports marketing mix elements

into developing solutions for top athletes competing in sports events. These top athletes train under experienced coaches, their teams are run by seasoned managers, their clubs are governed by leagues comprising industry experts that set rules and standards for conduct and commerce, their careers are managed by sports agents, and their efforts are cheered and jeered by fans.

## Product

In the twenty-first century, product is more broadly described as offerings that encompass both hard goods and services. In the context of sports marketing, products range from athletic shoes to sports agency services. The era of globalization has broken down trade barriers and strong competitors are evident in almost every country, so the minimum cost of entry for succeeding in sports marketing is to have high-quality offerings. The range of sports industry offerings is diverse:

- consumer products:
  - footwear;
  - apparel;
  - hard goods;
  - accessories;
- competitions and entertainment:
  - exhibitions;

- regular seasonal games and contests;
- championship events;
- mega-sports events;
- general fitness:
  - clubs;
  - coaches, trainers and instructors;
- media and content:
  - live sports programming;
  - talk shows;
  - software and game technologies;
  - broadcast and print sources.

## Price

Price remains the primary determinant of financial value for products. Price also guides the marketplace's understanding of quality and uniqueness. However, sports marketers must be careful not to inflate prices simply in an effort to convey higher quality or value. Charging high prices for a special event or product might initially suggest to the customer that they are getting a premium, distinctive offering, but marketers must ensure that the value is truly exceptional. In the early 2000s in the United States, a new football league called the XFL was launched with a major marketing campaign and the promise of better and more exciting football (as compared to the NFL, which was positioned by the XFL as boring and predictable). But the quality of player was inferior and it became obvious to the fans as they watched each week's games. The XFL folded as a league in it first year, partly because fans perceived that the value they received was not worth the price.[21]

## Place

Place describes how customers can purchase the products they seek and where the products are distributed so that they are easily found. Place comprises two primary channels: consumer and business. Traditional consumer products are distributed in retail stores, and business products are often distributed through field sales forces and/or professional intermediaries such as value-added resellers or technical consultants. The rapid growth of the internet and, more recently, digital and social media, has enabled people anywhere in the world to purchase the products they seek without having to physically visit a retail store. For sports fans, digital distribution allows them to receive real-time information updates about their favorite athletes, teams, and even products.

## Promotion

Promotion describes how sports marketers develop awareness about their offerings in the marketplace and develop profitable customers using marketing communications. Once narrowly defined as advertising, marketing communication is a vital component of any marketing strategy and has grown in sophistication as more marketing communication tools have emerged. Marketing communication encompasses traditional media (broadcast, print) and non-traditional/new media (social, digital, internet).

## 1.5 Cycle of value in sports

Live sports events reveal the interplay between four fundamental variables:

- athletes;
- fans;
- media;
- sports marketing.

This dynamic relationship among the four variables is known as the cycle of value and Figure 1.2 shows how they contribute to creating value in sports:

**Figure 1.2** The cycle of value

In essence, athletes attract fans, fans attract media, media attract sports marketers, and sports marketers attract athletes. The cycle of value is a vital dynamic in sports since it describes the interrelationship between the four key variables. The logic is clear, but turning this into a valuable investment for sports marketers is an ongoing challenge. The purpose of this book is to uncover and understand these variables and how they interact to affect value and sports marketing decision-making. We will learn about the role of each of these four variables and how they interact to develop and sustain value for sports marketers.

## 1.6    Sports value chain

The cycle of value is at the core of a more sophisticated concept known as the sports value chain, which is, in essence, a description of the interdependent links among the key components of the sports industry as shown in Figure 1.3.

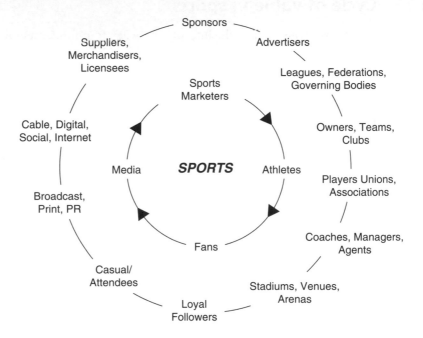

**Figure 1.3** The sports value chain

### Leagues, federations, governing bodies

Every major sport is governed by an organizational entity that prescribes the rules of competition, schedules games and matches, manages post-season championship play, and serves to protect its intellectual properties (trademarks, logos, slogans, colors, and similar key identifiers). Each governing body's rules and regulations can also affect how sports marketers develop their marketing activities. The governing bodies and league structures vary by sport, as examples later in this book will show.

## Owners, teams, clubs

Within most sports are teams and clubs run by individual or corporate owners (two notable exceptions are professional golf and professional tennis). Teams and clubs have developed fan followings over time, with the level of fan loyalty and size of their overall fan base dependent on their location, longevity, and history of success. Owners acquire athletes primarily through universities, developmental leagues, and trade, and the size of investments made in athletes, particularly acknowledged stars, is in the tens or even hundreds of millions of dollars. The best-known teams and clubs, such as the Premier League's Manchester United or Major League Baseball's New York Yankees, command premium valuations. *Forbes Magazine* publishes an annual list of the 'World's Most Valuable Sports Franchises'. In 2011 the top 50 were as shown in Table 1.1.

**Table 1.1** The top 50 teams and clubs

| Franchise | League | Owners | Value |
|---|---|---|---|
| 1 Manchester United | Premier | Glazer family | US$1.86 billion |
| 2 Dallas Cowboys | NFL | Jerry Jones | US$1.81 billion |
| 3 New York Yankees | MLB | Steinbrenner family | US$1.7 billion |
| 4 Washington Redskins | NFL | Dan Snyder | US$1.55 billion |
| 5 Real Madrid | La Liga | Club members | US$1.45 billion |
| 6 New England Patriots | NFL | Robert Kraft | US$1.37 billion |
| 7 Arsenal | Premier | Stanley Kroenke | US$1.19 billion |
| 8 New York Giants | NFL | John Mara, Steven Tisch | US$1.18 billion |
| 9 Houston Texans | NFL | Robert McNair | US$1.17 billion |
| 10 New York Jets | NFL | Robert Wood Johnson | US$1.14 billion |
| 11 Philadelphia Eagles | NFL | Jeffrey Lurie | US$1.12 billion |
| 12 Baltimore Ravens | NFL | Stephen Bisciotti | US$1.07 billion |
| 13 Ferrari | F1 | Fiat Group | US$1.07 billion |
| 14 Chicago Bears | NFL | McCaskey family | US$1.07 billion |
| 15 Denver Broncos | NFL | Patrick Bowlen | US$1.05 billion |
| 16 Indianapolis Colts | NFL | James Irsay | US$1.04 billion |
| 17 Carolina Panthers | NFL | Jerry Richardson | US$1.04 billion |
| 18 Tampa Bay Buccaneers | NFL | Glazer family | US$1.03 billion |
| 19 Bayern Munich | Bundesliga | Club members | US$1.03 billion |
| 20 Green Bay Packers | NFL | Shareholder-owned | US$1.02 billion |
| 21 Cleveland Browns | NFL | Randolph Lerner | US$1.02 billion |
| 22 Miami Dolphins | NFL | Stephen Ross | US$1.01 billion |
| 23 Pittsburgh Steelers | NFL | Daniel Rooney and Art Rooney II | US$996 million |
| 24 Tennessee Titans | NFL | Kenneth Adams, Jr. | US$994 million |
| 25 Seattle Seahawks | NFL | Paul Allen | US$989 million |

**Table 1.1** (continued)

| Franchise | League | Owners | Value |
|---|---|---|---|
| 26 Barcelona | La Liga | Club members | US$975 million |
| 27 Kansas City Chiefs | NFL | Lamar Hunt family | US$965 million |
| 28 New Orleans Saints | NFL | Thomas Benson | US$955 million |
| 29 San Francisco 49ers | NFL | Denise DeBartalo York and John York | US$925 million |
| 30 Arizona Cardinals | NFL | William Bidwell | US$919 million |
| 31 Boston Red Sox | MLB | John Henry and Thomas Werner | US$912 million |
| 32 San Diego Chargers | NFL | Alexander Spanos | US$907 million |
| 33 Cincinnati Bengals | NFL | Michael Brown | US$905 million |
| 34 AC Milan | Serie A | Silvio Berlusconi | US$838 million |
| 35 Atlanta Falcons | NFL | Arthur Blank | US$831 million |
| 36 Detroit Lions | NFL | William Clay Ford | US$817 million |
| 37 McLaren | F1 | McLaren Group | US$815 million |
| 38 Los Angeles Dodgers | MLB | Guggenheim Baseball Management | US$800 million |
| 39 Buffalo Bills | NFL | Ralph Wilson Jr. | US$799 million |
| 40 St. Louis Rams | NFL | Stanley Kroenke | US$779 million |
| 41 Minnesota Vikings | NFL | Zygmunt Wilf and Mark Wilf | US$774 million |
| 42 Chicago Cubs | MLB | Ricketts Family | US$773 million |
| 43 Oakland Raiders | NFL | Mark Davis | US$758 million |
| 44 New York Mets | MLB | Fred Wilpon and Saul Katz | US$747 million |
| 45 Jacksonville Jaguars | NFL | Wayne Weaver | US$725 million |
| 46 Chelsea | Premier | Roman Abramovich | US$658 million |
| 47 New York Knicks | NBA | Madison Square Garden | US$655 million |
| 48 Los Angeles Lakers | NBA | Jerry Buss and Philip Anschutz | US$643 million |
| 49 Juventus | Serie A | Agnelli family | US$628 million |
| 50 Philadelphia Phillies | MLB | David Montgomery and partners | US$609 million |

Source: Badenhausen (2011).

## Players' unions, associations

These are labor organizations whose purpose is to represent and protect players' interests concerning wages, working conditions, hours, and their rights as professional athletes.

## Coaches, managers, agents

Coaches and managers are concerned with team and individual player development, developing strengths and unique skillsets, and strategizing athlete/team performances throughout each season against each opponent. Agents are paid consultants/representatives of each athlete, helping negotiate their playing contracts and endorsement deals (agents receive a percentage of these). Agents help maximize the athlete's marketability during their primary playing years.

## Stadiums, venues, arenas

The stadiums, venues, and arenas where athletes and teams play are essential to sports marketing. Not only do they provide seating for fans, but they have facilities for owners and leagues to develop additional revenue streams through the sale of merchandise and food and beverage items. In addition, most sports facilities provide signage and similar marketing communications vehicles for corporate sponsors and advertisers. Additional revenues are often realized by offering pricing tiers based on seat type (standing, reserved, luxury box) and location. Furthermore, as the teams and athletes competing in stadiums, venues, and arenas develop over time, so too do the reputations of these facilities, leading to a phenomenon known as home team advantage (due to the presence and support of their home fans and the psychological comfort of playing in one's own facilities). Naming rights are often another way for owners of teams and facilities to generate additional financial gain for their sports franchises.

## Loyal followers

Sports fans are a type of customer in the classic business sense. While sharing some similarities with traditional business customers, loyal sports fans differ in that their commitment and devotion to their favorite team and/or athlete tends to remain steady, even when their favorites are underperforming. Finding similar loyalty from typical non-sports customers for a company whose products are of inconsistent quality is rare, particularly since most products have competitive substitutes that consumers will use if their previously favorite brand disappoints them. Given this, media companies such as television broadcasters, as well as advertisers and sponsors, find loyal sports fans to be a particularly attractive and valuable audience.

## Casual/attendees

Many sports fans are more casual and less loyal to their favorite teams and athletes. These fans may follow sports only occasionally, such as during big games with rivals, or during the end of season championships. Or, casual fans may have a light interest in a given sport and watch it if they are seeking an entertainment alternative. Even though they are not as committed as loyal sports fans, casual fans are still attractive and important to media companies and corporations since they typically represent a larger portion of the population than loyal sports fans, comprising a significant audience. There are also members of the viewing audience with little interest in sports, but who still watch them occasionally because of the social nature of the event (i.e., their friends are watching, or a unique entertainer will perform, or a special promotion is being advertised, or other similar appeals attract them etc.).

## Broadcast, print, PR

Broadcast, print and PR (public relations) are also known as traditional media because these have dominated the media landscape for decades and have well-developed methods for making full use of their media type for marketing communicators. Traditional media are particularly effective for raising awareness among large audiences and communicating a clear, simple message that is memorable. Sports marketers, particularly in Europe and North America, still significantly rely on traditional media to reach mass audiences. Most sports events are still broadcast through conventional television, or aired via radio.

## Cable, digital, social, internet

Since the advent of the commercial internet in the 1990s, the pace of technological change in media has been rapid, showing few signs of slowing down. Cable, as opposed to airwave broadcasts, has facilitated the rapid development of new programming in sports, increasing access around the world and allowing media companies and advertisers to tailor their messages to narrower audiences. The emergence of digital and social media in the 2000s has added to the range of tools sports marketers can use to appeal to various audiences. Digital and social media have also fostered a much stronger and more demanding consumer audience, effectively changing the relationship between organizations and their customers from one controlled by the organization to one controlled by customers. This change has also coincided with a shift from one way (from organization to market) to two-way simultaneous communications (an ongoing dialog between the organization and the marketplace). The result is that organizations (sports companies, teams, leagues etc.) are finding that they must listen far more actively to their customers than ever, otherwise the risk of a fan backlash increases noticeably. This is not meant to suggest that fans control the business decisions of their favorite organization (such as player trades); instead, the implication is that any sports organization, or athlete, must be far more attuned to the feedback from their fans to ensure their reputation and brand value remain strong.

## Suppliers, merchandisers, licensees

Suppliers, merchandisers, and licensees supply the products that sports fans and athletes buy. Sports governing bodies, teams (and owners), sporting goods manufacturers, food and beverage companies, and sports agents all play a role in generating additional revenues through officially approved products with protected trademarks, logos, and slogans purchased by sports fans. These offerings are an important mechanism for fans to stay connected to their favorite athletes and teams and to display their loyalty to others. A form of social pride is an important by-product of fans wearing and consuming the products of their favorite sports entity. These products also help reinforce the brand image of that sports franchise and often serve to inspire demand from other consumers.

## Sponsors

Sponsors are typically companies that wish to be associated with a given sports entity (league, event, team, athlete, coach etc.). Sponsors pay a fee for this right and, in the case of major sports events such as the Olympic Games and FIFA World Cup, companies invest in extended sponsorship relationships lasting years. The rationale for sports sponsorship is to raise awareness of the sponsoring entity and associate the values of the sponsored entity with their firm. Paying sponsorship fees represents only part of the investment. Sponsors then have to *activate* their sponsorship by spending additional money on buying media time, hiring an advertising agency, developing creative communications, and even developing and launching new products. Activation activities can cost another two to three times the initial sponsorship amount, but the potential benefits are significant when a sponsor/sports entity relationship succeeds.

## Advertisers

Advertisers are those organizations that seek to use a sports event, team or athlete to promote their products and/or companies. An obvious example is the stadium signage seen during the UK's Premier League and Europe's UEFA football matches. The Super Bowl game, pitting the top two teams from the USA's NFL, is known for being a successful event for companies to gain exposure. The Super Bowl is also well known for the unusually creative, even weird, company advertising. Not all advertisers are sponsors (nor do they have to be), but all sponsors advertise since they want to leverage their sponsorship investment to attract new customers, reinforce existing customers, and develop their brand image in front of a large audience.

## 1.7    Chapter summary

This chapter provided an overview of the sports industry, selected leading sports leagues around the world, the cycle of value in sports, and the sports value chain. The global sports industry represents billions of dollars in revenue with important interdependences between governing bodies, owners, sports teams/clubs, athletes, suppliers, media, and fans. Students of sports marketing will quickly learn to appreciate the complexity of the global sports industry and the potential value to the various stakeholders. Among the many challenges one can infer is how sports entities can sustain market interest in their offerings to ensure that companies are attracted to sponsorship, media companies are interested in broadcasting, and fans are devoted to viewing these events. Without question, the sheer diversity of sports around the world has attracted a wide range of fans and companies, each interested in following and being associated with sports.

**CASE STUDY 1**

# NASCAR

The National Association for Stock Car Auto Racing, better known as NASCAR, is a unique sports property that has been in existence since 1948.[22] It is a family-owned and -operated business venture that governs multiple auto racing events throughout the year and is the largest sanctioning body of stock car racing in the United States. Bill France Sr. began the body and to this day, the France family still owns and runs it.[23] From the days of its modest inception, the organization has grown to control over 1200 races in more than 30 states.[24] NASCAR has a reach that far exceeds the boundaries of the United States, however. While the majority of the races occur in the United States, a handful are in Canada and Mexico each year.[25] Thirty million people consider themselves avid fans of the sport.[26]

Currently, there are two different major national stock car circuits in the United States that NASCAR sanctions: the Sprint Cup Series and the Nationwide Series.[27] The Sprint Cup Series represents the highest level of competition in stock car racing in North America and the Nationwide Series is the step below that. In 2012, the Sprint Cup Series featured 36 races over ten months and has a cumulative points system (based on a driver's finish in each race) and significant cash prizes for those who do well. Most of the top tier drivers are signed by 'teams' that pay them a salary, bonuses, and outfit them for races. Each team also has its own particular brand and model of car. The top earning team in NASCAR is currently Hendrick Motorsports, which was worth $350 million in 2011, with $177 million in revenues.[28] Hendrick's drivers include Dale Earnhardt Jr., Jeff Gordon, and Jimmie Johnson.[29] Behind Hendrick Motorsports is Roush Fenway Racing, valued at $224 million and Richard Childress at $158 million.[30]

Many of the drivers enjoy significant benefits from being in the spotlight of their sport. Some of the sport's most famous drivers, including Dale Earnhardt Jr. and Jeff Gordon, have appeared in major motion pictures and television shows in addition to appearances on talk shows. In 2010, Dale Earnhardt Jr. was NASCAR's highest paid driver with earnings of $29 million.[31] In addition to the revenue he earns from his race performances, he also earns significant income from his racing team, Hendrick Motorsports (reportedly an eight-figure salary), and merchandise sales, which account for one-third of all NASCAR merchandise sold.[32] Over the course of his career, Jeff Gordon has racked up more that $117 million in race winnings alone.[33]

Perhaps the most impressive (and noticeable) feature of NASCAR races is the predominance of sponsorship within the sport. In 2011, 400 companies of all sizes spent a total of $3.51 billion on NASCAR sponsorship.[34] This total was up from a $3.37 billion spend in 2010, and $3.3 billion in 2009.[35] DuPont and the American Association for Retired Persons (AARP) each pledged $25 million in NASCAR sponsorships in 2011.[36] Sponsorship in this sport is so popular that even the United States Army plopped down a cool $8.4 million to sponsor Ryan Newman's No. 39 Chevrolet for 12 races in 2012.[37] The US National Guard, whose sports sponsorship budget was $54.5 million in 2012 pledged $26.5 million of that on NASCAR sponsorships.[38] Part of the reason that so many dollars are spent on NASCAR sponsorship is because NASCAR fans are known to be highly loyal to brands who sponsor NASCAR properties. Seventy percent of avid NASCAR fans say they are more likely to consider trying a product or service if that product or service is an official sponsor.[39] In addition, the sheer volume of eyeballs fixated on the cars, drivers, and the racetrack throughout these races (some of which are hours long) is extremely alluring for potential sponsors.

Television presence is another impressive feature of NASCAR's presence in the sports value chain. Behind only the National Football League, NASCAR has the second highest viewership in the country. Fox, Turner, and ESPN are currently NASCAR's television rights holders for the Sprint Cup Series.[40] Fox pays approximately $220 million per year, over eight years, to hold this title.[41] In total, NASCAR's broadcast agreements are worth $4.48 billion over eight years and expire in 2014. In 2011, Nielsen ratings on Fox's Sprint Cup Series broadcasts were on average 4.8 and each broadcast drew approximately 7.9 million viewers.[42] ESPN and ABC hold the rights for the Nationwide Series broadcasts and on average reel in Nielsen ratings of 1.7 and 2.4 million viewers.[43]

Beyond the sport of racing, NASCAR also operates a 150 000 square foot NASCAR Hall of Fame in Charlotte, North Carolina. In addition to a full service restaurant and 278-person theater, the Hall of Fame boasts 18 historic race cars and exhibits detailing 40 current and historic racetracks. The NASCAR Foundation also has a large footprint off the racetrack. Since 2006, the foundation has helped provide medical treatment to 19 000 kids at Speediatrics, which is a NASCAR-themed ward at the Halifax Medical Center in Daytona Beach, Florida. In 2012, NASCAR surpassed the $1 million mark of funds donated to the unit in the partenership.[44]

NASCAR venues hold some of the largest sports crowds. There are currently 27 active tracks in the United States, all with varying capacities and track shapes. The Indianapolis Motor Speedway is the largest spectator sporting facility in the world with a capacity of more than 250 000 permanent seats and annually hosts the Brickyard 400.[45] At the 2012 Brickyard 400, the track drew in approximately $9 million in ticket revenue, $6 million in television revenue, and $2 million in its new title sponsorship with Crown Royal.[46] Despite a struggling global economy, NASCAR races still drew 3.6 million people in 2010 with the average attendance at Sprint Cup Series races hovering between 75 000 and 150 000 attendees.[47]

Recently, however, NASCAR has faced trouble in a seemingly waning interest in the sport. Bad weather and declining interest in the 18–34 age demographic of the sport also led to an 8 percent decrease in viewership in 2011 and a 4 percent decrease in ratings.[48] More alarmingly, ticket revenues have sharply declined for the three major publicly owned race track companies and fell by 38 percent over the five-year span between 2007 and 2012.[49] In 2011, 35 of the 38 race weekends occurred at the one of the tracks owned by three major track ownership companies: SMI, ISC, and Dover Motorsports.[50] Brian France,

**CASE STUDY 1** *(continued)*

NASCAR's current CEO, blames the declining attendance revenue on the race weekend format and notes that attending a NASCAR race requires a greater fan expenditure in terms of travel and accommodation costs than most sporting events.[51] To combat these sinking ticket revenues both NASCAR and the racetracks have considered some creative options. NASCAR has shortened several races and is considering reducing the amount of races altogether.[52] At the Charlotte Motor Speedway, a large block of seats was removed and a luxury motor park now stands in its place.[53] In 2013, NASCAR will debut new car designs to also help spur greater interest in the sport.[54]

 **QUESTIONS**

1  Will these changes be enough to return NASCAR to its glory days?

2  Or could this shift in fan favoritism spell the end of America's oldest stock car racing circuit?

3  Discuss the potential impact of NASCAR's changes on fans and the media.

**CASE STUDY 2**

# Seattle SuperSonics' relocation to Oklahoma City

Not all sports teams are rooted in any singular city. While many teams have moved locations through the years, the SuperSonics' move from Seattle to become the Oklahoma City Thunder was one of the most controversial of all time.

In 2006, the 39th year of the team's history, Seattle SuperSonics were playing in the aged publicly funded KeyArena. The arena was the smallest arena in the National Basketball Association (NBA) with a capacity of 17 072. Sonics owner Howard Schultz approached the State of Washington to upgrade the facility but was rejected. With the team's lease of the KeyArena set to expire in 2010, Schultz was looking for a way to offload the team so he sold the team to the Professional Basketball Club LLC (PBC), which was an Oklahoma City-based investment group led by Clay Bennett.[55] When Bennett again approached the City of Seattle to build a $500 million arena complex and was denied, Bennett dropped a bomb on Sonics fans – he requested an arbitration between the City of Seattle and PBC to get the SuperSonics out of their lease at KeyArena and move the team to Oklahoma City.[56] The ensuing months were not pretty for the Seattle SuperSonics.

Bennett's initial request for arbitration was denied by a judge. Immediately afterward, the City of Seattle sued PBC to enforce the lease. This lawsuit came to an end, just hours before the judge was to announce her ruling, in the form of a complex settlement. PBC would have to pay the city $45 million to terminate its lease early, and Bennett would potentially have to pay an additional $30 million relocation fee to the NBA if another basketball team did not appear within five years.[57] The Sonics' history and colors would stay in Seattle, but Oklahoma City Thunder would begin playing during the 2008–09 season.[58] Only then could Oklahoma City begin to brand its new team, Oklahoma City Thunder and its arena, then the Ford Center.

Moving the Sonics to Oklahoma City was risky. The metropolitan Oklahoma City area only had approximately 1.2 million people and no major professional sports teams. While the city had temporarily hosted the Charlotte Hornets in 2005–07 and was home to the AFL's Oklahoma City Wranglers, a major professional sports team had never been an installment in the city. The arena that the team would play in was built in 2002, but it was not a brand new arena and didn't have the jaw-dropping allure of a brand new space.

Bennett played a very active role in building his new team from the ground up in Oklahoma City. Though most NBA owners leave business operations to a team president or executive, Bennett took charge of this role. His goal by the end of the team's first year was to turn a profit and to achieve that goal, he played a part in just about every aspect of the team's formation from choosing team colors, selling sponsorships, to hiring personnel.[59] Bennett helped negotiate the team's Fox Sports Net television deal and a $4 million tax credit from Oklahoma City. In addition to the tax credit, he also successfully guided a publicly funded deal through the City Council worth $121 million to renovate the Ford Center and to build the team's new practice facilities.[60] After its first year, the team was reportedly worth $300 million, up from the $268 million that the Seattle SuperSonics were worth in

**CASE STUDY 2** (continued)

its last season at KeyArena.[61] Perhaps even more telling statistics in the sports world, the Sonics sold 78 percent of their available tickets during their last season, whereas Thunder sold out the larger Ford Center almost immediately.

While Bennett had successfully put the financial pieces in place for Thunder to succeed, the big unknown was how Oklahoma City would react to its new team. Bennett was just coming out of two ugly seasons in Seattle and fans there vilified him for moving the team to Oklahoma. His new team needed to find ways to connect to their new fans. Over the course of the team's first few years in existence, he seems to have done just that. When Rumble the Bison was introduced as the team's mascot, the team used Twitter and Facebook not only to build awareness of the team and mascot, but also allow fans to connect with the team.[62]

In July 2011, Bennett announced that the arena that the team plays in would be renamed the Chesapeake Energy Arena in a deal that would last 11 years.[63] The deal was worth $3 million per year initially and has a 3 percent annual escalation cost. In 2012, in just the team's fifth year of existence, it was valued at $348 million and ranked 15 on the 'Forbes Most Valuable Team List', raking in $25 million in operating income.[64] All of the arena's 124 court-side seats are also exclusively available to those who sponsor the team.[65] The team has no internal inventory to dispense these seats on a game-by-game basis and must appeal to sponsors if a need should arise to allocate these seats differently. Even television viewership has been strong in Oklahoma City, which is the third smallest market in the NBA. During the 2012 play-offs, the Western Conference finals between Thunder and San Antonio Spurs averaged a 5.0 rating and 7.8 million viewers.[66]

Seattle hasn't completely faded from the picture entirely either. In 2009, just a year after the Sonics played their last season in Seattle, a group of loyal fans filmed a documentary called *Sonicsgate: Requiem for a Team*. The film aimed to 'build momentum for bringing an NBA team back to Seattle and restoring the 41-year legacy of the Seattle SuperSonics'. There is still a strong feeling of ill-will toward Clay Bennett and the Oklahoma City Thunder organization. Many people in Seattle admit that they can't imagine rooting for Oklahoma City Thunder and countless stories appeared in the media relating this sentiment in 2012 when the Thunder made the NBA Finals. There is also a current push to build a new arena and bring an NBA team back to Seattle. Led by Chris Hansen, a managing partner at Valiant Capital, the arena would be funded by $300 million in private investments with the remaining $200 million coming from King County bonds paid over 30 years and, eventually, tax revenues from the City of Seattle.[67]

**? QUESTIONS**

1  Does a team actually change when it moves locations?

2  What might be the most affected aspects of the sports value chain if a team moves locations?

3  If Seattle gets another NBA team, what are some of the key factors that the team needs to address to ensure success?

## NOTES

1  A.T. Kearney, Inc. (2011, p. 1).
2  Horrow and Swatek (2010).
3  Olympic Marketing Fact File (2012, p. 6).
4  FIFA.com (2010).
5  International Cricket Council (n.d.).
6  Brand Finance (2012); Gibson (2012).
7  Paddock Magazine (n.d.).
8  Chakrabarti (2010).
9  Marium (n.d.).
10  Balony (2011).
11  BtoB (2012).
12  *The Economist* (2011).
13  Burke (2012a).
14  Beasley (2010).
15  Ozanian (2012).
16  Cutler (2010).
17  TSN (2011).
18  New York Sports Journalism (2010).
19  Mickle and Ourand (2011).
20  'NASCAR racing statistics' (2012).
21  Ackman (2001).
22  'History of NASCAR' (2010).
23  Ibid.
24  Ibid.
25  NASCAR Racing Series (2010).
26  Badenhausen (2011).
27  NASCAR Racing Series (2010).
28  Badenhausen (2011).
29  Ibid.
30  Ibid.
31  Badenhausen (2012).
32  Ibid.
33  Ibid.
34  Park (2011).
35  Ibid.
36  Badenhausen (2011).
37  Long (2012).
38  Ibid.
39  Broughton (2010).
40  Mickle and Ourand (2012a).
41  Mickle and Ourand (2012b).
42  Mickle and Ourand (2012a).
43  Ibid.
44  'NASCAR foundation reaches $1m for speediatrics' (2012).
45  'FAQs about the Indianapolis Motor Speedway' (2012).
46  Schoettle (2012).
47  Peltz (2012).
48  Mickle and Ourand (2012a).
49  Scott and Dunn (2012).
50  Ibid.
51  Ibid.
52  Ryan (2012).

53  Scott and Dunn (2012).
54  Diaz (2012).
55  Johns (2007).
56  Ibid.
57  Pian Chan and Brunner (2008).
58  Ibid.
59  Lombardo (2008).
60  Ibid.
61  Helman (2012).
62  Maul (2009).
63  Burke (2012b).
64  Ibid.
65  Lombardo and King (2012).
66  Ourand and Lombardo (2012).
67  Booth (2012).

 **REFERENCES**

Ackman, Dan (2001), 'Top of the news: XFL exterminated', Forbes.com, 11 May 2001, accessed 11 December 2011 at http://www.forbes.com/2001/05/11/0511topnews.html.

A.T. Kearney, Inc. (2011), 'The sports market', accessed 13 May 2013 at http://www.atkearney.co.uk/documents/10192/6f46b880-f8d1-4909-9960-cc605bb1ff34.

Badenhausen, Kurt (2011), 'NASCAR's most valuable teams', Forbes.com, 23 February 2011, accessed 30 July 2012 at http://www.forbes.com/2011/02/23/nascar-most-valuable-teams-business-sports-nascar-11.html.

Badenhausen, Kurt (2012), 'NASCAR's highest paid drivers', Forbes.com, 22 February 2012, accessed 30 July 2012 at http://www.forbes.com/sites/kurtbadenhausen/2012/02/22/nascars-highest-paid-drivers/.

Balony, Buford (2011), '2011 Rugby World Cup is 2nd best of all time', Ozzie News, 31 March 2011, accessed 3 September 2011 at http://www.ozzienews.com/sport/2011-rugby-world-cup-is-2nd-best-of-all-time/.

Beasley, Bryan (2010), 'Sports media contracts: evaluating revenue to leagues and universities', BleacherReport.com, 29 December 2010, accessed 22 June 2011 at http://bleacherreport.com/articles/556188-sports-media-contracts-evaluating-revenue-to-leagues-and-universities.

Booth, Tim (2012), 'Seattle's basketball hopes sit with Chris Hansen', CBS Seattle, 22 June 2012, accessed 14 May 2013 at http://seattle.cbslocal.com/2012/06/23/seattles-basketball-hopes-sit-with-chris-hansen/.

Brand Finance (2012), 'Football brands (2012)', accessed 11 September 2012 at http://brandfinance.com/images/upload/brandfinance_football_brands_2012.pdf, 9.

Broughton, David (2010), 'Official brands get a good ride with NASCAR', Sports Business Daily, 28 November 2010, accessed 30 July 2012 at http://www.sportsbusinessdaily.com/Journal/Issues/2011/11/28/Research-and-Ratings/NASCAR-Sponsor-Loyalty.aspx.

BtoB (2012), 'PGA Tour offers marketers a major link to business decision makers', 14 March 2012, accessed 15 March 2012 at http://www.btobonline.com/article/20120514/MEDIAPOWER/305149946/pga-tour-offers-marketers-a-major-link-to-business-decision-makers#.

Burke, Monte (2012a), 'The richest tournaments on the PGA Tour', Forbes.com, 8 May 2012, accessed 13 May 2012 at http://www.forbes.com/sites/monteburke/2012/05/08/the-richest-tournaments-on-the-pga-tour/.

Burke, Monte (2012b), 'Getting to know the Oklahoma City Thunder', Forbes.com, 7 June

2012, accessed 31 May 2013 at http://www.forbes.com/sites/monteburke/2012/06/07/getting-to-know-the-oklahoma-city-thunder/.

Chakrabarti, Sumon K. (2010), 'Watchdog questions Commonwealth Games deals', Time.com, 26 October 2010, accessed 1 November 2011 at http://www.time.com/time/world/article/0,8599,2027349,00.html.

Cutler, Matt (2010), 'Big Four US sports enjoy sponsorship hike', IEG, 19 November 2010, accessed 22 January 2011 at http://www.sponsorship.com/About-IEG/IEG-In-The-News/Big-Four-US-Sports-Enjoy-Sponsorship-Hike.aspx.

Diaz, George (2012), 'NASCAR models for '13 will look more like passenger cars', *Chicago Tribune*, 1 August 2012, accessed 21 August 2012 at http://www.chicagotribune.com/sports/motorracing/sc-spt-0801-notes-autos-module--20120801,0,3082368.story.

'FAQs about the Indianapolis Motor Speedway' (n.d.), Indianapolismotorspeedway.com, accessed 30 July 2012 at http://www.indianapolismotorspeedway.com/about/35550-FAQ/.

FIFA.com (2010), '61st FIFA Congress FIFA financial report 2010', 31 May–1 June 2011, accessed 14 January at http://www.fifa.com/mm/document/affederation/administration/01/39/20/45/web_fifa_fr2010_eng[1].pdf.

Gibson, Owen (2012), 'Premier League lands £3bn TV rights bonanza from Sky and BT', *The Guardian*, 13 June 2012, accessed 21 June 2012 at http://www.guardian.co.uk/media/2012/jun/13/premier-league-tv-rights-3-billion-sky-bt.

Helman, Christopher (2012), 'The sordid deal that created the Oklahoma City Thunder', Forbes.com, 13 June 2012, accessed 21 July 2012 at http://www.forbes.com/sites/christopherhelman/2012/06/13/the-sordid-story-of-how-aubrey-mcclendon-and-pals-transformed-the-seattle-sonics-into-the-oklahoma-city-thunder/.

'History of NASCAR' (2010), NASCAR.com, 8 March 2010, accessed 24 July 2012 at http://www.nascar.com/news/features/history/.

Horrow, R. and K. Swatek (2010), *Beyond the Box Score: An Insider's Guide to the $750 Billion Business of Sports*, New York: Morgan James.

International Cricket Council (n.d.), 'Annual Report 2011–2012, accessed 11 September 2012 at http://static.icc-cricket.com/ugc/documents/DOC_5053F902931ACD247E88928C5B0FA3AD_1350473037465_438.pdf, 36.

Johns, Greg (2007), 'Bennett says Sonics going to Oklahoma', *Seattle Post-Intelligencer*, 2 November 2007, accessed 14 May 2013 at http://www.seattlepi.com/news/article/Bennett-says-Sonics-going-to-Oklahoma-1254432.php?source=mypi.

Lombardo, John (2008), 'Starting over', *Sports Business Journal*, 27 October 2008, accessed 21 July 2012 at http://www.sportsbusinessdaily.com/Journal/Issues/2008/10/20081027/SBJ-In-Depth/Starting-Over.aspx?hl=seattle%20supersonics&sc=0.

Lombardo, John and Bill King (2012), 'The action's on the floor', *Sports Business Journal*, 21 May 2012, accessed 21 July 2012 at http://www.sportsbusinessdaily.com/Journal/Issues/2012/05/21/Franchises/NBA-seats.aspx?hl=costs%20oklahoma%20city%20thunder&sc=0.

Long, Dustin (2012), 'U.S. Army to discontinue NASCAR sponsorship in 2013', USA Today, 11 July 2012, accessed 30 July 2012 at http://www.usatoday.com/sports/motor/nascar/story/2012-07-10/Army-wont-return-to-NASCAR-in-2013/56126666/1.

Marium (n.d.), 'IPL 5 broadcasting channels 2012', 3jig.com, accessed 27 June 2012 at http://www.3jig.com/sports/ipl-5-broadcasting-channels-2012.

Maul, Kimberly (2009), 'Sports entities must adapt a new game plan to reach fans', *PR Week*, 1 October 2009, 20.

Mickle, Tripp and John Ourand (2011), 'NASCAR viewership jumps 8%, halts long slide', *Sports Business Daily*, 5 December 2011, accessed 17 December 2011 at http://www.sportsbusinessdaily.com/Journal/Issues/2011/12/05/Leagues-and-Governing-Bodies/NASCAR.aspx.

Mickle, Tripp and John Ourand (2012a), 'NASCAR: no panic over dip in 18–34 demo', *Sports Business Journal*, 11 June 2012, 4.

Mickle, Tripp and John Ourand (2012b), 'Fox making strong bid to keep NASCAR', *Sports Business Journal*, 18 June 2012, 8.

'NASCAR Foundation reaches $1m for Speediatrics' (2012), Nascar.com, 25 July 2012, accessed 31 July 2012 at http://www.nascar.com/news/120725/nascar-foundation-donation-milestone-speediatrics/index.html.

NASCAR Racing Series (2010), NASCAR.com, 8 March 2010, accessed 24 July 2012 at http://www.nascar.com/news/features/nascar.series/index.html.

NASCAR Racing Statistics (2012), Statistic Brain, 15 March 2012, accessed 22 March 2012 at http://www.statisticbrain.com/nascar-racing-statistics/.

New York Sports Journalism (2010), 'Report: pro sports sponsorships are the real financial deal in NFL, MLB, NBA, NHL', IEG, 18 November 2010, accessed 2 July 2011 at http://www.sponsorship.com/About-IEG/IEG-In-The-News/Report--Pro-Sports-Sponsorships-Are-The-Real-Finan.aspx.

Olympic Marketing Fact File (2012), accessed 30 July 2012 at http://www.olympic.org/Documents/IOC_Marketing/OLYMPIC-MARKETING-FACT-FILE-2012.pdf.

Ourand, John and John Lombardo (2012), 'NBA's small markets hang tough in play-offs, but so do the League's TV ratings', *Sports Business Journal*, 2 July 2012, accessed 21 July 2012 at http://www.sportsbusinessdaily.com/Journal/Issues/2012/07/02/Media/NBA-ratings.aspx?hl=costs%20oklahoma%20city%20thunder&sc=0.

Ozanian, Mike (2012), 'The business of baseball 2012', Forbes.com, 21 March 2012, accessed 29 May 2012 at http://www.forbes.com/sites/mikeozanian/2012/03/21/the-business-of-baseball-2012/.

Paddock Magazine (n.d.), 'F1's record revenues', accessed 22 August 2012 at http://www.thepaddockmagazine.com/articles/features/f1-s-record-revenues.

Park, Clayton (2011), 'Fan loyalty to sponsors' products fuels NASCAR success', *Daytona Beach News Journal*, 20 February 2011, accessed 30 July 2012 at http://www.sponsorship.com/About-IEG/IEG-In-The-News/Fan-Loyalty-to-Sponsors--Products-Fuels-NASCAR-Suc.aspx.

Peltz, Jim (2012), 'NASCAR grapples with downshift in popularity', *LA Times*, 21 March 2012, accessed 30 July 2012 at http://articles.latimes.com/2011/mar/21/sports/la-sp-nascar-20110322.

Pian Chan, Shannon and Richard Brunner (2008), 'Sonics, city reach settlement', *Seattle Times*, 2 July 2008, accessed 21 July 2012 at http://seattletimes.nwsource.com/html/localnews/2008030229_sonitrial02.html.

Ryan, Nate (2012), 'NASCAR's Brian France says shortened races on the table', USA Today, 6 July 2012, accessed 21 August 2012 at http://www.usatoday.com/sports/motor/nascar/story/2012-07-06/CEO-brian-france-advocates-shorter-races-dismisses-caution-flags/56062950/1.

Schoettle, Anthony (2012), 'Brickyard 400 profitable despite falling crowds, experts say', *Indianapolis Business Journal*, 30 July 2012, accessed 31 July 2012 at http://www.ibj.com/nascar-in-indy-still-profitable-despite-falling-crowds--experts-say/PARAMS/article/35811.

Scott, David and Andrew Dunn (2012), 'NASCAR ticket revenue in sharp decline', *Charlotte Observer*, 8 July 2012, accessed 15 May 2013 at http://www.thatsracin.com/2012/07/07/91025/nascar-ticket-revenue-in-sharp.html.

TSN (2011), 'NHL announces 10-year TV deal with NBC and Versus', 19 April 2011, TSN, accessed 2 July 2011 at http://www.tsn.ca/nhl/story/?id=362861.

*The Economist* (2011), 'Beyond Tiger', 9 June 2011, accessed 23 June 2011 at http://www.economist.com/node/18805531.

# 2

# The sports marketing context

 **CHAPTER OVERVIEW**

Chapter 1 provided an overview of the sports industry, establishing the basic context to help sports marketers gain an understanding of the big picture. We will expand on the sports industry context in this chapter, comparing and contrasting it with non-sports businesses to give astute students a better understanding of those factors that make the sports industry unique, and begin analyzing the differences in organizational models across leagues. Each of these aforementioned areas are important pieces of information for sports marketers to grasp since the success of their decisions will depend partly on their ability to understand how the industry's different variables interact with each other and, where relevant, show how these factors compare to non-sports businesses. Gaining a deeper understanding of the industry will also assist sports marketers as they prepare their sports marketing plans. Particular emphasis will be on using the author's brand development framework, based on research of over 200+ companies and sports organizations around the world.

## 2.1 Comparing sports and non-sports industries

As an industry, sports share common interests with non-sports industries, yet they also have a unique set of competitive conditions that affect how sports marketers develop and implement their strategies. As Chapter 1 pointed out, the sports industry is complex and the success is dependent on appealing to the interests of fans, companies, and athletes alike. For students of sports marketing, they will become familiar with the similarities and differences between sports and non-sports industries. The comparison is important for understanding how sports marketing can be used to maximize company investments in sports entities.

## Similarities between sports and non-sports industries

### Strong leadership

Sports and non-sports companies share a common interest in strong leadership that provides a clear vision from which sound strategies can be developed to guide the direction of the enterprise. Strong leadership also guides how value is to be created by the company and which values define and animate the corporate culture within.

### Stakeholders as strategic assets

Stakeholders are the employees (management and non-management), customers, suppliers, government, trade associations, and shareholders. Each of these groups contributes to the companies' success in different ways (employees have the talent to realize the firm's ambitions; customers determine if the firm's offerings are valuable; suppliers ensure the quality of supporting components and ingredients are world class; government provides the protections and regulations that ensure competition is fair and that reasonable rules of conduct are followed; trade associations are typically membership organizations designed to promote the interests of the industry overall and the member companies within; and shareholders are investors that own part or all of the business, providing an importance source of capital), and their collective involvement can help to strengthen the overall enterprise.

### Importance of distinction

Sports and non-sports companies seek to create competitive advantage for themselves, and as a by-product, competitive disadvantage for their opponents, by developing unique and distinctive offerings. Distinction is typically seen as having a strong brand, whose qualities are clearly understood by the marketplace. Focusing on distinction enables companies to develop brand identities and reputations that resonate with the marketplace and make their offerings more recognizable compared to lesser-known competitors. Being distinctive means that companies must emphasize innovation in their offerings. Innovation is far more than simply being creative with advertising. True innovation must be reflected in the design of products and services that customers see as meaningful, relevant, and even surprising to them. Quality, too, is an important ingredient in creating and supporting a distinctive reputation. In the era of globalization, many companies around the world are capable of producing quality products, so quality is now a minimum cost of entry for any company today. A firm cannot remain distinctive if quality falls because there are too many eager and capable competitors ready to overtake a former quality leader. Recognized distinction can also reinforce a premium pricing strategy, which can positively affect the next area of commonality: revenue and profit growth.

### Ongoing pursuit of sound financial results

Finding new sources of revenue and having distinctive offerings that improve profit margins are essential to all businesses. Financial strength and growth enable companies to reinvest in the development of their business opportunities, develop their customer bases further, and enhance their market reputation. With an emphasis on innovation, companies can more credibly command higher prices than competitors because the perceived value from customers is greater.

### Development of trusted partnerships

Globalization has accelerated the entry of firms specializing in unique skills, whether those are in manufacturing, distribution, sourcing, marketing and more. Consequently, business growth often comes from the pursuit of new markets (geographically and/or customer type). Rather than attempting to own all of the areas of expertise (as vertical and horizontal integrators do), companies increasingly rely on the expertise of other firms to help in the development of market opportunities. With strong leadership, companies seek to build reputations as reliable and trustworthy partners since good relationships can positively affect how employees within each firm interact and make decisions on behalf of the overall partnership. Furthermore, trusted relationships can help reduce the inevitable tensions that arise when companies from different countries, with different cultures and practices, work together for a common interest.

## Differences between sports and non-sports industries

### Results and changes are more immediate

Sports businesses, particularly athletes and teams, face intense pressure to win, and to adjust quickly if results are not as expected. Athletes often find themselves removed from a game if their performance has not been up to par, or if they have committed a significant error. Non-sports businesses are often more forgiving of underperformance (up to a point), using mistakes as teachable moments from which future improvements and adjustments can be made.

## Sports owners are more hands-on

While sports and non-sports companies both have shareholders, non-sports companies typically have dispersed ownership, with shareholders owning very small percentages and very little if any input on day to day operations. Individual professional sports team ownership is concentrated (and less likely to be dispersed), with owners deeply involved in the decision-making on behalf of their teams. Sports owners are usually quite wealthy, accomplished and recognized business 'celebrities' and are more vocal about their ownership since the franchise(s) they own are seen as an extension of the personality and ego.

## Every decision is under the public microscope

In professional sports, athletes, teams, coaches and events operate under the equivalent of a public microscope, perpetually being examined and questioned about their performances and decisions by media and fans everywhere, creating unique pressures with outcomes that are both hard to predict and control. Such scrutiny changes the way sports marketing decisions are made as compared to non-sports industries. One can imagine how such scrutiny would alter the performance of non-sports companies if every employee's actions were similarly analyzed. As a result, sports franchises require people with the ability to withstand constant scrutiny and criticism. Of course, one could argue that the significant compensation professional athletes receive obligates them to relentless examination. High levels of athlete compensation makes them into far more valuable strategic assets for their organizations whose productivity and contributions directly affect the fortunes of the team on any given day, as opposed to regular employees of non-sports firms. Simply put, the higher compensation attracts greater scrutiny since the athlete is in effect the producer as well as the product and any underperformance means the sports franchise's assets are not adding the fullest value to the enterprise. Interestingly, sports franchise owners are not required to provide detailed financial statements (unless they are publicly traded), unlike publicly traded non-sports companies, thereby protecting them from the same level of scrutiny they, the media, and fans place on individual players. Despite these issues, companies find that using sports as a vehicle for marketing their brands and products is not just popular, but an important and valuable strategic investment.

## Higher-risk assets

Related to the previous section, athletes are critical strategic assets for their sports franchises, and a great deal of financial investment is tied to them through their playing contracts as well as any endorsements. Sponsoring companies and franchise owners have significant capital at risk if an athlete is injured or behaves in appropriately. Injury, of course, is hard to control since the pace of most sports is very fast and play is unpredictable – asset owners and sponsors simply have no way of knowing when a prized athlete is going to be injured and, as a consequence, how that will affect their investment (such as the impact on the rest of the team, fan interest, and media coverage, all of which are vital to helping create a return on investment when the athlete is otherwise healthy). Barring injury, owners and sponsors also face the risk of athletes behaving inappropriately (illegally, immorally, or irresponsibly). Such behavior can quickly create a negative perception about the athlete and the ensuing public backlash can directly affect the rest of the team and the sponsors as well. Non-sports businesses do not face a similar level of risk for their typical employee, which makes the management of sports franchises especially challenging.

### Share the wealth

Many sports leagues (the NFL is a good example) have revenue sharing and allocation agreements in an effort to ensure a more even distribution of financial proceeds to all teams in the league. Such financial engineering is designed to help small market teams (and teams with smaller budgets) stay competitive with large market, more financially successful clubs so that sports dynasties are hopefully avoided. As Roger Goodell, Commissioner of the NFL, stated in a 2012 interview with CBS's Show *60 Minutes*: 'It is a form of socialism. And it's worked quite well for us. So we try to combine socialism and capitalism. How can we socialize by sharing our revenue in a way that will allow every team the ability to compete?'[1]

While monopoly laws exist to prevent domination by any one company in an industry, non-sports businesses do not face revenue reallocation rules to the other firms in their industry to create competitive parity.

## 2.2    League structure and competition models

### Structure

The many professional sports leagues around the world feature structural and organizational characteristics common to all, as well as differences based partly on the unique traditions of each sport. The majority of the leagues are structured as distributed ownership models, meaning each team has its own ownership. In rare instances leagues may have a single entity ownership structure, whereby a main organizing body owns the teams and clubs within; or a hybrid ownership structure characterized by a single league ownership entity with individual team owners acting as shareholders. Irrespective of ownership structure, the sports governing bodies (leagues and/or associations) act as the central authority for rules of conduct to which all teams within adhere.

## Single entity ownership

The rationale supporting a single ownership league structure is to ensure competitive parity, especially in the league's formative stages, so that no one owner with a disproportionate amount of wealth can build a dominant franchise. Striving for competitive parity is an understandable need in a league's early years since league officials want to ensure that fans and sponsors have a reasonable assurance of their team succeeding and receiving media coverage. Competitive parity is not a guarantee of equal success for all teams, but in theory parity builds confidence that the end of season outcome is unpredictable. Examples of single entity ownership include:

- WNBA (Women's National Basketball Association), which had a single ownership structure at its founding (North America);
- MLS (Major League Soccer), which had a single ownership structure at its founding (North America).

## Distributed ownership

Distributed ownership means that each team is individually owned. Such a structure can confer obvious benefits to clubs with wealthier owners since they are in a position to offer more attractive salary packages to top tier athletes. However, competitive balance issues have arisen in which a small number of teams dominate over time. Leagues have put salary caps in place, penalizing teams financially by levying a luxury tax should they exceed the salary maximum. In addition, big market clubs have tended to generate a disproportionate share of broadcast and merchandise revenues, which can further enrich the wealthier clubs. The NFL has created broadcast and merchandising revenue sharing schemes to help reduce the revenue imbalances and help small market clubs remain financially competitive. Examples of distributed ownership include:

- NFL (National Football League – North America);
- CFL (Canadian Football League – North America);

- MLB (Major League Baseball –North America);
- NBA (National Basketball Association – North America);
- NBL (National Basketball League – Australia);
- NHL (National Hockey League – North America);
- AFL (Australian Football League – 'Aussie Rules');
- Nippon Professional Baseball (Japan);
- Premier League (UK);[a,b]
- La Liga (Spain);[a]
- Serie A (Italy);[a]
- Bundesliga (Germany);[a]
- IPL (Indian Premier League – India);
- F1 (Formula One Auto Racing – Worldwide).

Notes:
a. These are leagues within each country. Teams within each league are also part of UEFA, the Union of European Football Associations, which is a governing body for Europe's 53 national football associations.
b. The Premier League can also be considered a hybrid ownership in that while each club is individually owned and operated, the Premier League itself is also a corporation whose shareholders are the 20 member clubs in any given season.

## Hybrid ownership structure

This includes:

- WNBA (Women's National Basketball Association) (six teams with individual owners, six owned by NBA teams);
- MLS (Major League Soccer) (17 of 19 clubs in 2012 had individual owners).

Both the WNBA and MLS placed salary caps on the teams to keep costs under relative control and reinforce balance across the league. In 2008 the WNBA agreed to a new collective bargaining contract that would allow team payrolls to climb to $900 000 in 2013 (from $728 000 in 2007) and a maximum salary of $100 000+ for a veteran player of six years or more.[2] In 2007 MLS created the 'designated player' exception, which allowed teams to have one designated player outside the salary cap, enabling MLS teams to recruit top international stars. A portion of the designated player's salary is charged to the salary cap, with the team owner responsible for the remainder of the contract. The designated player rule has been modified over the years and in 2012 teams were allowed two designated players and the amount charged against the salary cap was based on the age of the player, with younger players' salary cap charges lower based on their ages (for 23 years+, the salary cap charge is $350 000; for players aged 21–23 the salary cap charge is $200 000; and for players and 20 or under, the salary cap charge is $150 000).[3]

## Competition

The most obvious differences among sports leagues pertain to determining champions at the end of each sport's season. In Europe, football clubs in their respective national leagues receive three points for each win, one point for a tie, and no points for a loss. At the end of the season the team with the most points is declared the champion. In the event of a tie, a single game play-off at a neutral site is held to determine league champion. European leagues also promote the best teams to the highest division and relegate the poorest performers to lower divisions.

In contrast, most North American leagues use a play-off system, pitting the top teams from the regular season against each other for several rounds of five- and seven-game play-off series. The two final teams play a best-of-seven games series to determine league champion, except for the NFL, where the Super Bowl game determines the winner. Australian sports leagues are similar to those in North America. The Indian Premier League, in which competing teams play a form of cricket called Twenty20, compete in two play-off rounds before the top two teams play for the championship.[4]

Understanding the characteristics of sports leagues around the world provides marketers with insights about each sport's unique competitive environment, which can then help guide decision-making for the most effective way to invest their sports marketing dollars.

## 2.3 Brand planning framework

Armed with a clearer understanding of the sports industry, sports marketers must begin developing a marketing plan for their organization. The purpose of a plan is to provide guidance for how to effectively use the sports marketing resources (people, capital, partnerships) in a way that not only improves short-term financial performance but also helps the organization build a strong and formidable brand for the long term. It is important to not only be aware of the role developing a strong brand can play in creating sustained and improved value, but to *think through* the implications and potential outcomes of the planning choices being made. The author has studied over 200 companies and sports teams around the world to help explain how the most successful among them have created significant value, both financially and in terms of a more positive reputation. The best-performing organizations studied excelled in four areas: *destiny, distinction, culture,* and *experiences.*[5] Sports marketers should first carefully consider each of the four areas outlined below for their organizations so that a robust and useful plan can then be developed. Much like entering a game without any knowledge of your team's strengths or a plan for neutralizing the capabilities of the opponent would likely lead to a disastrous loss, ignoring the brand planning framework means critical insights and understandings about the sports marketer's organization will be missed and the resulting planning tactics will be far off the mark for what is really needed to succeed. Figure 2.1 shows the four components of the brand planning framework:

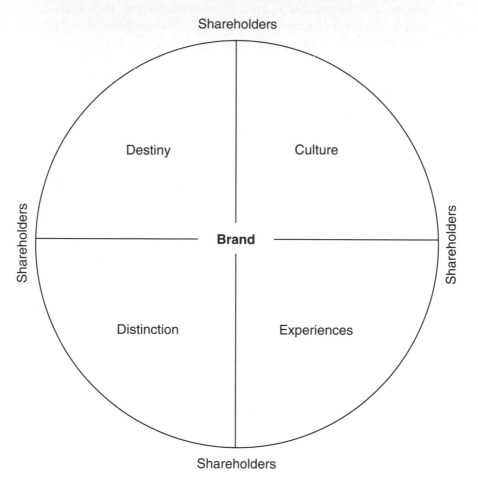

Source: Davis (2013). Derived from research by Davis, John A. in *Competitive Success – How Branding Adds Value.* Pp.95–118 (©2010 John Wiley & Sons).

**Figure 2.1** The four components of the brand planning framework

## Destiny

Destiny answers the question *why*? Why does the organization exist and why should people care? Destiny is similar, but not identical to vision. Destiny asks, what is the organization's ultimate, ideal destination if it were to truly have achieved all it could? In essence, and perhaps too simply, destiny is *extremely* long term. As should be readily apparent, an organization's destiny is never fully realized even though it strives continuously to achieve it. In contrast, vision describes the long-term (five to ten years) direction of the organization and may change over time as competitive, economic and social conditions warrant, providing relatively temporary guidance on the organization's pathway to its destiny.

### Example: Real Madrid

Real Madrid FC's destiny is unequivocally clear and has been since it was founded in 1902: 'To have respected players known for championship caliber football'.[6]

Real Madrid FC is one of the world's leading football clubs and, as shown in Chapter 1, one of its most valuable with a brand value of $1.45 billion. The club's destiny is neither mysterious nor complicated, but it is also not fully realized each year since other teams, such as Barcelona, rise to the occasion and win the La Liga title. Nevertheless, Real Madrid's destiny animates its direction and highlights that its ongoing ambition is to always play championship caliber football.

## Distinction

Distinction focuses organizational thinking and efforts around identifying *what* makes their company and/or products unique. Uniqueness requires substantial effort to develop, let alone sustain. As seen in Chapter 1, being unique compels organizations to focus on innovation and quality that matters to their customers and, thereby, distinguishes them from competitors. When distinction is successfully pursued, organizations are able to charge premium prices over comparable offerings from competitors, partly because the marketplace expects to pay more for an offering that stands apart.

### Example: Olympic Games

The Olympic Games are distinctive in the world of mega-sports events because of several factors: their 3000-year history; the 28 sports and 300+

events in every Summer Olympics and the seven sports and 80+ events in every Winter Olympics, making the Games unrivaled in tradition, variety of sports, and complexity; and the core set of values that define what being an Olympian is, understood across continents, countries, and cultures.[7]

## Culture

Culture explains *who* is involved in the success of the organization. Employees are directly involved, of course, and so are suppliers and shareholders, although more indirectly. Even customers (fans) can be considered a part of the organizational culture insofar as they become loyal followers that make a concerted effort to not just attend games or watch them on TV, but involve themselves more directly through social media and events. Customers of sports manufacturers can also be considered part of the organizational culture when they remain loyal to the firm's products and make consistent suggestions to improve offerings.

### Examples: Barcelona FC, Nike

Modern sports teams are increasingly less defined by the stability of their rosters, viewed instead through the lens of wins and championships. Nevertheless, teams do still try to build around a core group of stars, or even a single superstar, combining different talents in a way that can help establish a unique playing style that also permeates the overall culture. Barcelona FC is well known for its pinpoint, artistic passing, which is a distinctive skill set that has been built over time through its football academy, used for developing future stars.

Sports companies also work hard to develop rich cultures. Nike has historically sought employees who love sports, whether or not they have competed at the highest levels (although that is usually a positive attribute as well).

## Experiences

Experiences describe *how* the market will interact with the brand. As the term experience implies, an experience is a happening, a contact, or an occurrence that leaves an indelible impression, preferably favorable. Traditionally, interaction was primarily between the company's products and the customer (or the customer's usage of that product). In today's context, interactions between organizations and their offerings occur through many different mechanisms, more commonly called touchpoints. Touchpoints are where the customer and the organization meet. These can be in a tangible location, such as a retail store, or through intangible activities, such as services.

Experiences encompass a wide range of touchpoints, from advertising to sales people; from merchandise to attending a sports event, and so on.

*Example: F1*

An F1 motor race illustrates how sports experiences work. Over the course of a 19–20 race season, 12 teams with up to four drivers each compete for two championships: the driver's championship; and the constructor's championship. Each F1 race is held in a different country around the world and the race courses are as varied as the countries. Singapore began hosting the first night time race in the history of F1 racing in 2008, and the overall experience was enhanced by offering a racing atmosphere never previously seen in this sport. Combined with F1's known touchpoints (fast state of the art cars, loud engines, unpredictable action and results, sponsor signage, energetic announcers, pit stop dynamics, prestigious brands, exciting drivers etc.), fans enjoy a virtually non-stop sensory experience that leaves them exhilarated and exhausted. Each of these experience-based touchpoints develops and reinforces the sport's brand reputation.

The brand planning framework guides marketers in identifying the qualities and characteristics of their organization, knowledge of which then helps them develop specific actions to grow their businesses consistent with their organization's capabilities and ambitions. In addition, using the brand planning framework also helps ascertain the ways markets can most effectively build brand value.

## 2.4 Brand value framework

Sport, from sports products to sports events, is a big business and this is made abundantly clear when examining a vital measure of value known as *brand value*. The concept of brand value is deceptively simple: *brand value represents the total value of the brand, whether that brand is a single, well known product, or an entire company.*

The framework defines value along four dimensions as represented in Figure 2.2.

### Financial

Business people most commonly define value in financial terms. Financial value is both familiar and essential as a means of assessing whether the

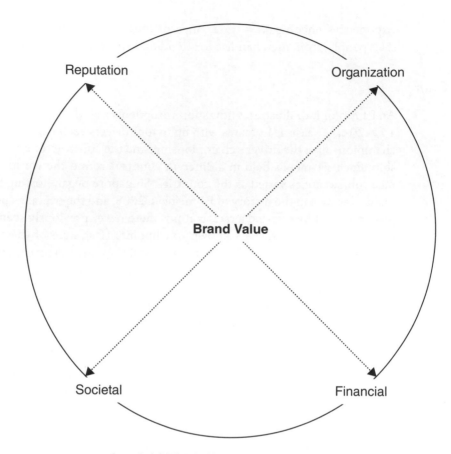

Reputation

Organization

**Brand Value**

Societal

Financial

Source: Davis (2013). Derived from research by Davis, John A. in *Competitive Success – How Branding Adds Value*. Pp.34–42 (©2010 John Wiley & Sons).

**Figure 2.2** The four dimensions of the brand value framework

marketing activities contribute to the growth of the brand. Financial value shows the measured numerical by-product of the sports marketer's actions. Brand Finance®, a global consultancy specializing in brand valuation, produces annual brand valuation surveys ranking the world's most valuable brands in their respective industries. As discussed in Chapter 1, brand value is a significant portion of total company value (also called 'market capitalization').

## Example: Top 50 football clubs

In 2012 Brand Finance ranked the top 50 football (soccer) clubs around the world based on brand value (Table 2.1).[8]

Reviewing the top 50 football clubs illustrates the importance of financial brand value. Developing and nurturing this value is a central part of any

**Table 2.1** Top 50 football clubs around the world, based on brand value

| Club/Team | Country | League | 2012 Brand Value |
|---|---|---|---|
| 1 Manchester United | UK | Premier | US$853 million |
| 2 Bayern Munich | Germany | Bundesliga | US$786 million |
| 3 Real Madrid | Spain | La Liga | US$600 million |
| 4 FC Barcelona | Spain | La Liga | US$580 million |
| 5 Chelsea | UK | Premier | US$398 million |
| 6 Arsenal | UK | Premier | US$388 million |
| 7 Liverpool | UK | Premier | US$367 million |
| 8 Manchester City | UK | Premier | US$302 million |
| 9 AC Milan | Italy | Serie A | US$292 million |
| 10 Schalke 04 | Germany | Bundesliga | US$266 million |
| 11 Borussia Dortmund | Germany | Bundesliga | US$227 million |
| 12 Tottenham | UK | Premier | US$225 million |
| 13 Inter Milan | Italy | Serie A | US$215 million |
| 14 Ajax | Netherlands | Eredivisie | US$184 million |
| 15 Olympique de Marseille | France | Ligue 1 | US$168 million |
| 16 Juventus | Italy | Serie A | US$160 million |
| 17 Hamburg SV | Germany | Bundesliga | US$153 million |
| 18 Olympique Lyonais | France | Ligue 1 | US$120 million |
| 19 Aston Villa | UK | Premier | US$87 million |
| 20 Newcastle United | UK | Premier | US$86 million |
| 21 AS Roma | Italy | Serie A | US$85 million |
| 22 SSC Napoli | Italy | Serie A | US$85 million |
| 23 Everton | UK | Premier | US$79 million |
| 24 SC Corinthians Paulista | Brazil | CB Serie A | US$77 million |
| 25 FC Girondins de Bordeaux | France | Ligue 1 | US$77 million |
| 26 PSV Eindhoven | Netherlands | Eredivisie | US$74 million |
| 27 FC Basel 1893 | Switzerland | Swiss Super | US$72 million |
| 28 VFB Stuttgart | Germany | Bundesliga | US$71 million |
| 29 West Ham United FC | UK | Premier | US$70 million |
| 30 Werder Bremen | Germany | Bundesliga | US$68 million |
| 31 Valencia CF | Spain | La Liga | US$68 million |
| 32 VfL Wolfsburg | Germany | Bundesliga | US$66 million |
| 33 Sunderland AFC | UK | Premier | US$66 million |
| 34 Fulham FC | UK | Premier | US$65 million |
| 35 Guangzhou Evergrande FC | China | Chinese Super | US$65 million |
| 36 Bayer 04 Leverkusen | Germany | Bundesliga | US$64 million |
| 37 Celtic | UK | Scottish Premier | US$64 million |
| 38 Paris Saint-Germain FC | France | Ligue 1 | US$64 million |
| 39 São Paulo FC | Brazil | CB Serie A | US$58 million |
| 40 Seattle Sounders FC | USA | MLS | US$58 million |
| 41 FC Zenit St. Petersburg | Russia | Russian Premier | US$56 million |

**Table 2.1** (continued)

| Club/Team | Country | League | 2012 Brand Value |
| --- | --- | --- | --- |
| 42 Stoke City FC | UK | Premier | US$55 million |
| 43 Hertha BSC Berlin | Germany | Bundesliga | US$55 million |
| 44 SC International | Brazil | CB Serie A | US$51 million |
| 45 Atlético de Madrid | Spain | La Liga | US$50 million |
| 46 Sevilla FC | Spain | La Liga | US$49 million |
| 47 CR Flamengo | Brazil | CB Serie A | US$46 million |
| 48 SS Lazio | Italy | Serie A | US$46 million |
| 46 ACF Fiorentina | Italy | Serie A | US$46 million |
| 50 Los Angeles Galaxy | USA | MLS | US$46 million |

sports marketer's responsibilities. However, financial value alone only shows a measured calculation. As with any business planning efforts, marketers must understand the surrounding business environment to gain a complete understanding of the contextual factors that influence financial value. The three other value-creating dimensions have a direct influence on the creation of financial value:

## Reputation

Trust is at the core of a brand's reputation. Business practitioners and academic researchers over the years have established that long-term business success is built on a foundation of trust. The level of trust between the brand and its stakeholders is a key factor in determining how successful, and influential, it is. Trust is essential when customers decide to purchase a company's offerings, and it is a necessary ingredient for productive business partnerships. Trust is developed and reinforced whenever a brand delivers on its promises to the market and is catalyst for promoting positive word of mouth. The development of trust must be consciously embedded in every activity the brand and its caretakers undertake and every touchpoint where the brand and its customers intersect, from products to delivery to advertising to support. Conversely, the absence of trust undermines the entire business and erodes relationships and market confidence, directly harming the brand's reputation and, ultimately, its financial value.

### Example: Tennis and golf

All sports rely on the intrinsic trust and integrity of the athletes within to ensure competition is fair and victory is achieved through honest, ethical means. Professional tennis and golf are each examples of how reputations and trust are made, and sometimes lost.

Consider what these sports share in common. They are not team sports, for the most part (the exceptions are Davis Cup and doubles in tennis, and the Ryder Cup in golf), pitting individuals against one another. In both sports it is the responsibility of the athlete to fairly track scores, and even signal their own mistakes. Certainly, with television cameras watching every move and various sport officials, evidence of cheating in these sports is scant. One can imagine, particularly in golf, if a player were to record the wrong score, or secretively move the ball to gain a better lie, how swift and stinging the rebuke would be from officials and fans if the transgression were discovered, never mind the penalties that the golfer would face from sponsors. Fortunately for both golf and tennis, very few examples of distrust have arisen over the decades. Conversely, the sport of cycling has seen a steady erosion of trust over the years as the performance enhancement substances scandals have seen one champion after another toppled due to anti-doping violations, with the most visible being Lance Armstrong, who chose to no longer fight allegations of doping and subsequently had his seven Tour de France titles stripped, as well as all other titles since 1998, among other penalties. Although cycling officials are attempting to fix their sport, the reputation damage from the past 20 years has undermined public trust, undoubtedly harming each of the sport's stakeholders, whether or not they have individually contributed to the scandals. Rebuilding a reputation is the most challenging turnaround facing any business, both sports and non-sports.

## Organization

Organizational value refers to the intangible benefits derived by employees, and as a consequence the organization, when their level of understanding about their brand's strategy, direction, and supporting marketing activities is crystal clear. To gain employee support on an organization-wide scale requires management to coherently and regularly communicate the key objectives being pursued and, just as importantly, the relevance of these objectives to the employees' daily efforts. When employees perceive that their contributions are meaningful and have a direct impact on the brand's success, then this often translates into a belief that they are part of a larger cause, well beyond simply doing one's job just to earn a wage. Successfully imbuing a sense of cause is one of management's greatest ongoing challenges, especially considering a concomitant pressure to focus purely on financial gain. Shareholders are interested in financial gain for obvious reasons, but organization leaders must also be concerned with how financial gain can be realized, and this means spending considerable effort and resources on inspiring employees to achieve something greater than just enhancing shareholder wealth. Gains in shareholder wealth are a by-product of management's success in motivating their organization to exceed expectations by creating a corporate culture that reinforces the rewards (psychic and financial) for being part of a significant cause.

### Example: Under Armour

Under Armour (UA) is a US-based athletic products company founded in 1996, with 2011 revenues of US$1.47 billion. The company specializes in sports apparel, footwear, and accessories. UA is known for having an intensely competitive corporate culture (like Nike) that aspires to not only be one of the world's leading sports brands, but to one day overtake them. Management seeks employees that love sports and have a desire to beat all competitors, irrespective of size. The company's founder, Kevin Plank, is well regarded for being driven and demanding while also being thoughtful and polite, in the context of sports, and his positive energy infuses the company's employees with a similar appetite for winning. From the top down, the company philosophy is for all employees to take responsibility and solve problems, not point fingers or blame outside factors. Management asks new employees 'What do you want to be?' and the company's retail employees ask the same question to customers, creating a consistent sense of commitment to setting ambitious goals and then finding ways to achieve them. UA is considered a great place to work, particularly for younger employees.[9]

## Societal

Societal value is created when a brand makes meaningful and relevant contributions to the communities it serves, above and beyond providing jobs and generating financial returns. The twenty-first century has witnessed a sea change in the marketplace's expectations of companies, demanding greater accountability and involvement in solving society's larger challenges, such as environmental, healthcare, humanitarian, education or energy issues. Corporate social responsibility (CSR) has been an important topic taught in business schools the past 25 years, reflecting society's interest in seeing companies use some of their profits to demonstrate integrity and leadership by example. CSR takes on many meanings, including how a company's network of suppliers ensure their

activities minimize harm and maximize good. Societal value is an especially pronounced expectation for those involved in sports, particularly the
athletes and teams, since they often receive substantial and disproportionate compensation rewards for their efforts. Athletes supply a social good
through their participation in sports and the ensuing entertainment value
it creates, but public sentiment encourages athletes to look beyond their
sport for ways to leverage their well-known personas to achieve a higher
level of social good in the world.

### Example: Green Sports Alliance

The Green Sports Alliance (www.greensportsalliance.org) was founded
in 2010 by six professional sports teams in the Pacific Northwest of the
United States, with the stated ambition to improve the environmental performance of sports facilities and operations. The Green Sports Alliance has
grown to over 50 professional teams, 45 sports venues, and 20 business partners (leagues, companies, and not-for-profit organizations). The Alliance
members collaborate on how to ensure sporting events are performed in a
way that minimizes environmental impact.

## 2.5  Advertising

Advertising remains an important part of total marketing activities since it
is how companies communicate about their offerings. The rapid emergence
of digital and social media offers sports marketers valuable new avenues for
engaging with their target audiences. All advertising spending was affected
by the 2008 global financial crisis worldwide, but sports advertising expenditures, particularly in the USA began to show impressive increases in
2010. Sports advertising increased 27 percent in 2010 over 2009 (and 22
percent over 2008), with the top 50 US advertisers spending a total of $6.6
billion. Ninety-two percent of these top 50 advertisers increased their sports
spending over 2009.

Table 2.2 compares sports leagues, including sponsorship revenues, ad
spending, total merchandise spending, and the unique characteristics of each
league.

Table 2.3 compares major sports events, including sponsorship revenues,
advertising revenues, broadcast revenues, and unique characteristics of the
event.

**Table 2.2** A comparison of sports leagues

| League/ Governing Body | # of Teams | # of TV Viewers | # of Social Media Users | Avg. Attendance Per Game | Champion-ship | Champion-ship Viewers | Total League Revenues |
|---|---|---|---|---|---|---|---|
| **(A2)** NFL | **(B2)** 32 | **(C2)** Average 17.5 million per game, over 200 million total in 2011 | **(D2)** 6 079 843 likes on Facebook (891 738 likes on Facebook for Super Bowl), 3 699 221 followers on Twitter, 5734 followers on Instagram, 55 998 on Google+ | **(E2)** 67 358 in 2011 | **(F2)** SuperBowl | **(G2)** 100 million+ (111.3 million record set in 2012) | **(H2)** $9 billion |
| **(A3)** EPL | **(B3)** 20 | **(C3)** 4.7 billion global in 2011 | **(D3)** 1 674 480 likes on Facebook, 312 155 followers on Twitter, 311 on Google+ | **(E3)** 34 601 in 2011/12 | **(F3)** Premier League Champion-ship | **(G3)** 650 million worldwide in 2012 | **(H3)** 2.5 billion in 2010/11 |
| **(A4)** IPL | **(B4)** 9 | **(C4)** 122.44 million in 2012 | **(D4)** 1 209 371 likes on Facebook, 340 525 | **(E4)** 32 182 attended Delhi Daredevils | **(F4)** IPL Champion-ship | **(G4)** 55.5 million | **(H4)** 10 billion in 2011 ($18 122 500) |

| Revenue Sharing Info. | Total Sponsorship Revenues | Total Advertising Revenues | Total Merchandise Revenues | Player Selection (highlights how drafts, or whatever mechanism are used to recruit players) | Broadcast Revenues (TV or digital rights deals) | Unique Characteristics |
|---|---|---|---|---|---|---|
| **(I2)** Players get 47% of league revenue, owners get 53% | **(J2)** $946 million in 2011 | **(K2)** $3 billion in 2011, $900.1 million in 2011 post-season | **(L2)** $2.5 billion in 2011 | **(M2)** Annual NFL Draft (every year during the off-season, a large pool of amateur players coming out of college enter themselves into the draft; selection order is the reverse order of finish at the close of the previous season though draft picks may be traded). Free Agency allows movement of players whose contracts are up | **(N2)** Combined national broadcasters paying $1.93 billion/year through 2013 and then escalating 7% annually up to $3.1 billion/year till 2022 | **(O2)** Most watched event in the world with 2012 Super Bowl; most watched sport in the USA |
| **(I3)** Domestic TV rights: 50% shared equally, 25% based on where team ends up rankings at end of season, 25% based on how often a team's matches are broadcast. Int'l TV rights, everything shared equally | **(J3)** $229 million in 2011 ($128 million in shirt sponsorships in 2012) | **(K3)**$155 million in 2010 | **(L3)** 168 milion in 2011 | **(M3)** Players can join a club at any age and work up through the levels of play the club offers. Transfers enable foreign players to play in the EPL and sometimes, EPL teams are fielded entirely of foreign players | **(N3)** £3 billion television deal over three years signed June 2012 | **(O3)** Promotion and relegation system where bottom three teams get 'relegated' to lower Football League Championship; top four teams in EPL play for UEFA Champions League title |
| **(I4)** 'The franchises will receive 80% of the television revenue over the | **(J4)** RS 800 crore in 2011 | **(K4)** $140 million in 2012 | **(L4)** Chennai Super Kings 2011 | **(M4)** There are five ways that a franchise can acquire a player: | **(N4)** $1.026 billion for ten years signed | **(O4)** The league plays an abbreviated |

**Table 2.2** (continued)

| League/ Governing Body | # of Teams | # of TV Viewers | # of Social Media Users | Avg. Attendance Per Game | Champion- ship | Champion- ship Viewers | Total League Revenues |
|---|---|---|---|---|---|---|---|
| | | | followers on Twitter, 285 on Google+ | vs Pune Warriors match in April 2012 | | | |
| **(A5)** NHL | **(B5)** 30 | **(C5)** Boston Bruins highest at average 112 000 per game | **(D5)** 2 500 830 likes on Facebook, 1 348 476 followers on Twitter, 73 000 followers on Instagram, 28 180 on Google+ | **(E5)** 17 455 in 2011/12 | **(F5)** Stanley Cup | **(G5)** Stanley Cup Playoffs 2012: 3.01 million | **(H5)** $3.3 billion in 2011/12 |
| **(A6)** MLB | **(B6)** 30 | **(C6)** NYY highest in 2011 at avg. 309 000 | **(D6)** 1 494 721 likes on Facebook, 2 352 248 followers on | **(E6)** 30 366 per game in 2011; 73 425 568 total for 2011 season | **(F6)** World Series | **(G6)** 2011 World Series averaged 16.6 million viewers; | **(H6)** $7.5 billion in 2011 |

| Revenue Sharing Info. | Total Sponsorship Revenues | Total Advertising Revenues | Total Merchandise Revenues | Player Selection (highlights how drafts, or whatever mechanism are used to recruit players) | Broadcast Revenues (TV or digital rights deals) | Unique Characteristics |
|---|---|---|---|---|---|---|
| first two years, 70% in the third and fourth years, 60% between years five and ten, and 50% from the 11th year onwards. In addition, they will also receive 60% of the sponsorship revenue during the first ten years, after which they will receive 50%' (League began in 2007) | | | merchandise sales = Rs 3.5 crore | in the annual auction, signing domestic players, signing uncapped players, through trading, and signing replacements | January 2008 | form of cricket called Twenty20 where the match is capped at 20 overs |
| **(I5)** Currently negotiating a new CBA that is set to expire 9/15/2012. Under previous CBA, players get 57% of hockey-related revenues | **(J5)** $356 million in 2010 | **(K5)** Not disclosed | **(L5)** $750 million in 2009 | **(M5)** Annual NHL Entry Draft (every year during the off-season, a large pool of amateur players enter themselves into the draft; selection order is the reverse order of finish at the close of the previous season though draft picks may be traded), Free Agency allows movement of players whose contracts are up | **(N5)** Ten years $2 billion signed in 2011 | **(O5)** Annual Winter Classic outdoor hockey game raked in $36 million for the city of Boston, MA in 2010 |
| **(I6)** Each team plays in 31% of local revenue into central pot. Pot is divided | **(J6)** $585 million in 2010 | **(K6)** $452 million in 2011 postseason | **(L6)** $2.82 billion in 2009 | **(M6)** Annual MLB Draft, Every year during the off-season, a large pool of amateur players | **(N6)** $701.7 million annually in national contracts | **(O6)** New York Yankees are tied for most valuable American |

**Table 2.2** (continued)

| League/ Governing Body | # of Teams | # of TV Viewers | # of Social Media Users | Avg. Attendance Per Game | Champion-ship | Champion-ship Viewers | Total League Revenues |
|---|---|---|---|---|---|---|---|
| | | | Twitter, 45 000 followers on Instagram, 1 066 191 on Google+ | | | Game 7 had 25.4 million | |
| **(A7)** NBA | **(B7)** 30 | **(C7)** Regular season games on TNT: 2.5 million | **(D7)** 14 269 038 likes on Facebook, 5 790 687 followers on Twitter, 259 000 followers on Instagram, 1 219 849 on Google+ | **(E7)** 17 274 in 2011/12 | **(F7)** NBA Finals | **(G7)** NBA Finals averaged 16.5 million viewers through first four games of 2012 Finals | **(H7)** $4.3 billion in 2011 |

| Revenue Sharing Info. | Total Sponsorship Revenues | Total Advertising Revenues | Total Merchandise Revenues | Player Selection (highlights how drafts, or whatever mechanism are used to recruit players) | Broadcast Revenues (TV or digital rights deals) | Unique Characteristics |
|---|---|---|---|---|---|---|
| equally among all teams. Central fund (including broadcast $$) is allocated based on each team's revenue. By 2016, the 15 largest market teams will no longer be eligible for revenue sharing | | | | enter themselves into the draft; selection order is the reverse order of finish at the close of the previous season though draft picks may be traded), Free Agency allows movement of players whose contracts are up | | sports team (ranked by Forbes) at $185 million |
| (I7) 'All teams to contribute an annually fixed percentage, roughly 50%, of their total annual revenue (minus certain expenses such as arena operating costs, into a revenue sharing pool). Each team then receives an allocation equal to the league's average team payroll for that season from the revenue pool. If a team's contribution to the pool is less than the league's average team payroll, then that team is a revenue recipient. Teams | (J7) $572 million in 2010 | (K7) $448.5 in 2011 post-season | (L7) $1.80 billion in 2009 | (M7) Annual NBA Draft & Draft Lottery. Every year during the off-season, a large pool of amateur players enter themselves into the draft. In the NBA Draft Lottery, the team with the worst record in the regular season has the most chances for the number one pick, while the team with the best record among the non-playoff teams has the least number of chances. The Lottery determines the order of selection for the first three teams only; the remaining non-playoff teams select in inverse order of their | (N7) $900 million in 2011/12 season | (O7) The NBA is the best-paid league per person at an average of $79 860 per week in 2012 |

**Table 2.2** (continued)

| League/ Governing Body | # of Teams | # of TV Viewers | # of Social Media Users | Avg. Attendance Per Game | Champion- ship | Champion- ship Viewers | Total League Revenues |
|---|---|---|---|---|---|---|---|
| **(A8)** WNBA | **(B8)** 12 | **(C8)** 12 ESPN broad- casts drew 270000 viewers | **(D8)** 410828 likes on Facebook, 306116 followers on Twitter, 3 on Google+ | **(E8)** 7800 | **(F8)** WNBA Finals | **(G8)** 2011 Finals averaged 515000 viewers; Game 3 had 600000 | **(H8)** Not disclosed |

| Revenue Sharing Info. | Total Sponsorship Revenues | Total Advertising Revenues | Total Merchandise Revenues | Player Selection (highlights how drafts, or whatever mechanism are used to recruit players) | Broadcast Revenues (TV or digital rights deals) | Unique Characteristics |
|---|---|---|---|---|---|---|
| that contribute an amount that exceeds the average team salary fund the revenue given to receiving teams' | | | | regular season records. Free Agency allows movement of players whose contracts are up | | |
| **(I8)** If average team ticket revenue exceeds the target applicable to such season, the WNBA shall pay an amount equal to 10% of the average to the Players' Association for distribution to players. (Target in 2008 was $2.5 million) | **(J8)** Boost Mobile partnership reputed to be in eight-figure range | **(K8)** Not disclosed | **(L8)** Not disclosed | **(M8)** Annual WNBA Draft & Draft Lottery. Every year during the off-season, a large pool of amateur players enter themselves into the draft. In the WNBA Draft Lottery, the team with the worst record in the regular season has the most chances for the number one pick, while the team with the best record among the non-playoff teams has the least number of chances. The Lottery determines the order of selection for the first four teams only; the remaining non-playoff teams select in inverse order of their regular season records. Free Agency allows movement of players whose contracts are up | **(N8)** Not disclosed | **(O8)** Longest running professional women's sports league in the United States |

**Table 2.2** (continued)

| League/ Governing Body | # of Teams | # of TV Viewers | # of Social Media Users | Avg. Attendance Per Game | Champion-ship | Champion-ship Viewers | Total League Revenues |
|---|---|---|---|---|---|---|---|
| (A9) La Liga | (B9) 20 | (C9) 50 million total world-wide | (D9) 1 125 921 likes, 333 938 followers, 14 000 followers on Instagram, 77 199 on Google+ | (E9) 30 372 in 2011/12 | (F9) Champion-ship | (G9) No champion-ship match, per se | (H9) 1.718 billion in 2010/11 |
| (A10) Serie A | (B10) 20 | (C10) | (D10) 735 521 likes on Facebook | (E10) 23 459 in 2011/12 | (F10) Champion-ship | (G10) No champion-ship match, per se | (H10) 1.553 billion in 2010/11 |
| (A11) Bundesliga | (B11) 18 | (C11) 18 million on average | (D11) 103 409 likes on Facebook, 43 367 followers on Twitter, 1000 on Google+ | (E11) 45 116 in 2011/12 | (F11) Champion-ship | (G11) No champion-ship match, per se | (H11) 1.941 billion in 2011/12 |
| (A12) F1 | (B12) 12 teams, 24 drivers | 527 million total world-wide in 2010 | (D12) 676 066 likes on Facebook, 103 869 followers on Twitter | (E12) 2012 Australian Grand Prix total attendance was 313 700 | (F12) FIA Formula One World Champion-ship | (G12) 527 million for over the course of 2010 FIA World Championship | (H12) $3.9 billion in 2009 |

| Revenue Sharing Info. | Total Sponsorship Revenues | Total Advertising Revenues | Total Merchandise Revenues | Player Selection (highlights how drafts, or whatever mechanism are used to recruit players) | Broadcast Revenues (TV or digital rights deals) | Unique Characteristics |
|---|---|---|---|---|---|---|
| (I9) Real Madrid and FC Barcelona end up with 50% of TV rights pot because TV deals are crafted by individual clubs | (J9) 62 million in 2012 for shirt sponsorships | (K9) Varies based on team, 148.8 million for Real Madrid in all marketing during 2011 | (L9) 190 million in 2010 | (M9) Players can join a club at any age and work up through the levels of play the club offers. Transfers enable foreign players to play in La Liga | (N9) Real Madrid raked in 183.5 million in 2010/11; FC Barcelona earned 183.7 million in 2010/11 | (O9) Real Madrid is the highest earning soccer club in the world announced in Deloitte's annual Football Money League |
| (I10) 'Income is to be distributed by taking into account surveys of supporter bases and audience ratings for live Serie A matches' | (J10) 79 million in 2012 for shirt sponsorships | (K10) | (L10) 77 million in 2010 | (M10) Players can join a club at any age and work up through the levels of play the club offers. Transfers enable foreign players to play in Serie A | (N10) $3.34 billion from 2013–15 for domestic TV rights | (O10) |
| (I11) All teams are 51% owned by members of the club. 100% of television revenues are shared equally in the league. Each team is imposed with strict financial guidelines they must meet | (J11) 121 million in 2012 for shirt sponsorships | (K11) 522.7million euros | (L11) 79326000 in 2011 | (M11) Players can join a club at any age and work up through the levels of play the club offers. Transfers enable foreign players to play in the Bundesliga | (N11) 519629000 in 2011/12 | (O11) Most profitable soccer league in Europe |
| (I12) Stipulated in Concorde Agreement, which is highly secret. Seventh Concorde Agreement to be signed in 2012. Prize money share goes with success; the champion | (J12) $887 million in 2011 | (K12) | (L12) 2011 Indian Grand Prix = Rs 60 crore | (M12) Teams maintain driver development programs | (N12) $450 million | (O12) Formula 1 had planned an IPO for $2.5 billion on the Singapore Exchange in May 2012 that was delayed |

**Table 2.2** (continued)

| League/ Governing Body | # of Teams | # of TV Viewers | # of Social Media Users | Avg. Attendance Per Game | Champion-ship | Champion-ship Viewers | Total League Revenues |
|---|---|---|---|---|---|---|---|
| **(A13)** NASCAR | **(B13)** 35 drivers in 2012 Sprint Cup | **(C13)** 6.5 million on average per race in 2011 | **(D13)** 3 143 536 likes on Facebook, 710 229 followers on Twitter, 606 953 on Google+ | **(E13)** 111 533 in 2011 | **(F13)** Sprint Cup Series 'Race for the Cup' | **(G13)** 2011 Race for the Cup Finale drew 10.5 million at peak, averaged 6.799 million | **(H13)** SMI – 2011 revenue = $505.8 million, ISC – 2011 revenue = $629.7 million, Dover Motorsports = $51.9 million |
| **(A14)** MLS | **(B14)** 19 | **(C14)** 291 000 in 2011 per game | **(D14)** 435 134 likes on Facebook, 113 134 followers on Twitter, 373 followers on Instagram, 504 614 on Google+ | **(E14)** 17 872 in 2011 | **(F14)** MLS Cup | **(G14)** 2011 MLS Cup 1.039 million | **(H14)** $15.6 million projected in 2011 |

Note: See the end of the chapter for a list of references for the table's data, with each cell of the table numbered in bold type corresponding to the references.

| Revenue Sharing Info. | Total Sponsorship Revenues | Total Advertising Revenues | Total Merchandise Revenues | Player Selection (highlights how drafts, or whatever mechanism are used to recruit players) | Broadcast Revenues (TV or digital rights deals) | Unique Characteristics |
|---|---|---|---|---|---|---|
| team receives more than lower placed teams, while there is another column rewarding teams with a long history of success (I13) 65% goes to tracks, 25% to teams.,10% to NASCAR | (J13) $3.51 billion in 2011 | (K13) | (L13) | (M13) No official draft; drivers must win on lower circuits to get connected to teams | (N13) $4.48 billion through 2014 for TNT, ESPN/ABC, and Fox | (O13) One in five Fortune 500 companies invest in NASCAR |
| (I14) Player contracts negotiated directly with the MLS; clubs owned and operated by the league itself | (J14) $44 million, ten-year record shirt sponsorship deal signed by LA Galaxy in 2012 | (K14) | (L14) $300 million in 2009 | (M14) MLS SuperDraft and youth development programs; expansion teams get first pick, following eight picks are currently held by clubs that did not qualify for the post-season, in reverse order of regular season finish. The remaining ten picks will be determined by the order in which teams are eliminated in the playoffs combined with reverse order of regular-season finish | (N14) $10 million television annually for three years | (O14)The MLS is a single entity league, meaning that teams are not privately owned but are owned by the MLS |

**Table 2.3** A comparison of sports events

| Event | Governing Body | # of TV Viewers | # of Social Media Users | # of Teams/ Countries |
|---|---|---|---|---|
| **(A2)** Summer Olympics | **(B2)** IOC | **(C2)** 2012 London Olympics – 219.4 total viewers in the USA | **(D2)** 3 643 551 likes, 1 573 243 followers for @london2012, 8665 followers for London2012 on Instagram, 792 970 on Google+ for London 2012 | **(E2)** 204 in 2012 |
| **(A3)** Winter Olympics | **(B3)** IOC | **(C3)** 2010 Vancouver Olympics – 1.8 billion worldwide | **(D3)** 3 643 551 likes on Facebook, 13 580 followers so far for @Sochi2014OC | **(E3)** 82 in 2010 |
| **(A4)** Youth Olympics | **(B4)** IOC | **(C4)** 2010 Singapore Games: 4.4 million viewers for live and video-on-demand at youtholympicgames. org; 247 million TV reach | **(D4)** 99 896 likes on Facebook (Singapore YOG has 111 837), 128 897 followers on Twitter | **(E4)** 205 in 2010, 84 in 2012 |
| **(A5)** SEA Games | **(B5)** Southeast Asian Games Federation | **(C5)** 106 000 | **(D5)** 5502 likes on Facebook, 48 on Google+ | **(E5)** 11 in 2011 |
| **(A6)** Commonwealth Games | **(B6)** Common- wealth Games Federation | **(C6)** Record: 2006 Sydney opening ceremony 3.56 million | **(D6)** 355 376 likes on Facebook, 41 494 followers on Twitter (for 2010 CWG), 40 on Google+ | **(E6)** 71 teams |

| # of Athletes | Sponsorship Revenues | Advertising Revenues | Merchandise Revenues | Broadcast Revenues (TV or digital rights deals) | Unique Characteristics |
|---|---|---|---|---|---|
| **(F2)** 10 000 athletes in 2012 | **(G2)** $957 million from TOP Program for 2009–12 quadrennium | **(H2)** NBC sold more than $1 billion in ad revenue in 2012; $850 million in 2008 | **(I2)** Expected over £80 million for London 2012 | **(J2)** $4.4 billion in US through 2020 | **(K2)** Brand value reputed to be worth $230 million; Beijing Games nearly became the first sporting event to earn $4 billion in revenues (it earned $3.9 billion) |
| **(F3)** 2566 in 2010 | **(G3)** $957 million from TOP Program for 2009–12 quadrennium | **(H3)** $782 million in US for NBC in 2010. | **(I3)** CAD $54.6 million | **(J3)** $4.4 billion in US through 2020 | **(K3)** Brand value reputed to be worth $93 million; Vancouver Games generated $2.56 billion in revenue |
| **(F4)** 3530 in 2010, 1059 in 2012 | **(G4)** $47 million in 2010 | **(H4)** n/a | **(I4)** n/a | **(J4)** n/a | **(K4)** In addition to sports competitions, the YOG have a simultaneous Culture and Education Program (CEP) that focuses on Olympism and Olympic values, skills development, well-being and healthy lifestyle, social responsibility and expression through digital media |
| **(F5)** 5219 in 2011 | **(G5)** n/a | **(H5)** n/a | **(I5)** n/a | **(J5)** n/a | **(K5)** While some events are mandatory, each host nation can pick and choose which events are part of their Games |
| **(F6)** 6000 in 2010 | **(G6)** $74 million in 2010 | **(H6)** Rs 1 billion in 2010 | **(I6)** Rs 80 lakh in 2010 | **(J6)** Rs 215 crore | **(K6)** There are only 53 Commonwealth nations, but some nations have multiple Commonwealth Games Associations |

**Table 2.3** (continued)

| Event | Governing Body | # of TV Viewers | # of Social Media Users | # of Teams/ Countries |
|---|---|---|---|---|
| **(A7)** FIFA World Cup | **(B7)** FIFA | **(C7)** FIFA 2010 World Cup – 2.2 billion viewers | **(D7)** 57 466 likes on Facebook for 2014 WC, 97 831 followers on Twitter for 2014 WC, 9 followers on Instagram for 2014 WC | **(E7)** 32 teams |
| **(A8)** Rugby World Cup | **(B8)** IRB | **(C8)** 4 billion over the course of the 2011 tournament | **(D8)** 1 743 903 likes on Facebook, 126 125 followers on Twitter | **(E8)** 20 teams |
| **(A9)** ICC World Cup | **(B9)** ICC | **(C9)** 1 billion people worldwide for 2011 final match | **(D9)** 42 760 (for 2015 WC) likes on Facebook, 399 123 followers on Twitter | **(E9)** 14 teams in 2011 |
| **(A10)** Euro 2012 | **(B10)** UEFA | **(C10)** Projected reach of 4.3 billion worldwide | **(D10)** 981 472 likes on Facebook, 31 802 followers on Twitter, 1 383 171 on Google+ | **(E10)** 16 teams |

Note: See the end of the chapter for a list of references for the table's data, with each cell of the table numbered in bold type corresponding to the references.

## 2.6   Chapter summary

This chapter introduced three important topics: a comparison of sports and non-sports leagues to explain the business characteristics they each have in common, plus their differences, highlighting the importance of understand-

| # of Athletes | Sponsorship Revenues | Advertising Revenues | Merchandise Revenues | Broadcast Revenues (TV or digital rights deals) | Unique Characteristics |
|---|---|---|---|---|---|
| **(F7)** ~736 | **(G7)** $1.6 billion at 2010 World Cup | **(H7)** $147.2 million for CCTV in China for 2010 World Cup | **(I7)** $35 million in US in 2010 | **(J7)** ESPN paid $1.85 billion in USA for 2018 and 2022 tournaments | **(K7)** Largest single-event sporting competition in the world with 208 member associations vying for 32 spots |
| **(F8)** 600 in 2011 | **(G8)** $80 million at 2011 RWC | **(H8)** €13 million in France in 2011 for TV1 | **(I8)** n/a | **(J8)** £82 million for 2007 RWC | **(K8)** 2011 Rugby World Cup was the largest sporting event ever staged in New Zealand, drawing 1.35 million spectators and $218 million in ticket revenue |
| **(F9)** 210 in 2011 | **(G9)** $500 million for eight-year deals expiring in 2015 | **(H9)** Rs 800 crore in 2011 | **(I9)** Rs 50 crore in 2011 | **(J9)** $1.1 billion through 2015 on ESPN Star Sports | **(K9)** The 2011 final match between India and Sri Lanka was one of the most watched television events ever in India |
| **(F10)** ~368 | **(G10)** $1.6 billion for total commercial revenues | **(H10)** £15m for ITV in the UK | **(I10)** Part of $1.6 billion commercial revenues | **(J10)** Part of $1.6 billion commercial revenues | **(K10)** UEFA spent $124 million as daily rate compensation to European clubs to release them to play in the tournament, compared to FIFA who will spend $79 million for the 2014 World Cup |

ing the sports context in making effective sports marketing decisions; the brand planning framework of *destiny, distinction, culture,* and *experiences,* which provides a set of strategic guidelines sports marketers can use in developing their sports marketing plan; and the brand value framework of *reputation, societal, organizational,* and *financial* to show that enhancing brand value for any organization interested in using sports marketing to improve its company's awareness and market performance is the result of these four components working with each other to create lasting value that is also measurable. Finally, this chapter also discussed advertising in the context of select sports leagues around the world as well as major sports events worldwide to show the scale and scope of investments in key marketing communications activities. This included two comparison tables to help readers gain a clearer sense of each sports entity's unique characteristics.

**CASE STUDY 1**

# AFL expansion

Australian Rules Football, also known as Australian Football, Aussie Rules, or just simply 'footy', first originated in Melbourne in 1858 as a game to keep cricketers fit during the winter months.[10] Although it is a truly indigenous Australian sport that is said to have been inspired by a form of football played by the Aborigines, the game has influences from European sports such as Gaelic football, popular in Ireland, and global sports such as rugby. In its modern form, footy would appear to be a hybrid of soccer, rugby, and Gaelic football.

Though an organized national league has been in existence since 1897, the current iteration of the Australian Football League (AFL) formed in 1990 and is the de facto world governing body of the sport.[11] A total of 18 clubs from across Australia currently participate in the annual league that culminates at the AFL Grand Final. Held at the Melbourne Cricket Ground (MCG) with an attendance of 99 537 in 2011, the AFL Grand Final is also the most popular domestic club championship event in the world.[12]

The AFL has seen sustained growth over the past decade. All levels of the sport (recreational through professional) generate about AUS$4 billion for the Australian economy each year.[13] But the financial impact does not stop there. The AFL's broadcast deal is worth AUS$1.253 billion through 2016 and corporate sponsorships also provide significant sums of money.[14] Though the official amount has not been disclosed, the AFL's title sponsor, Toyota, reportedly has a deal that will last through 2014 and is worth approximately AUS$ 8 million per year, making it the largest sponsorship for any sport in Australia.[15] The size of the AFL's fan base continues to grow as well. Across the country, matches attract over 7.4 million people per annum. AFL Club membership grew for the 11th straight season to 650 373 members, which means that one in every 34 Australians is part of an AFL club.[16] The AFL made AUS$159 million in payments to its clubs in 2011 and players earned AUS$164.83 million. The collective bargaining agreement set to run from 2012 to 2016 totalled AUS$1.144 billion in player payments and related benefits with the average AFL player earning AUS$300 000 by 2016.[17] Though the league reported a net loss in 2011, it was the first time in the decade that it had a poorly performing year, fiscally speaking. However, the AFL attributes the majority of the net loss to an increase in distributed funds to teams.[18]

Soon after it began in the mid-1800s, footy began making its ways overseas to countries such as New Zealand and South Africa in the 1880s with the help of Australian gold miners and soldiers. Currently, it is played all over the world and has managed to gain access to many countries. However, many of them do not have professional leagues or a well-established infrastructure. In order to promote and develop the game internationally, the AFL has extended its international arm to foster the sport's growth.[19] For the first time in 2011, participation in the sport topped 100 000 outside of Australia, which was a 54 percent increase over the previous year.[20] In addition, the fourth annual International Cup

**CASE STUDY 1** *(continued)*

was held in Sydney in 2011 and boasted the largest field the tournament has ever seen with 23 teams present (up from 16 the previous year). The tournament also had a women's division for the first time in the tournament's young history.[21]

Similar to other major professional sports, footy has many alluring characteristics that could seemingly catch hold worldwide. Fans will be able to associate themselves with national teams, league teams, and even individual players. The unique selling point of Australian Rules Football is its excitement, aggression, and uninterrupted flow of the game (unlike American football or baseball). With its increasing popularity worldwide, it would be a good way for sponsors to target various groups of audiences from locally established leagues to international competitions. Based on the success of the AFL over the past decade, revenues could be substantial once a certain level of popularity has been established in other countries. With big name sponsors like Toyota and Coca-Cola already on board to reap the benefits, it might not take long for other sponsors to see the potential value that footy can bring to them.

As the AFL continues to grow, it hopes to continue expanding the sport both in Australia and beyond, raising the important issue of how to go about expanding internationally.

 **QUESTIONS**

1 In order to grow abroad, what key strategic objectives should the AFL focus on?
2 Should the AFL consider making rule changes to make the game more appealing to international audiences?
3 How should the AFL devote its resources towards international expansion?

**CASE STUDY 2**

# NY Red Bulls

Since its inception in 1984, Red Bull has been one of the world's most popular energy drinks.[22] As of 2012, the brand dominates the energy drink market with a 40 percent market share.[23] A large part of Red Bull's success stems from its successful hard-driving, guerrilla marketing campaigns, especially in the sports industry. The company has financial stakes in extreme sports, four soccer clubs, and two Formula 1 teams.[24] The company's purchase and subsequent rebranding of the New York/New Jersey Metrostars in 2006 has been one of the most dominant shifts in the culture of a sports team in the world.

Prior to Red Bull's $150 million purchase of the team in 2006, the Metrostars were the only founding member of Major League Soccer (MLS) to have not won a significant trophy in the league.[25] However, almost as soon as the team was purchased, a cultural shift began to occur. On 8 April 2006, at the Red Bulls' first home game, the team debuted with newly branded kits featuring two red bulls clashing into a soccer ball with Red Bull's script predominantly featured above. At that game, 35 000 fans poured into Giants Stadium and were treated to a half-time performance by international music superstars Shakira and Wyclef Jean.[26] A few months later, the Red Bulls would break ground on their own $200 million, 25 000 seat arena, which would be completed in 2010.[27]

2010 proved to be a pivotal year in the transformation of the New York Red Bulls. In addition to beginning play in their new arena, many faces changed in the organization. To kick off the new team, Hans Backe was hired as the new head coach in January and immediately got to work restructuring the team.[28] International superstar Thierry Henry was acquired from FC Barcelona as the team's third ever designated player.[29] Just a few weeks later, the Red Bulls would announce that another FC Barcelona player, and Mexican national team captain, Rafa Márquez was joining the team, making the Red Bulls the first team in MLS history to have three active designated players.[30] A week after Márquez made his debut with teammate Henry, the Red Bulls would sell out their new arena for the first time on 14 August 2010, beginning a quantifiable upswing for the organization.[31] The Red Bulls would finish the 2010 season by clinching the Eastern Conference.[32] A year later, in 2011, the Red Bulls would continue to increase average attendance at their games from 18 441 in 2010 to 19 749 in 2011.[33]

In the early days of Red Bulls' team ownership, there was minimal activation of the energy drink with the team. That sponsorship landscape has changed dramatically as well. In 2012, Red Bull featured over 1 million branded cans with Rafa Márquez and 800 000 branded six-packs with Thierry Henry.[34] While this activation began initially in the New York area during the early part of the 2012, it spread as the season went on to the Western states.[35] In addition to outdoor advertising in New York featuring Red Bulls players and the drink, a nationally aired television commercial featuring the Red Bull Arena and Thierry Henry played for several weeks throughout the 2012 season.[36]

**CASE STUDY 2** *(continued)*

More importantly, the Red Bull Arena is turning into a 'place to be seen'. Demand for the Red Bull Arena's 30 luxury suites has gone up dramatically for all 18 home games of the MLS season. The club charged $75 000 for a season package in 2011, and doubled the price to $150 000 in 2012.[37] As a result of the team's increasing popularity, they were able to come to terms on a new three-year TV deal in 2011 with MSG Networks.[38] While terms of the deal were not disclosed, the deal did increase the number of games televised to 24, up from 22 the previous year.[39] Finally, it's clear that New York fans are buying in a heavily saturated sports market of nine other professional sports teams.[40] The Red Bulls have three different prominent fan clubs, the Empire Supporters Club, the Garden State Supporters, and the Viking Army, which combine to make up the 'South Ward' at the Red Bull Arena.[41] In total, these groups fill approximately 1500 seats at every home game, compared to about 20 seats when the Red Bulls played at Giants Stadium prior to 2010.[42] They're on their feet all 90 minutes of the game singing and chanting and Red Bulls players note that the South Ward is quite similar to the famous cheering sections present in European leagues.

 **QUESTIONS**

1   It's clear that something has caught on culturally in New York in the world of professional soccer. But is the cultural aspect enough to ensure success?
2   Do the Red Bulls need more wins on the field (i.e., fulfill a successful destiny) to be a truly profitable business enterprise?
3   Or do the experiences of the South Ward make up for other lagging brand framework dimensions?

**NOTES**

1   *60 Minutes* (2012).
2   Niesen (2012).
3   Slaton (2012).
4   S.A. (2012).
5   Davis (2010, p. 98).
6   Ibid., p. 99.
7   Davis (2012, p. 21).
8   Brand Finance (2012).
9   Mednik (2010); Lefton (2011); McCausland (2012).
10  'Australian Rules Football' (n.d.).
11  Ibid.
12  'Australian Football League Annual Report 2011', p. 61.
13  Ibid., p. 29.
14  Ibid., p. 68.
15  Fraser (2011).
16  AFL Annual Report 2011, p. 26.
17  Ibid., p. 7.
18  Ibid., p. 17.

19  'AFL International' (n.d.).
20  AFL Annual Report 2011, p. 74.
21  Ibid., p. 94.
22  'Red Bull GmbH Company Profile' (n.d.).
23  Ibid.
24  Robinson (2012).
25  Ibid.
26  'Red Bull GmbH Company Profile' (n.d.).
27  Ibid. See also 'Timeline' (2010).
28  'Red Bull GmbH Company Profile' (n.d.).
29  Robinson (2012).
30  Ibid.
31  Ibid.
32  'Red Bull GmbH Company Profile' (n.d.).
33  Oshan (2011).
34  Botta (2012, p. 9).
35  Robinson (2012).
36  Botta (2012, p. 9).
37  Robinson (2012).
38  Crupi (2012).
39  Ibid.
40  Robinson (2012).
41  Clark (2011).
42  Ibid.

## REFERENCES

'AFL International' (n.d.), AFLCommunityClub.com.au, accessed 27 May 2013 at http://afl communityclub.com.au/index.php?id=607.

'Australian Rules Football' (n.d.), *Encyclopaedia Britannica*, accessed 27 May 2013 at http://www.britannica.com/EBchecked/topic/44079/Australian-rules-football.

'Australian Football League Annual Report 2011', Australian Football League, accessed 8 July 2012 at http://mm.afl.com.au/portals/0/2012/afl_annual_report_2011.pdf.

Botta, Christopher (2012), 'Heck gets front-row look at passion of soccer fans in his role with New York Red Bulls', *Sports Business Journal*, 11 June 2012.

Brand Finance (2012), 'BrandFinance° Football 50 2012 – the world's most valuable football brands', accessed 1 July 2012 at http://brandirectory.com/league_tables/table/top-50-football-club-brands-2012.

Clark, Kevin (2011), '1,500 of New York's craziest fans', *The Wall Street Journal*, 31 May 2011, accessed 24 September 2012 at http://online.wsj.com/article/SB100014240527023036574 04576355752880654530.html.

Crupi, Anthony (2012), 'MSG re-ups with Red Bulls', *Ad Week*, 31 March 2011, accessed 24 September 2012 at http://www.adweek.com/news/advertising-branding/msg-re-ups-red-bulls-126120.

Davis, John A. (2010), *Competitive Success –How Branding Adds Value*, New York: John Wiley & Sons.

Davis, John A. (2012), *The Olympic Games Effect – How Sports Marketing Builds Strong Brands*, New York: John Wiley & Sons.

Fraser, Adam (2011), 'Toyota agree biggest sponsorship in Australian sport', Sportspromedia. com, 1 July 2011, accessed 8 July 2012 at http://www.sportspromedia.com/news/toyota_and_afl_agree_biggest_sponsorship_in_australian_sport/.

Lefton, Terry (2011), 'Under Armour tabs Optimum Sports for media buying', 6 June 2011, *Sport Business Daily*, accessed 29 September 2011 at http://www.sportsbusinessdaily.com/Journal/Issues/2011/06/06/Marketing-and-Sponsorship/UnderArmour.aspx.

McCausland, Christianna (2012), '2012 best places to work', February 2012, BaltimoreMagazine.net, accessed 3 May 2012 at http://www.baltimoremagazine.net/features/2012/02/2012-best-places-to-work.

Mednik, Max (2010), 'Lessons from Kevin Plank (Under Armour CEO)', 8 December 2010, accessed 23 September 2011 at http://www.maxmednik.com/1/post/2010/12/lessons-from-kevin-plank-under-armour-ceo.html.

Niesen, Joan (2012), 'WNBA finding success apart from NBA', 17 July 2012, FoxSports North, accessed 23 July 2012 at http://www.foxsportsnorth.com/07/17/12/WNBA-finding-success-apart-from NBA/landing_lynx.html?blockID=761959&feedID=5930.

Oshan, Jeremiah (2011), 'MLS attendance was up almost across the board in 2011', SB Nation, 24 October 2011, accessed 24 September 2012 at http://www.sbnation.com/soccer/2011/10/24/2511576/mls-attendance-up-2011-major-league-soccer.

'Red Bull GmbH Company Profile' (n.d.), Biz.Yahoo.com, accessed 24 September 2012 at http://biz.yahoo.com/ic/101/101316.html.

Robinson, Joshua (2012), 'In search of a (Red) Bull market', *The Wall Street Journal*, 18 April 2012, accessed 24 September 2012 at http://online.wsj.com/article/SB10001424052702303425504577352324048828262.html.

S.A. (2012), 'Not cricket', 3 May 2012, *The Economist*, accessed 23 May 2012 at http://www.economist.com/blogs/schumpeter/2012/05/indias-sports-leagues.

*60 Minutes* (2012), 'The NFL Commissioner: Roger Goodell', 29 January 2012, CBSNews, accessed 3 February 2012 at http://www.cbsnews.com/8301-18560_162-57367998/the-nfl-commissioner-roger-goodell/?pageNum=3&tag=contentMain;contentBody.

Slaton, Zach (2012), 'MLS payroll shows steady improvement, but still not world class', 26 May 2012, Forbes.com, accessed 29 2012 at http://www.forbes.com/sites/zachslaton/2012/05/26/mls-payroll-shows-steady-improvement-but-still-not-world-class/.

'Timeline' (2010), *Sports Business Journal*, 20 December 2010, accessed 24 September 2012 at http://www.sportsbusinessdaily.com/Journal/Issues/2010/12/20101220/2010-Year-in-Review/Timeline.aspx?hl=red%20bull%20arena&sc=1.

## REFERENCES FOR TABLE 2.2

*NFL*

B2   NFL.com (n.d.), National Football League, accessed 2 August 2012 at http://www.nfl.com.

C2   'NFL sees highest viewership average since '89; local markets up' (2012), *Sports Business Daily*, 6 January 2012, accessed 2 Aug 2012 at http://www.sportsbusinessdaily.com/Daily/Issues/2012/01/06/Media/NFL-Ratings.aspx.

D2   Facebook, Twitter, Instagram, Google+

E2   'NFL Attendance Report 2011' (n.d.), ESPN.com, accessed 8 August 2012 at http://espn.go.com/nfl/attendance/_/year/2011.

G2   de Moraes, Lisa (2012), 'Super Bowl XLVI: biggest TV audience ever', *Washington Post*, 6 February 2012, accessed 2 August 2012 at http://www.washingtonpost.com/blogs/tv-column/post/super-bowl-xlvi-no-tv-ratings-record/2012/02/06/gIQAVAD6tQ_blog.html.

H2   Fendrich, Howard (2012), 'NFL's ratings, revenue, popularity grow and grow',

FoxNews.com, 3 February 2012, accessed 8 August 2012 at http://www.foxnews.com/
sports/2012/02/03/nfls-ratings-revenue-popularity-grow-and-grow/.

**I2**    Farmer, Sam (2011), 'First vote on labor deal by NFL players expected Monday', *Los
Angeles Times*, 24 July 2011, accessed 11 August 2012 at http://articles.latimes.com/2011/
jul/24/sports/la-sp-0725-nfl-labor-20110725.

**J2**    Chipps, William (2011), 'Sponsorship spending on U.S. pro sports leagues and teams to
grow 7.9 percent in 2011', Sponsorship.com, IEG Press Release 3 October 2011, accessed
13 August 2012 at http://www.sponsorship.com/About-IEG/Press-Room/Sponsorship-
Spending-On-U-S--Pro-Sports-Leagues-An-1.aspx.

**K2**    Thomaselli, Rich (2011), 'Over $12bn at stake if NFL lockout prevents 2011
season', *Advertising Age*, 10 January 2011, accessed 13 August 2012 at http://
adage.com/article/news/12b-stake-nfl-lockout-prevents-2011-season/148093/;
'Kantar media releases March madness advertising trends report', Kantar Media, 5
March 2012, accessed 14 August 2012 at http://kantarmediana.com/intelligence/
press/2012-march-madness-advertising-trends-report.

**L2**    Cheng, Andria (2012), 'Game changer: Nike unveils new NFL gear', *Wall Street Journal*,
3 April 2012, accessed 14 August 2012 at http://articles.marketwatch.com/2012-04-03/
industries/31279965_1_nike-shares-big-sales-retail-sales.

**M2**    Gray, Andy (2010), 'English Premier League draft: can an NFL-style draft system work
in the EPL?' BleacherReport.com, 6 October 2010, accessed 15 August 2012 at http://
bleacherreport.com/articles/484332-premier-league-draft-can-an-nfl-style-draft-system-
work-in-the-epl.

**N2**    Associated Press (2011), 'NFL renews television deals', ESPN.com, 11 December
2011, accessed 3 August 2012 at http://espn.go.com/nfl/story/_/id/7353238/
nfl-re-ups-tv-pacts-expand-thursday-schedule.

**O2**    Associated Press (2012), 'Super Bowl sets ratings records again', ESPN.com, 6 February
2012, accessed 13 August 2012 at http://espn.go.com/nfl/playoffs/2011/story/_/
id/7546470/2012-super-bowl-new-york-giants-new-england-patriots-sets-ratings-
record-3rd-straight-year.

*EPL*

**B3**    'Clubs'(n.d.), PremierLeague.com, accessed 2 August 2012 at http://www.premierleague.
com/en-gb/clubs.html.

**C3**    Lipton, Martin (2011), 'Prem officially world's most viewed league with TV audience
of 4.7 BILLION', *Mirror*, 11 October 2011, accessed 8 August 2012 at http://www.
mirrorfootball.co.uk/news/The-Premier-League-is-watched-by-a-global-audience-4-7-
BILLION-according-to-new-survey-article810710.html.

**D3**    Facebook, Twitter, Google+

**E3**    'Barclays Premier League stats 2011–12' (n.d.), Soccernet.ESPN.com, accessed 13
August 2012 at http://soccernet.espn.go.com/stats/_/league/eng.1/year/2011/
barclays-premier-league?cc=5901.

**G3**    Lord, David (2012), 'Manchester set a club television audience world record', *The Roar*,
2 May 2012, accessed 8 August 2012 at http://www.theroar.com.au/2012/05/02/
manchester-set-a-club-television-audience-world-record/.

**H3**    'Annual review of football finance 2012' (2012), Deloitte LLP, 31 May 2012.

**I3**    'Premier League broadcasting revenue: how is it distributed?' (n.d.), *The Guardian*,
accessed 12 August 2012 at http://www.guardian.co.uk/news/datablog/2011/oct/12/
football-broadcasting-deal-liverpool.

**J3**    Lusbec, Karl (2012), 'The top 10 shirts sponsorship deals: EPL clubs (still) very attractive', Karl's Football Lounge, 7 August 2012, accessed 13 August 2012 at http://karllusbec.wordpress.com/2012/08/07/the-top-10-shirts-sponsorship-deals-epl-clubs-still-very-attractive/; 'Premier League tops shirt sponsorships; Bundesliga gets more per team' (2012), *Sports Business Daily*, 21 June 2012, accessed 11 August 2012 at http://www.sportsbusinessdaily.com/Global/Issues/2012/06/21/Marketing-and-Sponsorship/Shirts-Europe.aspx.

**K3** Thomaselli, Rich (2010), 'If English soccer can take in $155m from sponsored jerseys, what about NBA, NHL?' Advertising Age, 4 October 2010, accessed 13 August 2012 at http://adage.com/article/news/nba-nfl-follow-english-soccer-sponsor-jerseys/146264/.

**L3** Cutler, Matt (2011), 'La Liga topples Premier League as Europe's top merchandise division', Sport Business, 23 February 2011, accessed 14 August 2012 at http://www.sportbusiness.com/news/183139/la-liga-topples-premier-league-as-europe-s-top-merchandise-division.

**M3** Gray, Andy (2010), 'English Premier League draft: can an NFL-style draft system work in the EPL?' BleacherReport.com, 6 October 2010, accessed 15 August 2012 at http://bleacherreport.com/articles/484332-premier-league-draft-can-an-nfl-style-draft-system-work-in-the-epl.

**N3** Gibson, Owen (2012), 'Premier League lands £3bn TV rights bonanza from Sky and BT', *The Guardian*, 13 June 2012, accessed 3 August 2012 at http://www.guardian.co.uk/media/2012/jun/13/premier-league-tv-rights-3-billion-sky-bt.

**O3** 'Who qualifies to play in Europe?' (n.d.), PremierLeague.com, Barclays Premier League, accessed 15 August 2012 at http://www.premierleague.com/en-gb/fans/faqs/who-qualifies-to-play-in-europe/.

*IPL*

**B4** 'Teams' (n.d.), Iplt20.com, accessed 2 August 2012 at http://www.iplt20.com/teams.

**C4** Engineer, Tariq (2012), 'TV ratings for IPL continue to fall', ESPNcricinfo.com, 20 April 2012, accessed 3 August 2012 at http://www.espncricinfo.com/indian-premier-league-2012/content/story/561971.html.

**D4** Facebook, Twitter, Google+

**E4** Ali, Qaiser Mohammad (2012), 'IPL 2012: revenue from Delhi Daredevils–Pune Warriors tie may have broken records', *India Today*, 24 April 2012, accessed 11 August 2012 at http://indiatoday.intoday.in/story/ipl-revenue-from-daredevils-pune-warriors-tie-may-break-records/1/185821.html.

**G4** 'Record reach for IPL 5 final; beats IPL 4 rating' (2012), BestMediaInfo Bureau, 7 June 2012, accessed 8 August 2012 at http://www.bestmediainfo.com/2012/06/record-reach-for-ipl-5-final-beats-ipl-4-rating/.

**H4** 'BCCI will make Rs 1000 cr from IPL 4' (2011), *The Hindu Business Line*, 6 May 2011, accessed 11 August 2012 at http://www.thehindubusinessline.com/industry-and-economy/marketing/article1997048.ece?css=print.

**I4** 'IPL lays out revenue-sharing plan with franchises' (2007), ESPNcricinfo.com, 18 December 2007, accessed 11 August 2012 at http://www.espncricinfo.com/ipl/content/story/326200.html.

**J4** Mehta, Shramana Ganguly and Meenakshi Verma Ambwani (2011), 'IPL-4 to match advertising revenues from ICC World Cup 2011', *The Economic Times*, 4 April 2011, accessed 11 August 2012 at http://articles.economictimes.indiatimes.com/2011-04-04/news/29380323_1_associate-sponsors-airtel-digital-television-ipl-4.

**K4** Engineer, Tariq (2012), 'Stadium crowds show IPL the money', ESPNcricinfo.com,

14 June 2012, accessed 15 August 2012 at http://www.espncricinfo.com/magazine/content/story/568291.html.

**L4**   'India Cements sees 15–20% rise in revenues' (2012), *Business Standard*, 29 March 2012, accessed 14 August 2012 at http://www.business-standard.com/india/news/india-cements-sees-15-20-rise-in-revenuesipl/469355/.

**M4**   Gollapudi, Nagraj (2009), 'Slow trading with all eyes on auction', ESPNcricinfo.com, 23 January 2009, accessed 15 August 2012 at http://www.espncricinfo.com/ipl2009/content/story/387453.html.

**N4**   'India cricket chiefs sell rights to Sony and World Sport Group' (2008), *The Australian*, 15 January 2008, accessed 15 August 2012 at http://www.theaustralian.com.au/news/billion-dollar-rights-deal-for-ipl/story-e6frg7mo-1111115320967.

*NHL*

**B5**   'Teams' (n.d.), NHL.com, accessed 3 August 2012 at http://www.nhl.com/ice/teams.htm?nav-tms-main.

**C5**   Ourand, John (2012), 'Penguins stay atop NHL in local TV ratings', *Sports Business Journal*, 9 April 2012, 23.

**D5**   Facebook, Twitter, Instagram, Google+

**E5**   'NHL Attendance Report 2011–2012' (n.d.), ESPN.com, accessed 8 August 2012, http://espn.go.com/nhl/attendance/_/year/2012.

**G5**   'Stanley Cup final hits five-year low in ratings, viewership' (2012), Sports Media Watch, 14 June 2012, accessed 4 August 2012 at http://www.sportsmediawatch.com/2012/06/2012-stanley-cup-final-hits-five-year-low-in-ratings-viewership/.

**H5**   Botta, Christopher (2012), 'Nearing milestone, Bettman says focused on NHL's future', *Sports Business Journal*, 25 June 2012, 1.

**I5**   Boden, Chris (2012), 'Revenue sharing an issue as NHL lockout looms', CSNChicago.com, 9 August 2012, accessed 11 August 2012 at http://www.csnchicago.com/hockey-chicago-blackhawks/blackhawks-talk/Revenue-sharing-an-issue-as-NHL-lockout-?blockID=754215&feedID=10334.

**J5**   Chipps, William (2011), 'Sponsorship spending on U.S. pro sports leagues and teams to grow 7.9 percent in 2011', Sponsorship.com, IEG Press Release, 3 October 2011, accessed 13 August 2012 at http://www.sponsorship.com/About-IEG/Press-Room/Sponsorship-Spending-On-U-S--Pro-Sports-Leagues-An-1.aspx.

**L5**   Rovell, Darren (2010), 'MLB will beat NFL in licensing revenue in '10', CNBC.com, 14 June 2010, accessed 15 August 2012 at http://www.cnbc.com/id/37692194/Publication_MLB_Will_Beat_NFL_In_Licensing_Revenue_In_10.

**M5**   'NHL draft history' (n.d.), NHL.com, accessed 15 August 2012 at http://www.nhl.com/futures/drafthistory.html.

**N5**   Botta, Christophe (2012), 'Nearing milestone, Bettman stays focused on NHL's future', *Sports Business Journal*, 25 June 2012, 1.

**O5**   Maynard, Michelle (2012), 'What's a hockey game worth?', *The Atlantic*, 2 January 2012, accessed 15 August 2012 at http://www.theatlanticcities.com/arts-and-lifestyle/2012/01/what-hockey-game-worth/846/.

*MLB*

**B6**   'Team-by-team information' (n.d.), MLB.com, accessed 4 August 2012 at http://mlb.mlb.com/team/index.jsp.

**C6**   Ourand, John (2011), 'Troubled Mets, Dodgers take local ratings hit', *Sports Business Journal*, 11 June 2011, 1.

**D6**  Facebook, Twitter, Instagram, Google+

**E6**  'MLB turnstile tracker' (2011), *Sports Business Journal*, 3 October 2011, 43.

**G6**  McCarthy, Michael (2011), 'Cards' game 7 win most-watched since Red Sox in '04', USA Today, 29 October 2011, accessed 8 August 2011 at http://content.usatoday.com/communities/gameon/post/2011/10/world-series-game-7-tv-ratings-st-louis-cardinals-texas-rangers/1#.UCMIQHA6-Kw.

**H6**  Bauman, Mike (2011), 'Selig shares praise of historic 2011 season', MLB.com, 26 December 2011, accessed 8 August 2012 at http://mlb.mlb.com/news/print.jsp?ymd=20111225&content_id=26234614&vkey=news_mlb&c_id=mlb.

**I6**  Slowinski, Steve (2012), 'Revenue sharing', Fangraphs.com, 21 March 2012, accessed 11 August 2012, at http://www.fangraphs.com/library/index.php/business/revenue-sharing/.

**J6**  Chipps, William (2011), 'Sponsorship spending on U.S. pro sports leagues and teams to grow 7.9 percent in 2011', Sponsorship.com, IEG Press Release, 3 October 2011, accessed 13 August 2012 at http://www.sponsorship.com/About-IEG/Press-Room/Sponsorship-Spending-On-U-S--Pro-Sports-Leagues-An-1.aspx.

**K6**  'Kantar media releases March Madness advertising trends report' (2012), Kantar Media, 5 March 2012, accessed 14 August 2012 at http://kantarmediana.com/intelligence/press/2012-march-madness-advertising-trends-report.

**L6**  Rovell, Darren (2010), 'MLB will beat NFL in licensing revenue in '10', CNBC.com, 14 June 2010, accessed 15 August 2012 at http://www.cnbc.com/id/37692194/Publication_MLB_Will_Beat_NFL_In_Licensing_Revenue_In_10.

**M6**  'Major league draft' (n.d.), *New York Times*, accessed 15 August 2012 at http://topics.nytimes.com/topics/news/sports/baseball/majorleague/draft/index.html.

**N6**  Brown, Maury (2012), 'New MLB national TV deals would reach $1.75–$2.5 billion a year', BizofBaseball.com, 9 July 2012, accessed 15 August 2012 at http://bizofbaseball.com/index.php?option=com_content&view=article&id=5704:new-mlb-national-tv-deals-could-reach-175-25-billion-a-year&catid=26:editorials&Itemid=39.

**O6**  Badenhausen, Kurt (2012), 'Manchester United tops the world's 50 most valuable sports teams', Forbes.com, 16 July 2012, accessed 15 May 2013 at http://www.forbes.com/sites/kurtbadenhausen/2012/07/16/manchester-united-tops-the-worlds-50-most-valuable-sports-teams/.

*NBA*

**B7**  'Teams' (n.d.), NBA.com, accessed 5 August 2012 at http://www.nba.com/teams/.

**C7**  Mamudi, Sam (2012), 'LeBron James, Heat power NBA TV ratings', *Wall Street Journal*, MarketWatch, 22 June 2012, accessed 5 August 2012 at http://articles.marketwatch.com/2012-06-22/industries/32364181_1_nba-playoffs-nba-tv-boston-celtics.

**D7**  Facebook, Twitter, Instagram, Google+

**E7**  'NBA Attendance Report 2012' (n.d.), ESPN.com, accessed 8 August 2012 at http://espn.go.com/nba/attendance.

**G7**  Mamudi, Sam (2012), 'LeBron James, Heat power NBA TV ratings', *Wall Street Journal*, MarketWatch, 22 June 2012, accessed 5 August 2012 at http://articles.marketwatch.com/2012-06-22/industries/32364181_1_nba-playoffs-nba-tv-boston-celtics.

**H7**  Lombardo, John (2011), 'Drama sells for NBA', *Sports Business Journal*, 18 April 2011, 1.

**I7**  Lombardo, John (2012), 'Inside NBA's revenue sharing', *Sports Business Journal*, 23 January 2012, 1.

**J7**  Chipps, William (2012), 'Sponsorship spending on U.S. pro sports leagues and teams to grow 7.9 percent in 2011', Sponsorship.com, IEG Press Release, 3 October 2011, accessed 13 August 2012 at http://www.sponsorship.com/About-IEG/Press-Room/Sponsorship-Spending-On-U-S--Pro-Sports-Leagues-An-1.aspx.

**K7** 'Kantar media releases March Madness advertising trends report' (2012), Kantar Media, 5 March 2012, accessed 14 August 2012 at http://kantarmediana.com/intelligence/press/2012-march-madness-advertising-trends-report.

**L7** Rovell, Darren (2010), 'MLB will beat NFL in licensing revenue in '10', CNBC.com, 14 June 2010, accessed 15 August 2012 at http://www.cnbc.com/id/37692194/Publication_MLB_Will_Beat_NFL_In_Licensing_Revenue_In_10.

**M7** 'Basketball 101: NBA draft' (n.d.), NBA.com, accessed 15 August 2012 at http://www.nba.com/bobcats/draft_basketball_101.html.

**N7** Berger, Ken (2012), 'Stern calls flopping "Trickery," says lockout didn't kill NBA's cashcow', CBSsports.com, 12 June 2012, accessed 15 August 2012 at http://www.cbssports.com/nba/blog/ken-berger/19341150/stern-calls-flopping-trickery-says-lockout-didnt-kill-nbas-cash-cow.

**O7** Harris, Nick (2012), 'REVEALED: the world's best paid teams, Man City close in on Barca and Real Madrid', SportingIntelligence.com, 1 May 2012, accessed 15 August 2012 at http://www.sportingintelligence.com/2012/05/01/revealed-the-worlds-best-paid-teams-man-city-close-in-on-barca-and-real-madrid-010501/.

*WNBA*

**B8** 'WNBA teams' (n.d.), ESPN.com, accessed 5 August 2012 at http://sports.espn.go.com/wnba/teams.

**C8** 'WNBA experiences more growth', ESPN.com, 2 September 2011, accessed 5 August 2012 at http://espn.go.com/wnba/story/_/id/6923070/attendance-tv-viewership-rise-again-wnba.

**D8** Facebook, Twitter, Google+

**E8** 'WNBA experiences more growth', ESPN.com, 2 September 2011, accessed 5 August 2012 at http://espn.go.com/wnba/story/_/id/6923070/attendance-tv-viewership-rise-again-wnba.

**G8** 'WNBA finals: mixed numbers for final two games', Sports Media Watch, 11 October 2011, accessed 8 August 2012 at http://www.sportsmediawatch.com/2011/10/wnba-finals-mixed-numbers-for-final-two-games/.

**I8** 'Collective Bargaining Agreement 2008' (2008), Women's National Basketball Association, 24 January 2008, accessed 10 August 2012 at http://www.wnbpa.org/storage/WNBA-WNBPA%20CBA%202008.pdf.

**J8** Lombardo, John (2011), 'WNBA lands Boost Mobile as top sponsor', *Sports Business Journal*, 22 August 2011, 1.

**M8** 'Top college prospects invited to attend 2012 WNBA draft presented by Boost Mobile' (n.d.), WNBA.com, accessed 15 August 2012 at http://www.wnba.com/draft/2012/prospects_invited_to_draft_2012_04_11.html.

**O8** Pelton, Kevin (2012), 'Title IX: 40 years of progress but more to come', StormBasketball.com, 12 June 2012, accessed 15 August 2012 at http://www.wnba.com/storm/news/titleix_feature_120621.html.

*La Liga*

**B9** 'La Liga teams' (n.d.), FoxSports.com, accessed 4 August 2012 at http://msn.foxsports.com/foxsoccer/laliga/teams/.

**C9** 'La Liga ended with 3.6 million more viewers over last season' (n.d.), European Professional

Football Leagues, accessed 11 August 2012 at http://www.epfl-europeanleagues.com/la_liga_viewers.htm.

**D9**   Facebook, Twitter, Instagram, Google+

**E9**   'Spanish La Liga stats 2011–12' (n.d.), Soccernet.espn.com, accessed 11 August 2012 at http://soccernet.espn.go.com/stats/_/league/esp.1/year/2011/spanish-primera-division?cc=590, 1.

**H9**   'Annual review of football finance 2012' (2012), Deloitte LLP, 31 May 2012.

**I9**   Lowe, Sid (2011), 'Barcelona and Real in La Liga of their own with the rest nowhere', *The Guardian*, 7 September 2011, accessed 10 August 2012 at http://www.guardian.co.uk/football/blog/2011/sep/07/la-liga-barcelona-real-madrid.

**J9**   'Premier League tops shirt sponsorships; Bundesliga gets more per team' (2012), *Sports Business Daily*, 21 June 2012, accessed 11 August 2012 at http://www.sportsbusiness daily.com/Global/Issues/2012/06/21/Marketing-and-Sponsorship/Shirts-Europe.aspx.

**K9**   'Real Madrid annual report 2010–2011' (2011), September 2011, 91.

**L9**   Cutler, Matt (2011), 'La Liga topples Premier League as Europe's top merchandise division', Sport Business, 23 February 2011, accessed 14 August 2012 at http://www.sportbusiness.com/news/183139/la-liga-topples-premier-league-as-europe-s-top-merchandise-division.

**N9**   'Fan power: football money league 2012' (2012), Deloitte LLP, February 2012.

**O9**   Ibid.

*Serie A*

**B10**   'Serie A teams' (n.d.), FoxSports.com, accessed 4 August 2012 at http://msn.foxsports.com/foxsoccer/seriea/teams/.

**D10**   Facebook

**E10**   'Italian Serie A attendance 2011–12', Soccernet.espn.com, accessed 11 August 2012 at http://soccernet.espn.go.com/stats/attendance/_/league/ita.1/year/2011/italian-serie-a?cc=5901.

**H10**   'Annual review of football finance 2012' (2012), Deloitte LLP, 31 May 2012.

**I10**   Cutler, Matt (2011), 'Serie A's 20 clubs have finally reached an agreement to settle the long-running dispute about the distribution of media-rights income in Italian football', SportBusiness.com, 12 July 2011, accessed 11 August 2012 at http://www.sportbusiness.com/news/183942/peace-at-last-as-serie-a-clubs-agree-revenue-sharing-deal.

**J10**   'Premier League tops shirt sponsorships; Bundesliga gets more per team' (2012), *Sports Business Daily*, 21 June 2012, accessed 11 August 2012 at http://www.sportsbusinessdaily.com/Global/Issues/2012/06/21/Marketing-and-Sponsorship/Shirts-Europe.aspx.

**L10**   Cutler, Matt (2011), 'La Liga topples Premier League as Europe's top merchandise division', Sport Business, 23 February 2011, accessed 14 August 2012 at http://www.sportbusiness.com/news/183139/la-liga-topples-premier-league-as-europe-s-top-merchandise-division.

**N10**   Associated Press (2011), 'Serie A sells domestic TV rights for $3.34 billion', *Washington Post*, 22 September 2011, accessed 15 August 2012 at http://www.washingtontimes.com/news/2011/sep/22/serie-a-sells-domestic-tv-rights-for-334-billion/.

*Bundesliga*

**B11**   'Clubs and players' (n.d.), Bundesliga.com, accessed 4 August 2012 at http://www.bundesliga.de/en/liga/clubs/.

**C11**   'Update 1: auction for Bundesliga broadcast rights heats up' (2012), Reuters.com, 2 April 2012, accessed 12 August 2012 at http://www.reuters.com/article/2012/04/02/germany-bundesliga-deutschetelekom-idUSL6E8F22FU20120402.

**D11**   Facebook, Twitter, Google+

**E11**   'Number of spectators' (n.d.), Deutscher Fussball-Bund, accessed 8 August 2012 at http://www.dfb.de/?id=380609.

**H11**   Tom Bender (ed.) (2012), 'Bundesliga report 2012', DFL Deutsche Fussball Liga GmbH, 23 January 2012, 8.

**I11**   Skinner, James (2010), 'German model highlights Man Utd dilemma', Bbc.co.uk, 29 March 2010, accessed 15 August 2012 at http://news.bbc.co.uk/sport2/hi/football/europe/8589872.stm.

**J11**   'Premier League tops shirt sponsorships; Bundesliga gets more per team' (2012), *Sports Business Daily*, 21 June 2012, accessed 11 August 2012 at http://www.sportsbusinessdaily.com/Global/Issues/2012/06/21/Marketing-and-Sponsorship/Shirts-Europe.aspx.

**K11**   Tom Bender (ed.) (2012), 'Bundesliga report 2012', DFL Deutsche Fussball Liga GmbH, 23 January 2012, 8.

**L11**   Ibid.

**M11**   Jackson, Jamie (2010), 'Germany provide the blueprint for England's academy system', *The Guardian*, 3 July 2010, accessed 15 August 2012 at http://www.guardian.co.uk/football/2010/jul/04/germany-youth-development-england.

**N11**   Tom Bender (ed.) (2012), 'Bundesliga report 2012', DFL Deutsche Fussball Liga GmbH, 23 January 2012, 8.

**O11**   'Annual review of football finance 2012' (2012), Deloitte LLP, 31 May 2012.


*Formula 1*

**B12**   'Teams' (n.d.), Formula1.com, accessed 4 August 2012 at http://www.formula1.com/teams_and_drivers/.

**C12**   'Thrilling 2010 season boosts Formula One TV audiences' (2011), Formula1.com, 21 January 2011, accessed 8 August 2012 at http://www.formula1.com/news/headlines/2011/1/11660.html.

**D12**   Facebook, Twitter

**E12**   Langmaid, Aaron (2012), 'Right on track for a blast at Albert Park', *Herald Sun*, 19 March 2012, accessed 15 August 2012 at http://www.heraldsun.com.au/sport/right-on-track-for-a-blast-at-albert-park/story-fn7q3txe-1226303405298.

**G12**   'Thrilling 2010 season boosts Formula One TV audiences' (2011), Formula1.com, 21 January 2011, accessed 8 August 2012 at http://www.formula1.com/news/headlines/2011/1/11660.html.

**H12**   Ludvig, Sonja (2009), 'Formula 1's global revenues are $3.9 billion', Deloitte.com, Deloitte Press Release, 5 August 2009, accessed 9 August 2012 at https://www.deloitte.com/view/en_BA/ba/press/ba-press-releases-en/21e3f75d99efd110VgnVCM100000ba42f00aRCRD.htm.

**I12**   Allen, James (2011), 'F1 turnover tops $1 billion again as teams' share rises', 6 April 2011, accessed 11 August 2012 at http://www.jamesallenonf1.com/2011/04/f1-turnover-tops-1-billion-again-as-teams-share-rises/.

**J12**   Edgecliffe-Johnson, Andrew (2012), 'Media rights: pay TV deal changes the game for a sport hungry for revenues', *Financial Times*, 15 March 2012, accessed 8 August 2012 at http://www.ft.com/cms/s/0/26559306-6e30-11e1-baa5-00144feab49a.html#axzz22xqJqiba.

**L12**   Pinto, Viveat Susan and Ranju Sarkar (2012), 'Brands queue up for their share of Formula 1 pie', *Business Standard*, 29 October 2012, accessed 13 August 2012 at http://www.business-standard.com/india/news/brands-queuefor-their-shareformula1-pie/453937/.

**M12**   'Our drivers of the future' (n.d.), Caterham F1 Team, accessed 15 August 2012 at http://www.caterhamf1.com/team/driver-development-program/driver-develop ment-program.

**N12** Edgecliffe-Johnson, Andrew (2012), 'Media rights: pay TV deal changes the game for a sport hungry for revenues', *Financial Times*, 15 March 2012, accessed 8 August 2012 at http://www.ft.com/cms/s/0/26559306-6e30-11e1-baa5-00144feab49a.html#axzz22x qJqiba.

**O12** Venkat, P.R. (2012), 'Formula One may restart IPO late in 2012', *The Wall Street Journal*, 13 June 2012, accessed 15 August 2012 at http://online.wsj.com/article/SB1000142405 2702303734204577464292348447640.html.

### NASCAR

**B13** 'Drivers', NASCAR.com, accessed 4 August 2012 at http://www.nascar.com/drivers/ list/cup/dps/.

**C13** Badenhausen, Kurt (2012), 'All of NASCAR gets a boost with a Dale Earnhardt win', Forbes.com, 17 June 2012, accessed 12 August 2012 at http://www.forbes.com/sites/ kurtbadenhausen/2012/06/17/all-of-nascar-gets-boost-with-dale-earnhardt-win/.

**D13** Facebook, Twitter, Google+

**E13** 'NASCAR's TV ratings rise after three-year decline' (2011), NASCAR.com, 14 June 2011, accessed 8 August 2012 at http://www.nascar.com/news/110614/ratings- increase-2011/index.html.

**G13** Gorman, Bill (2011), 'NASCAR Chase finale earns ESPN's largest NASCAR Sprint Cup viewership ever', TV By The Numbers, 22 November 2011, accessed 8 August 2011 at http://tvbythenumbers.zap2it.com/2011/11/22/nascar-chase-finale-earns-espn% E2%80%99s-largest-nascar-sprint-cup-viewership-ever/111600/.

**H13** '2011 financial results' (2012), International Speedway Corporation, 26 January 2012, accessed 11 August 2012 at http://www.internationalspeedwaycorporation.com/ Articles/2012/01/2011-Financial-Results.aspx; '2011 annual report' (n.d.), Dover Motorsports Incorporation, accessed 12 August 2012 at www.dovermotorsports.com/ DMS_AnnReport_2011.pdf.

**I13** Smith, Michael (2010), 'NASCAR markets new production space', *Sports Business Journal*, 4 January 2010, accessed 9 August 2012 at http://www.sportsbusinessdaily.com/Journal/ Issues/2010/01/20100104/This-Weeks-News/NASCAR-Markets-New-Production- Space.aspx?hl=NASCAR%20revenue&sc=1.

**J13** Greenberg, Karl (2011), '2011 auto racing sponsors head up the asphalt', Mediapost, 11 February 2011, accessed 14 August 2012 at http://www.sponsorship.com/About-IEG/ IEG-In-The-News/2011-Auto-Racing-Sponsors-Head-Up-The-Asphalt.aspx.

**L13** Badenhausen, Kurt (2010), 'NASCAR's most valuable teams', Forbes.com, 24 March 2010, accessed 15 August 2012 at http://www.forbes.com/2010/03/24/nascar-most- valuable-teams-business-sports-nascar-10-teams.html.

**N13** Pockrass, Bob (2012), 'ISC hopes NBC sports network is player in TV rights negotiations', Sporting News NASCAR, 5 July 2012, accessed 10 August 2012 at http://aol.sportingnews.com/nascar/story/2012-07-05/nascar-tv-rights-nbc-sports- network-isc-financial-report-ticket-revenue-down.

**O13** 'More than 100 Fortune 500 companies in NASCAR' (2012), NASCAR.com, NASCAR Official Release, 17 July 2012, accessed 10 August 2012 at http://www.nascar.com/ news/120717/nascar-fortune-500-investments/index.html.

*MLS*

**B14** 'Clubs' (n.d.), MajorLeagueSoccer.com, accessed 5 August 2012 at http://www.mlssoccer.com/clubs.

**C14** Spanberg, Erik (2012), 'Soccer's new stage', *Sports Business Journal*, 4 March 2012, 15.

**D14** Facebook, Twitter, Instagram, Google+

**E14** 'MLS turnstile tracker' (2011), *Sports Business Journal*, 7 November 2011, 9.

**G14** 'Ratings: ACC Championship Game, Notre Dame on NBC, MLS Cup' (2011), Sports Media Watch, 16 December 2011, accessed 8 August 2012 at http://www.sportsmediawatch.com/2011/12/ratings-acc-championship-game-notre-dame-on-nbc-mls-cup/.

**H14** Constable, Phil (2011), 'Power ranking the leagues: EPL vs Serie A vs La Liga vs Ligue 1 vs MLS', Bleacherreport.com, 26 April 2011, accessed 11 August 2012, http://bleacherreport.com/articles/678848-power-ranking-the-leagues-epl-vs-serie-a-vs-la-liga-vs-ligue-1-vs-mls/page/2.

**I14** '2012 MLS SuperDraft set for January 12 in Kansas City' (2012), 21 October 2012, accessed 15 August 2012 at http://www.portlandtimbers.com/news/2011/10/2012-mls-superdraft-set-jan-12-kansas-city.

**J14** Eisenmenger, L.E. (2012), 'LA Galaxy sign MLS record $44 million sponsorship deal with Herbalife', *The Examiner*, 22 March 2012, accessed 11 August 2012 at http://www.examiner.com/article/la-galaxy-sign-mls-record-44-million-sponsorship-deal-with-herbalife.

**L14** Meyer, Harris (2009), 'Adidas banks on World Cup marketing to rally global sales', Oregon Live, 5 December 2009, accessed 15 August 2012 at http://www.oregonlive.com/business/index.ssf/2009/12/adidas_banks_on_world_cup_mark.html.

**M14** '2012 MLS SuperDraft set for January 12 in Kansas City' (2012), 21 October 2012, accessed 15 August 2012 at http://www.portlandtimbers.com/news/2011/10/2012-mls-superdraft-set-jan-12-kansas-city.

**N14** Spanberg, Erik (2012), 'Soccer's new stage', *Sports Business Journal*, 4 March 2012, 15.

**O14** Mickle, Tripp and Liz Mullen (2010), 'MLS labor agreement continues league's evolution', *Sports Business Daily*, 29 March 2010, accessed 15 August 2012 at http://www.sportsbusinessdaily.com/Journal/Issues/2010/03/20100329/This-Weeks-News/MLS-Labor-Agreement-Continues-Leagues-Evolution.aspx?hl=MLS%20single%20entity&sc=0.

 **REFERENCES FOR TABLE 2.3**

*Summer Olympics*

**C2** Sherman, Alex and Andy Fixmer (2012), 'NBC says London Games were most watched U.S. televised event', Businessweek.com, 13 August 2012, accessed 15 August 2012 at http://www.businessweek.com/news/2012-08-13/nbc-says-london-games-were-most-watched-u-dot-s-dot-televised-event.

**D2** Facebook, Twitter, Instagram, Google+

**E2** 'London 2012 Olympics close with spectacular ceremony', BBC, 13 August 2012, accessed 19 August 2012 at http://www.bbc.co.uk/news/uk-19236754.

**F2** Ibid.

**G2** 'IOC marketing media guide: London 2012' (2012), International Olympic Committee, 2 July 2012, 6.

**H2** Poggi, Jeanine (2012), 'So much for #NBCfail: Olympics ratings soar', Advertising Age, 6 August 2012, accessed 19 August 2012 at http://adage.com/article/media/nbcfail-olympics-ratings-soar/236524/.

I2    'IOC marketing media guide: London 2012' (2012), International Olympic Committee, 2 July 2012, 47.

J2    Poggi, Jeanine (2012), 'So much for #NBCfail: Olympics ratings soar', Advertising Age, 6 August 2012, accessed 19 August 2012 at http://adage.com/article/media/nbcfail-olympics-ratings-soar/236524/.

K2    Schwartz, Peter J. (2010), 'The world's top sports events', Forbes.com, 5 March 2010, accessed 19 August 2012 at http://www.forbes.com/global/2010/0315/companies-olympics-superbowl-daytona-worlds-top-sports-events.html.

*Winter Olympics*

C3    'Marketing report Vancouver 2010' (2010), International Olympic Committee, 6 July 2010, 28.

D3    Facebook, Twitter

E3    'Factsheet: Vancouver facts & figures' (2011), International Olympic Committee, February 2011, 1.

F3    Ibid.

G3    'IOC marketing media guide: London 2012' (2012), International Olympic Committee, 2 July 2012, 6.

H3    James, Meg (2011), 'Comcast to invest additional $300 million for NBCUniversal programming', *Los Angeles Times*, 5 May 2011, accessed 19 August 2012 at http://articles.latimes.com/2011/may/05/business/la-fi-ct-comcast-20110505.

I3    Brumwell, Chris (2010), '2010 Winter Games delivered on budget, leaving strong sport legacy and some of Canada's finest hours on the world stage', Newswire.ca, 17 December 2010, accessed 19 August 2012 at http://www.newswire.ca/en/story/664169/2010-winter-games-delivered-on-budget-leaving-strong-sport-legacy-and-some-of-canada-s-finest-hours-on-the-world-stage.

J3    Poggi, Jeanine (2012), 'So much for #NBCfail: Olympics ratings soar', Advertising Age, 6 August 2012, accessed 19 August 2012 at http://adage.com/article/media/nbcfail-olympics-ratings-soar/236524/.

K3    Schwartz, Peter J. (2010), 'The world's top sports events', Forbes.com, 5 March 2010, accessed 19 August 2012 at http://www.forbes.com/global/2010/0315/companies-olympics-superbowl-daytona-worlds-top-sports-events.html.

*Youth Olympics*

C4    'Blazing the trail' (2011), 2010 Singapore Youth Olympic Games Official Report, 23 March 2011, 199.

D4    Facebook, Twitter

E4    'Blazing the trail' (2011), 2010 Singapore Youth Olympic Games Official Report, 23 March 2011, 179; 'About Innsbruck 2012' (n.d), Innsbruck2012.com, accessed 19 August 2012 at http://www.innsbruck2012.com/en/about_us.

F4    Ibid.

G4    'Sponsoring the Winter YOG' (n.d.), Sports Marketing Frontiers, accessed 19 August 2012 at http://frontiers.sportbusiness.com/frontloaded/head-to-head/sponsoring-winter-yog.

K4    'It's a high level sport and much more' (n.d.), Youth Olympic Games, International Olympic Committee, accessed 19 August 2012 at http://www.olympic.org/content/yog_/yog-2/page/its-a-high-level-sport-and-much-more/.

*SEA Games*

**C5**  Ika, Aprillia(2011), 'SEA Games generates high number of TV viewers', Indonesia FinanceToday.com, 28 November 2011, accessed 19 August 2012 at http://en. indonesiafinancetoday.com/read/14083/SEA-Games-Generates-High-Number-of-TV-Viewers.

**D5**  Facebook, Google+

**E5**  'Indonesia 2011' (n.d.), OCAsia.org, Olympic Council of Asia, 19 August 2012 at http://www.ocasia.org/game/GameParticular.aspx?SYCXGjC0df9FinVzEIKang==.

**F5**  Ibid.

**K5**  Navarro, June (2012), 'SEA Games schedules more Olympic sports', SportsInquirer.net, 20 July 2012, accessed 20 August 2012 at http://sports.inquirer.net/53499/sea-games-schedules-more-olympic-sports.

*Commonwealth Games*

**C6**  Lord, David (2012), 'Manchester set a club television audience world record', TheRoar.au, 2 May 2012, accessed 19 August 2012 at http://www.theroar.com.au/2012/05/02/manchester-set-a-club-television-audience-world-record/.

**D6**  Facebook, Twitter, Google+

**E6**  'Frequently asked questions' (n.d.), Commonwealth Games Federation, accessed 19 August 2012 at http://www.thecgf.com/faq/.

**F6**  'India prepares for Commonwealth Games' (2010), Boston.com, 1 October 2010 accessed 19 August 2012 at http://www.boston.com/bigpicture/2010/10/india_prepares_for_the_commonw.html.

**G6**  'Commonwealth Games revenue pleases officials' (2010), DNAIndia.com, 6 May 2010, accessed 19 August 2012 at http://www.dnaindia.com/sport/report_commonwealth-games-revenue-pleases-officials_1379596.

**H6**  Mukherjee, Sharmistha (2010), 'DD set to cross Games revenue target', Business-Standard.com, 10 October 2010, accessed 19 August 2012 at http://www.business-standard.com/india/news/dd-set-to-cross-games-revenue-target/410846/.

**I6**  'OC faces shortfall in meeting revenue targets' (2010), IndianExpress.com, 26 September 2010, accessed 19 August 2012 at http://www.indianexpress.com/news/oc-faces-shortfall-in-meeting-revenue-targets/688220/0.

**J6**  'Dismal revenue collection for Games organizing committee' (2010), IndiaToday.in, 31 October 2010, accessed 19 August 2012 at http://indiatoday.intoday.in/story/dismal-revenue-collection-for-games-organizing-committee/1/118425.html.

**K6**  'Frequently asked questions' (n.d.), Commonwealth Games Federation, accessed 19 August 2012 at http://www.thecgf.com/faq/.

*FIFA World Cup*

**C7**  'Almost half the world tuned in at home to watch 2010 FIFA World Cup South Africa' (2011), Fédération Internationale de Football Association Media Release, 11 July 2011, accessed 15 August 2012 at http://www.fifa.com/worldcup/archive/southafrica2010/organisation/media/newsid=1473143/index.html.

**D7**  Facebook, Twitter, Instagram

**E7**  'FIFA World Cup' (n.d.), FIFA.com, accessed 20 August 2012 at http://www.fifa.com/aboutfifa/worldcup/index.html.

**F7**  Ibid.

**G7**  Chipps, William (2010), 'FIFA secures $1.6 billion in World Cup sponsorship revenue', Sponsorship.com, 3 June 2010, accessed 19 August 2012 at http://www.sponsorship.

com/About-IEG/Press-Room/FIFA-Secures-$1-6-Billion-in-World-Cup-Sponsorship. aspx.

**H7** Madden, Normandy (2010), 'CCTV will make $147 million from World Cup ads', *Advertising Age*, 30 June 2010, accessed 19 Aug 2012 at http://adage.com/china/article/ fast-facts/cctv-will-make-147-million-from-world-cup-ads/144717/.

**I7** Rodrigues, Aaron (2010), 'Now even official merchandise for the Commonwealth Games is under a cloud', Moneylife.in, 3 August 2010, accessed 19 August 2012 at http://www. moneylife.in/article/now-even-official-merchandise-for-the-commonwealth-games-is- under-a-cloud/7832.html.

**J7** Associated Press (2011), 'FIFA completes World Cup TV deals', ESPN.com, 27 October 2011, accessed 19 August 2012 at http://espn.go.com/sports/soccer/news/_/ id/7154917/fifa-completes-185-billion-world-cup-tv-deals.

**K7** 'FIFA World Cup' (n.d.), FIFA, accessed 20 August 2012 at http://www.fifa.com/about- fifa/worldcup/index.html.

*Rugby World Cup*

**C8** 'Heineken extends Rugby World Cup sponsorship for RWC 2015 in England' (2011), Heineken Press Release, 21 October 2011.

**D8** Facebook, Twitter

**E8** 'Rugby World Cup – the origins' (2011), RugbyWorldCup.com, IRB, 12 August 2011, accessed 20 August 2012 at http://en.rugbyworldcup.com/home/history/origins. html.

**F8** Baynes, Dan (2011), 'Rugby World Cup teams Select 30-man squads to contest event in New Zealand', Bloomberg.com, 24 August 2011, accessed 27 May 2013 at http://www. bloomberg.com/news/2011-08-25/rugby-world-cup-teams-select-30-man-squads-to- contest-event-in-new-zealand.html.

**G8** Okunniwa, Tove (n.d.), 'Tackling the opportunity of rugby sponsorship', MEC:Access, accessed 19 August 2012 at http://www.mecglobal.com/assets/assets/Uploads/ Reports/Resources/MEC-Access-RWC-Sept-11-FINAL.PDF.

**H8** 'Consolidated revenue held steady at €2,620m' (2012), TF1, TF1 Press Release, 16 February 2012.

**J8** 'Media groups in showdown over web advertising' (2011), *The Sydney Morning Herald*, 26 August 2011, accessed 20 August 2012 at http://www.smh.com.au/business/media- groups-in-showdown-over-web-advertising-20110825-1jc8d.html.

**K8** Cutler, Matt (2012), 'New Zealand's Rugby World Cup exceeds financial expectations', SportBusiness.com, 23 March 2012, accessed 20 August 2012 at http://www.sportbusi- ness.com/news/185279/new-zealand-s-rugby-world-cup-exceeds-financial-expectations.

*ICC World Cup*

**C9** Marks, Vic (2011), 'India v Pakistan: ultimate cricket Derby brings two countries to a standstill', *The Guardian*, 30 March 2011, accessed 20 August 2012 at http://www.guard- ian.co.uk/sport/2011/mar/30/india-pakistan-ultimate-cricket-derby.

**D9** Facebook, Twitter

**E9** 'ESPN cric info World Cup 2011' (n.d.), ESPNcricinfo.com, accessed 20 August 2012 at http://www.espncricinfo.com/icc-cricket-world-cup-2011.

**F9** Suhalb, Hilal (2011), 'Sri Lanka name 2011 ICC World Cup squad', IslandCricket. com, 7 January 2011, accessed 20 August 2012 at http://www.islandcricket.lk/news/ srilankacricket/87670107/sri-lanka-name-2011-icc-cricket-world-cup-squad.

**G9** 'ICC set to cash in on sponsorship rights' (2007), ESPNcricinfo.com, 18 January 2007, accessed 20 August 2012 at http://www.espncricinfo.com/ci/content/story/276853. html.

**H9**    Chandran, Anushree and Gouri Shah (2011), 'Sponsorship revenue, viewership set to rise from last tournament', *The Wall Street Journal*, 9 February 2011, accessed 20 August 2012 at http://www.livemint.com/2011/02/09214932/Sponsorship-revenue-viewershi.html.

**I9**    'ICC earns \$321.2 million from 2011 World Cup' (2012), Indiantelevision.com, 30 June 2012, accessed 20 August 2012 at http://www.indiantelevision.com/headlines/y2k12/june/jun301.php.

**J9**    Mahalingam, T.V. and Anusha Subramanian (2011), 'The game's biggest year ever', BusinessToday.intoday.in, 6 February 2011, accessed 20 August 2012 at http://business-today.intoday.in/story/huge-money-at-stake-in-icc-world-cup-ipl4/0/12525.html.

**K9**    'World Cup final had highest rating: TAM' (2011), *Economic Times*, 7 April 2011, accessed 20 August 2012 at http://articles.economictimes.indiatimes.com/2011-04-07/news/29392442_1_peak-rating-highest-rating-star-cricket.


*UEFA Euro 2012*

**C10**    Gindrat, François (2012), 'UEFA's battle for its brand', *WIPO Magazine*, February 2012, accessed http://www.wipo.int/wipo_magazine/en/2012/02/article_0008.html.

**D10**    Facebook, Twitter, Google+

**E10**    'Final UEFA Euro 2012 squads confirmed' (2012), UEFA.com, 29 May 2012, accessed 20 August 2012 at http://www.uefa.com/uefaeuro/news/newsid=1803170.html.

**F10**    Ibid.

**G10**    Dunbar, Graham (2012), 'Euro 2012 earns elite-level income and TV ratings', Associated Press, 5 June 2012, accessed 20 August 2012 at http://sports.yahoo.com/news/euro-2012-earns-elite-level-200526556--sow.html.

**H10**    McCabe, Maisie (2012), 'ITV set for £15m euro 2012 boost', Mediaweek.co.uk, 25 June 2012, accessed 20 August 2012 at http://www.mediaweek.co.uk/news/1137870/.

**I10**    Dunbar, Graham (2012), 'Euro 2012 earns elite-level income and TV ratings', Associated Press, 5 June 2012, accessed 20 August 2012 at http://sports.yahoo.com/news/euro-2012-earns-elite-level-200526556--sow.html.

**J10**    Ibid.

**K10**    Ibid.

# 3

# Sports histories and sports fans

 **CHAPTER OVERVIEW**

Our emphasis in the first two chapters was on understanding the overall context of the sports industry, the major sports leagues, and the sports brand planning framework since each of these areas help inform the marketing analysis marketers must make as they evaluate how to effectively allocate their sports marketing investment. In this chapter we will expand our description of the origins of several of the world's sports to help describe the factors that attracts fans to each sport. We will then focus on customers and fans since they are the primary target audience that sports marketers are attempting to serve. Value is created in sports marketing when stakeholders', particularly customers' (since they typically support the value proposition by purchasing the goods and creating a financial transaction), needs are met, so we look at how marketing segmentation approaches apply to the world of sports. The most popular sports in the world are laden with rich traditions that their respective fans support and follow with enthusiasm, and sports marketers will be well served in their marketing efforts by paying close attention to each sport's historical legacies.

## 3.1 Development of selected sports

### Cricket

The origins of cricket are clouded, with some historical literature suggesting the sport began sometime in the Dark Ages. Perhaps more accurately, early variations of the sport most resembling its current form were played in Surrey, England around 1550, or roughly at the mid-point of the Tudor dynasty. Cricket quickly grew in popularity and became a prominent activity outside of school for males from young boys to young men. The first team to leave England for overseas play was in 1859 when an English cricket team played in the USA and Canada. In 1882 Australia defeated England in England and a subsequent mock obituary notice was placed in the *Sporting*

*Times*, inspiring a now famous cricket event called 'The Ashes'. The notice read:

> In Affectionate Remembrance
> of
> ENGLISH CRICKET,
> which died at the Oval
> on
> 29th AUGUST 1882,
> Deeply lamented by a large circle of sorrowing
> friends and acquaintances
> R.I.P.
> N.B. – The body will be cremated and the
> ashes taken to Australia.[1]

The Ashes is a biennial event and as of 2011 66 Ashes series had been played, with Australia leading England 31–30, with five draws. Cricket is governed by the ICC (International Cricket Council), which has 104 member nations. There are three forms of cricket: Test cricket (five days), One Day Internationals (ODI), and Twenty20. Of the 104 nations in the ICC, ten are considered full members, which means they are eligible to field teams in each of the three forms of the sport.[2] The full members are:

- Australia;
- Bangladesh;
- England;
- India;
- New Zealand;
- Pakistan;
- South Africa;
- Sri Lanka;
- West Indies;
- Zimbabwe.

The next level of ICC membership is called Associate and Affiliate. These members are not allowed to play Test, but if they perform well in the quadrennial ICC World Cricket League, they are then awarded recognition as an ODI team. The top six teams from the ICC World Cup Qualifier are granted the right to play both ODI and Twenty20, wherein they can then play full members in those two forms of the sport. India was crowned ICC World Cup Champion by virtue of its victory over Sri Lanka in Mumbai in April 2011, setting off a feverish national celebration that lasted for days across the country.[3]

For sports fans outside of cricket's main participating countries, the game appears perplexing and obscure, with odd terminology and complex scoring rules. But for the sport's loyal fans, cricket is their passion and a key part of their lives and identity.

## Baseball

Like cricket, baseball's exact origins are subject to some interpretation. Antecedents of baseball were seen in England in the eighteenth century, but the modern form of the sport appears to have emerged in the United States in the mid-nineteenth century. While cricket and baseball share a basic ancestry of a round ball being hurled at a target, the two sports differ significantly in how they are played, scored, and the length of game time (Test matches in cricket lasting five days whereas most baseball games are over after three hours).

Professional baseball, now known as Major League Baseball (MLB), was founded in 1869. In the early 1900s two separate leagues were formed, the American and National Leagues. The winners of each league would meet in the World Series, the sport's season-ending championship. Both leagues remained separate, with independent executive teams governed by a league president. A common baseball Commissioner overseeing the sport and adjudicating conflicts between the two leagues began formally in 1903. In 2000 the two leagues dissolved their respective independent offices and presidencies, joining together as one entity governed by the Commissioner. Since the mid-1990s, MLB has been criticized by fans and media alike because of the increased use of performance-enhancing drugs by many prominent players, which has coincided with a barrage of recording-breaking performances, affecting the sport's popularity.[4]

Also like cricket, baseball enjoys a loyal, even rabid, fan base. Similar to cricket, baseball's rules seem complex and even arcane to outsiders, but baseball's diehard baseball fans love the sport's traditions, memorize a wide and varied range of sport statistics, and believe fervently in the sport's reputation as America's favorite pastime.

## Football (Soccer)

Football's origins, like those of cricket and arguably baseball, were in England. In the mid-1800s the sport was played throughout England, and was enjoyed especially by university students. The sport has grown into the world's most popular sport. According to FIFA (*English*: The International

Federation of Association Football), more than 265 million people from its 207 member associations play the sport each year.[5] The professional leagues are most popular in Europe and South America, although growing interest has been seen in Asia as well, with the launch of professional leagues in Korea (1983), Japan (1992), Singapore (1996), and China (2004) since the 1980s. The major European Leagues are characterized by having both a league structure and a governing body in which teams from different country leagues are members of the main governing body:

- *UEFA* (Union of European Football Associations). UEFA is the leading body for all football in Europe, with 53 national associations under its purview.[6]
- *FA* (Football Association – the governing body in England and all football clubs from the various English leagues are members):[7]
  - Premier League (a separate entity comprising the UK's top 20 teams);
  - FL (Football League – UK league containing 72 teams in three divisions below the Premier League level [Championship; League 1; League 2]);
- La Liga (Spain), Primera Division – 20 clubs:[8]
  - La Liga, Secunda Division –22 clubs;
- Serie A (Italy) – 20 clubs;[9]
- Bundesliga (Germany) –18 clubs:[10]
  - Second Bundesliga – 18 clubs;
- Eredivisie (Netherlands) – 18 clubs:[11]
  - Eerste Division – 18 clubs.

Soccer fans are well known for their fierce loyalties, and occasional violent outbursts (most commonly referred to as hooliganism), in support of their favorite clubs. Italy's Serie A (and Serie B, second division) matches cancelled all matches in 2007 following the death of a police officer during a game between Palermo and Catania. Italy is not alone as a site of soccer-related conflict. Other instances of unruly and even deadly fan behavior have been witnessed around the world, highlighting one of the risks companies confront when investing in sports marketing.[12]

## Basketball

Basketball began in 1891 when Dr. James Naismith, a physical education instructor in Massachusetts, wanted to keep his students fit during the long New England winters so he attached two peach baskets to the end walls of an indoor gym and the sport was born. The game evolved over the decades, but it wasn't until the 1950s that a consistent size, shape, and color for the basketball was designed. This simple change ushered in the era of more dribbling by individual players, allowing them to move up and down court more easily with greater control over the ball. Prior to this, basketballs varied a bit in their design and the game was characterized by more passing than dribbling.[13]

In 1932 FIBA (Fédération Internationale de Basket-ball Amateur) was founded by seven countries in Europe (Switzerland, Portugal, Greece, Romania, Czechoslovakia, Italy, Latvia) and one in South America (Argentina), with authority over amateur players. FIBA men's basketball was first played in the Olympics in Berlin in 1936. In 1989 FIBA changed its charter, no longer distinguishing between amateur and professional players, paving the way for professionals to play in the Olympics.[14]

The NBA (National Basketball Association) was officially formed in 1949 from the merger of two earlier professional leagues, the National Basketball League and the Basketball Association of America. In 1967 a rival league was launched, called the ABA (American Basketball Association), which enjoyed early success, but in 1976 it merged with the NBA. The ABA was the catalyst, however, for a number of important changes in the NBA, including slam dunks, faster offensive playing, a three-point arc, and the addition of teams in southern US cities.[15]

While both FIBA and the NBA represent basketball, there are many differences between the two organizations' game rules. Interested readers are encouraged to review the following links to compare the two:

http://www.fiba.com/asp_includes/download.asp?file_id=518;
http://sports.yahoo.com/blogs/olympics-fourth-place-medal/breaking-down-rule-play-differences-between-nba-fiba-213638219--oly.html.

## F1

F1 (Formula 1) began formally in 1950, although an earlier version of racing, called Grand Prix Motor Racing, was popular for nearly 20 years in the 1920s and 1930s. The term 'Formula' refers to the unique vehicle specifications the sport's 12 racing teams are required to meet. The sport has undergone many changes over the years, perhaps none more important than those introduced by Bernie Ecclestone in the 1970s. Prior to Ecclestone's arrival F1 drivers could choose which races they wished to enter and negotiated terms with the individual promoters of each race. While there was a loyal fan following, it was eclectic, mostly European, relegated to the cities in which the races were held, and perceived as a sport only for the very rich. Ecclestone determined that the future success depended on getting all teams to participate in all races. He reasoned that this commitment from the teams would build confidence from sponsors that the teams and drivers were reliable, which would help improve fan loyalty, increase overall fan numbers, and thereby make the sport more attractive to TV broadcasters as well. His changes took many years to enact, but in short, Ecclestone transformed the sport from a regional novelty event to a true professional league with a more formalized set of rules. TV interest grew, sponsorship investments increased, and the sport's popularity grew around the world. During his early years in the sport, Ecclestone progressed from being an owner of one of the racing teams to eventually taking over as CEO of Formula One Management, Formula One Administration, and Formula One Constructors' Association, all three of which are in the Formula One Group of Companies. The Formula One Group is responsible for overseeing the FIA F1 World Championship every year, comprising two individual world championships: the drivers and the constructors.[16] Twelve teams compete in 20 races each season, and the top ten finishers receive points as follows:

| | |
|---|---|
| 1st: 25 points | 6th: 8 points |
| 2nd: 18 points | 7th: 6 points |
| 3rd: 15 points | 8th: 4 points |
| 4th: 12 points | 9th: 2 points |
| 5th: 10 points | 10th: 1 point |

Each team is allowed two drivers. If those two drivers finish in the top ten, then they each receive the points associated with their particular order of finish per the scale above, and the points then count toward the drivers' championship. In this example, since both are from the same team, then the combination of their two-point totals are awarded toward the constructors' championship. F1 has become one of the largest and most popular sports while also nurturing an image as the world's most prestigious racing sport.[17]

## Football (US)

US football is the by-product of both rugby football and association football (soccer) from the UK. Early forms of the sport emerged in the mid-1800s, with the first official university-level football game held in New Jersey on 6 November 1869 between Princeton University and Rutgers University. In the 1880s, a now legendary football coach from Yale named Walter Camp introduced new rules, including allowing a forward pass, a required distance (five yards in the first years of the new rule, which evolved into the ten yards common today) to be covered by the offensive team within a limited number of plays called downs (or the ball would be relinquished to the opponent), and a specific start point for the offensive and defensive teams called the line of scrimmage. These changes marked the first serious departure of the US version of the sport from its rugby and soccer heritage.[18] The sport's popularity grew in the early 1900s, as did the violent nature of its style of play. Deaths occurred occasionally (33 in 1908 alone), so additional rules were introduced along with padding and other protective equipment.

The first professional league began in 1920 with 11 teams, taking on the name 'National Football League' in 1921. The college game was more popular, but an increasing number of college stars joined professional teams afterward, propelling fan interest. By 1950 professional football had become a mainstream sport, and the advent of television brought fans in huge numbers.[19] As discussed earlier in this book, the NFL has worked hard to establish parity in the league in an effort to keep small market teams competitive, with revenue sharing as one of the primary tools for achieving league balance. Revenue sharing remains controversial to many fans, and is quite different than the relegation system employed in most European soccer leagues (wherein the bottom three clubs in the highest division drop down to the second division, replaced by the top performers in the second division).

## 3.2    Fan segmentation

Classic marketing theory relies on four segmentation approaches in identifying customers, describing customer groups based on common characteristics:

- demographics: age, ethnicity, income, gender, occupation, religion;
- geographics: country, region, city, local;
- psychographics: lifestyle, interests, activities, values, opinions;
- behavioral: intended use, usage rates, brand loyalty, benefits sought.

### Demographics

Major League Baseball offers a good example of how customer demographic information is described. According to the Sports Business Research Network, the average attendance per game in 2011 was nearly 42 000 fans, up from 29 463 fans in 2005. Sixty-two percent of attending fans are male. Male fans have been between 57 percent and 62.2 percent of the attending fan population since 2005. In 2011, the age groups represented were as follows:

| <18–34 (16–34 in 2009) (13–24 in 2011) | 44.9% |
| 35–49 | 27.8% |
| 50+ | 27.2% |

Salary and income levels represent another useful demographic:

| Under $25 000 | 10.7% |
| $25 000–$49 999 | 18.5% |
| $50 000–$99 999 | 33.8% |
| $100 000+ | 37.0% |

For sports marketers these findings help in not just understanding the basic demographic composition of the attending fans, but they also provide marketers with data about the size of different audience types, which can help determine whether a particular fan group is large enough to merit the marketer's efforts. The baseball statistics cited above can be further enhanced by reviewing the trends in each demographic category over the past few years to determine if the number is growing or shrinking. A decreasing number does not necessarily mean that the sports marketer should ignore that audience. A deeper analysis of the fan data is warranted since it might reveal how fan tastes have changed, which, therefore, could have influenced the changes in the demographics. Astute sports marketers would question whether an alternative marketing approach might improve fan response and thus turn around a previously declining demographic group's interest. Correspondingly, additional analysis may confirm that the demographic changes are structural and permanent, indicating that the sports marketer's attention ought to be focused on the growing demographic groups.[20]

## Geographics

The NFL (National Football League) fan statistics for 2011 show the percentage of fans from each geographic region of the United States, by live attendance and by TV viewing, shown in Table 3.1.[21]

**Table 3.1** Percentage of NFL fans by live attendance and TV viewing

| Region | Live Attendance | TV Viewing |
| --- | --- | --- |
| Northeast | 18.7% | 16.8% |
| North Central | 28.1% | 23.6% |
| South | 35.2% | 37.7% |
| West | 18.1% | 21.9% |

As for sports marketers interested in football participation in general (not limited to the NFL), the geographic participation percentages are as shown in Table 3.2.

**Table 3.2** Geographic participation percentages

| Region | Participation |
| --- | --- |
| New England (5.1% of US pop.) | 2.1% |
| Middle Atlantic (14% of US pop.) | 14.4% |
| East North Central (16.5% of US pop.) | 15.3% |
| West North Central (7.1% of US pop.) | 8.4% |
| South Atlantic (18.8% of US pop.) | 22.6% |
| East South Central (6.2% of US pop.) | 5.4% |
| West South Central (11.1% of US pop.) | 8.6% |
| Mountain (6.3% of US pop.) | 11.3% |
| Pacific (14.9% of US pop.) | 11.9% |

Detailed percentage participation breakdowns by state, counties, and cities are also available. The benefit for marketers is that this information helps them begin to understand the market characteristics for football fans (or any sport's fans) and participants. Combining geographic data with demographic would add important insight, further helping marketers develop a complete picture of the marketplace and enabling them to select the most attractive markets for their particular offerings.[22]

## Psychographics

Another layer of information marketers seek is psychographics segmentation. Since psychographics are concerned with lifestyle and personality characteristics (is a person bold, timid, artistic, methodical etc.?), data gathering is more challenging because the insights are qualitative and descriptive, whereas demographic and geographic research concerns quantitative and tangible characteristics. Psychographic data enhances the sports marketer's understanding of the target audience's profile, providing in-depth customer knowledge that can be used to develop and align their offerings to maximize their appeal and generate long-term financial gains.

## Behavioral

Behavioral segmentation describes how customers behave toward and/or respond to offerings. Sports fans exhibit specific behaviors that reveal their need for and response to sports events. A sport fan's needs are categorized in three areas, validation, pleasure and arousal, and each need consists of underlying motives. While sports fans can be described in even greater detail, these three categories capture many of the most consistently familiar fan qualities, as shown in Table 3.3.

**Table 3.3** Three categories of a sport fan's needs

| Need | Underlying Motive Examples |
| --- | --- |
| Validation | Self-esteem |
| | Group affiliation |
| | Companionship |
| Pleasure | Entertainment |
| | Aesthetics |
| Arousal | Escape |
| | Eustress |

Source: Kahle and Close (2010).

*Validation* describes how a fan uses sports as a means to prove one's worth, typically through their association with a favorite team and/or athlete, as well as in a larger social context with others that also support the same athletes. We see validation in consumers' product choices from many industries, not just sports. Wearing a Rolex watch, using Apple iPads, buying premium wine are all different examples of how consumers reflect their sense of self, their identity, to others, just as affiliating with a sport, team or athlete does.

*Self-esteem* describes how fans take great pride in the successful performance of their favorite sports teams and athletes, with any wins leading to increased community support, exemplified by improved sales of team-related merchandise. Robert Cialdini et al. conducted pathbreaking studies on theories of cognition in an effort to explain how individuals gain self-worth from membership in select groups (Cialdini et al., 1976). Called 'basking in reflected glory' (BIRG), the studies showed that people like to be associated with success, gaining a vicarious thrill from another's success, even if they did not have any direct or even indirect influence on the sports' entities accomplishments. To an extent, this phenomenon can also help explain the gains companies seek when sponsoring a major sports event such as the Olympic Games, FIFA World Cup, or the Super Bowl. Conversely, people will also try to distance themselves from poor performers, exhibiting a phenomenon known as 'cutting off reflected failure' (CORF).[23]

*Companionship* refers to fans' enjoyment from seeing the sports event with others, including the pre-during and post-game socializing, sharing the sports event with friends as well as with fellow fans they don't know as well, or at all.

*Affiliation* describes the shared sense of community ('we are in this together') that unites fans, especially during success. Interestingly, failure leads fans to commiserate together, playing the proverbial 'armchair quarterback' (a term that describes a fan's second guessing of a team or athlete's performance, as if they could actually help the team improve if only they were in charge) and having their frustrations affirmed by others.

*Pleasure* describes the joy and pleasure fans derive from watching sports. Sports are both competitive, igniting strong passions, and entertaining, inspiring the fans' sense of spectacle and performance. The combination of sports and entertainment is evolving around the world, perhaps best accentuated by India's IPL (Indian Premier League) and Bollywood combination and the NBA's pre-game fireworks and during-game fan engagement activities. Sports clubs and their owners have invested resources in recent years in upgrading or even developing new sports facilities, designed to create better access to concessions and merchandise, improve access to and from the venues, enhance seating, and offer more appealing visual displays around the sports field and in the public areas and walkways.

*Entertainment* is one of the most powerful reasons sports fans attend games. Fans cheer their team on to win and expect the contest to provide a strong dose of excitement and unpredictability that serves as a catalyst to their overall enjoyment. As mentioned in the previous paragraph, entertainment can also extend beyond the play of the athletes themselves and into the between-play activities designed to engage fans, such as having them participate in quick games and contests designed to award prizes for achieving a specified outcome.

*Aesthetics* describes a fan's deep appreciation for the quality of the athlete's performances, much like art aficionados admire artistic expression and wine connoisseurs compliment a given wine's taste and complexity. When a team or individual athlete performs spectacularly well, fans' sense of awe and amazement tends to increase, with a sense that no mere mortal could perform such a feat.

*Arousal* is exemplified by fans' feeling of excitement, increased energy levels and a general sense of elation that is a by-product of watching a favorite sport. Part of this is the sense of wonder over what is going to happen next: for US fans, the 2008 Gold Medal-winning performance by the men's $4 \times 100$ relay swim team when the USA beat the French team by only 0.13 of a second; in 2012 in London, the French got their revenge, beating the USA by 0.45 of second to win the gold.

*Escape* refers to the feeling fans have of breaking free from their normal, hectic lives. Sports provide a form of relief where fans can be distracted, temporarily causing their concerns to recede, even for a short time.

*Eustress* describes beneficial psychological stress, such as sports fans enjoying the suspense and even cathartic rush of watching a sport. The typical, unpredictable ebb and flow that animates a team's performance throughout a game also causes different levels of stimulation within fans.[24]

# 3.3  Fan types

Sports marketers devote significant portions of their overall marketing budget to turn fans into profitable customers. As studies show, fan profiles vary around the world and depend on the characteristics being investigated. For example, is the sports marketer interested in the depth of fan commitment to the sport? Do they want to understand fan motivation for watching their favorite sport, and the type of motivation that inspires their behavior? Are they interested in fan personality types? Do they want to learn about fan identification with their team's success? Each of these themes, and dozens more, have been researched by leading academics and practitioners. Specific fan characteristics have been studied in depth in various sports around the world yielding an interesting, if complex and even contradictory set of understandings about fans. For our purposes, the studies of sports fan profiles have been broadly summarized into three layers, described by the intensity of their interest, from most intense, to least intense, as illustrated by Figure 3.1.

The three layers are:

- intense enthusiasts;
- shared enthusiasts;
- casual enthusiasts.

## Intense enthusiasts[25]

Intense enthusiasts (IE) are avid sports fans. IEs are the most loyal, characterized by ongoing support of their favorite sport, team and athletes, irrespective of success. IEs have a strong interest in sports and, if they are adults,

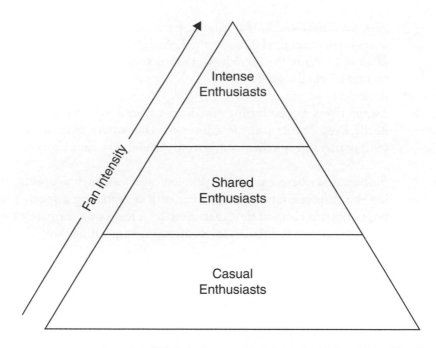

Source: Davis (2013). Derived from research by Davis, John A. in *The Olympic Games Effect – How Sports Marketing Builds Strong Brands*. Pp.236–238 (©2012 John Wiley & Sons).
**Figure 3.1** Layers of sports fan profiles

are the most likely to have played competitive sports in their youth and may still compete through adult leagues. Staying fit is a priority for IEs as well, finding time to exercise several times each week. However, IEs are not exclusively physically active as many simply love sports passionately. While they may have a favorite sport that becomes their primary focus, their love of sports is so strong that they will follow different sports each season throughout the year, and are often quite knowledgeable about statistical details from each sport. They are comfortable watching sports by themselves, but viewing with fellow IEs, and sports fans in general, is most common, reflecting the needs described in the previous chart for validation, pleasure, and arousal.

## Examples

IEs are a combination of sports geek, athlete (or wannabe), team player and loner, loud and quiet. They are indisputably passionate. Positive fan behavior is found everywhere in the cheers, merchandise purchases, fantasy leagues, social events before and after games, fan clubs, and, in university athletics, alumni and booster groups. IE fans around the world are banding together to support positive initiatives designed to make games more enjoyable. In Australia, fans of Melbourne Victory, an Australian Football League club, enthusiastically supported efforts in 2011 to prescribe how fans ought to behave.[26]

Negative behavior is also apparent and, at times, has forced restrictions on fans to quell the most egregious transgressors. In Northern Ireland for example, new laws were introduced in rugby, soccer, and Gaelic games in an effort to discourage misbehavior. Items thrown by fans that could result in injury can result in fines of £1000 or more. Use of fireworks can result in a three-month prison term, as can possession of alcohol in private hire vehicles.[27] In Scotland, new legislation aimed at stamping out fan bigotry often found in chants and songs is on the rise as well.[28]

## Shared enthusiasts[29]

Shared enthusiasts (SEs) are less intense than IEs, but they still share a common love of sports. Whereas the IEs are equally comfortable by themselves or in groups, SEs prefer, if given a choice, group and shared community sports experiences (hence their designation) over individual ones. SEs have a strong interest in their fitness and health, just as IEs do. SEs won't dedicate the same hours watching or attending sports events, but they will review highlights of their favorite every few days and increase their efforts when a unique opportunity arise or their favorite team is playing.

### *Example*

> In Europe if you are dancing in the team bus before a World Cup final match it would be viewed as not concentrating. But in Brazil if you are not speaking and laughing on the bus that is seen as being afraid.[30]

Football (soccer) fans in Europe and South America are legendary for their support of their national teams. While the observation above could easily describe IEs as well, the group setting described represents classic SE fan behavior. They enjoy the camaraderie of the collective experience and behave according to cultural norms that dictate 'good fan behavior'.

## Casual enthusiasts[31]

Casual enthusiasts (CEs) are even more relaxed about following sports, paying occasional attention if time permits and doing so is convenient. CEs are found in the same social and professional circles as IEs and SEs, but they are equally likely to be completely disconnected from the first two more committed fan types, with entirely different social and professional networks. CEs may go for weeks ignoring sports until a surprising or fascinating story emerges that rekindles their interest and/or when 'water cooler' conversations (professional socializing at work) pique their interest in a particular sports story. CEs are the most likely to be the least athletic, although fitness is still important for many of this fan type as well.

## Example

In 2003 the first regular season outdoor NHL (National Hockey League) game (called the 'Heritage Classic' at the time) between the Montreal Canadiens and the Edmonton Oilers attracted 57 000 fans, despite the fact that the temperature was well below zero. The US TV network NBC (National Broadcasting Company) and the NHL saw an opportunity to create a new annual event that would appeal to even the most casual fan, and the 'Winter Classic' was born. The first Winter Classic in 2008 in Buffalo, New York was held while snow fell, and still attracted over 71 000 fans. As John Collins, the NHL's Chief Operating Officer said:

> It made it look phenomenal on TV. There were some issues for the ice crew,
> but it was definitely part of the charm and part of the reason even casual fans
> actually stopped when they were channel-surfing. It was incredibly compelling – a
> phenomenal celebration of hockey.

Fan attendance has remained strong and, in 2011, TV viewership of this game exceeded 4.5 million, higher than the NHL had witnessed for any regular season game in 36 years.[32]

Each of these segmentation approaches are used by marketers either individually or in combination, depending on the customer audience profile information needed to make the integrated marketing communication plan effective. Customer identification is a step by step process designed to reveal characteristics and insights about customers that a company can then use in developing their business and marketing strategies. Marketers are also using the segmentation analysis to determine if the attractiveness of the customer market is matched by the company's ability to satisfactorily address the customers' needs. Assuming sports marketers learn from their customer analysis that additional investment is needed to design a proper marketing campaign, then the company's management must decide whether the increased spending will yield positive financial returns, warranting the extra investment in the first place.

## 3.4 Using customer needs to refine marketing execution

Earlier in this chapter customer needs were described using three main categories: validation, pleasure, and arousal. As marketers gather their market research, they will look even deeper into each segment's needs to also reveal insights about the product-specific needs sought. For example, the needs of customers of athletic footwear will vary depending on their usage profile (such as: are they active athletes placing rigorous demands on the footwear each day, or are they casual mall walkers merely seeking comfort?). Such market research information can be either company initiated or through third party market research firms. The results will help sports marketers tailor their marketing tactics to appeal to each segment's needs. The opposite is also true – the information may identify those segments that are either harder to service or are entirely unattractive before further resources are expended on attracting them.

Table 3.4 is a simplified example of how a sports marketer might organize their research findings based on each segment and the associated needs.

**Table 3.4** Segment needs analysis

| Needs | Intense Enthusiasts | Shared Enthusiasts | Casual Enthusiasts |
|---|---|---|---|
| Superior quality | ✓ | | |
| Product guarantees | ✓ | | |
| Real-time service | ✓ | | |
| Low price | | | ✓ |
| Loyalty programs | | ✓ | |
| Lifestyle fit | ✓ | ✓ | |
| Validation | ✓ | ✓ | |
| Pleasure | ✓ | | |
| Arousal | ✓ | ✓ | ✓ |

Source: Davis (2012, pp. 283–5).

By understanding each segment's needs and expectations sports marketers will be able to develop more effective marketing communications, and even product adaptations, to meet customer needs. The IE segment seeks satisfaction on most need categories. IEs have high expectations for their sports products and, like technology early adopters, tend to be well informed about their favorite sports, exhibiting a depth of knowledge non-IEs might describe as 'geeky'. Since IE customer's expectations are higher for their favorite sports offering, they are more willing to pay a premium price. IEs seek validation, pleasure, and arousal, indicating a desire for not only deep immersion into the sport psychologically, but also an inclination to have feelings of excitement and sharing with other like-minded people. Sports marketers would be wise to shape their marketing offering (the product, communications, service, and support) accordingly to address the IE segment's needs.

In this example the SE segment prefers loyalty programs and lifestyle fit, suggesting that if the sports offering matches their needs, they may become loyal customers. SEs also seek the companionship of others, which is a key characteristic of those seeking a shared experience with others and helps affirm their sense of identity. In this example, SEs also enjoy the sense of escape watching sports provides as well as the adrenalin-induced suspense characteristic of unscripted events. Given the need differences between IEs and SEs, the marketing team will need to market differently to each, adjusting their marketing programs just enough to show the SEs that they are understood.

Finally, the CE segment seeks low prices and arousal. The CE's interest is piqued when pricing is accessible, and there is a feeling of freedom and release from their everyday lives. While product quality and lifestyle fit may be of interest, these qualities are not as actively sought as much as affordable prices and a sense of departure, even though the latter is temporary.

The needs research discussed up to this point gives marketers invaluable insights about their target audience. Another area that is often underexplored, but ultimately essential to business success, is measuring the company's past success in attracting profitably customers from each segment to help determine how to take full advantage of growth opportunities in the future. Three measures that provide marketers with useful information are:

- market share of each segment;
- revenues represented by each segment;
- profit represented by each segment.

## Market share of each segment[33]

An important and ongoing objective is to outperform the competition. Besting competitors can be assessed many ways, including financial, reputation, and awareness. Measuring market share is a familiar and important way to compare the sports marketer's company to their competition, and doing this by customer segment can reveal a firm's advantages and disadvantages.

The following questions will help sports marketers understand their market share and determine how to plan for market share gains:

1. Can we gain market share versus our competitors if we succeed in winning over these customers?
2. What are the market share gains, if any, we can reasonably expect?
3. Is it reasonable to expect any market share gains in the short term?
4. What is our competition doing that is affecting their success with each segment?
5. Are there gaps or opportunities in our offering that can be addressed?
6. Are the relative market shares indicative of product quality, effective marketing communication, service delivery, or some combination of these?

When a sports marketer thinks through the complexities of how to increase market share, the segment needs' research discussed in the previous section takes on added importance and usefulness. There are likely very good reasons why the company is more successful selling to one segment versus another and why the competitors excel with certain segments, and knowing whether each segment's needs were adequately addressed by existing marketing programs (and how the competitors' marketing efforts are refined to address their segments) will indicate where adjustments to the marketing program can be made. Market share analysis is helpful here.

As an example, assume a sports marketer has invested in sponsoring the MLB World Series. Our now familiar fan types IE, SE, and CE describe their target audiences, and the sports marketer wants to see how their firm's market share compares to their main competitors (A, B, C in this example). To measure market share performance in each segment, the sports marketer divides her company's sales to each segment by total market sales in that same segment, as shown by this equation:

$$\text{Market share } (\%) = \frac{\text{Total company sales to segment (IE or SE or CE)}}{\text{Total market sales to segment (IE or SE or CE)}}$$

$$(3.1)$$

If the sports marketer sold \$23 000 000 to Segment IE, and total market sales to Segment IE were \$65 000 000, then the company's market share of Segment IE is 4.6 percent:

$$\text{Market share } (\%) = \frac{\$23 000 000}{\$65 000 000} = 0.354 \text{ or } 35.4$$

$$(3.2)$$

The same calculation would help measure the market share of Competitors A, B, and C in Segment IE, as follows:

$$
\begin{array}{lll}
\text{Competitor 1:} & \$15\,000\,000 \\
\text{Competitor 2:} & \$17\,500\,000 \\
\text{Competitor 3:} & \$9\,500\,000 & \text{(3.3)}
\end{array}
$$

Their respective market shares would be:

$$
\text{Competitor 1:} \quad \frac{\$15\,000\,000}{\$65\,000\,000} = 0.23 \text{ or } 23\% \tag{3.4}
$$

$$
\text{Competitor 2:} \quad \frac{\$17\,600\,000}{\$65\,000\,000} = 0.27 \text{ or } 27\% \tag{3.5}
$$

$$
\text{Competitor 3:} \quad \frac{\$9\,500\,000}{\$65\,000\,000} = 0.146 \text{ or } 14.6\%
$$

This simple market share analysis provides an important gauge of competitive strength and relative market position. The same approach would be applied to measuring segments SE and CE as summarized in Table 3.5.

**Table 3.5** Segment share analysis

|  | Intense Enthusiasts | Shared Enthusiasts[a] | Casual Enthusiasts[a] |
| --- | --- | --- | --- |
| Sports marketer | $23 million/35.4% | $10 million/15.4% | $19 million/29.2% |
| Competitor 1 | $15 million/23% | $44 million/67.7% | $4 million/6.2% |
| Competitor 2 | $17.6 million/27% | $8 million/12.3% | $30 million/46.1% |
| Competitor 3 | $9.5 million/14.6% | $3 million/4.6% | $12 million/18.5% |

Note: a. The figures for SE and CE segments were plugged in to complete the illustration, and total market sales for each segment was also assumed to be $65 000 000 to simplify the analysis.

Source: Davis (2012, pp. 287–8).

The data in the segment share analysis is also useful in showing the percentage of total sales each customer segment represents to the sports marketer's overall sales:[34]

$$
\begin{array}{ll}
\text{Segment IE:} & \$23 \text{ million} \\
\text{Segment SE:} & \$10 \text{ million} \\
\text{Segment CE:} & \$19 \text{ million} \\
\text{TOTAL SALES} & \$52 \text{ million}
\end{array}
$$

Each segment's percentage contribution to total company sales can now be calculated (the numerators and denominators are in $ millions):[35]

$$\text{Segment IE:} \quad \frac{\$23}{\$52} = 0.442 \text{ or } 44.2\% \qquad\qquad (3.6)$$

$$\text{Segment SE:} \quad \frac{\$10}{\$52} = 0.192 \text{ or } 19.2\% \qquad\qquad (3.7)$$

$$\text{Segment CE:} \quad \frac{\$19}{\$52} = 0.366 \text{ or } 36.6\% \qquad\qquad (3.8)$$

The resulting percentages are known as *internal market share*. Knowing this gives marketers additional insight into the relative impact of each segment on the company's overall success.

Reviewing the number of customers in each segment and their respective contribution to profitability helps construct the company's segment contribution analysis. The sports marketer in this example has the following data:[36]

Segment IE    250 customers    $2.3 million in profits
Segment SE    110 customers    $900k in profits
Segment CE    430 customers    $1.2 million in profits

As Table 3.6 shows, there are 790 total customers and $4.4 million in total profits.

**Table 3.6** Segment contribution analysis

|  | Intense Enthusiasts | Shared Enthusiasts | Casual Enthusiasts | TOTAL |
|---|---|---|---|---|
| Customers | 250 | 110 | 430 | 790 |
| Revenues | $23 million | $10 million | $19 million | $52 million |
| Profits | $2.3 million | $900k | $1.2 million | $4.4 million |

Source: Davis (2012, p. 289).

The sports marketer now knows the number of customers in each segment and the financial contribution each segment makes. Knowing the number of customers by segment is important as it helps the company's sales management plan its customer account management needs, the corresponding sales force structure and, when combined with the earlier needs analysis, the type of customer support and service to offer. Since companies seek to improve their financial performance, asking several more questions are helpful:

## Revenues

1. Is the number of available customers in the segment (either business or consumer) large enough to continue developing growth opportunities?
2. If not, then is there additional potential for revenue growth with each individual customer (can the company increase its share of customer wallet)?

## Profits

1. How can profitability with each segment be improved over time?
2. Are these customers high-end, high-margin customers with whom the company can cultivate a premium image, or are they volume customers requiring the firm to secure sizable contracts to ensure a reasonable profit?
3. How will winning over more of each segment's customers affect the company's brand reputation?

The preceding analysis is designed to provoke exploration into each segment's past contribution and future potential for growth. A segment with a large number of customers but lower revenues may initially suggest a lower amount per purchase, but marketers would want to learn if adjusting their marketing approach could yield positive improvements, which could rapidly grow revenues and profits since a large customer base already exists. One can imagine variations on this line of reasoning that, when considered in total, can enhance the sports marketing activities and lead to profitable growth and market share gains.

## 3.5    Customer cycle and brand growth

Sports marketing investments are pursued partly to help position a company, its products, and its overall brand reputation. When positioning efforts are effective, then they help stimulate existing and new customer interest. The customer cycle in brand building describes the progression of the customer's relationship with the company (Figure 3.2).

The customer cycle in brand building shows three possible outcomes at each stage:

- continue moving the relationship forward;
- lose the relationship;
- continue moving forward and refer a prospective customer.

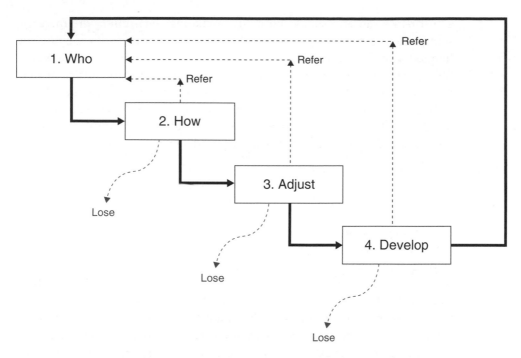

Source: Davis (2013). Derived from research by Davis, John A. in *Competitive Success – How Branding Adds Value*. Pp.252–257 (©2010 John Wiley & Sons).

**Figure 3.2** Customer cycle in brand building

## Who

The 'who' describes the customer. This information results from the market research activities.

## How

'How' describes how the brand is positioned/will be positioned and the marketing communications tactics used to attract to customers. Ineffective marketing communication efforts may hasten the customer's departure before they have a chance to progress through the cycle, whereas compelling marketing can capture the customer's attention early and ensure they remain with the company as the relationship is being developed. If the customer's experience is positive then marketers hope that the customer will refer other prospective customers.

## Adjust

It is rare that a marketing activity remains unaltered, even in the midst of execution. As sports marketers gain feedback on the market's response, adjustments can and should be made, including: fine-tuning the message, subtly altering packaging and/or retail channel distribution, changing the frequency of the message, and altering the marketing mode used. However, fine-tuning is not the same as a complete overhaul of the marketing campaign. When customers are at this stage in the cycle, they have already signaled their willingness to stick with the sports marketer's company. Therefore, any customer loss at this point should be reviewed to determine if any of the adjustments caused the customer to leave (or, was the loss attributed to competitor inroads?).

## Develop

At this point, customers are well established and confident in the sports marketer's company, so the marketing focus should emphasize more of a one-to-one relationship between the company and the customer. Such emphasis fosters customer loyalty and builds customer equity (the sum of the lifetime values of the brand's customers)[37] and increases the sports marketer's share of the customer's wallet (a measure that indicates how much of the customer's spending is directed to the company as a percentage of their total spending). Increases in share of customer wallet can occur by the sports marketer's efforts to further fine-tune the product offerings and marketing communications. However, if the customer leaves at this stage, then the company must carefully examine the reasons for the loss (assuming that the customer was profitable and important).

## 3.6 Questions for customer planning

1. What segments are being targeted?
   a  What do the customers have in common?
2. What is known about them?
   a  What are their needs?
   b  Your market share?
   c  Their contribution to the brand's revenues/profits?
   d  Does the segment match the firm's ability to deliver?
3. Has each customer target been evaluated and scored/rated?

## 3.7 Chapter summary

In Chapter 3 we learned more about the connection between sports and sports fans. Specifically, we gained insight into the distinctive histories of key sports such as basketball, F1, and cricket, which provides important context about why each sport has evolved into the modern equivalent we see today. The historical legacy of each sport explains part of their appeal. Understanding how each sport relates to its fans is useful for sports marketers as they develop their marketing plans. Deep customer research that identifies demographics, psychographics, behavior and geography is vital for helping marketers understand the characteristics of their target audiences. Furthermore, we saw that sports fan descriptions provide even richer insights about their qualities and their level of interest (as intense, shared or casual enthusiasts). With this knowledge of each sport and their respective histories, coupled with customer analyses that reveal important profile characteristics, marketers can more effectively begin to set goals for financial growth, determine competitive strategies, and develop techniques for creating lasting and profitable customer relationships.

## CASE STUDY

# Monaco Grand Prix

Since 1929, the Monaco Grand Prix has built a brand as the 'jewel in Formula 1's crown'.[38] While it is one of the oldest unchanged races on the Formula 1 circuit, the race that blasts through the streets of Monaco is perhaps the most important grand prix in the FIA World Championship series if for no other reason than its prestige. The Monaco Grand Prix also takes full advantage of its relative importance to the F1 circuit. Many other grand prix must pay upwards of $40 million just to have the rights to host an F1 race; Monaco's sanctioning fee is nothing.[39] The event, which costs about $40 million to stage, is able to essentially cover its costs through ticket sales, but it does receive a small subsidy from the government.[40] Organizers of the Monaco GP have negotiated the right to retain $10–15 million in revenues from the sale of trackside signage.[41] The race is also part of the Triple Crown of motorsports along with the Indianapolis 500 and the Le Mans 24 Hour.[42]

A large part of the Monaco GP's global appeal is the accompanying glitz and glamour. Monaco is a tax haven and many wealthy individuals choose to live there.[43] The backdrops for the street circuit therefore are filled with multimillion-dollar yachts in the harbor, dramatic cliffs, and luxurious homes. The royal family of Monaco has also supported the race since its inception and not only attend every year, but also play an active role in the race by presenting the trophy to the victor at the end.[44] For nearly 30 years, Princess Grace, the actress turned Monaco royalty, handled the role of presenting the trophy.[45] Because of the international prestige and Monaco's reputation for being an 'adult playground' due to its casino, celebrities from all over the world come to Monaco each year to take part in the festivities surrounding the race. Very often, business is conducted in the less formal atmosphere and corporations view the event as a unique way to wine and dine their customers. The official capacity of the grandstands is only 37 000, but there are around 200 000 spectators who attend the event over its four days as they watch from the balconies of buildings and boats in the harbor.[46] In addition, approximately 1.2 million viewers worldwide tune into over 900 hours of television coverage.[47]

Another part of Monaco's appeal is the unique nature of the race. The race is unlike any other grand prix in that it is shorter (260 total kilometers vs 305 total kilometers for all other races), and is one of the slowest and most challenging grand prix because of the tight turns in the race and a tunnel, which requires drivers' vision to adjust rapidly. The track has 19 corners, and drivers have to shift gears over 4000 times over the course of the entire race.[48] Still, drivers tout the race as a necessary item on their bucket lists despite F1 legend Nelson Piquet once describing the race as 'like trying to ride your bicycle around your living room'.[49]

With the race serving as a prime example of excess, some find the continued staging of the Monaco GP difficult to swallow. The Principality, which has a normal population of only 33 000, swells to over 100 000 on Sunday of the race weekend.[50] Prince Albert II of Monaco is a fervent supporter of the grand prix, but he is also a strong supporter of environmentalism.[51] With global climate change at the forefront of the major global issues, it's

## CASE STUDY (continued)

certainly conceivable that the long-term viability of the Monaco GP could be questioned when the current contract expires in 2020.[52] Finally, the infrastructure strain placed on the event is not getting easier. Race organizers are confined to only six weeks for constructing and two weeks for deconstructing the race course.[53] About 1100 tons of grandstands, 900 tons of pit garages and 33 kilometers of barriers are part of this construction and deconstruction effort.[54] On top of those inconveniences, the streets that make up the Circuit de Monaco are closed during the race, construction, and deconstruction times.

 **QUESTIONS**

1   What are some ways the Automobile Club de Monaco can continue to create value for citizens of Monaco in their efforts moving forward with the Monaco Grand Prix?

2   Many of the fans at the Monaco Grand Prix are not citizens of Monaco. What are some ways to engage with them throughout the year to extend the excitement of the event beyond the weekend it occurs?

3   Given Prince Albert's environmental concerns should F1 consider new rule changes to acknowledge increasing interest in these issues? How might such a decision affect F1 racing team sponsors?

4   How could environmental concerns affect F1 and fan interest over the next ten years?

**NOTES**

1   Briggs (2009).
2   International Cricket Council (n.d.).
3   Ibid.
4   'History of the game' (n.d.).
5   Kunz (2007).
6   UEFA (n.d.).
7   'Leagues' (n.d).
8   Soccer-Spain (n.d.).
9   Serie A (n.d.).
10  Bundesliga (n.d.).
11  Eredivisie (n.d.).
12  Parrinello (2007).
13  NBA (2006).
14  FIBA (n.d.).
15  NBA (2006).
16  Williamson (n.d.).
17  F1 (n.d.).
18  'A brief history of football' (n.d.).
19  Ibid.
20  'Market research/demographics: baseball – MLB attendance. . .' (n.d.).
21  'Market research/demographics: NFL fan market summary' (n.d.).

22  Ibid.
23  Snyder et al. (1983).
24  Kahle and Close (2010).
25  Davis (2012, p. 268).
26  'Fans welcome say in crowd management' (n.d.).
27  'New laws for sports fans; legislation aims to stamp out bad behavior at grounds' (2011).
28  'Fans in protest at ban on chants' (2011).
29  Davis (2012, pp. 269–70).
30  Arajujo (2006).
31  Davis (2012, p. 270).
32  Carchidi (2012).
33  Davis (2012, pp. 285–8).
34  Ibid.
35  Ibid., p. 288.
36  Ibid.
37  Rust et al. (2004).
38  'Ecclestone indicates that Europe will play lesser role as F1's future race sites' (2011).
39  Sylt and Reid (2010).
40  Ibid. See also Allen (2012).
41  Allen (2012).
42  'Monaco Grand Prix' (n.d.).
43  Spurgeon (2008).
44  Allen (2012).
45  Ibid.
46  Sylt and Reid (2010).
47  Ibid.
48  Spurgeon (2008).
49  Widdows (2011).
50  Sylt and Reid (2010).
51  'Missions and objectives' (n.d.).
52  'Black Book Formula 1' (n.d.).
53  Sylt and Reid (2010).
54  Ibid.

 **REFERENCES**

'A brief history of football' (n.d.), HistoryofFootball.com, accessed 14 November 2011 at http://www.historyoffootball.net/history_of_football.html.

Allen, James (2012), 'Unique location bestows glamour', *Financial Times*, 25 May 2012, accessed 15 May 2013 at http://www.ft.com/cms/s/0/5d6619dc-a4c3-11e1-9908-00144feabdc0.html#axzz2TT4ETwBB.

Arajujo, Leonardo (2006), in A. Benson and J. Sinnott, 'Why are Brazil so good?' BBC, accessed 15 May 2013 at http://news.bbc.co.uk/sport1/hi/football/world cup 2006/teams/brazil/4751387.stm.

'Black Book Formula 1' (n.d.), F1BlackBook.com, accessed 30 September 2012 at http://www.f1blackbook.com/circuits_and_races/monaco/.

Briggs, Simon (2009), 'The Ashes: what are the origins of the England–Australia rivalry?', 23 July 2009, *The Telegraph*, accessed 28 September 2011 at http://www.telegraph.co.uk/sport/cricket/international/theashes/5893794/The-Ashes-What-are-the-origins-of-the-England-Australia-rivalry.html.

Bundesliga (n.d.), 'League', Bundesliga.com, accessed 11 November 2011 at http://www.bundesliga.com/en/league/.

Carchidi, Sam (2012), 'How the Winter Classic snowballed' (2012), *The Philadelphia Inquirer*, 1 January 2012, accessed 15 May 2013 at http://articles.philly.com/2012-01-01/sports/30579183_1_snow-globe-effect-nhl-winter-classic-citizens-bank-park.

Cialdini, Robert B. Richard J. Borden, Avril Thorne, Marcus Randall Walker, Stephen Freeman and Lloyd Reynolds Sloan (1976), 'Basking in reflected glory: three (football) field studies', *Journal of Personality and Social Psychology*, **34**(3).

Davis, John A. (2010), *Competitive Success – How Branding Adds Value*, New York: John Wiley & Sons.

Davis, John A. (2012), *The Olympic Games Effect – How Sports Marketing Builds Strong Brands*, New York: John Wiley & Sons.

'Ecclestone indicates that Europe will play lesser role as F1's future race sites', *Sports Business Daily*, 30 November 2011, accessed 30 September 2012 at http://www.sportsbusinessdaily.com/Daily/Issues/2011/11/30/Leagues-and-Governing-Bodies/F1.aspx?hl=monaco percent20f1&sc=0.

Eredivisie (n.d.), 'Premier League clubs', Eredivisie.nl, accessed 11 November 2011 at http://eredivisielive.nl/eredivisie/.

Fans in protest at ban on chants' (2011), *Sunday Express*, 2 October 2011.

'Fans welcome say in crowd management' (n.d.), *The Age* (Melbourne, Australia), 22 February 2011, accessed 1 August 2012 at http://www.theage.com.au/sport/a-league/fans-welcome-say-in-crowd-management-20110221-1b2jg.html. 2012/08/01.

FIBA (n.d.), 'FIBA history', accessed 3 September 2011 at http://www.fiba.com/pages/eng/fc/FIBA/fibaHist/p/openNodeIDs/5683/selNodeID/5683/fibaHist.html.

F1 (n.d.), 'Points', F1.com, accessed 14 November 2011 at http://www.formula1.com/inside_f1/rules_and_regulations/sporting_regulations/8681/.

'History of the game' (n.d.), MLB.com, accessed 10 November 2011 at http://mlb.mlb.com/mlb/history/index.jsp.

International Cricket Council (n.d.), 'ICC members countries', accessed 3 March 2012 at http://www.icceap.com/overview.php.

Kahle, Lynn R. and Angeline G. Close (2010), *Consumer Behavior Knowledge for Effective Sports and Event Marketing*, New York: Taylor and Francis Group, LLC, pp. 74–5.

Kunz, Matthias (2007), '265 million playing football', July 2007, *FIFA Magazine*, accessed 10 November 2011 at http://www.fifa.com/mm/document/fifafacts/bcoffsurv/emaga_9384_10704.pdf.

'Leagues' (n.d), TheFA.com, accessed 12 November 2011 at http://www.thefa.com/Leagues/Respect/NewsAndFeatures/2012/devon-cfa-video.aspx.

'Market research/demographics: baseball-MLB attendance...' (n.d.), SBRnet.com, accessed 3 August 2012 at http://www.sbrnet.com/research.asp?subrid=521.

Market research/demographics: NFL fan market summary' (n.d.), SBRnet.com, accessed 3 August 2012 at http://www.sbrnet.com/research.asp?subrid=722.

'Missions and objectives' (n.d.), FPA2.com, Prince Albert II of Monaco Foundation, accessed 30 September 2012 at http://www.fpa2.com/missions-and-goals.html.

'Monaco Grand Prix' (n.d.), Monaco.mc, Automobile Club de Monaco, accessed 30 September 2012 at www3.monaco.mc/monaco/gprix/why.html.

NBA (2006), 'History of the basketball', 28 June 2006, NBC.com, accessed 3 September 2011 at http://www.nba.com/features/ball_timeline_060228.html.

'New laws for sports fans; legislation aims to stamp out bad behaviour at grounds', *Belfast Telegraph*, 1 August 2011), accessed 1 August 2012 at http://www.highbeam.com/doc/1P2-29275679.html.

Parrinello, Antonio (2007), 'Police officer killed in riots; all Serie A and B matches suspended',

3 February 2007, USAToday, accessed 12 November 2011 at http://usatoday30.usatoday.com/sports/soccer/europe/2007-02-02-italy-riots_x.htm.

Rust, Roland T., Valarie A. Zeithaml and Katherine N. Lemon (2004), 'Customer-centered brand management', *Harvard Business Review*, **82**(September), 68–75.

Serie A (n.d.), 'Lega Serie A – the profile', Serie A.com, accessed 12 November 2011 at http://www.legaseriea.it/en/lega-serie-a.

Soccer-Spain (n.d.), 'First Division league table', Soccer-Spain.com, accessed 12 November 2011 at http://www.soccer-spain.com/ssdocs/table1.php.

Spurgeon, Brad (2008), 'Grand Prix races abound, but there's only one Monaco', *New York Times*, 23 May 2008, accessed 30 September 2012 at http://www.nytimes.com/2008/05/23/sports/23iht-SRPRIX.1.13153775.html?pagewanted=1&_r=2.

Snyder, C.R., R.L. Higgins and R.J. Stucky (1983), *Excuses: Masquerades in Search of Grace*, New York: Wiley-Interscience.

Sylt, Christian and Caroline Reid (2010), 'Monaco's pulling power', ESPNF1.com, 14 May 2010, accessed 30 September 2012 at http://en.espnf1.com/monaco/motorsport/story/17098.html.

UEFA (n.d.), 'UEFA member associations', UEFA.com, accessed 12 November 2011 at http://www.uefa.com/memberassociations/index.html.

Widdows, Rob (2011), 'Monaco challenge remains unique', Motorsport, 24 May 2011, accessed 30 September 2012 at http://www.motorsportmagazine.com/f1/monaco-challenge-remains-unique/.

Williamson, Martin (n.d.), 'A brief history of Formula One', ESPNF1.com, accessed 2 November 2011 at http://en.espnf1.com/f1/motorsport/story/3831.html.

# 4

# Fans – delivering value through deep relationships

**CHAPTER OVERVIEW**

Sports marketing success requires a combination of a structured plan along with a tolerance for uncertainty. As we have discussed, companies using sports to elevate their image, improve their reputation, and expand their business opportunities have to think carefully about how to authentically align their brand with that of the sports property and weigh the pros and cons of investing in sports for the long term. Fans are inextricably linked to the company/sports-entity relationship because their very presence is the reason that sports have grown into one of the most successful and attractive industries in the world. Understanding why sports fans are passionate about their sports should, indeed must, be a key concern for companies if they want to understand how to develop true customer loyalty. Sports, more than any other industry, inspire a unique and deep relationship with their customers (fans), and the lessons can prove invaluable to companies seeking robust growth. In this chapter, we go beyond Chapter 3's analysis of customer markets to examine how sports, and sports marketing, can deliver increased value through deeper customer relationships.

## 4.1 Understanding why sports are so appealing to fans[1]

### Uncertainty as a motivator

Companies regularly ask how they can develop deeper and more profitable relationships with their customers, knowing that their financial success over time will be the result of their efforts to identify, attract, and nurture their customer base. Fans that support a favorite league, team or athlete do so for a variety of complex psychological and social reasons. Our intent here is not to dissect what is discussed in texts devoted to consumer psychology, but to generally explain why sports are so appealing to fans so that marketers can then assess whether linking their company to sports will lead to long-term value gain. As marketers evaluate using sports entities in their marketing activities, they must confront their own challenging questions as well as those from their finance and accounting departments, about how to minimize the risk inherent in being associated with a sports property. Yet risk and sense of uncertainty are vital contributors to the appeal fans find in the sports they follow. It is important for marketers to know that while fans mostly do not consciously follow a sport due to the uncertainty of outcomes, it is precisely that uncertainty that engages fans at a deeper level with the sports entities they follow, as opposed to the less engaged involvement they feel when buying non-sports consumer products. In fact, people seek predictability and certainty when purchasing non-sports consumer products mostly because they expect the item to work, otherwise they will return it for reimbursement. Sports fans do not seek reimbursement when their favorite sports entity fails. Failure is understood to be a normal part of sports, just as reliability is considered a normal expectation of non-sports products, although extended underperformance does cause many fans to lose interest, with the exception of the most die-hard (whose suffering is even considered a badge of honor). With that said, sports fans do not seek sports entities that are failing, nor do they want their favorites to fail, but they also understand that not every sports entity will enjoy perfect success every game, let alone every season. Sports are more complex products, with success dependent on training, opponents, team mates (for team sports), strategy, ability to adjust quickly, individual athlete mood and emotion, surprising performances during a game, and even fan reaction in the stadium. That very uncertainty foments curiosity that whatever has occurred in previous games, perhaps next time it will be different.[2]

This points to an important distinction about sports as a product versus non-sports products: sports are unique partly because they are not the result of an automated manufacturing process. Instead, the sports 'product' is really a fluid, dynamic entity whose performance does indeed change, and these very changes add dimension and attributes to the core product (players, plays, team chemistry etc.). This applies to individual sports as well, such as individual events in track and field and swimming. Michael Phelps was expected to have another good Olympics when he competed in London 2012, although some fellow competitors questioned his level of dedication and fitness in the months leading up the Games.[3] He did go on to become the most decorated medal winner in Olympic history, winning two silver medals and four gold medals, giving him 18 gold medals and 22 Olympic medals overall in his storied career.[4] But the surprise came in his signature event, the 200m butterfly, when he was out-touched at the end by Chad le Clos of South Africa, finishing second to the surprised and elated South African swimmer.[5] Phelps still had a great Olympics, and Olympic career, and Le Clos' surprising finish suggested that an exciting new swimming chapter might be beginning.

## Seeking drama[6]

What constitutes drama in sports? Qualities include: surprise, demonstrations of physical prowess, artfully executed on-field (or on-court) plays, a sense of energy, inevitable disappointments, visual and aural spectacles that enhance fan experience, and comfort from knowing that the athletic performances are unscripted. Each of these factors, and more, create a sense of drama about how athletes and teams are going to play. Loyal fans know the day-to-day status of their favorite sports entities, but what they don't know is how changes to the product's ingredients (switching players, changing strategy) will affect the recipe for success. This drama is an essential reason why sports are so appealing to fans – they see sports as a form of entertainment, but certainly not in the scripted sense. While scripted entertainment, such as movies, theatrical productions, and professional wrestling has wide appeal as a form of story telling, unscripted entertainment via sports provides a very different type of story telling, one where the outcome is anything but confirmed and likely scenarios are subject to the real-time dynamics of sport as it is played. Athletes do not follow rigid scripts, with the exception of sports like gymnastics and synchronized swimming, and this iterative dynamic is appealing to fans. Athletes and teams do have a general strategy about what is to be accomplished and how for each competition, influenced by the characteristics of each opponent as well as their own objectives, with constant adjustments made based on of-the-moment circumstances. Their training certainly helps ensure that required behaviors and skills are automatic, and their preparation also enables the athletes to more effectively improvise during a game, knowing that their base of skills is solid and reliable. For fans this ongoing interplay of influencing variables is a vital and compelling aspect of watching sports and fuels their expectations that any competition is likely to be exciting, tension filled, and dramatic, with the hope that their favorite emerges victorious.[7]

In 2011, India won the Cricket World Cup at home, beating Sri Lanka and thereby winning their first World Cup title since 1983.[8] India's victory was not necessarily a surprise because their teams had been among the very top in the world for years, but the absence of a victory for nearly 30 years, coupled with playing at home, certainly added vital dramatic ingredients that fostered a palpable sense of anticipation and expectation that 2011 could and would be different. When India's victory was achieved, the national outpouring was unprecedented, with people countrywide and Indians worldwide celebrating in the streets and creating an informal national holiday. Sponsors were elated. LG India became a sponsor of India's cricket team in 1998 and stated that sales of flat panel displays rose 10–15 percent during the 2011 World Cup series. Hyundai was another sponsor of cricket in India and saw added value as well:

> 'With India winning the World Cup our move of sponsoring the tournament has paid off. We are sponsors with ICC till 2015, so it includes the T20 World Cup and the Women's World Cup. As for local events we are already on-air sponsors with the IPL. We are also looking at increasing our association with IPL but no deals have been finalized yet', said a Hyundai spokesperson.[9]

## Sports intensify fan aspirations[10]

World-class athletes perform athletic feats that are well beyond what the average fan can do, serving as a form of aspiration that appeals to fans. Fans admire the athlete's exploits, recognizing the extreme physical challenges being faced, while occasionally also presuming a certain level of expertise by vocalizing how the athlete should have done better. Such behavior is known as 'armchair quarterbacking', a US sports term that describes spectators and viewers who offer their own opinion and advice despite not having the requisite expertise (the term 'quarterback' is a reference to the leader of the offensive team, responsible for calling plays and determining in real time how to execute the play as it unfolds while the opposition simultaneously attempts to disrupt the play). Fan intensity manifests itself in occasional near mimicry, gesticulating as if they are the player, enjoying a vicarious sense of shared exertion as well as exhilaration of the athlete's own actual effort. Sports become a catalyst for change, partly influenced by short-term adrenalin boosts from watching events unfold, inspiring fans to seek their own improvement and fulfill their ambitions. As fans watch top athletes perform, many understand that such accomplishment comes at great sacrifice, serving as a useful metaphor for achieving success in their own lives. Of course, sports tend to inspire short bursts of emotion in fans that also serve to inflate a fan's sense of achievement, subsiding in the hours and days following the event. Aspiration can be longer lasting if the fan's favorite team or athletes continue to perform at a sustained level of excellence, creating a halo effect over fans and thereby possibly inspiring new, or at least modified behaviors that could lead to improvement in their own lives. But mostly fans gain a sense of aspiration that lasts for the duration of the competition itself, and perhaps a bit beyond, and it is another reason why sports are attractive to watch. Another dimension of aspiration is evidenced by the purchase of favorite team and player merchandise, such as shirts and kits.[11] Manchester

United was valued by *Forbes Magazine* as the most valuable sports franchise in the world at US$2.23 billion and their revenues include merchandise sales. Nike is responsible for the team's merchandise sales, estimated to be valued at $39 million per year as part of an agreement that runs through 2015.[12]

## Fans as arbiters of quality[13]

While fans don't play their favorite sports at the same level as dedicated professionals, some have experience playing at a high amateur level, which provides them with fair insight into the ingredients required for the highest quality play. Even those that did not play sports but have been committed followers gain a solid understanding of the factors needed for a game to be considered high quality. Fans can quickly assess if the level of play is substandard and are invariably vocal when sports violate their sense of fair play and integrity. During the 2012 London Olympics four teams of badminton doubles were disqualified (two from Korea, one from China, and one from Indonesia) due to deliberate efforts they made to play poorly in order to secure a more favorable seeding in the next round of competition.[14] Fans jeered and booed, shouting their displeasure, knowing that they were witnessing substandard play. Such displays of poor sportsmanship run afoul of the ideals the Olympics represent.

A decade before in the USA a new professional football league was launched called the XFL (Extreme Football League). The objective of the league as expressed by its founder Vince McMahon (owner of World Wrestling Entertainment) and his joint venture partner NBC was to introduce a higher quality, more exciting, colorful, and aggressive form of professional football as a response to what McMahon perceived to have been the NFL's increasingly dull and uninspired style of play. Using ambitious marketing campaigns and relentless promotions, the XFL generated early fan interest in the weeks and months before the league launched. The league had eight teams and the first week of the season saw sold-out games everywhere and high TV viewership ratings. Unfortunately, with each successive week fan interest declined dramatically, and the league collapsed by the end of its first season. There were several reasons for the failure of the XFL, including the timing of the league (held in the spring, which is not a traditional football season for US sports fans) and a sense that entertainment and showmanship were more important than the game itself.[15] But the biggest contributor to the league's demise was the uninspired, even poor quality of play fans saw on the field. Despite the promises of a new and better caliber of football, the actual product was equivalent to that of a small college conference and not professional grade.[16]

In 2012 the NFL risked fan and sports media ire when a professional referees' strike resulted in the league substituting replacement referees without professional experience. While the same high-quality athletes continued to play, the replacement referees served as a negative distraction by repeatedly making poor calls during games, some of which affected the outcome of games, and even more importantly, risked severe injury to players since many rules of conduct were not enforced, thereby encouraging players to increase their aggressiveness in a league already known for being high risk and even dangerous as a sport. This altered the quality of play, and while TV viewership and even ticket sales remained strong during the referees' strike, many pundits and fans wondered how long the NFL's gold-plated brand reputation would last if the strike were not resolved.[17] Fortunately, by the end of September 2012 the impasse was overcome and the regular referees returned, signaling a returning to a more consistent quality of play and officiating.

When fans know that athletes, their teams, and league represent the highest quality, then their commitment level remains stable and may also increase.

## Sports foster individual identity and social affiliation[18]

Sports research consistently shows that fans derive both individual and social/group benefits from being followers. On an individual basis, sports can serve as catalyst for enhancing one's esteem, akin to the halo affect described earlier. Our individual identities are linked to a wide array of factors (what we wear, say, do) and sports, in effect, provide a short cut in helping people reinforce a desired identity. When one says they are a fan of rugby, others make quick and often unconscious associations and even judgments about the person.[19] Furthermore, sports provide a measure of relief and escape for individual fans, offering an energetic and vibrant distraction from life's daily pressures.

At the same time, sports foster social affiliation and group identity based on the shared experience multiple fans have in supporting the same sport, or club, or athlete. Indeed, people may not know each other in a social setting until one's sports preferences are stated, whereby the proverbial ice is broken and each person is more freely able to socialize knowing they are part of a group with common likes. Such social identity also creates expectations about fans that support opposing teams and competitors, fueling rivalries and inspiring the boisterous atmosphere associated with games. Social affiliation, and even individual identities, can lead to extreme behaviors from fans that may cause injury or undermine the reputation of the sport. Hooliganism is a pejorative term that has been associated with some countries participating in European football. Both the UK and Italy have had reputations for unruly fan behavior that has led to injury or even death on occasion. The UK strengthened security personnel and cameras in stadiums, which has led to reductions in fan violence. In 2006 and 2007 Italian football matches confronted occasional fan riots that led to banning fans from matches and the reputation of Italian football, once Europe's pre-eminent league, suffered as a consequence.[20]

## 4.2    How psychology influences fan loyalty[21]

### Repetition vs commitment

As we have explained so far, a fan's love of sports is based on the interplay of several important factors that help to inspire fan following. Loyalty is something most organizations wish to develop with their customers, followers, and fans. However, marketers will sometimes mistake purchase as a sign of loyalty, but loyalty is the result of more complex interactions between the sports entity and the fans that go beyond mere purchase. One may purchase an item more than once, but the repeat business is not necessarily a sign of loyalty if the product purchased is the only offering of its kind, whereas repeat purchases of the same product when the customer has many competitive offerings to choose is a much stronger indicator of loyalty. In this instance, the consumer is aware of alternatives but continues to purchase the same product, which is a stronger indicator of psychological commitment. Psychological commitment is an important objective marketers should attempt to stimulate and encourage in their sports marketing plans.[22] While sports fans have a variety of choices of teams and even sports to follow, loyalties are not just based on frequent purchase, or repeated purchase from an array of choices. Psychological commitment may in fact be a by-product of a fan's family's history of support for a particular sport or team, adding yet another dimension to complement repeat purchases in a world of choice. Alternatively, a fan's social group may also induce loyal support for a sports entity as a form of subtle peer pressure by encouraging loyalty because everyone else is already committed. However, the loyalty is earned, true sports fans have it. They purchase the tickets and cable TV subscriptions of their favorite teams, even though they have choices. Why do fans follow the New York Mets when the New York Yankees are just a short drive away? Or why do fans prefer the Los Angeles Dodgers over the Los Angeles Angels? Or the San Francisco 49ers over the Oakland Raiders? Given the selection, the choices have been made and fan favorites result from peer group influence, family preferences, geographic proximity as well as the sports entity's reputation, traditions, storyline, and more. Sports marketers have a rich set of attributes to parlay into a successful sports sponsorship if they pay attention to the reasons why fans are so loyal.

## Reluctance to consider alternatives[23]

Since sports appeal to the fans' sense of excitement and entertainment, as well as their individual identity, a reasonable question is whether fans can be persuaded to change loyalties, just as companies try to encourage brand switching from competitors. Interestingly, a fan's loyalty is often so deeply intertwined in their worldview that alternatives are almost inconceivable, even if the alternative is a superbly coached, successful sports property. Bombarding prospective fans with an onslaught of clever and persuasive marketing communications is not likely to dislodge a loyal fan. Nor will a poor performance, or a succession of poor performances. Fans tend to stick to their teams because of the alchemic mix of emotion, social and familial associations, the aforementioned storyline, and even pure stubbornness. Peripheral fans, or those described as casual enthusiasts in Chapter 3, may drift away if their sports property consistently underperforms, but the deeply committed fans remain, despite the almost irrational nature of their commitment. The lesson for companies is apparent: such abiding loyalty represents significant potential sources of growth for years, even decades. But achieving this for non-sports companies is far rarer than their sports counterparts. This unique fan loyalty and the generally popular and emotionally powerful appeal of sports are essential factors attracting companies to be associated with sports. If a sports marketing relationship blossoms into ongoing success, then the company's reputation is often reshaped, and more closely associated with the qualities of the sports property.

## Personalized experiences[24]

Given the characteristics that describe fan interest and loyalty, sports entities are keenly interested in reinforcing fan appeal and gaining deeper commitment from fans by building relationships using marketing tools in traditional and digital/social media, and turning events into memorable experiences. The traditional and digital/social media tools will be explored in detail later in this book, but it is important to understand that today's fans respond better to marketing that does not interrupt their enjoyment of sport. Fans want their favorite brands, in sports and even non-sports, to communicate with them based in ways consistent with the fan's communication preferences. Digital technology allows companies and sports properties to track how fans seek information and communication.[25] Amazon.com is one of many firms that use personalization techniques to encourage customers to keep using their services without necessarily interrupting the way they shop. After each visit to Amazon.com, customers leave a digital footprint about their online behavior, ranging from length of time on a particular page or product, to purchase choices, to the transitions customers make between different areas of the site, or even to other sites away from Amazon. The resulting digital footprint provides the company with data about that customer and is automatically added to their profile so that when they return next time, the company is able to tailor its recommendations based on the accumulation of the customer's previous experiences. This personalized response provides a positive experience and encourages their repeat business and loyalty, thereby building the relationship even though there has been no direct person-to-person contact between the company and the customer. There are several relevant objectives sports marketers need to pursue to develop a positive customer experience that leads to loyalty and profitable growth for their companies:

- Make the experience accessible and understandable, not inaccessible and complex. This means marketers themselves must be crystal clear on their own objectives first before designing marketing campaigns and techniques.
- Develop a robust data gathering method that is based on the company's long-term objectives. This would include capturing measures of marketing campaign performance so that they can be tracked at any given time and significant deviations from expectations can be quickly addressed.
- The best customers expect their favorite brands and sports properties to know them and not annoy them. Interruption marketing *interrupts*, which aggravates customers. Sports marketers need to emphasize participation and invitations so that customers believe they are being asked, and not told.
- The best customers will have a very different profile than more casual and less frequent customers and the sports marketer must understand these differences in order to develop effective marketing approaches to each type of customer. Digital and social media are very useful vehicles for learning about these differences.
- Like any relationship, ups and downs occur, so marketers must analyze data over time, and not just overnight. Significant and rapid customer changes should not be ignored and may require the marketer to adjust quickly, but too much adjustment can lead to confusion, leaving customers to wonder what the company is trying to do.
- Learn how customers learn. Sports fans are as varied as the sports and athletes they follow. How they become knowledgeable about sport says a great deal about how they learn, and not everybody learns the same

way. The marketer must review the customer information they gather to help create marketing activities that can provide a useful educational function.

● Be innovative and adjust the customer experience based on their known behaviors as gathered through digital and traditional marketing.

● Find ways to include important business collaborators and partners in the customer development effort.

Sports fan behavior and their level of interest is connected to their social network, their self-image, their aspirations, and the level of their interest intensity in sport. The marketer's task is to gather as much information as possible to understand their various customer audiences and how those audiences might perceive the company's sports marketing activities.

## 4.3    Chapter summary

Sports and non-sports marketing both rely on segmentation, targeting, and positioning, which are familiar analytical frameworks for identifying the best customers. Part of the reason companies seek to align themselves with sports entities is because of the intense passions fans display, which is uncharacteristic of customers of non-sports products. Therefore, the sports marketer has an opportunity to take advantage of the sports entity's unique attraction for fans by finding ways to have their own company develop marketing and customer programs that deepen their relationship well beyond the more traditional customer development programs that are designed to inspire product purchase. Knowledge of the psychological components of a sports fan's loyalty can provide non-sports companies with compelling new ways to strengthen the relationship and loyalty from their customers while also potentially gaining the fans of the sports entity as new customers.

**CASE STUDY**

# Vancouver Canucks fans

To simply play any sport, any game or match typically only needs the necessary equipment and players. However, to play any sport in any professional sports league, fans are an essential part of any sport equation. In Canada, ice hockey is king and millions of people tune into National Hockey League (NHL) games every year. In 2011, when the Vancouver Canucks and Boston Bruins competed in the Stanley Cup Finals, Game 7 drew the second-largest sport television viewership of 8.76 million Canadians.[26] While there are seven Canadian teams in the NHL, the Vancouver Canucks fans in particular are known for their antics. Canucks fans have packed the Rogers Arena since 14 November 2002 and sold out 361 regular season games and 45 post-season games since then.[27] In 2011, the Canucks raised prices by 3.5 percent and still had a 98 percent renewal rate, showing that their fans don't mind price increases to see hockey.[28] That year, the Canucks offered perks such as seat upgrades for pre-season games, pre-game skate sessions and customizable ticket designs for those who renewed their season tickets.[29] A year later in 2012, despite a potential labor dispute impending, the Canucks renewed 97 percent of their season ticket holders.[30]

While the Canucks are lucky in the sense that they are in a market of devoted hockey fans who seem to follow the team despite never having won the Stanley Cup, they still make efforts to cultivate their fans. The Canucks operate Facebook, Twitter, Instagram, Google+, Foursquare, and YouTube accounts that strive to bring the best hockey content to their fans. In addition, they have their own Fan Zone social media platform that allows Canucks fans to connect with one another.[31] On the contests and promotions side, the Canucks have a Kids Club, which offers children in the Vancouver area an opportunity to connect with the team in a more age-appropriate way. The team's mascot, Fin Orca, is a large part of the Kids Club outreach, but he also provides an emotional touchpoint for fans of all ages. They have a separate Twitter account devoted exclusively to sharing information about their contests and promotions.

Canucks fans are also credited with beginning the tradition of waving towels above their heads to spark rallies in game play. The tradition dates back to the Western Conference finals of 1982 when coach Roger Neilson hung a towel from a hockey stick and waved it as a surrender flag to protest at poor officiating.[32] The act got him ejected from the game, and fans soon followed his example when the team returned to Vancouver for Game 3 to show their solidarity with their team's leader by waving white towels above their heads.[33] The tradition lives on in Vancouver during the play-offs and a towel is placed on every seat in the Rogers Arena, which seats 18 890 people, prior to each game.[34] Other NHL teams and teams in other professional sports have since copied this fan antic.

The Vancouver Canucks are also host to two of the most famous fans in sports. Force and Sully, better known as 'The Green Men', are two guys who wear green spandex body suits that cover their entire bodies (including their faces) and taunt opposing team players when they are in the penalty box. What started in 2009 as a prank stemming from the television

**CASE STUDY** *(continued)*

show *It's Always Sunny in Philadelphia* has turned into a huge rallying point for Canucks fans.[35] Force and Sully continue to attend Canucks games but have added additional props, such as cardboard cutouts of famous people wearing Canucks jerseys, and continue to taunt players as they spend their time in the box.[36] Not only do Force and Sully heckle penalized players at the Rogers Arena, but in the past they have travelled with the Canucks in a few of their play-off runs to continue their antics in other cities as well.[37] In 2011, the Green Men were banned by the NHL from touching the glass of the penalty box or doing handstands and spurred an outcry of support from their fans on social media.[38] The Green Men have also been honored by ESPN via induction into the sports network's first class of their 'Hall of Fans'.[39] The new institution, which was designed to 'honor and recognize extraordinary stories of fandom', was decided through over 50 000 votes cast over ten days. The Green Men were selected as one of the top three and were chosen as the only Canadian and hockey representatives to the fan hall of fame.[40]

The Canucks place significant importance on giving back to their community. With multiple charitable arms, the club's efforts are focused on supporting children's health and wellness, fostering the growth of hockey, and encouraging education in their home province of British Columbia.[41] During the 2010–11 season, the Canucks raised a record $4.2 million for the Canucks for Kids Fund.[42] They annually donate $40 000 worth of autographed merchandise to local charities and fundraisers.[43] In addition to access to a free education center for low-income families and year-round hockey camps for all ages, the Canucks' charitable footprint in Vancouver is wide and growing.[44]

While no team likes to lose, the Vancouver Canucks of the NHL really don't like to lose because of their unfortunate fan history of rioting after losses in the Stanley Cup Finals. In 1994, fans took to the streets after the Canucks lost to the New York Rangers in Game 7 of the Stanley Cup finals. Then, again in 2011, the Canucks lost to the Boston Bruins in Game 7. What started as a few fans setting fire to a stuffed bear to symbolize the Bruins turned into a $3 million destruction spree.[45] Damage was done to 89 businesses, 113 cars, and 58 people were injured in the hours following the loss.[46] The Vancouver police pegged 15 000 criminal acts in their investigations and has spent $5 million in their ongoing investigations of the riots, which was $2 million above their normal operating budget for violence and arson.[47] In the wake of the riots, the Canucks issued a statement condemning the fans' behavior, But it's clear that the only control that the Canucks have over their fans' passion is on the ice.

 **QUESTIONS**

1  Where should teams draw the line between inspiring passionate fans (such as the Green Men) and condemning acts of violence (such as the 2011 riots)?
2  In a collision sport like hockey, is it the responsibility of the teams to place less emphasis on the physical nature of the sport in marketing efforts?
3  How important is fan education?
4  What are some ways that teams can creatively educate their fans?

**NOTES**

1  Bee and Havitz (2010).
2  Ibid.
3  Pioch (2012).
4  Farber (2012).
5  'Chad le Clos beats Michael Phelps for 200m butterfly gold' (2012).
6  Bee and Havitz (2010).
7  Ibid.
8  'World Cup sponsors are cock-a-hoop' (2011).
9  Ibid.
10  Bee and Havitz (2010).
11  Ibid.
12  Badenhausen (2012).
13  Bee and Havitz (2010).
14  Greene (2012).
15  Lobdell (2009).
16  Ibid.
17  Greenfield (2012).
18  Bee and Havitz (2010).
19  Rowe (2012).
20  Zeller (2007).
21  Bee and Havitz (2010).
22  Ibid.
23  Ibid.
24  Davis (2010, pp. 215–32).
25  Ibid., pp. 309, 314.
26  'Game 7 smashes hockey night in Canada record' (2012).
27  Fung (n.d.).
28  Dreier (2011).
29  Ibid.
30  Mullen (2012, p. 38).
31  'Stay connected' (n.d.).
32  Jory (2011b).
33  Ibid.
34  Ibid. See also 'Rogers Arena' (n.d.).
35  Jory (2011a).
36  Ibid.
37  Wyshynski (2012).
38  Ibid.
39  Hudak (2012).
40  Ibid.
41  'Community partnerships' (n.d.).
42  'Coast to coast: take me out to the tablet' (2011).
43  'Community partnerships' (n.d.).
44  Ibid.
45  Mann (2011).
46  Ibid. Also see 'Hockey riot damage numbers emerging' (2012).
47  'Hockey riot damage numbers emerging' (2012).

**REFERENCES**

Badenhausen, Kurt (2012), 'Manchester United tops the world's 50 most valuable sports teams', Forbes.com, 16 July 2012, accessed 23 July 2012 at http://www.forbes.com/sites/kurtbaden-hausen/2012/07/16/manchester-united-tops-the-worlds-50-most-valuable-sports-teams/.

Bee, C.C. and M.E. Havitz (2010), 'Exploring the relationship between involvement, fan attraction, psychological commitment and behavioral loyalty in a sports spectator context', *International Journal of Sports Marketing & Sponsorship*, **11**(2), 140–57.

'Chad le Clos beats Michael Phelps for 200m butterfly gold' (2012), BBC.com, 31 July 2012, accessed 31 July 2012 at http://www.bbc.co.uk/sport/0/olympics/18902357.

'Coast to coast: take me out to the tablet' (2011), *Sports Business Journal*, 1 August 2011, 22.

'Community partnerships' (n.d.), Canucks.NHL.com, accessed 16 September 2012 at http://canucks.nhl.com/club/page.htm?id=40190.

Davis, John A. (2010), *Competitive Success – How Branding Adds Value*, New York: John Wiley & Sons.

Dreier, Fred (2011), 'NHL: renewal rate at more than 90 percent', *Sports Business Journal*, 3 October 2011, 6.

Farber, Michael (2012), 'In passing the torch, Phelps caps career as most decorated Olympian', SportsIllustrated.com, 4 August 2012, accessed 4 August 2012 at http://sportsillustrated.cnn.com/2012/olympics/2012/writers/michael_farber/08/04/michael-phelps-final-swim/index.html.

Fung, Daniel (n.d.), 'Game notes', Canucks.NHL.com, accessed 18 September 2012 at http://canucks.nhl.com/club/page.htm?id=39654.

'Game 7 smashes hockey night in Canada record' (2012), CBC.ca, 16 June 2012, accessed 18 September 2012 at http://www.cbc.ca/sports/hockey/stanleycup/story/2011/06/16/sp-nhl-game7-ratings-us.html?cmp=fb-cbcsports

Greene, Richard Allen (2012), 'Olympic badminton players disqualified for trying to lose', CNN.com, 2 August 2012, accessed 3 August 2012 at http://edition.cnn.com/2012/08/01/sport/olympics-badminton-scandal/index.html.

Greenfield, Karl Taro (2012), 'The NFL fiasco: why referees are like Chicago teachers', Bloomberg Businessweek, 25 September 2012, accessed 28 September 2012 at http://www.business-week.com/articles/2012-09-25/the-nfl-fiasco-why-referees-are-like-chicago-teachers.

'Hockey riot damage numbers emerging' (2012), UPI.com, 19 April 2012, accessed 8 September 2012 at http://www.upi.com/Top_News/World-News/2012/04/19/Hockey-riot-damage-numbers-emerging/UPI-36431334858163/.

Hudak, Kristen (2012), 'These three answer the call to the "Hall of Fans"', ESPN.com. 5 September 2012, accessed 16 September 2012 at http://frontrow.espn.go.com/2012/09/these-three-answer-the-call-to-the-hall-of-fans/.

Jory, Derek (2011a), 'Force & Sully', Canucks.NHL.com, 11 January 2011, accessed 15 September 2012 at http://canucks.nhl.com/club/news.htm?id=513183.

Jory, Derek (2011b), 'Towel power', Canucks.NHL.com, 6 June 2011, accessed 15 September 2012 at http://canucks.nhl.com/club/news.htm?id=558295.

Lobdell, Josh (2009), 'Why did the XFL fail?' Examiner.com, 10 October 2009, accessed 15 March 2012 at http://www.examiner.com/article/why-did-the-xfl-fail.

Mann, Camille (2011), 'Vancouver Canucks fans riot after losing Stanley Cup final', CBSNews.com, 16 June 2011, accessed 13 September 2012 at http://www.cbsnews.com/8301-504083_162-20071569-504083.html.

Mullen, Liz (2012), 'Most NHL clubs say season tickets selling well', *Sports Business Journal*, 18 June 2012, 38.

Pioch, Evan (2012), 'U.S. swimmer questions Phelps' work ethic', NBC.com, 26 July 2012, accessed 27 July 2012 at http://www.nbcwashington.com/news/sports/US-Swimmer-Questions-Phelps-Work-Ethic-163885236.html.

'Rogers Arena' (n.d.), ESPN.com, accessed 15 September 2012 at http://espn.go.com/travel/stadium/_/s/nhl/id/22/rogers-arena.

Rowe, Jessica (2012), 'Irish rugby fans upset by drunk stereotype', NZ3News.com, 22 December 2012, accessed 22 December 2012 at http://www.3news.co.nz/Irish-rugby-fans-upset-by-drunk-stereotype/tabid/423/articleID/258314/Default.aspx.

'Stay connected' (n.d.), Canucks.NHL.com, accessed 15 September 2012 at http://canucks.nhl.com/club/page.htm?id=60933.

'World Cup sponsors are cock-a-hoop' (2011), The Hindu Business Line, 4 April 2011, accessed 23 September 2011 at http://www.thehindubusinessline.com/industry-and-economy/marketing/article1599743.ece.

Wyshynski, Greg (2012), 'Vancouver Green Men, Canucks fans fight NHL ban on antics', Sports.Yahoo.com, 2 May 2012, accessed 16 September 2012 at http://sports.yahoo.com/nhl/blog/puck_daddy/post/vancouver-green-men-canucks-fans-fight-nhl-ban-on-antics?urn=nhl,wp3963.

Zeller Jr., Tom (2007), 'Italy confronts its soccer hooliganism', 8 February 2007, *The New York Times*, accessed 9 November 2011 at http://thelede.blogs.nytimes.com/2007/02/08/italy-confronts-its-soccer-hooliganism/.

# 5

# Association benefits of sports marketing

 **CHAPTER OVERVIEW**

We now have a good understanding of the sports market, its key value chain members, and differences across sports and leagues. We have also learned about the unique histories of select sports and how those histories have influenced fan attraction and loyalty. When companies are deciding whether to invest in sports marketing, their understanding of the broader sports market as discussed so far can give them a competitive edge because the knowledge will provide insight into the positive association benefits they may derive if they plan carefully.

## 5.1 Effective sports marketing

Effective sports marketing planning helps marketers fully leverage their sports marketing investment because the thought process involved requires them to consider several possible outcomes from their actions. As a marketer weighs different tactics in their pursuit of using sports to enhance their company's reputation and ultimately increase value, one consideration that will regularly reappear concerns the unpredictability of the sport entity they are using for marketing purposes. Will that entity (athlete or team) perform worse, better, or as expected? What are the implications of each? How will our association with that entity change marketplace perceptions of our company? Clearly, there are many reasons why companies use sports as a vehicle to market their offerings. One is to reach the sports entity's fan base, assuming, of course, that the company's market research indicates that the fan base is a good target audience for the company's products. Another reason is to link the company with the sponsored sports entity in the customer's mind. As discussed earlier in this book, customers buy when they trust the entity from which they are buying. The absence of trust means a customer is highly unlikely to purchase unless they are desperate. Trust is most often developed from experience, such as a customer's use of a company's products, but trust is also a function of the larger reputation the organization has amongst the general public. When a company decides to use sports to market their offerings, they are hoping that the qualities associated with that sports entity 'rub off' on them as well. This rub off is commonly referred to as *association benefits* – by being associated with the sports entity, that entity's qualities cast a positive glow over its various business relationships. The converse is true as well when a sports entity is the subject of controversy, then that controversy is likely to spill over onto its network of businesses.

We have emphasized the importance for understanding a sport's history as a means for developing marketing campaigns that are not only aligned with the values and legacy of the sports entity, but also improve the relevance of the marketer's offerings to the target audience. Being relevant means that the product is useful to the customer.

To create a relevant connection between their company and customers, marketers must have a clear understanding of their company's strategic brand objectives and a thorough understanding of customer needs so that the right marketing programs can be developed to convincingly attract customers. Developing strategic brand objectives will be discussed more in subsequent chapters about the specifics of the actual sports marketing plan. In the meantime, it is important that readers understand that the brand objectives provide guidance that inspires the tactical steps needed to grow the business and, eventually, increases brand value.

Three concepts are useful at this point:

- positioning;
- awareness;
- market growth.

Each of these is familiar to marketers as they are used in pre-planning, planning, execution, and post-execution review. When positioning is clear, and properly supported by the marketer, then market awareness can develop more effectively, helping to elevate the company's presence in the marketplace, which, in turn, can facilitate future growth opportunities. We will revisit these throughout the book.

## 5.2   Positioning

Positioning describes how a company is anchored in the target audience's minds. This is a very important point to understand and to think through thoroughly during pre-planning because a common mistake companies make is to view positioning as something they do to the product, such as its location in a store, a website, or through marketing communication campaigns such as advertising. If, for example, Company A positions their offerings as the most innovative through advertising in a sports team's brochures or at the team's home stadium, but consumers believe that Company B's offerings are more innovative, then A's efforts to control their positioning will not be seen as credible. Instead, Company A would want to consider how to reinforce the positioning already fixed in the target audience's mind. Perhaps Company A is known for great service, in which case their marketing communications ought to convey this. Positioning can be supported by the company's choice of marketing programs (advertising, social media, star athlete endorsers, promotions etc.), which will be discussed in detail later in this book. For now, it is important for marketers to be aware of their actual market position before embarking on the development of a detailed plan because any marketing tactics subsequently implemented will either support the company's known position or at least serve to begin getting consumers to view them differently (but the latter has to be backed up by changes in product, or any other part of the marketing mix, if it is to be believable). When a company uses sports marketing to reinforce their positioning, then they are hoping the association with the sports entity will improve recognition of their brand and enhance brand value. This is why it is critically important that marketers do *not* try to force a position on the marketplace through overstated advertising messages or unproven promises, especially if their current reputation is contrary to the new position the company wishes to have. If the marketer seeks to use sports marketing to facilitate a positioning change, then this must be supported through a broader set of activities that clearly demonstrate the company is making a concerted effort to shift and that the marketing communications conveying this are not just hype to attract attention.

To develop a memorable position in the consumer's mind, the marketer must research the attributes and characteristics associated with both their own company and the sports entity they choose to sponsor. When these factors are known then the effort to reinforce the company's position using the sports entity will appear more natural, thereby helping to build emotional connections to consumers.

## Example: Visa

In 2012, Visa had the largest share of the worldwide purchase transactions market of both credit and debit cards at 64.67 percent, followed by

MasterCard at 25.57 percent. Sports have been integral to Visa's marketing strategy, helping the company increase its visibility over the past 25 years. The company's sports marketing efforts are centered around its TOP sponsorship of the Olympics, FIFA World Cup, the National Football League, the National Hockey League and the National Hockey League Players' Association, and Copa Santander Libertadores (an international soccer tournament featuring 38 teams from South America and Mexico). These various sports marketing activities are implemented through sponsorships and over the years the broad-based exposure from repeated advertising and promotions has helped raise Visa's brand preference scores (a measure of loyalty that indicates consumer preference for one brand versus the offerings of competitors) to over 50 percent, rating Visa as the 'best overall card', a strong position to have in the marketplace.[1]

## 5.3    Awareness

Awareness describes the degree to which consumers identify the company, its brand(s) and products, and associates these with familiar characteristics and qualities. The need to develop awareness with customers may seem self-evident, since consumers would have a hard time asking for or purchasing something they do not know exists, but the process of doing so requires carefully creating marketing programs designed to foster lasting, favorable memories. Aided and unaided awareness are the most common types measured (these are also known as aided or unaided recall). Aided awareness is measured by first showing survey respondents a product, ad, brand name, or trademark and then asking them when they recall last seeing it. Unaided awareness tests ask respondents if they recall *any* product, ad, brand name or trademark they have recently seen.

### Examples: Coca-Cola and Samsung

Coca-Cola has had a marketing relationship with the Olympics since 1928, elevating its Olympic marketing when it became a TOP sponsor in 1986. TOP is an acronym for The Olympic Partners, which is the highest and most prestigious sponsorship level for the Olympic Games. TOP sponsors have exclusive worldwide rights in their product category to be associated with the Olympics. Prior to the 1994 Olympics in Lillehammer, consumers were asked to name brands associated with the Olympics. Coca-Cola was correctly identified as a TOP sponsor, with 22 percent unaided and 69 percent aided awareness. Interestingly, Pepsi was also mentioned, incorrectly, as an Olympic sponsor, with 14 percent unaided and 54 percent aided awareness scores. This apparent confusion may be the result of category bleed, whereby a market's leading brands are so visible and associated with each other that consumers assume that if one is involved then so is the other. Ambush marketing (a practice by which a company tries to associate itself with a sports property unofficially, without paying for the rights, to be discussed in a later chapter) may also be a factor.[2]

In 1996, Samsung began revamping the company to improve its position as a leading global brand, with a key objective to overtake Sony (the market leader at the time) as the world's most valuable consumer products company business and, in the process, increase its brand value. Samsung signed an agreement to become an Olympic TOP sponsor in 1997 in the wireless communications category, joining Visa and Coca-Cola and other leading global companies. Since 1997, the company's market awareness has increased substantially. During the 2000 Sydney Olympic Games, Samsung's unaided awareness increased from 5 percent rise to 16.2 percent. Awareness grew again during the 2004 Summer Olympics in Athens, from 57 percent to 62 percent. Since 1999 Samsung's brand value has grown from just over $3 billion to US$38.2 billion.[3] Samsung's TOP sponsorship of the Olympics has been so successful that the company agreed to extend it through the 2016 Olympics. Samsung management believes its association with the Olympics has been an important part of its marketing efforts to reshape the company and its image. The Olympics are one of several sports partnerships Samsung has. Others include:[4]

- Asian Games (since 1986);
- World Hockey (since 2003);
- Hansol Korea Open, a WTA event (since 2005);
- Chelsea FC, a Premier League team (since 2005);
- Asian Football Confederation (since 2006);
- Korean Football Association (since 2006);
- IAAF (International Association of Athletics Federations) (since 2009);
- CAF (Confederation of African Football) (since 2010);
- Asian Amateur Championship, for young professional golfers (since 2010).

Plus several other football sponsorships:

- Olympiacos FC;
- Inter Milan;
- Chivas FC Mexico;
- Real Madrid;
- Spain National Team;

- Palmieras FC Brasil;
- Bolivar FC Bolivia;
- Romania National Team;
- Portugal National Team;
- Universitari Peru.

## 5.4    Market growth

Market growth describes changes, either increases or decreases, in business activity year over year, either in units sold or total dollar volume. Market growth can also be measured by comparing market share (total company sales as a percentage of the total market) year by year.

### *Examples: Visa and Samsung*

Visa's 2012 market share of 64+ percent reflects long-term market share growth from 1986 when its market share was 33 percent, an increase that coincides with its sports marketing investments, including the Olympics and, since 2010, the FIFA World Cup. Total transaction volume (comprising payments and cash transactions) grew from US$111 billion to US$6.3 trillion during this time, and the total number of cards issued grew from 137 million to 2.0 billion.[5]

Samsung's mobile phone market share increased from 5 percent in 1999 to 17.7 percent in 2011, and sales increased from 17 million units to nearly 314 million units during that time.[6] In the first quarter of 2012 Samsung's global mobile phone market share increased again, to 20.7 percent, making the company number one worldwide, ahead of Nokia at number two (19.8 percent) and Apple number three (7.9 percent).[7]

Before embarking on developing a detailed marketing plan, an invaluable exercise (that saves significant time and conceivably money later on) is for marketers to identify the different growth choices available and, from those, devote part of the business plan to those that appear to have the greatest opportunity for sustained success and that match well with the company's and sports entity's common values.

The Ansoff Matrix[8] (Figure 5.1) is a helpful framework for determining product and market growth choices, and the resulting marketing implications. The matrix organizes the growth choices on two intersecting dimensions: (1) product (horizontal axis); and (2) market (vertical axis).

|  | **Current Products** | **New Products** |
|---|---|---|
| **Current Markets** | A<br><br>**Grow in Current Markets**<br>Increase market share<br>Increase product usage | B<br><br>**Product Development**<br>Add product features<br>New generation products |
| **New Markets** | C<br><br>**Market Development**<br>Expand geographically<br>Identify new segments | D<br><br>**Diversification**<br>Related<br>Unrelated |

Source: Ansoff (1957).

**Figure 5.1** Growth choices

## Quadrant A: Grow in current markets

Quadrant A focuses on how to grow by selling current products into current markets. There are two ways to accomplish this: (1) increase market share and (2) increase product usage. In addition the marketer must look at the most effective tools for increasing market share and/or usage.

### Increase market share

This requires taking share and/or customers away from competitors.

### Implications for sports marketing

Marketers must design their sports marketing strategy to convince customers to switch. This includes having a clear understanding of their company's strengths and competitor vulnerabilities and crafting the marketing communications plan to take advantage of these differences.

### Example: Visa

Visa's market share growth the past 25 years has come at the expense of its rivals, including MasterCard and American Express. Visa decided to raise awareness about the company's credit cards by using sports sponsorships to highlight the many locations where Visa cards could be used. The sports sponsorships included increased advertising with a message that Visa cards could be used anywhere the customer wanted and, over time, the company's market share increased.[9]

## Increase product usage

This means inspiring existing customers to buy more of the company's products:

### Implications for sports marketing

Company management must understand their customer segments thoroughly if they are to persuade their own customers to buy more.

### Example: Sports drinks

Sports drink manufacturers regularly run television advertisements showing athletes using their beverages to replenish important fluids and nutrients lost during physical activity. These ads are intended to convey the health benefits successful athletes enjoy from these drinks, with the implication that average consumers will gain the same benefit. Over the years the imagery in sports drink ads has expanded to include kids, adults, and families consuming these same beverages, signaling that a larger audience beyond athletes can benefit as well, inspiring additional purchases by the same customers.

## Tools for Quadrant A growth

Since this quadrant is restricted to gaining additional growth from selling the same products into the same markets, the marketer's most effective tools for increasing market share and/or usage are: market research, increased advertising and field sales programs, and price changes:

- *Market research.* Additional market research will help marketers gain a better understanding about the kinds of marketing media and marketing message combinations that might cause consumers to switch brands and/or also encourage increased usage by existing customers.
- *Increased advertising and field sales programs.* Assuming the marketer is convinced that growth is possible by selling current products to customers in current markets, then increasing the investment in advertising and field sales programs can increase awareness and conceivably alter customer purchase and usage patterns. To be successful requires more than simply spending more money on advertising. Marketers will need to invest in improved creative communications, new advertising mediums

(print, broadcast, digital, social), and field sales programs (such as internal incentive programs designed to increase rewards given to sales people for selling more of the current product into current markets).

- *Price changes.* Marketers can also adjust price (probably down, since a price increase is unlikely to induce customers to purchase more) to encourage brand switching and increased usage. If the new price is below the competition's, then growth is likely, assuming that product quality is comparable and consumers are indifferent to brand. The downside is that once prices are lowered, customers will expect them to remain at the new, lower level because any price increase, even back to the previous price, will cause consumers to seek added value, otherwise they may switch to a competitor.

## Quadrant B: Product development

In this quadrant marketers are selling new or improved products to current markets. There are two ways to accomplish this: (1) add product features and (2) new generation products. In addition, the marketer must look at increasing investment in marketing tools and activities.

### Add product features

This means increasing (and probably improving) the product's features as a means of conveying added value and distinguishing the offerings from those of competitors.

### Implications for sports marketing

Innovation involves some risk since the implied changes may or may not be accepted by the marketplace. As with most marketing growth opportunities, marketers must know the profiles of their segments and also be clear about factors that distinguish their company from competitors in order to help determine which innovations are most likely to succeed.

### Example: Nike and Apple

When Nike and Apple combined running shoes and Apple iPods by embedding a sensor in the shoe that transmitted workout data to the iPod, it created a novel way for fitness buffs to keep track of their workouts and assess their progress over time. The resulting product, called Nike+iPod, enhanced the benefits athletes received from each product and increased their respective perceived values, helping both companies to grow sales.[10]

## New generation products

This refers to developing entirely new products.

### Implications for sports marketing

With both new features and entirely new products, company management must commit to a more complex and expensive product strategy since money will be spent on explaining the new product features and/or the new products to existing and/or competitor customers (to increase share) while also implementing the other facets of the sports marketing plan.

### Example: LZR

For decades swimming convention said that competitive swimmers performed best in briefs (for men), and minimal torso and waist suits for women. In early 2008 Speedo, the swimwear and accessories maker, launched the LZR, a body length swimsuit. It was billed as the world's fastest swimsuit. Later that same year, 33 of the first 36 Olympic swimming medals in Beijing were won by athletes wearing the LZR[11] and by summer 2009 more than 120 world records were broken by athletes wearing the LZR and similar advanced materials swimsuits from competitor manufacturers.[12] The suit featured superior technology and a patented manufacturing process that minimized seams. The result for swimmers was reduced drag and greater buoyancy. Swimmers not sponsored by Speedo were at a clear competitive disadvantage. In July 2009, swimming's governing body FINA ruled that suits for male swimmers could only cover from the waist to the knee and for female swimmers the area from the shoulder to the knee. This decision outlawed full body suits and the LZR's brief brush with history was over. The LZR's innovations were impressive, although as the Italian national swim coach Alberto Castagnetti said, the LZR was akin to 'technological doping'.[13]

## Tools for Quadrant B growth

Quadrant B seeks growth from selling innovation to existing customers. This requires investment increases in any or all of the following areas: market research; R&D; increased advertising and field sales programs; price changes; and/or channel development:

- *Market research.* In support of innovation, market research will often emphasize uncovering latent, or unknown, customer needs and unique new ways to solve vexing problems. Detecting latent needs is not easy. Marketers must not only sift through qualitative and quantitative data, but they must also be attuned to trends and changes in the marketplace as well as needs not addressed by competitors.

- *R&D.* The aforementioned market research findings can help the company's product scientists and engineers direct their efforts toward the as yet untapped market opportunities. At the same time, market research is not always a requirement for true innovation. Sometimes the spark of an idea occurs as product specialists, engineers, and designers independently conceive of imaginative new solutions, without any direct input from the marketplace.

- *Increased advertising and field sales programs.* Any new offerings, whether new product features or entirely new products, require marketing communications designed to excite and inform the market about the innovation. Innovative products often require innovative and creative advertising and sales programs in order to properly seed the offerings into the market and generate early demand. For innovations to have mass appeal, marketers have to hope that viral marketing (word of mouth) spreads quickly and favorably, boosting demand further.

- *Price changes.* Product innovations provide an opportunity for companies to charge a premium. In some technology markets, such as mobile software, innovations in the form of downloadable apps may be free to encourage fast adoption, with charges applied as users upgrade to a more sophisticated version, growing sales rapidly thereafter.

- *Channel development.* If an innovation is added to a current product, then existing channels will need educating and perhaps even additional support to encourage their placement of the offerings in their outlets.

## Quadrant C: Market development

This quadrant directs company management attention on finding new markets for current products. This is accomplished in two ways: (1) expand geographically and (2) identify new segments. In addition, the marketer must increase investment in marketing activities and tools.

### *Expand geographically*

This type of growth means identifying new places (region, country) where the customers are similar to existing customers in existing markets.

*Implications for sports marketing*

Growing in new geographies increases the marketer's logistical and operational challenges, including determining how to address possible language and culture differences, especially as demand grows.

*Example: Li Ning*

Li Ning, the Chinese athletic footwear and apparel company, grew quickly following the 2008 Beijing Olympics. The company's profile was heightened when Li Ning, the eponymous founder of the company, lit the Olympic torch after floating on a wire high above the Bird's Nest stadium and there were high expectations that the company would leverage its Olympics exposure to enter new markets, including the USA. But in 2011 the company's profits declined 65 percent and its ambitious expansion plans slowed dramatically. In 2012 the company chose to focus on stabilizing its domestic business, since both Adidas and Nike had continued to grow there following the 2008 Olympics. Part of Li Ning's challenge was overcoming markets that have been dominated by Nike and Adidas for decades. At the same time, a few Chinese consumer products confronted other issues about quality and safety that may have unintentionally tainted Li Ning's emerging brand.[14]

## Identify new segments

New segments can be in existing or new geographies. Either way, marketers will need more research findings about the new and different customer groups being pursued and their associated characteristics.

*Implications for sports marketing*

New segments can be in existing or new geographies. If the segment(s) are in existing geographies, then management must focus on making the products relevant to the new segments. If the segments are in new geographies, then management has to emphasize product relevance given the new cultural and language context.

*Example: Endorsement*

Athletic footwear companies like Nike, Adidas and Puma sponsor athletes to associate their products with top athletes and their success. Athlete endorsers' use of the footwear is a form of association and endorser marketing, viewed by sports marketers as integral to persuading consumers that their own sports success may be improved by wearing the same products as their favorite athlete. Athlete endorsers are particularly useful when launching new products since they bring added attention to the latest footwear innovations and designs.[15]

## Tools for Quadrant C growth

Quadrant C seeks growth from selling current products to new customers. This requires investment increases in any or all of the following areas: market research; increased advertising and field sales programs; price changes; and/ or channel development:

- *Market research.* Needless to say, marketers depend on high-quality research insights about their target customers. The decision to market to a new segment, or a new geography, should be made after investigating the new market's characteristics. The new research can also provide important new understandings about similarities across segments that can be leveraged and differences that can be exploited.
- *Increased advertising and field sales.* Entering a new geography or appealing to a new segment means marketing communication activities will be oriented toward educating and informing as part of an effort to raise awareness to the new audiences. This includes crafting field sales activities to incentivize the right behaviors that lead to market penetration.
- *Price changes.* Given that current products are being sold, price changes should be considered only if necessary. Any difference from existing pricing in other markets will cause one group of customers to feel disadvantaged versus another. In very unique situations price changes to encourage purchases, such as a target audience located in an isolated area with little interaction with other existing customers. This is a highly unusual likelihood in today's globalized world where prices and information are shared instantly via mobile communications and digital technology.
- *Channel development*: New customer segments are sometimes serviced by different channels, so marketers will need to assess whether channel development is warranted.

## Quadrant D: Diversification

Selecting this quadrant means developing entirely new products for entirely new markets. There are two ways: (1) related and (2) unrelated. In addition, the marketer must seek to increase investment in marketing activities and tools.

## Related

This means developing new products for new markets, but within the same industry.

### Implications for sports marketing

In this case, companies must be careful not to dilute or erode the company's current brand position or detract from the sports sponsorship effort. This is akin to launching a new company, albeit in a familiar industry, so it is a major effort unto itself, let alone the existing effort to execute on the sports sponsorship properly. It is unlikely a company would do this as a linked growth strategy to the sports sponsorship since they are fundamentally two separate business efforts.

### Example: Bloomberg

In 2011 Bloomberg, the business and financial information company, received one of the '10 Most Innovative Companies' awards by *Fast Company Magazine*. The award recognized the company's Bloomberg Sports division, which was first launched in December 2009, for its pioneering Bloomberg Sports Front Office product suite. The suite offers sports fans tools that can quickly analyze sports data used in fantasy sports decision-making. For Bloomberg this opened up a new market segment with an innovative new offering designed to tap into the most ardent sports fans' love of statistics. The new Sports Front Office product suite is consistent with Bloomberg's overall reputation as a statistical data company, applying its number crunching expertise to new applications for new markets.[16]

## Unrelated

This is pure pioneering work in both new products and new markets.

### Implications for sports marketing

This is the highest-risk growth choice of all and, as such, requires extraordinary dedication and resources (financial, people, energy, time) in order to succeed. The risk for sports marketers is introducing a new offering for a new market with no recognizable connection to the company's core business. Examples of success are few and far between, so the best examples tend to be at least peripherally related to the company's known areas of expertise.

*Example: Nike*

In 2010 Nike launched a new division called Digital Sport, directed to develop new technologies and devices to help athletes track their performances. The previously mentioned Nike+ running sensor embedded in the shoe was a logical connection to the core sports market. Nike+ was followed by a new device called the FuelBand, designed to track energy output. While certainly a new type of device and technology for Nike and its more familiar athletic footwear and apparel markets, the FuelBand represents a unique way to capture the imagination of a broader consumer market attracted to unusual gadgets. One does not typically think of Nike as a device technology company, so Digital Sport represents an interesting new opportunity for Nike.[17]

## Tools for Quadrant D growth

Quadrant D growth will come from selling new innovations to new markets, whether related to the company's core business, or unrelated. Similar to Quadrant B, this requires investment in: market research; R&D; increased advertising and field sales programs; price setting; and/or channel development. The difference is that the size and scale of the investment required to achieve growth from a Quadrant D strategy is likely to be substantially higher:

- *Market research.* Innovation requires that marketers remove as much uncertainty as possible from their business decisions, which means that research should be directed toward helping companies identify the target customers with the willingness to purchase something new and unknown. Latent needs research, as with Quadrant B, is useful to gather. At the same time, marketers will have to rely on their own experience and the market conditions at the time the innovation is ready for launch to determine how best to market it.
- *R&D.* Whereas Quadrant B focuses R&D efforts on offerings for existing markets, Quadrant D is a wide open opportunity, and an equally wide open prospect for failure. Not knowing which audience may purchase the offering can be liberating for product experts, freeing them to pursue pure innovation without worry about market guidelines, so the marketer's challenge is how to translate something completely new to a world unprepared for it.

- *Increased advertising and field sales programs.* In addition to creative new advertising and field sales programs, marketers may also use product demos and free trials to encourage consumer experimentation and then purchase.
- *Price setting.* Innovation usually equals premium pricing, unless a business argument can be made to capture a large number of customers with low or no price and then follow up with more expensive, value-added upgrades.
- *Channel development.* New products for new markets require an intensive channel development effort to encourage channel members to take a risk by selling the product. If the innovator is a known, established, and credible company, then new innovation may be more readily accepted than innovation from a start-up.

## 5.5 Chapter summary

Sports marketing is an attractive way for companies to gain valuable benefits from associating with a known sports entity. Benefits include having the qualities and values associated with the sports entity being connected to the sports marketer's company, helping the market perceive the company in a different and more positive light. As with any marketing, sports marketers must consider positioning, awareness development, and market growth objectives in their planning efforts. Positioning refers to the market's perception of the company and/or its offerings vis-à-vis competitive alternatives (i.e., is the offering viewed as a better, higher quality, more distinctive specialty offering, or as a parity, equal quality, commodity offering etc.). Awareness development describes the sports marketer's efforts to increase the market's knowledge of the company and its offerings to increase the likelihood that the sports marketer's products will be among the top choices when making a purchase decision. Market growth delineates the different market and product development alternatives that the sports marketer's company must weigh in determining how best to take advantage of their relationship with the sports entity. There are four main growth choices: growth in existing markets; product development; market development; or diversification. Each of these choices have specific implications for how sports marketers will focus their marketing communication and product development activities, and the decision as to which growth choice, or combination of growth choices, will depend on the company's strategic needs and the sports entity's most effective areas of strength in terms of its reputation in the market, its locations, and the type of customer audience it attracts.

---

**CASE STUDY**

# The Tiger Woods scandal

While many professional athletes' personal lives often fly under the radar, the sports world's superstars must constantly cope with being in the spotlight at all times. In 2009, Tiger Woods was just that: a superstar. As of June 2013, he had 104 professional wins, 78 of which were on the PGA Tour.[18] He had won 14 major tournaments, which was (and still is) the second highest of any professional golfer.[19] He had won ten Player of the Year Awards from the Golf Writers Association of America (GWAA) in 2009.

Woods was an extraordinarily marketable athlete. As soon as he stepped onto the professional golf stage in 1996, he began breaking records. First, he landed a $40 million Nike contract in 1996.[20] Then in 1997, he became the first black player, and the youngest player ever to win the Masters Tournament, which he did by a record 12 strokes.[21] In addition to nine annual money titles,[22] he also grossed approximately $110 million a year in endorsement deals from companies including Nike, Gillette, Accenture, American Express, and AT&T.[23] He was the highest paid athlete of all time and the first athlete ever to eclipse the $1 billion mark in 2009, according to Forbes.com.[24] In addition to his impressive golf resume, Woods had also gained a reputation of having outstanding character. The Tiger Woods Foundation had worked with 10 million kids since its inception in 1996 and, to date in 2009, had given away $2 million in scholarships to inner city kids.[25] He married Swedish former model Elin Nordegren in 2003 and in 2007 they had their first of two children, Sam. Tiger Woods was on top of the world.

But then, in November 2009, his entire world would come tumbling down. On 27 November Woods crashed his SUV into a fire hydrant on his street and soon thereafter the media in the United States revealed that he had had several marital transgressions.[26] Woods then disappeared from sight. He canceled appearing at his own golf tournament, the Chevron World Challenge, on the 30th, days after the accident citing injuries from the accident.[27] As a result of his withdrawal, the tournament even offered $20 000 worth of refunds to those who had purchased tickets hoping to see Woods play.[28] On 2 December, Woods publicly acknowledged on his website that he had made mistakes and just nine days later, he announced that he would be taking an indefinite leave of absence from the game of golf and entering rehab.[29]

Almost immediately after Woods announced that he would be taking a break from golf his sponsors began to back-pedal and his halo began to fade. Within a week after Woods's announcement of taking an indefinite break from golf, Gillette issued a statement on 12 December 2009 that it would be limiting the golfer in its print, television, and online advertisements.[30] On 13 December global consulting firm Accenture became the first sponsor to drop Woods in the wake of his scandal.[31] Tag Heuer was the next sponsor to drop Woods on 18 December,[32] and then, on 23 December, Gillette announced that it would not re-sign Woods, in effect also dropping him from their marketing campaigns.[33] Other companies to follow suit in dropping Woods over the following months included AT&T and Gatorade.[34]

**CASE STUDY** *(continued)*

All four of these sponsors dropped Tiger Woods without him having played a single round of golf since the scandal.

Two sponsors, EA Sports and Nike did stick with Woods through his tumultuous time, perhaps because they had tied up so much equity in the golfer. EA Sports annually produces a golf video game called Tiger Woods PGA Tour. In the wake of the scandal, sales of the 2011 version of the game plummeted 60 percent worldwide.[35] For the 2011 version of the game, Woods shared the cover with Irish golfer Rory McIlroy, but EA Sports decided to drop Woods's face from the front cover for the 2012 edition in hopes of reinvigorating sales.[36] Nike had famously signed Woods to massive contracts. After his initial $40 million contract expired, the athletic company re-signed him in 2000 for reportedly $105 million over five years[37] and then renewed again in 2005 under the same stipulations. However, reports surfaced in 2010 that Nike also slashed his paycheck by 50 percent to approximately $10 million a year for his public behavior after the scandal broke.[38] Still, Woods is a key part of Nike's entire golf division. His clothing line, the Tiger Woods Collection, debuted in 1999 as Nike Golf's 'top-of-the-line apparel'.[39] Though recently the division has battled an economic recession, it still earns Nike more than $650 million annually in revenue, and Woods's line accounts for approximately 10 percent of Nike's overall golf sales.[40]

Woods's purse strings weren't only harmed by losses in endorsement dollars. His five-month hiatus from playing golf coupled with ensuing poor play meant that Woods's prize earnings also plummeted. Woods went from earning $10.5 million in prize money in 2009, to $660 000 in 2011.[41] In 2010 he was 68th on the PGA Tour money list, which was his lowest ranking ever.[42] His golf ranking slid from #1 in the world in 2009, to a low of #58 in 2011.[43] Also during 2010 he shot his highest score ever, 298, at Bridgestone, which was 18 over par and 30 shots behind the winner of the tournament.[44]

As a result of Woods's demise, the PGA Tour also took a hit. Even before the scandal it was clear how important Woods was to the game of golf. Events that Woods played in during 2009 drew 30 million more viewers on network television than those he didn't play in.[45] In addition, those events that he skipped earned as much as 50 percent less revenue than those he played in.[46] Television viewership took a drop in 2010, falling to 2.040 million[47] from 3.6 million in 2009.[48] Nielsen ratings also dipped to 1.4[49] down from 2.4 in 2009.[50] In 2011, prior to the PGA Tour's television deal expiration in 2012, tour officials even acknowledged that they would wait as long as they could before renegotiating the television deals so that Woods would have ample time to return to top form.[51] The scandal was also a divisive subject for players on the tour. After being away from the game for just two months, Phil Mickelson, a long time rival of Woods, went on the record saying that 'the game of golf need[ed] him back'.[52] However, other high profile golfers, such as Ernie Els and Tom Watson, criticized Woods during his absence from the course.[53]

Tiger Woods's halo extended well beyond the world of golf. Bill Sanders, a writer for the *Sports Business Journal* went so far as to dub the entire 12-month span between the fall of 2009 and fall of 2010 as the 'Tiger recession'.[54] Shortly after the tabloid *The National*

## CASE STUDY *(continued)*

*Enquirer* broke the story about the scandal, TMZ, another popular gossip source in the United States announced that it would start a TMZ Sports division to better track the personal lives of athletes around the globe.[55] One study conducted by two professors at the University of California, Davis estimated that Woods's scandal cost his sponsors' companies' shareholders up to $12 billion.[56] But the question still remains as to whether on-field marketability or off-field marketability is more important to sponsors.

 **QUESTIONS**

1   Do you think the companies that stopped sponsoring Tiger Woods following his 2009 scandal were most concerned about the future of their market position, market awareness, or market growth opportunities? Explain your answer.
2   The PGA Tour faced several problems related to the Tiger Woods scandal, including significantly reduced TV viewership and decreased tournament revenues. What could PGA Tour officials have done differently to offset the dramatic, negative impact resulting from Tiger's personal challenges?
3   Does Tiger Woods's 2009 scandal harm him irreparably, or temporarily? What might make a company want to sponsor Tiger again? What are the potential association benefits (and risks) future sponsors face when sponsoring Tiger Woods?

### NOTES

1   'About Visa – additional sponsorships' (n.d.); Griffin(2012).
2   'Olympics, what Olympics? Sponsors, what sponsors?' (1994).
3   Brand Finance (2012).
4   Samsung website (n.d.).
5   Visa website (n.d.).
6   Gartner website (2012a).
7   Gartner website (2012b).
8   Ansoff (1957).
9   Davis (2012).
10  Kraft (2006).
11  Goodgame (2008).
12  Shipley (2009).
13  Associated Press (2008).
14  Sauer (2012).
15  Fogelson (2009).
16  Bloomberg.com (2011).
17  Cendrowski (2012).
18  'Report: Tiger richest athlete in history'(2009); 'About Tiger Woods' (n.d.).
19  Posnanski (2013).
20  Badenhausen, Kurt (2009).
21  Ibid.
22  Ibid.

23  Diaz (2009).
24  Badenhausen (2009).
25  Horrow and Swatek (2008).
26  DiMeglio (2009).
27  McCarthy (2010).
28  McCarthy (2009).
29  'Tiger taking "indefinite break" to save marriage' (2009).
30  Diaz (2009).
31  'Accenture ends sponsorship of Tiger Woods' (2009).
32  'Tag Heuer to drop Tiger Woods from U.S. campaigns' (2009).
33  Gloster (2009).
34  Belson (2011).
35  Caulfield (2011).
36  Ibid.
37  DiCarlo (2004).
38  Roberts (2011).
39  Sherman (2010).
40  Ibid.
41  Belson (2011).
42  'Tiger's year of turmoil, by the numbers' (2010).
43  'Tiger Woods moves to 50th in rankings' (2011).
44  'Tiger's year of turmoil, by the numbers' (2010).
45  Show (2009a).
46  Ibid.
47  Smith (2011, p.6).
48  Sandomir (2010).
49  Smith (2011, p.6).
50  Show (2009b).
51  Smith (2011, p.6).
52  'Mickelson hopeful of Woods' return' (2010).
53  'Watson: tiger should "clean up his act"' (2010); 'Els blasts Tiger's "selfish" timing' (2010).
54  Sanders (2010).
55  Ibid.
56  'Tiger Woods study cost shareholders up to $12b: study' (2009).

 **REFERENCES**

'About Tiger Woods' (n.d.), www.tigerwoods.com, accessed 30 May 2013 at http://web.tiger-woods.com/aboutTiger/bio.

'About Visa – additional sponsorships' (n.d.), Corporate.visa.com, accessed 23 July 2012 at http://corporate.visa.com/about-visa/brand-and-sponsorships/additional-sponsorships.shtml.

'Accenture ends sponsorship of Tiger Woods' (2009), NBCNews.com, 13 December 2009, accessed 28 August 2012 at http://www.msnbc.msn.com/id/34406263/#.UD24YkQ6-Kw.

Ansoff, H.I. (1957), 'Strategies for diversification', *Harvard Business Review*, **35**(2), 113–24.

Associated Press (2008), 'Speedo suit expected to help swimmers rewrite records in Beijing', CBCSports, 11 April 2008, accessed 21 March 2011 at http://www.cbc.ca/sports/amateur/story/2008/04/11/swim-records-beijing.html.

Badenhausen, Kurt (2009), 'Sports' first billion-dollar man', Forbes.com, 29 September 2009, accessed 28 August 2012 at http://www.forbes.com/2009/09/29/tiger-woods-billion-business-sports-tiger.html.

Belson, Ken (2011), 'Hints of a comeback as Woods secures deals', *New York Times*, 24 November

2011, accessed 29 August 2012 at http://www.nytimes.com/2011/11/25/sports/golf/woods-begins-comeback-with-new-sponsorship-deals.html.

Bloomberg.com (2011), 'Bloomberg Sports named one of 10 most innovative companies', Bloomberg.com, 17 May 2011, accessed 4 July 2012 at http://www.bloomberg.com/news/2011-03-17/bloomberg-sports-named-one-of-10-most-innovative-companies.html.

Brand Finance (2012), 'Best global brands 2012', BrandFinance.com, accessed 3 October 2012 at http://brandirectory.com/profile/samsung.

Caulfield, Peter (2011), 'Tiger Woods face dropped from latest version of EA Sports golf video game; Masters flag in his place', *New York Daily News*, 6 January 2011, accessed 29 August 2012 at http://articles.nydailynews.com/2011-01-06/entertainment/27086597_1_elin-nordegren-golf-game-tiger-woods-pga-tour.

Cendrowski, Scott (2012), 'Nike's new marketing mojo', 13 February 2012, accessed 11 May 2012 at http://management.fortune.cnn.com/2012/02/13/nike-digital-marketing/.

Davis, John A. (2012), *The Olympic Games Effect – How Sports Marketing Builds Strong Brands*, New York: John Wiley & Sons, pp. 245–59.

Diaz, Michael (2009), 'Gillette benches Tiger Woods', *The Boston Globe*, 12 December 2009, accessed 28 August 2012 at http://www.boston.com/news/local/breaking_news/2009/12/gillette_benche.html.

DiCarlo, Lisa (2004), 'Six degrees of Tiger Woods', Forbes.com, 18 March 2004, accessed 29 August 2012 at http://www.forbes.com/2004/03/18/cx_ld_0318nike.html.

DiMeglio, Steve (2009), 'Woods crash did $3200 damage to hydrant, tree', USAToday.com, 3 December 2009, accessed 28 August 2012 at http://www.usatoday.com/sports/golf/pga/2009-12-02-woods-crash-damage_N.htm.

'Els blasts Tiger's "selfish" timing' (2010), ESPN.co.uk, 18 February 2010, accessed 28 August 2012 at http://www.espn.co.uk/golf/sport/story/7601.html.

Fogelson, Dave (2009), 'Athlete endorsement deals evolve in post-"Shoe Wars" era', *Sports Business Journal*, 18 May 2009, accessed 25 March 2011 at http://m.sportsbusinessdaily.com/Journal/Issues/2009/05/20090518/Opinion/Athlete-Endorsement-Deals-Evolve-In-Post-Shoe-Wars-Era.aspx.

Gartner website (2012a), 'Gartner says worldwide smartphone sales soared in fourth quarter of 2011 with 47 percent growth', Gartner.com, 1 February 2012, accessed 22 February 2012 at http://www.gartner.com/it/page.jsp?id=2017015.

Gartner website (2012b), 'Gartner says worldwide sales of mobile phones declined 2 percent in first quarter of 2012; Previous year-over-year decline occurred in second quarter of 2009', 16 May 2012, accessed 3 June 2012 at http://www.gartner.com/it/page.jsp?id=2017015.

Gloster, Rob (2009), 'Tiger Woods' Gillette endorsement ends next week as part of plan in 2009', Bloomberg.com, 23 December 2009, accessed 28 August 2012 at http://www.bloomberg.com/news/2010-12-23/gillette-carries-out-plan-to-drop-tiger-woods-as-endorser-at-end-of-year.html.

Goodgame, Clayton (2008), 'High-tech swimsuits: winning medals too', 13 August 2008, *Time*, accessed 21 March 2011 at http://www.time.com/time/world/article/0,8599,1832434,00.html.

Griffin, Donal (2012), 'MasterCard falls as quarterly revenue misses estimates', 1 August 2012, accessed 4 August 2012 at http://www.businessweek.com/news/2012-08-01/mastercard-profit-beats-estimates-amid-debit-market-share-gains.

Horrow, Rick and Karla Swatek (2008), 'Who benefits from Tiger Woods' scandal?' BloombergBusinessweek, 10 December 2008, accessed 28 August 2012 from http://www.businessweek.com/lifestyle/content/dec2009/bw20091210_272903.htm.

Kraft, Harvey (2006), 'The Nike+ iPod partnership strategy: develop unique lifestyle relationships', Marketingprofs.com, 20 June 2006, accessed 14 July 2010 at http://www.marketing-profs.com/6/kraft1.asp.

McCarthy, Michael (2009), 'Tiger Woods won't play in Chevron World Challenge', USAToday.com, 1 December 2009, accessed 28 August 2012 at http://www.usatoday.com/sports/golf/pga/2009-11-30-chevron-world-challenge_N.htm.

McCarthy, Michael (2010), 'Financial impact for golf felt all around with Tiger Woods gone', USAToday.com, 28 January 2010, accessed 29 August 2012 at http://www.usatoday.com/sports/golf/pga/2010-01-28-golf-without-tiger_N.htm.

'Mickelson hopeful of Woods' return' (2010), Golf.com, 27 January 2010, accessed 29 August 2012 at http://www.golf.com/ap-news/mickelson-hopeful-woods-return.

'Olympics, what Olympics? Sponsors, what sponsors?' (1994), Performance Research, accessed 11 May 2012 at http://www.performanceresearch.com/olympic-sponsorship-lillehammer.htm.

Posnanski, Joe. (2013), 'Will Woods break Nicklaus' majors record', GolfChannel.com, 11 April 2013, accessed 27 May 2013 at http://www.golfchannel.com/news/joe-posnanski/will-tiger-woods-break-jack-nicklaus-majors-record/.

'Report: Tiger richest athlete in history' (2009), ESPN.com, 9 October 2009, accessed 28 August 2012 at http://sports.espn.go.com/golf/news/story?id=4524640.

Roberts, Daniel (2011), 'Is Tiger Woods running out of money?', Fortune.com, 15 July 2011, accessed 29 August 2012 at http://features.blogs.fortune.cnn.com/2011/07/15/is-tiger-woods-running-out-of-money/.

Samsung website (n.d.), accessed 8 March 2012 at http://www.samsung.com/us/aboutsamsung/.

Sanders, Bill (2010), 'How impact of "Tiger recession" changed athlete marketability', Sports Business Journal, 2 August 2010, accessed 29 August 2012 at http://www.sportsbusinessdaily.com/Journal/Issues/2010/08/20100802/From-The-Field-Of/How-Impact-Of-Tiger-Recession-Changed-Athlete-Marketability.aspx.

Sandomir, Richard (2010), 'PGA says viewership decline shouldn't be costly in TV talks', New York Times, 19 August 2010, accessed 29 August 2012 at http://www.nytimes.com/2010/08/20/sports/golf/20sandomir.html?_r=0.

Sauer, Abe (2012), 'China's Li Ning tower wobbles', 9 July 2012, accessed 4 August 2012 at http://www.brandchannel.com/home/post/2012/07/09/Li-Ning-Struggles-070912.aspx.

Sherman, Alex (2010), 'Tiger Woods fans snub shirts as golfer has worst year of his career', Bloomberg.com, 24 August 2010, accessed 29 August 2012 at http://www.bloomberg.com/news/2010-08-24/tiger-fans-snub-shirts-as-golfer-has-worst-year-of-his-career.html.

Shipley, Amy (2009), 'High-tech swimsuits still causing a splash', The Washington Post, 23 June 2009, accessed 21 March 2011 at http://www.washingtonpost.com/wp-dyn/content/article/2009/06/22/AR2009062202810.html.

Show, Jon (2009a), 'Where does humbled Tiger (and his image) go from here?' (2009), Sports Business Journal, 7 December 2009, accessed 29 August 2012 at http://www.sportsbusiness-daily.com/Journal/Issues/2009/12/20091207/This-Weeks-News/Where-Does-Humbled-Tiger-And-His-Image-Go-From-Here.aspx?hl=tiger%20woods%20ea%20sports&sc=0.

Show, Jon (2009b), 'Woods revives PGA Tour ratings', Sports Business Journal, 5 October 2009, accessed 29 August 2012 at http://www.sportsbusinessdaily.com/Journal/Issues/2009/10/20091005/This-Weeks-News/Woods-Revives-PGA-Tour-Ratings.aspx.

Smith, Michael (2011), 'PGA tour rides ratings rebound into TV talks', Sports Business Journal, 16 May 2011, 6.

'Tag Heuer to drop Tiger Woods from U.S. campaigns' (2009), NBCNews.com, 18 December 2009, accessed 28 August 2012 at http://www.msnbc.msn.com/id/34482270/#.UD2-8EQ6-Kw.

'Tiger taking "indefinite break" to save marriage' (2009), NBCSports.com, 12 December 2009, accessed 29 August 2012 at http://nbcsports.msnbc.com/id/34386014/.

'Tiger's year of turmoil, by the numbers', NBCSports.com, 25 November 2010, accessed 29 August 2012 at http://nbcsports.msnbc.com/id/40345914/ns/sports-golf/.

'Tiger Woods moves to 50th in rankings', ESPN.com, 13 November 2011, accessed 29 August 2012 at http://espn.go.com/golf/story/_/id/7231583/tiger-woods-moves-50th-official-world-golf-rankings.

'Tiger Woods study cost shareholders up to $12b: study' (2009), ABS-CBNNews.com, 30 December 2009, accessed 28 August 2012 at http://www.abs-cbnnews.com/business/12/30/09/tiger-woods-scandal-cost-shareholders-12-b-study.

Visa website (n.d.), accessed 23 July 2012 at http://corporate.visa.com/_media/visa-corporate-overview.pdf.

'Watson: Tiger should "clean up his act"', ESPN.com, 3 February 2010, accessed 28 August 2012 at http://sports.espn.go.com/golf/news/story?id=4882736.

# 6

# Sports marketing measures

**CHAPTER OVERVIEW**

In Chapter 2 we introduced the brand planning framework: *destiny, distinction, culture, experiences* to describe the practices top brands use to build their reputations and how the framework can help marketers maximize the return on their sports investments. The brand value framework followed, introducing the four dimensions of value: *reputation, organizational, societal, financial*, giving marketers an important set of criteria to guide progress toward their growth objectives, while explicitly highlighting that aiming for a financial outcome is only one part of the value development effort. For measurable financial value to be improved, sports marketers need to think through and plan how their sports investment will add value in each of the first three areas of value. The two frameworks are designed to work together since brand planning success will be based on the value created, and value creation occurs after a comprehensive brand plan is developed. We then showed the importance of understanding the historical legacies of selected sports to provide marketers with a solid contextual foundation for aligning their sports marketing efforts more effectively with target audiences, describing sports fan types and the customer identification process required in pre-planning. This led to a discussion in Chapter 5 about positioning pre-planning, including weighing market growth options for sports marketers based on the Ansoff matrix, using current and new products sold in current and new markets as a blueprint for determining the opportunities that are most important for the marketer's company. In this chapter we will discuss the pre-planning measures for evaluating the organization's current market position that are important in developing and refining the actual marketing strategies and tactics employed.

## 6.1 Strategic measures

Preparing for successful a sports marketing effort starts with developing a coherent, long-term direction. The brand-planning framework described destiny as a framing theme that answers the question, *why do we exist*? This is more than a philosophical, or navel-gazing exercise. Every successful organization understands its ultimate purpose and reason to exist, but a common mistake is to assume the primary motivation organizations have is to make money. Making money is obviously important, indeed necessary, for surviving, let alone thriving. But making money is not a motivating rationale for the firm's existing since revenues can be generated selling almost anything. The importance of focusing on the organization's destiny is to identify what the firm could ultimately achieve over time and how the results would benefit stakeholders. Therefore, destiny becomes the driver for every strategy and action that follows and helps the firm organize its capabilities around making progress toward it.

## Awareness

Developing and strengthening awareness is fundamental to any organization's pursuit of growth and serves as a useful strategic starting point in developing strategic objectives. After all, even the most innovative, highest quality product ever invented will fail if people don't know it exists. Therefore, marketers will almost invariably look for ways to improve awareness, whether it is of new products from an existing company, or an entirely new company. For those organizations already well known, the sports marketing activities would be a vehicle for broadening the organization's awareness levels beyond its current customer base with new uncommitted customer audiences, or strengthening the firm's reputation in its core market segments by attracting customers currently buying competitor brands. There are two different types of awareness designed to measure prior knowledge of an entity (such as a brand, product, ad campaign, sports team etc.): recall and recognition. Recall, also known as unaided awareness, describes a person's ability to name a specific offering from a particular industry when asked questions like 'Can you name a brand from XYZ industry?' Recognition, also called aided awareness, refers to a person's ability to recognize a specific offering after being prompted by questions such as 'Do you recognize brand ABC?'

As with any marketing research, marketers must be careful in the design of the questionnaires and surveys since respondents will often want to sound knowledgeable. In other words, people may answer yes, even if they have never heard of the organization in order to appear informed. There are different survey techniques requiring careful survey design and question construction that marketers can employ but are beyond the scope of this book. Suffice to say that measuring awareness is a good starting point, assuming of course that marketers are confident their research findings accurately reflect market awareness levels. However, having high awareness levels does not mean the customer intends to purchase.

## Negative associations and awareness

Consumers in the market may be aware of a sports entity because of its notoriety, creating a negative association that is detrimental to the brand. In Major League Baseball (MLB) in North America, a decade-long series of reports about the use of performance-enhancing substances, along with seemingly superhuman athletic accomplishments has led some fans to conclude that the sport is tainted. A similar situation has affected professional cycling, in which many of the sport's stars over the last 20 years have been implicated for using banned substances.[1] Italian professional football, known as Serie A, has confronted numerous match-fixing scandals in the 2000s, which have undermined fan confidence in the league.[2] Sports fans around the world are aware of MLB, cycling, and Italian football, but not necessarily for positive reasons. However, it must be stated that many of the athletes in these sports, and others, compete honestly without the aid of banned substances. The unfortunate consequence of a negative association is that the public's memory tends not only to last, but often amplifies the banned activity, overwhelming the stories of athletic achievement of those competing honorably.

Negative associations have also impacted sports product manufacturers. When Nike was associated with controversial labor practices in its contracted factories in Asia, the company quickly came under fire from customers, human rights groups, and even governments. Since Nike has been the market leader for more than two decades, it become a lightning rod for criticism, even though its competitors often manufactured their products in the same regions of the world, and sometimes the same factories. Interestingly, Nike does not own any of the factories where its products are made, nor have they for several decades. The responsibility for management of factory workers lies with the local owners of factories in those countries, however, Nike, and its competitors, were blamed since their manufacturing contracts essentially implied their financial support of controversial labor tactics. The negative association has not caused the company's growth to slow over time, but it did inspire the company to seek more specific labor improvements from contracted factory management and to make overt changes to its outsourcing selection efforts in general.[3]

Olympic corporate sponsors known as TOP (The Olympic Partners) face regular scrutiny for their association with the Olympics. The 2008 Olympic Torch Relay had three TOP sponsors supporting it, Coca-Cola, Samsung and Lenovo, and all three were targeted by human rights groups seeking independence for Tibet from China. Human rights advocates urged boycotts of the sponsors' products and they disrupted the torch relay several times in an effort to draw larger media attention as well.[4] Human rights groups in India demanded that the International Olympic Committee (IOC) cancel Dow Chemical's 2012 Olympic sponsorship since the company's Union Carbide division was responsible for the 1984 Bhopal chemical disaster that led to thousands of deaths and severe disabilities for thousands more. Dow argued that they were not responsible for the Bhopal disaster since they had acquired Union Carbide in 1999, 15 years after the disaster, and that all legal claims had been settled prior to their acquisition. Dow remained a TOP sponsor for the 2012 London Olympics, despite the protests in India.[5]

The Olympic TOP sponsors and Nike and its competitors are examples of companies in sports, or using sports to market their offerings, which confronted visible negative associations. While the negative associations did not permanently damage their brands, and despite that these companies were not directly responsible for the negativity being pinned on them, it is clear that in the mind of some groups these companies bear direct responsibility. As a result, the companies have to figure out how to deal with the negative associations, whether through significant changes to the company or to their business relationships or even through alternative marketing communications, each of which alters the sports marketing strategies they had hoped to pursue.

## The benefits of high awareness of sports

The good news for sports marketing advocates is that most leagues, teams, clubs, and many athletes are well known and tend to have positive associations, thanks to decades of investment in developing athletes and clubs to compete at the highest levels combined with today's new and traditional media to help spread the word. This widespread familiarity is a key reason that more companies are increasingly investing in sports marketing to raise their brand profiles. Most athletes and teams that have transgressed have received the enmity of fans everywhere, usually causing management and owners to change course and refocus on the traditions that first made them successful. Even people who are not sports fans will usually have basic awareness of known sports entities. Therefore, instead of trying to raise even broader awareness of a known sports entity, such as the Premier League's Manchester United (ManU), sports marketers will instead concentrate their awareness-building activities around the club's many programs, including ManU's Official Membership Club, which is an annual fee program that provides the club's fans with discounts on ManU games, merchandise, and food as well as the club's official magazine.[6]

*Awareness: GoDaddy.com – even in sports, sex sells*

When the dotcom bubble burst at the turn of the twenty-first century, many sports marketers had written websites out of the sports sponsorship mix. The internet domain registrar and web-hosting company GoDaddy.com had been in existence for a few years, but it entered the sports marketing space with great fanfare in 2005. At the 2005 Super Bowl, GoDaddy purchased airtime during the famous game.[7] The advertisement featured former WWE wrestler Candice Michelle at a censorship hearing experiencing various wardrobe malfunctions as she demonstrated in a sexually suggestive manner what she would be doing in an impending Super Bowl commercial. Fox (the broadcaster of the Super Bowl that year) pulled the commercial after having shown it once in the broadcast. Later, AdStore CEO Paul Cappelli said 'we honestly weren't trying to make a commercial that would get rejected, but we were making a commercial that we hoped would get noticed'.[8]

Since that first infamous commercial, GoDaddy has made a habit of purchasing Super Bowl ad time and filling it with scantly clad women, known as 'GoDaddy girls'. It is also the title sponsor of the GoDaddy Bowl, a college football bowl game played between the Mid-American and the Sun Belt conferences,[9] and has sponsored race driver Danica Patrick since 2006.[10] Something seems to be working for GoDaddy. Its annual sales in 2011 hit $1.14 billion, up from $493 million in 2007[11] and it was named in *Fortune Magazine*'s '100 Best Companies to Work For' list in 2012.[12]

## From awareness to preference

As shown in Chapter 5, awareness is a basic measure of familiarity and prior knowledge of a product, service or company. Having a target audience that is aware of an organization's offerings is necessary for ensuring that organization's survival, but awareness alone is an insufficient guarantee of growth and profitability. We are all aware of innumerable products and services that we will never buy. Therefore, marketers need to use awareness as a base from which marketing programs are designed to transform awareness into *preference*. Preference indicates the target audience prefers the sports brand versus alternatives, giving marketers a critical advantage in ultimately persuading those customers to actually purchase.

## 6.2    Brand Contribution and Review Analysis

The findings from the marketer's awareness research guide the type of marketing programs that are implemented. To achieve awareness goals requires that marketers have a firmer understanding of the tangible and intangible factors that contribute to their company's overall brand reputation, and/or the reputation of the brands within. A diagnostic tool called Brand Contribution and Review Analysis (BCRA) (see Box 6.1) is well suited to this purpose. The BCRA is a highly practical tool, enabling marketers to more effectively determine sports marketing investment decisions, resource allocation, brand repositioning, and even divestments. The information required in the BCRA should be easily accessible, from a combination of the company's finance and accounting department to surveys of employees, customers, and suppliers about the company's reputation. For the BCRA to be truly useful marketers must be as accurate as possible with reliable data and survey findings. In other words, don't plug in answers if the evidence does not exist because then the BCRA will convey a misleading picture of the brand, making any sports marketing decisions moot.[13]

Working on the BCRA accomplishes two important tasks: (1) finding the right quantitative data that describes the brand's financial contribution and share; (2) conducting surveys with proper question methodology to gather qualitative insights about management/employee, customer, supplier perceptions of the brand's strengths and weaknesses.

The BCRA helps marketers gain a better understanding of how their company is performing internally, giving them more confidence in aligning their sports marketing plan with their company's strategy. This internal review is an important step toward creating a sports marketing plan that ultimately enhances the firm's reputation and brand value. At this point marketers need to turn their attention to understanding external factors and setting relevant goals to improve their market position.

## Market share and relative market share[14]

Market share and relative market share both describe how well the sports marketer's company is doing as a percentage of total sales (in dollars or units) versus their competitors, with one difference: market share shows how a company is doing compared to the total market, whereas relative market share describes how a company is doing versus its biggest competitor.

### Market share

Market share is calculated easily by dividing the company's sales by total market sales using this formula:

BOX 6.1

# BCRA

*Financial (annual)*
Revenues (attributed to the brand)          $_____
*Subtract* brand-specific marketing costs    $_____
Gross brand contribution                     $_____

---

Brand contribution as % of firm's total revenues       _____%
Brand contribution as % of firm's total profits       _____%
Brand market share                           _____%

---

Brand value increase/decrease            $_____ & _____%

---

| *Brand* | 1 = poor 5 = excellent |
|---|---|
| Market awareness | 1 2 3 4 5 |
| Contribution to company reputation | 1 2 3 4 5 |
| Reputation with customers | 1 2 3 4 5 |
| Reputation with suppliers | 1 2 3 4 5 |
| Reputation with employees | 1 2 3 4 5 |
| Ability to extend/stretch | 1 2 3 4 5 |
| Clear differentiation | 1 2 3 4 5 |

| *Product* | 1 = poor 5 = excellent |
|---|---|
| Quality | 1 2 3 4 5 |
| Reliability | 1 2 3 4 5 |
| Relevance to customers | 1 2 3 4 5 |
| Clear connection to product category | 1 2 3 4 5 |
| Addresses specific needs | 1 2 3 4 5 |
| Compares favorably to competitors | 1 2 3 4 5 |

| *Brand management* | Yes | No |
|---|---|---|
| Strong team | ___ | ___ |
| Good decision-making | ___ | ___ |
| Realistic business plans | ___ | ___ |
| Proactive | ___ | ___ |
| Profitable business | ___ | ___ |
|    Improved over prior years? | ___ | ___ |
| Handles crises well | ___ | ___ |
| Flexible | ___ | ___ |
| Communicative | ___ | ___ |
| Measures results | ___ | ___ |
| Good internal reputation | ___ | ___ |

➡

←

|                                      |       |       |
|--------------------------------------|-------|-------|
| Good industry reputation             | ___   | ___   |
| Retraining needed                    | ___   | ___   |
|   Explain briefly _____ |       |       |

| *Strategic*                          | *Yes* | *No*  |
|--------------------------------------|-------|-------|
| Good growth prospects                | ___   | ___   |
|   Revenues                 | ___   | ___   |
|   Profits                  | ___   | ___   |
|   Customers                | ___   | ___   |
| Favorable economic conditions        | ___   | ___   |
| Advances firm's strategic objectives | ___   | ___   |
| Relevant to brand's market segments  | ___   | ___   |
| Favorable market trends              | ___   | ___   |
| Overlap with firm's other brands     | ___   | ___   |
|   Is this a problem?       | ___   | ___   |
| Growth potential in new geographies  | ___   | ___   |
| Growth potential to new customer segments | ___ | ___ |

| *Customer*                           | *Gain?* | *Loss?* |
|--------------------------------------|---------|---------|
| Number of customers                  | ___     | ___     |
| Market share                         | ___     | ___     |
| New segments                         | ___     | ___     |
| Revenues per customer                | ___     | ___     |
| Profits per customer                 | ___     | ___     |
| Share of customer wallet             | ___     | ___     |
| Needs fulfilled                      | ___     | ___     |

| *Market*                             | *High* | *Low* |
|--------------------------------------|--------|-------|
| Growth potential                     | ___    | ___   |
| Competitive threats                  | ___    | ___   |
| Supplier strength                    | ___    | ___   |
| Regulatory restrictions              | ___    | ___   |
| Environmental concerns               | ___    | ___   |
| Socio-cultural benefits              | ___    | ___   |

| *Marketing*                          | *Yes* | *No*  |
|--------------------------------------|-------|-------|
| +                                    |       |       |
| Receiving appropriate advertising support | ___ | ___ |
| Influential customers                | ___   | ___   |
| Consistent marketing communications  | ___   | ___   |
| Clear brand message                  | ___   | ___   |
| –                                    |       |       |
| Unplanned additional sales force effort | ___ | ___ |
| Uneven channel support               | ___   | ___   |

→

←

| | Favorable | Not favorable |
|---|---|---|
| Confusing and/or overlapping offerings | —— | —— |
| Product quality problems | —— | —— |
| Unreliable suppliers | —— | —— |
| Unexpected competitor moves | —— | —— |
| *Marketing (cont.)* | *Favorable* | *Not favorable* |
| Company press | —— | —— |
| Industry press | —— | —— |
| Customer support and satisfaction | —— | —— |
| Word of mouth | —— | —— |
| *Corporate* | *Yes* | *No* |
| Overt senior management support | —— | —— |
| External corporate crises/challenges | —— | —— |
| Shareholder support | —— | —— |
| Employee turnover | —— | —— |
| Internal operations challenges | —— | —— |
| Budget support for growth plans | —— | —— |

$$M_{it} = \frac{S_{it}}{\Sigma S_{it}} \qquad (6.1)$$

Where:

$M_i$ = company $i$'s market share in time $t$ expressed in percentage terms;
$S_i$ = sales of company $i$ in time $t$ (in units or dollars);
$\Sigma S_t$ = sum of all sales in time $t$ (in units or dollars).

Market share is an important measure of a company's (and/or its products') market position and also serves as one indicator of how well a marketing strategy may be working. However, as an indicator only, market share does not reveal enough nuanced insight to tell marketers where obvious strengths and weaknesses lie, particularly since each time market share is measured it reflects a snapshot in time. To gain better intelligence on their company's performance a marketer would be well advised to compare several years of market share data to determine trends. Also, market share trends need to be examined to identify factors that inspired any changes that occurred over the years:

● Did market share increase due to price reductions? If so, were those price reductions still profitable? Price reductions to increase market share are a common tactic, but can have unfortunate side-effects. Customers will expect future reductions before purchasing again. Customers may balk at any price increases that are not also accompanied by value-added improvements in the product.

- Is the product category in the late maturity or even decline phase of its lifecycle, suggesting that market share increases may reflect competitors' abandoning the market and given only a temporary boost to the marketer's company?
- Are they market share changes (whether increases or decreases) expected, or unexpected? If unexpected, then what are the reasons for the surprising changes and are those permanent and/or sustainable? Were the changes due to the company-led factors or competitor-led factors?
- Do market share changes reflect larger changes in customer preferences?

Market share is a commonly used measure in most business planning. At the strategic level of planning, where goals and objectives are described, market share represents a target to be achieved typically over several years, although there are certainly examples of products that increase share in shorter time frames due to their quality, uniqueness, and/or ability to address a need.

## Relative market share

Relative market share measures the company's market share against that of its closest competitor:

$$\text{Relative market share } (I) \ (\%) = \frac{\text{Brands market share } (\$, \#)}{\text{Largest competitors market share } (\$, \#)}$$

(6.2)

One may reasonably ask what benefits arise from measuring relative market share. The measure sheds light on how the marketer's company is doing compared to its key competitor *in a specific category*. The result can also partly explain why a company is able to charge higher prices and have a premium position in the market (or, conversely, why they are underperforming).

Using both of these market share measures allows marketers to not only see how well they are competing for market share compared to competitors, but they can also set goals for improvement, which will influence how they develop their sports marketing activities to achieve the strategic brand value objectives.

## Brand development index and category development index[15]

The brand development and category development indexes identify and measure the strengths and weaknesses of a company's customer segments from a brand and category perspective. For sports marketers, these measures can be particularly useful in gaining a preliminary understanding of how effective their past marketing efforts have been in establishing a unique position in the marketplace for their brands and within specific product categories, thereby revealing how to use their sports marketing investments to improve the company's performance in both the brand and category areas.

### Brand development index (BDI)

The BDI measures a brand's effectiveness in penetrating a specific customer segment as compared to its performance across the entire market (such as French sports equipment company Babolat's success in selling to high school tennis players). In the numerator, the brand's sales to a group or a segment of customers are divided by the total households in that group. This is then divided by the denominator, which is the result of total brand sales divided by total households in the market:

$$\text{BDI} = \frac{[\text{Brand sales to group (\#)/Households in group (\#)}]}{[\text{Total brand sales (\#)/Total Household (\#)}]} \quad (6.3)$$

The results from the BDI calculation can show which customer segments represent the highest sales per capita in comparison to the market overall (assuming the marketer has data on each specific target segment and can therefore employ this measure for each segment). The result should indicate those customer segments where the brand has the greatest potential to gain additional growth.

### Category development index (CDI)

The CDI measures the marketer's sales strength to a select segment of customers in a particular product category (such as court sports equipment) relative to total households in that same segment, which is then divided by the result of total category sales divided by total households in the market:

$$\text{CDI} = \frac{[\text{Category sales to group (\#)/Households in group (\#)}]}{[\text{Total category sales (\#)/Total household (\#)}]}$$

$$(6.4)$$

Both BDI and CDI enable the sports marketer to see how their brands and products are selling to specific groups of customers, and how those results compare to total category sales to the entire market. Similar to the market share and relative market share measures, marketers will be able to use the findings most effectively if they have several years of data to compare.

So far we have started broadly by discussing market awareness, and then preference, as important pieces of information to learn and as objectives to achieve for guiding the direction of the sports marketing plan. We then looked at the marketer's efforts to understand more about their company's internal strengths and weaknesses by using the Brand Contribution and Review Analysis tool. The findings would logically compel marketers to understand more about their current market share vis-à-vis competitors and set future goals accordingly. From there we then discussed how marketers should measure the performance of the company's offerings as brands and within product categories. This has given us a good overview of various strategic measures related to general market conditions and the company's specific performance within. By understanding both the brand and category development indexes, we are building a more complete customer picture. Now our attention will shift to understanding a very important measure for long-term, sustained success: customer lifetime value.

## Customer lifetime value (CLTV)

When businesses focus on long-term value gain then they must also consider how to maximize their customer relationships. CLTV measures the long-term value derived from loyal customers and the costs of acquiring those customers. Two approaches for measuring CLTV that are based on the present value of future cash flows expected from a given customer will be discussed.

### CLTV approach 1[16]

This first approach measures the dollar value (typically, the flow of profits from the accumulation of purchases over time) from a customer's long-term relationship with a company and also includes a value for new customers referred by loyal customers, reinforcing the added value to the company from their relationship with the referring customer. Approach 1 only focuses on the added value derived from new customer referrals and does not contemplate how companies could also derive value from cross- or up-selling opportunities, which are alternative considerations in determining lifetime value:

$$CLTV = [(M - C) \times (P \times Y) - A + (A \times N)] \times F \qquad (6.5)$$

Where:
$M$ = average amount of money spent per purchase;
$C$ = average costs to service each purchase;
$P$ = number of purchases per year;
$Y$ = number of years managers expect to keep this customer;
$A$ = new customer acquisition cost;
$N$ = number of new customers referred by original customer;
$F$ = customer adjustment factor for the period of time being evaluated.

Allen Weiss, Professor of Marketing at the USC Marshall School of Business, describes $F$, the customer adjustment factor, as follows:

> [F] captures changes in a customer's behavior over time. If you estimate that the customer will increase the money spent per visit over time (because you estimate you will increase their loyalty), then put in a higher number – say, 1.4. If you estimate the customer will decrease their spending over time, put in a lower number – say, 9. This is obviously a subjective estimate.

Therefore, one is considered steady state, so there is no corresponding adjustment. Because the correction factor is subjective, based on the marketer's judgment, one can easily understand the importance of qualitative and quantitative measures in the analysis. The variables are then grouped into individual equations related to the customer purchase patterns over time, as well as the benefits derived from loyal customer referrals:

$M - C$ = the average gross profit per customer visit;
$P \times Y$ = total number of visits over the customer's lifetime;
$A \times N$ = the amount of money saved by the customer's referral.

The result provides an *estimate* of CLTV since a precise metric depends also on actual customer behavior, the actual contributions of referred customers, and accurate financial data of each purchase over time.

## Approach 2[17]

As the term customer lifetime value implies, there is potential financial gain for companies that focus on maximizing customer retention and, correspondingly, minimizing customer defection. The marketer's plans for customer retention should be designed to do more than just maintain a constant level of purchases; instead, their marketing programs should encourage increasing the purchases from loyal customers through cross-selling (selling similarly priced complements) and up-selling products (selling a more expensive product or complement).

The second approach uses a constant customer defection rate, a constant net margin, and a discount rate:

$$CLTV = m/(k + d) \tag{6.6}$$

Where:
$m$ = constant net margin (profits – retention costs);
$k$ = discount rate;
$d$ = constant defection rate.

Since each customer's contribution can be increased through cross-selling and up-selling, a constant growth rate $g$ is factored into the equation:

$$CLTV = m/(k + d - g) \tag{6.7}$$

Also, since a customer's growth in value is not likely to remain constant over time, the growth rate is subtracted. If the marketer cannot find ways to regularly add value that encourages additional purchases from loyal customers, then any increases from cross- or up-selling will decrease over time since each additional purchase becomes less valuable (known in economics as diminishing marginal utility).

The implications of nurturing customer lifetime value are self-evident. By developing their sports marketing programs to foster customer loyalty, marketers can inspire significant gains in customer purchases and also develop a reliable financial base that is, in effect, an annuity for their company.

Presuming marketers are successful in strengthening customer lifetime value, and in the process increase customer referrals as well, then understanding overall market growth is also an important measure.

## Market growth[18]

We discussed reviewing several years of market share data to determine trends that can help marketers gauge where customer interest lies, market growth is a good companion measure. At a minimum as a market grows, then marketers will want their market share to remain constant. Ideally, as the market grows, the marketer is also implementing new programs designed to increase share so that the momentum from market growth is reflected in increased share. Market growth is calculated by dividing the total sales in the target market this year total sales in the preceding year:

$$G_m = \frac{R_I}{R_L}$$ (6.8)

Where:
$G_m$ = % market growth;
$R_I$ = market dollars/units increase this year;
$R_L$ = market dollars/units last year.

Historical growth rates are not guaranteed to continue into the future, so marketers must not depend on it to drive sales for their company as well. This is why it is so important that marketers carefully consider how their sports marketing investment can produce growth and share increases for their company, even if the market overall shows signs of slowing growth or even retraction. However, by knowing their company's growth rate marketers will be able to see what the pattern has been for several years and how this compares not just to their company's historical average, but to that of competitors as well, acting as an indicator of overall market dynamics such as: the market's potential (the total number of customer in the target market segment), the level of customer penetration (how many customers have entered the market), and the rate of customer entry (how quickly new customers enter the market).

Growth can also be measured with specific customers using a measure known as share of wallet (also known as share of customer).

## Share of wallet/share of customer[19]

Any marketing activity is pursued to help companies grow. With more companies using sports marketing to improve their appeal to the marketplace and attract new customers, a logical question is whether there is a positive impact with existing customers as well. Share of wallet measures the depth of a customer's commitment to the company's products by calculating the percentage increase of the customer's total purchases of those products. Sales to the customer are divided by the sum of all customer spending:

$$S_i = \frac{S_{it}}{\sum Mi_t}$$ (6.9)

Where:

$S_i$ = share of customer $i$ (in percentage terms);
$S_{it}$ = sales to customer $i$ in time $t$ (in units or dollars);
$\Sigma M_t$ = sum of all customer spending in the category in time $t$ (in units or dollars).

The distinction between market share and share of customer should be clear. Market share measures an individual company's share of total market sales whereas share of customer calculates share at the individual customer account level, measuring the percentage share of the total dollars for a product. Share of customer indicates if the sports marketing programs have been successful at persuading a customer to purchase a larger share of the company's products over competitors. Share of customer is also useful for evaluating individual sales representatives since the result suggests how successful they have been in deepening their relationship with the customer.

## Market penetration[20]

Market penetration measures the number of people that buy a product one or more times during a specified period of time divided by the total target market population.

There are three market penetration formulas that are commonly used: market penetration, brand penetration, and penetration share:

*Market penetration*

$$M_p = \frac{C_c}{T_p} \qquad (6.10)$$

Where:

$M_p$ = market penetration %;
$C_c$ = customers that have purchased a product in the category (#);
$T_p$ = total market population (#).

*Brand penetration*

$$B_p = \frac{C_b}{T_p} \qquad (6.11)$$

Where:

$B_p$ = brand penetration %;

$C_b$ = customers that have purchased the brand (#);
$T_p$ = total market population (#).

*Penetration share*

$$P_s = \frac{B_p}{M_p} \qquad (6.12)$$

Where:
$P_s$ = penetration share %;
$B_p$ = brand penetration %;
$M_p$ = market penetration %.

*OR*

$$P_s = \frac{C_b}{C_c} \qquad (6.13)$$

Where:
$P_s$ = penetration share %;
$C_b$ = customers that have purchased the brand (#);
$C_c$ = customers that have purchased a product in the category (#).

Measuring market penetration can help marketers determine whether their sports marketing emphasis should be on taking customers from their competitors or on growing the category by attracting new customers.

## 6.3 Chapter summary

Marketers are accountable to their company's senior management for the plans and recommendations they make in their sports marketing plans. The need to establish growth-oriented goals is coupled with the need to measure progress toward those goals and evaluations of the marketing programs upon completion. Marketers must always be cognizant that their decisions and plans are intended to add value to their company that is measurable through customer gains, category development, market share growth, brand penetration, and, ultimately, brand value enhancement. The measures discussed in this chapter are useful for most marketing planning purposes, but they are by no means the only measurement tools available. However, the absence of a methodical system of measures makes sports marketing expenditures much harder to justify.

**CASE STUDY**

# Visa

In 1986, Visa was the third largest credit card company in the world, trailing behind American Express and MasterCard. While different iterations of the Visa card had been in existence since 1958, Visa branded credit cards had only been in existence since 1976.[21] The privately owned company was at a juncture. At the time, Visa's market share was 20.3 percent, with American Express and MasterCard coming in at considerably higher percentages of the market.[22] Annual transaction volume for Visa in 1986 was $111 billion.[23] When the TOP program was hatched in 1985, Visa was not the International Olympic Committee's first choice. In fact, Juan Antonio Samaranch, then the President of the IOC, sent a rare personal letter to American Express soliciting its official sponsorship of $8 million.[24] Luckily for Visa, American Express rejected the deal and the IOC surged ahead to sign a global deal with Visa.

Visa became one of the first TOP sponsors in December 1985 with an initial investment of $14.5 million.[25] At the time, Visa had already been working on a campaign aimed at American Express, so the company was thrilled to be able to roll out a 'Bring your Visa card, because the Olympics don't take American Express' campaign.[26] It made its debut at the 1988 Calgary Winter Games, with banks in fewer than five countries participating in marketing programs.[27] Its campaign had several important objectives: to chip away American Express's title as the top credit card in the world, and in doing so, to increase brand awareness. Visa developed and closely followed sponsorship criteria to best implement its strategies moving forward. The thorough criteria it established would be vital in ensuring positive results moving forward (Figure 6.1).

Source: Davis (2013).
**Figure 6.1** Visa sponsorship criteria

| Visa Sponsorship Criteria | | | | | | | | | |
|---|---|---|---|---|---|---|---|---|---|
| Brand Fit | Usage Stimulation | Event History/Credibility | Broad Reach | Governing Body Control | Advocacy Creation | Low Risk | Event's Marketing Plan | Ease of Implementation | Strong Member Interest |

Visa immediately began to see results from its TOP sponsorship. In the first three years of its relationship with the IOC, Visa's global sales increased 18 percent, which was 6 percent more than the company had forecasted.[28] During its Olympic promotions, card

**CASE STUDY** (continued)

volume increased 21 percent.[29] Visa soon became the number one credit card in the world, and has held the title ever since.

Throughout its ensuing Olympic campaigns, Visa has steadily increased its awareness among consumers. At the 2004 Games in Athens, Visa achieved 87 percent consumer awareness, which was the highest level of awareness among all Olympic sponsors.[30] Visa again achieved this honor at the 2010 Vancouver Games with a 66 percent awareness rate.[31] Despite holding the reins as the top credit card in the world, Visa's Olympic sponsorship objectives have not remained stagnant. Initially, Visa simply wanted to increase brand awareness. But as time wore on, Visa refined its Olympic objectives to differentiate itself from its competition. As one Visa executive stated, 'Our campaign for the 1988 Calgary Olympics was all about branding and we focused on the 17 days surrounding the games. Then in 1994, we saw that Visa was going to have to adapt its marketing. . .and spread its efforts over a much longer period'.[32] Transaction volume for Visa has since ballooned from its modest 1986 days to $5.6 trillion.[33] At the 2012 Olympics, $1.4 billion in payments were Visa transactions.[34]

A major part of Visa's continued success is the breadth and the scope of its Olympic partnership. In addition to its status as part of the TOP program, Visa also has taken significant initiative to extend its involvement with the Olympic movement far beyond the sidelines of the playing field. In 1994, Visa launched a children's art program called the 'Visa Olympics of the Imagination'.[35] As part of this program, children learned about the Olympic movement and were simultaneously entered into an art competition with the chance to win a trip to the Olympics.[36] According to Visa, more than a million children have participated in the program, with 181 children from 48 different countries attending the Olympics as a result.[37] Visa also became the first global sponsor of the International Paralympic Committee in 2002. As part of its sponsorship of various Paralympic athletes and federations, Visa sent more than 300 athletes and staff to the 2004 Athens Paralympic Games from the British Paralympic Association.[38] In 2006, Visa became the presenting sponsor of the International Paralympic Committee Hall of Fame, thus further 'reaffirm[ing] its commitment to the Paralympic Movement and to Paralympic athletes of the past, present, and future'.[39] Because it reaches many different groups through these additional sponsorships, Visa is better able to drive brand awareness and foster lasting connections with its consumers.

The Olympic partnership has become so ingrained in Visa that in 2010, the company launched its first ever Olympic-themed global marketing campaign.[40] Called 'Go World', the campaign seeks to elicit an emotional response from viewers with actor Morgan Freeman (in the United States) narrating sepia-toned images of athletes succeeding in their various athletic pursuits. The company continued this campaign through the 2012 London Games and enhanced the channels that it was offered through by ramping up its social media presence through its Team Visa campaign. In a campaign described as 'social-by-design',[41] consumers could 'cheer' for Team Visa athletes (athletes who Visa sponsored) and watch exclusive content on YouTube. Visa's campaign generated 59 million cheers and 47 million views on its YouTube channel.[42]

## CASE STUDY *(continued)*

Visa became a publicly traded company with a successful $17.9 billion IPO in March 2008. At the time it was the largest IPO in US history, but it spelled a new era for Visa executives. As a result of the IPO, Visa executives needed to prove the value of the TOP sponsorship to shareholders. While the exact terms of the TOP sponsorship deals are not released, it is estimated that Visa spends around $100 million for each Olympic quadrennial to have the right to use the Olympic rings, which Visa has the rights to through 2020.[43] But when the deal comes back up for renegotiation, will the astronomical fees that go with an Olympic sponsorship be too high? Brand Finance, an international brand valuation consultancy, estimates that the brand value of the Olympics at $47.6 billion, which is greater than the valuation of all of its sponsors combined.[44] Will there ever be a limit to how much a company, like Visa, will be willing to spend on this relationship?

 **QUESTIONS**

1 If you were Visa's CEO, what questions would you ask your Chief Marketing Officer if you wanted to understand how Visa is deriving value from its Olympic sponsorship?
2 What benefit would the 'Visa Olympics of the Imagination' have provided the company given that children were not their target audience? Can this be perceived negatively? If so, how?
3 What are the intangible factors that create brand value for the Olympics? For Visa? Describe.

## NOTES

1 Christopher (2012).
2 Hughes (2012).
3 'Nike's new labor practices' (1998).
4 Bowley and Sullivan (2008).
5 Mail Today Reporter (2012).
6 'General information' (n.d.).
7 'Censorship' (2005).
8 'Ads that caught our eye' (2005).
9 Love (2010).
10 'Danica Patrick' (n.d.).
11 Vance (2012).
12 'GoDaddy' (2012).
13 Davis (2010, pp. 83–6).
14 Farris et al. (2006, pp. 19–20).
15 Ibid., pp. 23–5.
16 Weiss (2005).
17 Reibstein and Srivastava (2004, pp. 8–9).
18 Best (2005, pp. 72–3).
19 Harte-Hanks Research & Analytics (n.d.); Davis (2005, pp. 167–8).
20 Ansoff (1957); Kotler et al. (2003); Best (2005, pp. 86–7); Davis (2005, pp. 35–9; 2013, pp. 34–6).

21  'History of Visa' (n.d.).
22  Davis, John A.(2012, p. 255).
23  Foster and Chang (2003).
24  Mickle (2010).
25  Ibid.
26  Ibid.
27  'Visa and the Olympic Games fact sheet' (2012).
28  Mickle (2010).
29  Ibid.
30  Davis (2012, pp. 254–5).
31  Ibid.
32  Ibid., p. 246.
33  Ibid., p. 254.
34  Babwani (2012).
35  Davis (2012, p. 256).
36  Ibid.
37  Ibid.
38  Ibid., p. 257.
39  Paralympic.org (n.d.).
40  Mickle, Tripp (2012, p. 1).
41  Bulik (2012).
42  Kwang (2012).
43  Bean, Susan (2012).
44  Mann (2012).

## REFERENCES

'Ads that caught our eye' (2005), *Sports Business Journal*, 26 December 2005, accessed 31 August 2012 at http://www.sportsbusinessdaily.com/Journal/Issues/2005/12/20051226/The-Year-In-Sports-Business-2005/Ads-That-Caught-Our-Eye.aspx?hl=godaddy&sc=0.

Ansoff, H.I. (1957), 'Strategies for diversification', *Harvard Business Review*, **35**(2), 113–24.

Babwani, Sakina (2012), 'London 2012 Olympics: Visa account holders contribute $1.4 billion to UK's tourism economy', *Economic Times*, 13 August 2012, accessed 31 August 2012 at http://articles.economictimes.indiatimes.com/2012-08 13/news/33182612_1_visa-accounts-visa-europe-payment-innovations.

Bean, Susan (2012), 'The competitiveness of Olympic advertising', PRWeekUS.com, 3 August 2012, accessed 31 August 2012 at http://www.prweekus.com/the-competitiveness-of-olympic-advertising/article/253231/.

Best, R.J. (2005), *Market-based Management: Strategies for Growing Customer Value and Profitability*, Upper Saddle River, NJ: Pearson Education, pp. 72–3.

Bowley, Graham and John Sullivan (2008), 'Officials expect Olympic torch to continue on route', *New York Times*, 9 April 2008, accessed 3 May 2011 at http://www.nytimes.com/2008/04/09/world/09torch.html.

Bulik, Beth Snyder (2012), 'Visa's "social-by-design" effort makes its debut on global stage', AdAge.com, 28 May 2012, accessed 31 August 2012 at http://adage.com/article/cmo-interviews/visa-s-social-design-effort-makes-debut-global-stage/234985/.

'Censorship' (2005), GoDaddy.com, accessed 31 August 2012 at http://videos.godaddy.com/super-bowl-commercials.aspx. Video.

Christopher, Craig (2012), 'Tour De France. The unfair consequences of cycling's doping scandals', BleacherReport, 17 June 2012, accessed 23 June 2012 at http://bleacherreport.com/articles/1224827-tour-de-france-the-unfair-consequences-of-cyclings-doping-scandals.

'Danica Patrick' (n.d.), GoDaddy.com, accessed 31 August 2012 at http://videos.godaddy.com/danica-media.aspx.

Davis, John A. (2005), *Magic Numbers for Consumer Marketing*, New York: John Wiley & Sons, pp. 167–8.

Davis, John A. (2010), *Competitive Success – How Branding Adds Value*, New York: John Wiley & Sons, pp. 83–6.

Davis, John A. (2012), *The Olympic Games Effect – How Sports Marketing Builds Strong Brands*, New York: John Wiley & Sons, p. 255.

Davis, John A. (2013), *Measuring Marketing – 110+ Key Metrics Every Marketer Needs*, Singapore: John Wiley & Sons, pp. 34–6.

Farris, Paul W., Neil T. Bendle, Phillip E. Pfeifer and David J. Reibstein (2006), *Marketing Metrics: 50+ Metrics Every Executive Should Master*, Upper Saddle River, NJ: Pearson Education.

Foster, David and Victoria Chang (2003), 'Visa sponsorship marketing', Harvard Business Publishing, Stanford University Graduate School of Business, Case: SPM-5.

'General information' (n.d.), Manchester United.com, accessed 11 June 2011 at http://www.manutd.com/en/Club/FAQs/One-United-Membership.aspx.

'GoDaddy' (2012), Fortune.com, 6 February 2012, accessed 31 August 2012 at http://money.cnn.com/magazines/fortune/best-companies/2012/snapshots/93.html.

Harte-Hanks Research & Analytics (n.d.), 'Market segmentation/share of wallet: understanding the characteristics of high-potential customers', accessed 16 May 2013 at http://www.scribd.com/doc/102640761/Share-of-Wallet-Case-Study.

'History of Visa' (n.d.), Visa.com, accessed 31 August 2012 at http://corporate.visa.com/about-visa/our-business/history-of-visa.shtml.

Hughes, Robert (2012), 'As Euro 2012 nears, troubling issues surface', *New York Times*, 29 May 2012, accessed 30 May 2012 at http://www.nytimes.com/2012/05/30/sports/soccer/30iht-soccer30.html.

Kotler, P., M.L. Siew, H.A. Swee and C.T. Tan (2010), *Marketing Management: An Asian Perspective*, Upper Saddle River, NJ: Prentice Hall, p. 137.

Kwang, Kevin (2012), 'Olympics bring gold for web advertisers', ZDnet.com, 15 August 2012, accessed 31 August 2012 at http://www.zdnet.com/olympics-bring-gold-for-web-advertisers-7000002644/.

Love, Tom (2010), 'GoDaddy announce College Bowl sponsorship', SportsProMedia.com, 19 October 2010, accessed 31 August 2012 at http://www.sportspromedia.com/news/godaddy_announce_college_bowl_sponsorship/.

Mail Today Reporter (2012), 'India ups Dow heat on International Olympic Committee', MailOnlineIndia, 27 January 2012, accessed 3 May 2011 at http://www.dailymail.co.uk/indiahome/indianews/article-2093012/India-ups-Dow-heat-International-Olympic-Committee.html.

Mann, Juliet (2012), 'Chasing the gold dust of "Brand Olympics"', CNN.com, 27 July 2012, accessed 31 August 2012 at http://edition.cnn.com/2012/07/26/business/business-olympics-brand/index.html.

Mickle, Tripp (2010), '25 years ago, IOC's TOP teetered, then thrived', *Sports Business Journal*, 21 June 2010, accessed 31 August 2012 at http://www.sportsbusinessdaily.com/Journal/Issues/2010/06/20100621/This-Weeks-News/25-Years-Ago-Iocs-TOP-Teetered-Then-Thrived.aspx?hl=visa%20olympic&sc=0.

Mickle, Tripp (2012), 'Visa goes for gold', *Sports Business Journal*, 23 July 2012, 1.

'Nike's new labor practices' (1998), *The New York Times*, 18 May 1998, accessed 11 June 2011 at http://www.nytimes.com/1998/05/18/opinion/nike-s-new-labor-practices.html.

Paralympic.org (n.d.), 'About', International Paralympic Committee, accessed 31 August 2012 at http://www.paralympic.org/Athletes/Halloffame.

Reibstein, D. and R. Srivastava (2004), 'Metrics for linking marketing to financial performance', working paper submitted to Marketing Science Institute, 19 October 2004, pp. 8–9.

Vance, Ashlee (2012), 'The challenge of classing up GoDaddy', BloombergBusinessweek.com, 24 May 2012, accessed 31 August 2012 at http://www.businessweek.com/articles/2012-05-24/the-challenge-of-classing-up-go-daddy#p1.

'Visa and the Olympic Games Fact Sheet' (2012), Visa.com, accessed 31 August 2012 at http://corporate.visa.com/newsroom/media-kits/olympic.shtml#sponsor.

Weiss, Allen (2005), 'What are your customers really worth?', Marketingprofs.com, 25 January 2005, accessed 17 July 2011 at http://www.marketingprofs.com/5/weiss7.asp.

# 7

# Sports marketing strategy and activation planning

 **CHAPTER OVERVIEW**

> To this point we have said that creating value is one of the key outcomes resulting from sports marketing activities. Creating value concerns how companies add value for stakeholders (employees, customers, suppliers etc.). In this respect, value creation is a by-product of the contribution and impact the organization hopes to achieve from its sports marketing efforts. To create value entails having the right combination of competencies and skills internally. In this chapter we will expand on the idea of creating value by focusing the sports marketing planning efforts on understanding the company's long-term objectives, described as *destiny* in Chapter 2 and continued in depth here; and the qualities that make the company unique, described as *distinction* in Chapter 2, and explored here in greater detail. To create value a company must have a clear picture in mind for how its sports marketing activities will foster sustained benefits over time.

## 7.1 Contribution and impact

Contribution and impact describes how the organization intends to advance its interests and positively affect customers and even society at large over time. The following questions will help sports marketers focus on how their plans will contribute to the growth and success of the organization:

1  *What advances does the organization hope to introduce through its sports marketing activities?*

Not every sports marketing-related action needs to be linked to a new advancement in products or services. But it is incumbent on organizations to consider how they are going to use sports marketing activities to position themselves as unique, and worthy of the public's attention, and the launch of new offerings are one way to do this. At the 2012 London Olympics,

Samsung and Visa partnered to offer a new mobile payment services plat-form. Since both companies are TOP (The Olympic Partners) sponsors, the highest sponsorship category for the Olympics, their collaboration enabled them to reach an enormous global audience, demonstrate their ability to work together, and introduce a useful new product associated with the world's most recognized and prestigious sports event.

2   *Will the sports marketing efforts open up new business opportunities?*

As we saw in Chapter 5, the Ansoff matrix helps marketers identify growth opportunities. In the context of sports marketing, these opportunities can be in the form of new products, as discussed in question 1 above, and/or new markets. Arguably, whenever a sports event occurs, whether it is a game that is part of the regular season schedule or is an end of season championship like the National Football League's Super Bowl, the potential to reach new customers increases for any organization using that event to market them-selves. Certainly the end of season contests attract the largest audiences, attracting a much wide range of customer segments than during the season, including 'fair weather fans' who watch because the event brings together the top competitors in the sport. A marketer that markets during the National Football League's (NFL's) Super Bowl, Major League Baseball's MLB's) World Series, FIFA World Cup, or the Olympic Games is paying a premium with the expectation that the additional cost is more than offset by appealing to a larger audience that ultimately purchases the company's products.

3   *Does the advancement enrich customers' lives? Reduce anxiety or stress? Extend enjoyment?*

The ubiquitous beer advertising around the world in almost every major sports league cannot easily be defended as selling product advancements that enrich people's lives. But beer advertising does attempt to link sports and beer with being social and having a good time. Sony, as one of the main spon-sors of the FIFA World Cup, launched a new 3D viewing experience for the 2010 FIFA World Cup in South Africa. The company had seven pairs of 3D cameras filming 25 of the World Cup matches, which were then broadcast to 3D channels worldwide. At the same time, Sony introduced new 3D TVs, and the combined 3D effort was intended to enhance the viewing experience.[1]

4   *What problem(s) or opportunities is the company addressing?*

As a TOP sponsor, Coca-Cola has used the Olympics to raise awareness about the company's work in corporate social responsibility. To illustrate, the rise of public concern about sustainability and environmental issues has placed intense scrutiny on the business practices of most companies, particularly those with a significant global presence. Challenged by Greenpeace in the early 2000s, Coca-Cola committed to using its Olympic sponsorship to demonstrate its increased work in green business practices. All equipment used on behalf of its Olympic sponsorship at the 2006 Winter Olympics in Turin was HFC (hydrofluorocarbon) free.[2] The company then launched a new line of HFC-free vending machines at the 2010 Winter Olympics in Vancouver,[3] in conjunction with VANOC's (Vancouver Olympic Committee's) vision for having a green Games. Coca-Cola also announced a public commitment to convert 100 percent of its vending machines around the world to HFC-free technology by 2015. The Olympics provide one of the largest media platforms in the world, let alone sports, accentuating Coca-Cola's commitment and also cleverly associating the company with the Olympics' recognized reputation as a high-integrity event.

## 5 How will competitors respond?

No sensible company pursuing growth will simply ignore competitor actions. Attempts to increase market share will undoubtedly provoke competitors to react both to protect their interests and reposition their products more favorably. When marketers use sports as a platform for promoting their company's offerings the opportunity exists to change, improve and/or enhance their market position at the expense of the competition. Marketers must be cognizant of this and prepare for competitor responses, even though they remain busy implementing their own plans. This is not to suggest that marketers must pay more attention to competitors than to customers or overall market conditions, but it is to suggest that almost any programs implemented to stimulate growth must include contingency plans to minimize competitor responses. In 2012, Merrell, a Michigan-based maker of outdoor footwear and apparel, was sued by adidas for introducing a shoe called the 'Glove' with an exoskeleton design that adidas claims infringed on its three-stripe mark.[4] Merrell has been making outdoor footwear since its founding in 1981 and has established itself as a high-quality brand in the outdoor footwear market. Adidas was founded in 1949 and has grown into the world's second largest athletic shoe brand behind Nike. The outcome of the lawsuit was not known at the time of this research, but the issue relates to whether Merrell's design (irrespective of intent) might confuse consumers.

As companies weigh their sports marketing choices marketers will need to carefully evaluate the closeness of fit between their company and the sports entity being sponsored. In Chapter 2 we introduced the brand planning framework of *destiny, distinction, culture,* and *experiences.* Destiny and distinction play a particularly important role early on in the planning process when evaluating the fit between the company and the sports entity being sponsored, both of which we will now discuss in depth.

## 7.2    Destiny

Destiny describes management's aspirations for the future of the brand – often a very distant and almost unreachable future, but also one that drives strategy and inspires employees. Management's efforts to articulate the company's destiny acts as a type of guidance over strategic decisions and the company's long-term direction. There are four parts to understanding a company's destiny and the destiny of a sports property as well: *ultimate dream; values; creating value;* and *personality.*

### Ultimate dream

The ultimate dream describes the long-term ambition for the organization. This is not a mere mission statement, but a much more far-reaching statement of purpose that serves to both guide and inspire the organization for years, if not generations of future employees and related stakeholders. As marketers plan the activation of their sports marketing activities, they need to pay heed to how these activities will advance their company toward the ultimate dream. It is tempting to think only short term, and thereby how to increase sales with a burst of excitement. But the challenge is how to sustain that excitement over time. Long-term gain is the marketer's real goal. Coca-Cola has worked for decades to be more than a carbonated beverage company. The company's management wants its many different brands (far more than just cola products) to be a regular part of everyone's lifestyle. The company has been an Olympic sponsor since 1928, one of the longest continuous marketing relationships in the world. In addition, Coca-Cola has been a sponsor of the FIFA World Cup since 1974, NBA (National Basketball Association) since 1985, NASCAR (National Association for Stock Car Auto Racing) since 1998, and the NCAA (National Collegiate Athletic Association) since 2002.[5] Each of these sports sponsorships not only broadly associates the company with several of the world's leading sports organizations, but specifically facilitates the sale of Coca-Cola's wide range of products at sports venues around each of these sports properties. Each of these sports entities are followed by loyal fans whose love of that sport is deep and often longlasting. The sport is part of their lives and, as such, Coca-Cola (the company overall and not just their cola beverages) becomes part of the fan's lifestyle.

The following questions will help sports marketers gain important insight into their organization's ultimate dream:[6]

1. Why does the company exist?
2. Can you identify and describe the company's aspirations for the future?
3. What is management's view of the world?
4. What is the company resolved to accomplish?
5. Is there a collective will to succeed?
6. What is the firm's direction for the next few years?
7. Is it obvious to employees why the destiny is important to the success of the company?
8. Does the company encourage collaborative work to achieve its destiny?
9. Is the firm's destiny practical and viable given the competitive environment?
10. Is the firm's destiny clearly understood internally? Can it be easily described to others?

Marketers need to evaluate similar questions regarding the sports entity:

1. How or why was the sports entity started?
   a Who were the founders?
   b What inspired the original property?
   c What types of athletes competed?
2. What is the guiding philosophy of the sports entity?
   a What is the entity's ultimate ambition (i.e., biggest, best etc.)?
   b What does it stand for (i.e., sportsmanship, teamwork etc.)?
3. What are the objectives of the sports entity?
   a What communities does it attract (i.e., local, regional, national, global?)
   b What are its general aims (i.e., raise money, increase awareness, attract volunteers etc.)?
   c Is it for-profit or not-for-profit? How does this affect your decision?
   d Does it benefit a cause (i.e., disease, social/political or economic problems etc.)?
4. What are the sports entity's social connotations?
   a How is it perceived (i.e., positive, controversial, innovative etc.)?
   b Does the event enjoy status appeal?

## Values[7]

Most organizations have a set of values intended to inspire people internally while explaining to the outside world the standards that are important to the company's long-term success. To be taken seriously, organizations must do more than list values on their website; they must live by their values, demonstrated by their actions, otherwise the organization will be viewed as disingenuous and, ultimately, untrustworthy. When planning sports marketing activities, an important consideration is determining how to align the values of the marketer's organization with those of the sports entity being sponsored. Alignment does not mean artificially forcing one organization's views onto another. Nor does it mean that a perfect, word for word alignment must exist for the sports marketing relationship to be seen as genuine. Instead, alignment refers to two or more organizations in a sports marketing relationship having a relatively similar set of standards. Fortunately, most values tend to have universal qualities that appeal across countries and social groups (for example, integrity, honesty, care for others, and sustainability), so identifying each organization's values is reasonably easy to do. The harder part is determining whether the organizations are genuine in their commitment to those values. However, we will assume that most are indeed sincere in honoring their values statements and are therefore trying to find sports marketing opportunities that simply seem to be a good fit and that are consistent with the public's image of each organization.

The Emirates Group, which includes Emirates Airlines, has been involved in sports marketing since 1987, embracing those sports events that share values similar to those of Emirates. The company values are based on *responsibility* and *community initiatives*. In terms of responsibility, Emirates views business ethics as paramount to its ongoing growth and success. Within responsibility, the company stresses taking great care of its employees by providing generous compensation and benefits and a work environment that encourages employees to take care of each other in the same way they would wish to be treated as customers. Additionally, the company focuses on air travel in the most modern, fuel-efficient aircraft in the industry, reducing the environmental impact as compared to most rival carriers. With respect to community initiatives, Emirates concentrates on healthcare and education for the world's most disadvantaged youth.

Emirates Group sponsors a variety of sports and cultural events that are arguably aligned with their own corporate values, including:

- football (soccer);
- rugby;
- tennis;
- horse racing;
- golf;
- cricket;
- sailing;
- Australian Rules football;
- arts and culture.

Within each of these events Emirates is a partner with numerous clubs and events. Of course, a vital part of Emirates' sponsorship strategy is associating the company with those events whose audiences and fans are most in line with the company's target customers. Companies support sponsorships because of the association benefits, and as a way to demonstrate their commitment to the same issues valued by their target audience. With sports and culture/arts events as important vehicles for sharing Emirates' values and its services, the company has been able to build a consistent image over the decades of an organization that is deeply involved in the communities it serves.[8] The questions below will help marketers identify and align their organization's values with those of the sports entities being considered:[9]

1.  Can you identify and describe the organization's values?
2.  What evidence exists that these values are deeply embedded, or not, in the culture?
3.  Does the CEO and senior management espouse the values directly?
4.  Are senior management perceived as credible advocates of the values?
5.  Are the organization's practices transparent?
6.  Does the organization have a strong values-based reputation?
7.  Which values are most important in aligning with the proposed sports properties? Why? Will the fit be perceived as forced, or natural?

These next questions will help the marketer conduct a similar values review of the proposed sports entity:

1.  What values best represent this entity (i.e., virtue, purity, honor, integrity etc.)?
    a   Who associated with this entity, past or present, embodies these values (i.e., athletes, fans, community leaders)?
2.  Are the sports entity's values widely known?
    a   Who communicates the values?
    b   How are the values communicated?
3.  Are the values an authentic, genuine reflection of the entity's leaders and their behaviors?
    a   What are the backgrounds of the current and historical leaders and organizers of the sports property?
    b   Do the leaders live the values themselves in their other work?
4.  Does the sports property consistently uphold its values through its practices (communication, partnership with suppliers/sponsors, reputation with the market etc.)?
    a   Are the entity's communications consistent with its image and history?

b   Do the various stakeholders associated with the sports entity uphold the same values? If not, are there any stakeholders whose association might be negative or controversial?

## Creating value[10]

Creating value refers to the organization's efforts to offer goods and services that enhance the lives of their customers. In a narrow sense, creating value can describe products. More broadly, creating value means the company is focused on improving the lives of all stakeholders and society at large. As one considers the myriad of leading companies that use sports marketing, it is hard to imagine any whose offerings do not create value in one way or another. Top companies rarely emerge based on luck. Indeed, their success is the result of trial and error, and learning from errors, which results in continuous improvement and an ongoing effort to enhance the value users derive while also improving the financial performance of the company.

Hero MotoCorp is an automotive company in India that is the team sponsor of the Mumbai Indians, one of nine Indian Premier League (IPL) Twenty20 cricket clubs. The three-year sponsorship deal commenced in 2011 and is valued at approximately $5 million per year.[11] The Mumbai Indians were the Twenty20 winners of the IPL Champions league (the IPL is a new league launched in 2008 and has quickly grown into one of the richest sports leagues anywhere). The team is located in a major business and tourism center for India and, perhaps even more importantly, they have Sachin Tendulkar, one of the all-time great players and a recognized superstar in cricket (Test and Twenty20). The Mumbai Indians play an exciting brand of cricket that has created deep fan loyalty and offered a unique combination of sports and entertainment, with the largest fan base (2.5 million Facebook fans as well) in the IPL. Part of the team's entertainment appeal is due to its location in the Indian capital of music and movies, with the club's matches punctuated by the periodic playing of Bollywood songs.[12] Hero MotoCorp is the Indian market leader of two and three-wheeled vehicles with 56 percent market share[13] and was involved as an IPL sponsor from the league's inception. The IPL has emerged as one of the great sports events for Indian cricket fans and has attracted many of the sport's leading players from teams around the world, due mostly to a creative blend of high-quality play and an irreverent use of Bollywood entertainment, creating unique value for fans. The following questions are designed to help marketers understand how their organization creates value:[14]

1.  What type of sports entity would provide credibility consistent with how the company creates value?

2. How will the company extend its success to other markets?
3. Where will the impact be noticed? Internally? In the market?
4. How can the sports marketing efforts affect market share?
5. Can the firm support rapid growth if the impact is strong?
6. Will the effect on financials be small or large?
7. Evaluate the firm's abilities, on a 1 to 5 scale (1 = poor, 5 = excellent) in its ability to: *create, compete, control,* and *collaborate.*

Here are corresponding questions marketers need to consider about the proposed sports marketing opportunity:

1. How does the sports property create value (financial, community support, benefit a cause, market exposure, sport reputation enhancement etc.)?
   a   What are its revenue sources?
   b   What are the specific ways the entity actually benefits its stated cause (i.e., how are the proceeds spent, is there transparency in the use of proceeds, does the event attract media attention that thereby attracts donors etc.)?
2. Who have been the past winners and/or notable competitors?
   a   Are these athletes well known?
   b   What are their reputations?
   c   Have any of the previous competitors achieved distinction outside this event?
3. Does the sports entity have ongoing awareness? If so, what type?
   a   Does it enjoy top of mind awareness recall (the first sports entity that comes to mind when a person is asked) or dominant awareness recall (the only entity recalled)?
   b   Is the awareness recognition based (meaning that a person has to be prompted before the sports properly comes to mind)?
4. Is this awareness positive or negative?
   a   If positive, are the associations with this sports entity likely to directly or indirectly benefit your company?
   b   If negative, are the associations likely to harm your company's reputation (i.e., scandals, controversies etc.)?

## Personality[15]

A company's personality is evidenced by its distinctive character. Every company has a personality, but the marketer's challenge is to make it compelling and relevant to the marketplace. Cultivating an identifiable personality is an ongoing exercise in delivering what the market expects, if not more. If the company is seen as innovative, creative, and cool, as Apple is, then our expectations are that Apple will continue to be that way. Since the death of Steve Jobs in 2011, many expect the personality and character of the company to change over time, which is likely since its most identifiable brand champion is no longer around to guide. At the same time, if a company has invested in cultivating a strong personality, then arguably its corporate DNA is deeply embedded with its uniquely identifiable characteristics and reflected by the continued activities and behaviors of its many employees and leaders. P&G (Procter & Gamble) has been around for more than 160 years, but mostly known as the parent company overseeing a house of brands. Since the company became an Olympic TOP sponsor in 2010 it has begun developing a corporate personality around its care and concern for moms. This effort came to life in the months leading up to and then during the London 2012 Olympic Games, represented by its 'Thank You Mom' campaign that shows images of Olympic moms, and even non-Olympic moms, as the behind the scenes reasons why their kids succeed. The campaign is enabling a repositioning P&G from being a behind-the-scenes corporate parent to a leading supporter of the needs of moms everywhere, using many of the company's iconic brands. Interestingly, prior to this campaign, many people did not know which specific world-renowned brands P&G owns, so the 'Thank You Mom' message is connecting the company and its brands for the first time to many audiences around the world. Detailed studies of the 'Thank You Mom' campaign have not been completed, but one can imagine a strong and positive emotional connection being made between the company and consumers around the world.[16] There are five traits that help bring a company's personality to life:

## Actions

Companies, like people, become known by their actions and associated qualities. Mercedes Benz is a company whose every product and accompanying advertising reinforces a sense of class and sophistication. The company's sports marketing activities are centered around golf, where they now sponsor three of the four majors, and auto racing, where they sponsor or co-sponsor three of the 12 F1 racing teams. Every action the company takes consistently supports the company's overall image of respectability.

## Intellect

IBM has a reputation for nurturing *thinking* leaders inside its company, and its corporate image leans toward being thoughtful, even cerebral. IBM sponsors the Masters Golf Tournament, one of golf's four majors and a tournament known for requiring the very best mental game from the sport's top players.[17]

GE (General Electric) has long been recognized as superb in developing talented leaders who move into important CEO positions either with GE or other leading companies. As a TOP sponsor for the Olympics, GE is aligning its corporate reputation for talent development with the known qualities Olympic athletes have, including dedication, overcoming challenges, competing to improve and best the opponents, and similar characteristics associated with developing top performers.[18]

### Emotions

A company's emotional qualities are usually captured best by affective messages designed to tug at the audience's heartstrings. These messages can be effectively conveyed using vivid images, evocative language, and colorful storytelling. Sports teams around the world highlight excitement, energy, and competitive rivalry to stoke fan enthusiasm, and companies that sponsor teams or leagues are doing so to tap directly into fan emotions, hoping to connect their company to those same, deeply stirring feelings.

### Instincts

Instinct refers to an organization's ability to anticipate possible future events, and even attempt to persuade target audiences that the company's description of the future is the one they, as possible customers, ought to embrace. This subtle, or perhaps not so subtle, effort to cajole large segments of the market is a pivotal aspect of marketing, and sports marketing can serve as a particularly useful approach for persuading consumers. Instinct can confirm the market's own assumptions and, if proven true, affirms the company's role in accurately anticipating the eventual outcome. Puma is a sponsor of Jamaican sprinter Usain Bolt, whose exciting performances in three sprint events at the 2008 Beijing Olympics (100 m, 20 m, 4 x 100 m relay) resulted in three gold medals. He then repeated this performance at the 2012 London Olympics, becoming the first 'triple double' sprinter (three gold medals in the same three events during back to back Olympics). Puma is a far smaller competitor compared to rivals Nike and adidas, but its disproportionate support of Usain Bolt (relative to other athletes it sponsors) has helped the company appear prescient, even implying that its products are a key reason for Bolt's success.[19]

### Authenticity

In the social media and digitally connected world of the twenty-first century, consumers are increasingly skeptical of an organization's claims, preferring to listen to those in their social networks to get honest information. Authenticity refers to the business practices undertaken by an organization that reflect known qualities and values, affirming the core identity as perceived by the marketplace. Carlsberg is one of Europe's leading beers, with a tradition dating back to 1847. For several decades the company has used the tagline 'Probably the Best Beer in the World', suggesting humility (versus brashness). Carlsberg has been an active sponsor of FIFA World Cup, UEFA (Union of European Football Associations), and European football clubs, connecting the company to the sport's passionate fans supporting some of the most storied sports clubs in the world competing in a sport with deep and rich traditions.[20]

Authenticity, or more precisely the lack of it, can also harm an organization's reputation. The XFL (Extreme Football League) in the USA is a classic example. Lasting less than a year, the sport promised hard-hitting, extreme football and fan excitement, even mixing in raw and sometimes crude entertainment during timeouts as a means of increasing fan interest. The league witnessed strong support during its first week and then watched as fan interest declined precipitously every week thereafter, leading just a few months later to the league (co-founded by WWE [World Wrestling Entertainment] founder Vince McMahon and NBC) disbanding. The reason was plain enough: in its early promotions the XFL promised 'smash mouth' football of the highest quality. Unfortunately, as fans witnessed, the caliber of the players and consequently, the quality of the games, was decidedly mixed, even poor. The XFL's promises of superb, exciting football were quickly perceived as false claims and the league gained a quick reputation for being inauthentic.[21]

A company's personality should not be mistaken for a superficial exercise in creating false impressions just for the sake of creating interest. Customers will quickly be able to distinguish fakery from authenticity. Marketers need to assess their company's personality so that any marketing communications, sports or non-sports, is seen as genuine and credible. At the same time, while personality is an influential consideration when considering sports marketing activities, it may not always be a deciding factor, as the dozens of sponsors of EPL (English Premier League), NBA, NFL, F1 and other major sports events show. Not every sponsor pays attention to whether the personality of their company is consistent with that of the sports entity. Furthermore, the absence of a clear personality match between the company and the sports entity does not mean the sponsorship should be avoided. In such circumstances marketers will need to decide if the sports property reaches the right audience and represents the overall values their company supports. These questions will help marketers more clearly identify their company's personality:[22]

1. Can you describe the company's personality? What evidence do you have that supports this?
2. Is it distinctive? To employees? To customers? To other stakeholders?
3. List the traits associated with each sub-component (actual traits, not wishful thinking etc.): *actions, intellect, emotions, instincts, authenticity*.
4. Are these traits consistent with perceptions in the public and internally?
5. Are the traits positive? Negative? How would the sports marketing efforts change or improve negative ones?

As before, here are corresponding questions in assessing the sports entity's personality:

1. What are the most common associations with this sports entity historically?
2. How would you describe this sports property's personality (friendly, intense, elitist, accessible, competitive, casual, quirky, predictable etc.)?
3. Do the entity's stakeholders (athletes, sponsors, suppliers, fans) share similar personality characteristics

## 7.3    Distinction

Chapter 2 introduced the concept of *distinction*, noting that *true* distinction is substantive, involving meaningful product innovation along with marketing communications that skillfully present the company in a genuine and relevant way. If a company believes distinction can be achieved by sponsoring sports events, then the market must recognize that this distinction exists, and has not been invented for the convenience of a short-term sports marketing tactic. Furthermore, the company's distinctive position must also *resonate* with consumers, inspiring emotional connections that give the company and its offerings meaning and creating an attraction beyond the satisfaction of basic needs. There are four components of distinction: *heritage, context, goals,* and *positioning*.[23]

### Heritage[24]

Leadership in any company does not make decisions in a vacuum. Consideration is given to larger contextual factors that could influence the company's long-term growth prospects and are invariably part of any decision calculus. When marketers are weighing their sports marketing options, they are doing so in part based on their understanding of the company's *internal context*. Each organization has a unique set of customers, product lines, long-standing traditions and management practices that exert varying degrees of influence on the growth strategies being considered. Furthermore, effective decision-making almost invariably reflects a combination of historical precedent and current market conditions. This historical precedent, comprised of highly valued traditions and qualities unique to the firm, is the equivalent of each succeeding management's inheritance, and management has an obligation to honor reasonable traditions, particularly those that have enabled the firm to hone a distinctive reputation, since that reputation, born from years of experience launching products and services and delivering on customer expectations in the process, is integral to explaining the firm's competitive advantage. At the same time, being cognizant of their firm's heritage helps marketers make decisions consistent with the company's traditions, which makes gaining internal support easier and, ultimately, facilitates market growth since customers trust the company to do the things they have come to expect while also delighting them with product innovation and similar surprises that give customers more reasons to support the company. Sports marketing options must be viewed through the lens of the impact on the firm's heritage to judge whether it would enhance the perceived reputation of the firm, or result in contradictory or even negative perceptions. Heritage is comprised of three important sub-components: *uniqueness*; *precedents*; and *core competencies*.[25]

## Uniqueness

Many factors affect a company's distinction as perceived by the market. The marketer's job is to identify the brand's known reputation *in general* and the contributing factors (long-standing product reputation, consumer preference, analyst opinions, service expertise etc.), determine if the reputation can be improved and growth therefore positively impacted, and decide how a sports marketing investment will support and reinforce the firm's uniqueness.

## Precedents

As discussed earlier, management is responsible for both honoring the company's traditions while finding growth opportunities for the future. Companies are comprised of formal and informal decision-making processes. However, whether formal or informal, there is an internal understanding of *the way the company does business*, and this understanding informs and animates most of the internal dialogs in and between meetings. As marketers consider their sports marketing options, they must think about how and whether their ideas align with the company's decision-making precedents. Honoring the traditions of the past should not be construed as a reason for rigid and inflexible decision-making or as a rationale to avoid new approaches for raising the firm's profile. Instead, being respectful to the past is meant to suggest that the company consider marketing activities that are not in direct contradiction to the firm's known reputation. This is a delicate decision-making balance and as marketers consider their sports marketing activities they must also consider the known reputations of the sports entity and their own firm, respectively. Departure from past practice can often be strategically important and could set the firm up for a more promising future. In these instances the marketer must see the sports marketing options in the larger context of parallel activities the company is pursuing to change its fortunes for the better (new products, acquisitions, appealing to new markets, taking advantage of competitor mis-steps, new service approaches, technological changes etc.).

## Core competencies

Most companies seek a relatively common set of core competencies: respected service, quality products, customer relationships etc.). Distinction lies in how the company deploys the talents of its employees, which is usually linked to strategies that are intended to guide internal behaviors and, eventually, the introduction of profitable products that are perceived as truly distinctive and relevant to customers in the marketplace. Marketers are not always in a position to alter the mix of skills inside their companies, but to the extent that the company has developed a reputation for being special then the marketer has an opportunity to include these unique qualities in the marketing communications implemented in the market. Like an athlete's own personal back story, a company can and should harness its unique qualities to help customers gain a clearer sense of why they are different.

The following questions will assist marketers in their sports marketing planning:

1. What makes the company special?
2. What have been the company's historical decision-making tendencies?
3. What are the company's distinct core competencies that contribute to making the company special?

Adidas and FIFA World Cup share a long relationship around football (soccer), the world's most popular sport. Adidas has designed footwear, apparel, and ball products for football (soccer) for more than 60 years. The company's global soccer market share is estimated at 38 percent, with Nike close behind at 36 percent.[26] Adidas began its relationship with FIFA in 1970 and has been a key sponsor of the FIFA World Cup ever since. Additionally, adidas has used its sponsorship to launch new products.[27] The FIFA World Cup was first played in Uruguay in 1930 and has been played every four years since, with the exception of 1942 and 1946 due to World War II and its aftermath.[28] Adidas has respectable and long history as a premier athletic goods maker, demonstrating its commitment to the rich traditions of football. Both FIFA and adidas are unique, with significant historical legacies that are intertwined, and a set of core competencies developed over decades of investment in football.

## Context[29]

Sports marketing investments should not be approached as if they were a one-time promotion or as a way to derive association benefits for the sponsoring company based on a perceived alignment between the company and the sports entity if no such alignment actual exists in practice. While it may be understandable that a company would want to be associated with a sports property, like the Olympics, FIFA World Cup, or the IPL, success will be based on whether the public sees the sponsorship as consistent with both organizations' known reputations. In other words, hoping that sports marketing will help a wayward company build a new image is unrealistic unless there are legitimate efforts underway across the company to change the way it does business. Developing a distinctive reputation by using sports marketing activities as part of a larger overall set of business growth and development plans means management must make decisions based on the business conditions in which their company competes. Conversely, creating strategies while ignoring the larger competitive environment is an empty exercise, risking placing planning efforts at peril because important new opportunities, areas of legitimate differentiation, and the development of solutions that are relevant to the market will be missed. Sports marketing planning must examine the overall market situation to gauge how effective the company is and has been in developing a distinctive reputation.

One helpful framework for evaluating the market context is to use the PEST (Political, Economic, Socio-cultural, Technological) model used in marketing for understanding macroeconomic and environmental factors. Political factors include learning whether the government and its policies support or hinder business and sports growth. Economic factors include understanding business conditions, interest rates and exchange rates, since each will reveal insights into the potential for companies to grow and invest. Socio-cultural factors describe customs and traditions in the marketplace and any demographic trends that could impact business. Technological factors are those that indicate the level of technical infrastructure sophistication, R&D investments, local worker technical competencies and skillsets, and any bias for or against innovation. Important context questions for marketers to ask are:

1. Is the market growing, stagnating, or declining?
2. What are the competitors' strengths and weaknesses?
3. Are our company's products specialties or commodities relative to the competition? If it is on the commodity end, is it possible to recapture a specialty position?
4. What is the size of investment needed to make the sponsorship as successful as possible?
5. What demographic and similar market trends are taking place that may affect the company's business?
6. Are the cultural differences likely to inhibit, or enhance the company's growth prospects?
7. How important are sports in the lives of those in the target market?
8. Will the sports marketer be seen as an outsider (pretender) or an authentic contributor to the sport and local market?

As the questions indicate, the sports marketer's decision of where to invest can get complicated quickly. F1 is among the world's most watched and followed sports, particularly outside the United States (where auto racing fans prefer NASCAR). In 1968, the first sponsor appeared on an F1 car (Gold Leaf cigarettes). As of 2010 more than 140 companies were F1 sponsors, raising the question of whether the sponsorships were worth the investment for each of those companies, and for F1 as well. There are approximately 20 F1 races held each year in cities around the world, so the market context differs by location. However, the common contextual factor is the prestigious reputation of F1 racing and the fact that the races are held in diverse, exotic locales like Singapore, Monte Carlo, and São Paolo. Each of the 140+ sponsors understandably hopes their sponsorship investment will yield positive returns. The challenge is how to distinguish one's company when competing for attention with 140 other sponsors. This is not even about being perceived as a specialty. Instead, the concern is whether the company will be perceived *as anything* other than a logo on the side of a car traveling at 200 mph. In this regard marketers should consider if the competitive market is too crowded. Another issue is related to trends for the sports property. AT&T was the title sponsor of the AT&T Williams F1 racing team from 2007 to the end of 2011 at a reported cost of $7 million per year (those are the sponsorship rights fees and do not include activation costs). $7 million is a relatively afford-able investment in the world of F1 racing, where title sponsors of other F1 teams pay as much as $50 million). During AT&T's tenure as title sponsor the AT&T Williams racing team never won an F1 title, reducing the visibil-ity and press coverage of the Williams racing team, undoubtedly a factor in AT&T's decision not to renew its title sponsorship after 2011.[30]

## Goals[31]

Goals provide a sense of direction for sports marketing planning by describ-ing intended future results. It is most effective is to consider a sequence of goals: short term, medium term and long term:

- *Short term.* Less than one year, these are typically the most achievable. For sports marketers, first-year goals may be as simple as targeting an increase in market awareness about the company as a result of the sports sponsorship.
- *Medium term.* One to two years, these are transition goals intended to help the firm progress from the short term to long term. Continuing with the previous example, sports marketers would seek higher awareness levels and also set increases in revenues (for example).
- *Long term.* Two years or more; while two years may not seem long term, globalization and technology have combined to compact time frames. The pace of change in many businesses is simply too fast to allow for much long-term detailed planning beyond two to four years. Long-term goals include changes in: distribution; unit sales; market share; revenues; profits; brand preference; brand value.

Table 7.1 is designed to illustrate the sequence of goals in greater detail. Marketers will want their sports marketing goals to help facilitate proper organizational alignment, including implementation and timetable ramifica-tions that, in turn, will impact the specific sports marketing tactics chosen.

The following questions will help marketers in planning their goals:[32]

1. Are our goals realistic?
   a Short term?
   b Medium term?
   c Long term?
2. Do our goals match our brand development needs?
3. If we achieve the goals in three to five years, how will the brand have changed?

**Table 7.1** Sports marketing goals planning

| | Customers | Products | Marketing Communications | Financial |
|---|---|---|---|---|
| Short term (<1 year) | Research new customers<br>Identify new retail channel partners | Develop new product plans for current and new customers<br>Source materials and manufacturing<br>Produce sample products/demos<br>Test product | Develop communications brief<br>RFP (request for proposal) to 3–5 marketing agencies<br>Select agency of record<br>Test market creative ideas, including social media | Invest $X in R&D<br>Get senior management buy-in<br>Measure initial brand value with outside valuation firm |
| Medium-term (1–2 years) | Secure distribution with top 3–5 accounts in target market<br>Review progress in field sales | Plan production run of #X units<br>Review progress with production team and suppliers | Roll-out initial media blitz in target market<br>Adjust campaign based on response<br>Review progress with agency | X% revenues from new customers<br>Review progress with senior management |
| Long-term (>2 years) | Expand to new geographies and top 10–20 accounts<br>Review progress with field sales | Expand production by #X units with each product<br>Add 1–2 product extensions<br>Review progress with production team and suppliers | Adjust and expand media plan to new geographies<br>Review progress with agency | Increase market share by X%<br>Assess progress in brand value growth<br>Review progress with senior management |

Source: Davis (2010, p. 158).

## Positioning[33]

A strategic position is described as owning a unique and memorable place in the customer's mind. Part of the rationale for using sports marketing is to help companies improve their image and position in the market. The following questions are useful in evaluating positioning activities:

*Give the brand meaning*

1. Is the company's market differentiation understood internally throughout the entire organization?
2. Does the company's position serve as a source of inspiration?
3. Is the firm's value proposition clear?

*Inspire and strengthen the brand*

1. Does the company's differentiation clearly help focus attention on appropriate internal operating activities that are consistent with the meaning and personality of the company?
2. Does the company's position attract the kinds of external business partnerships needed to reinforce integrity and differentiation?
3. Is it clear how sports marketing activities will support and further develop the company's uniqueness?
   a What is the risk that improper marketing program choices might devalue or harm the company's position?

*Advance brand addition and protect growth*

1. Does the company's position suggest a clear set of dos and don'ts for growing the business?
2. Are the line and product category extensions achievable?
   a Are the extensions likely to be profitable?
   b Will the extensions block or hinder competitors?
   c If so, will the company's uniqueness remain, or is there risk of diluting its long-term image?

*Boost brand recognition*

1. Are the company's associated identities memorable?
   a Logos?
   b Slogans?
   c Imagery?

    d   Extended relationships (partners, suppliers etc.)?
2. Do they conjure positive or negative associations with customers?
3. Are the company's partners knowledgeable of its reputation?

*Brand worth and usefulness*

1. Does the company's position signal to value chain participants (suppliers, distribution partners, ad agencies, logistics providers) how they are expected to add value?
2. Is the company considered reputable and helpful to society?
3. Does the company's position clarify how sports marketing activities fit into the company's overall financial and growth goals?

## 7.4   Chapter summary

When developing their business plans, sports marketers have to consider a series of important questions that support the rationale for the sports marketing investment and will ultimately affect the choice of marketing tactics developed to maximize the association with the sports entity. A vital component in this planning is for the sports marketer to understand the factors that make their company unique and, similarly, the characteristics that make the sports entity unique. Analyzing the assets that make a company and a sports entity distinctive involves understanding four areas: the ultimate dream; values; creating value; and personality. Each of these helps sports marketers break down their marketing plans into clearly understood, detailed profiles of their organization and/or that of the sports entity. The analyses conducted will provide important insights about their own organization so that marketing tactics, such as advertising and related marketing communications, are consistent with the qualities that make the sports marketer's firm unique. This will also ensure that the association with the sports entity is perceived more authentically, and not contrived, which can further enhance the brand reputation of the company.

**CASE STUDY**

# Tsingtao Beer

In 2005, the Tsingtao Brewery Company needed a facelift. At that point, the company had seen some success. It was the oldest brewery in China, founded by German settlers in 1903.[34] By output, it was also the largest brewery in China and often emphasized this distinction. However, it struggled with its brand image. It was often described as 'getting old' and Tsingtao's CEO, Sun Mingbo, even described his company's own product as 'my dad's beer'.[35] Yanjing Brewing Company, a Beijing-based brewery, was the recommended beer of choice for most Chinese people. It was favored by 80 percent of people living in Beijing and positioned itself as the patriotic beer with its 'Toast for China' campaign.[36] In addition, Yanjing was served in all Olympic venues (hotels and athletic facilities) through its partnership with the Beijing Tourism Group.[37] Three years from that point, the country of China would be thrust onto the world's stage with the 2008 Olympic Games taking place in Beijing. Tsingtao saw this as the perfect opportunity to reposition its brand and turn the company into a global powerhouse.

On 11 August 2005, Tsingtao and the Beijing Organizing Committee for the Olympic Games (BOCOG) announced their partnership.[38] Tsingtao's efforts to become the dominant beer brand in China weren't going to be easy. Within the beer sponsorship category, BOCOG had also completed deals with Yanjing (one day prior to Tsingtao's deal) and Budweiser.[39] While Budweiser had obvious international brand awareness, Yanjing had a strong grasp on China. Moving forward, Tsingtao decided it would reach out to younger consumers. A strong emphasis was placed on Tsingtao's new tagline, 'Passion, Dreams and Success' as Tsingtao prepared to reposition itself on the Olympic stage. Tsingtao had some experience with sports sponsorship on the Chinese national level. In 2003, it began sponsoring the Xiamen International Marathon and added the Chinese Tennis Open in 2004.[40] However, it had never participated in any sports property as global as the Olympics.

To tackle this massive challenge, Tsingtao developed a four-year marketing plan to best prepare and execute its Olympic strategy. A bolder, younger strategy was employed to better connect with its new target demographic. In 2006, it kicked off the strategy with its 'Light the Passion' campaign. Key components of this strategy included sponsoring the Chinese delegation to the 2006 Torino Olympic Games, and an Olympic Caravan that toured China, visiting 36 cities, to create excitement and spread knowledge about the Olympic Games. In addition, Tsingtao joined Hunan TV in sponsoring a television show called 'Tsingtao Beer – I Am the Champion'.[41] The show emphasized a national fitness campaign in the spirit of the upcoming Olympic Games and was seen by millions of Chinese citizens.[42] Finally, Tsingtao sponsored CCTV's FIFA World Cup program 'Hero of the Ball,' which was complemented by special edition packaging in honor of the FIFA World Cup.

The following year, in 2007, Tsingtao's strategic theme was 'Spread the Passion'. It sponsored the Chinese diving team, one of the most successful teams of all sports in the

**CASE STUDY** *(continued)*

country, at the 2007 FINA World Diving Championships.[43] In addition, it sponsored a television show called *Qing-Guo-Qing-Cheng*. The show was designed to introduce China's cities to the world and featured popular business leaders, Chinese celebrities, city officials, and everyday citizens.[44] It was co-sponsored by the National Geographic Channel, the United Nations World Tourism Organization, and the United Nations Development Programme, thereby projecting Tsingtao onto a truly global stage.[45] It also continued its sponsorship of 'I Am the Champion' and the Olympic Caravan, but altered the locations it would attend.

During 2008, which was year three of its multi-year strategy, Tsingtao was driven by the theme 'Release the Passion'. First, it launched 'Global Collection of Olympic Passion', a program designed to serve as a collection of Olympic-spirited images and videos. It ramped up its Olympic Caravan presence, sending out 20 to reach 1000 towns. As an incentive for its distributors, it invited those top performers globally to join it in Beijing for the Olympics. 'I Am the Champion' continued, with winners getting the chance to attend an Olympics Victory banquet with the Chinese diving team. Its activations during the Olympics were felt all over the city of Beijing. In Beijing's Chaoyang Park, Tsingtao opened an Olympic Games Experience Center. The Center featured games, Olympic history, Tsingtao beer tasting, and live television broadcasts of the Olympic Games. It also set up 15 smaller cultural areas around Beijing that offered live television viewing of Olympic events. All of these activations invited both Chinese and foreign visitors the opportunity to experience the new brand. 2009 was the fourth and final year of Tsingtao's Beijing Olympic campaign and focused its efforts on transitioning to other sports sponsorships. As such, 'Interpret the Passion' was the chosen theme of the brewing company.

In total, Tsingtao spent approximately $58.31 million on its Beijing Olympic campaign. The company is adamant, however, that these investments paid off. Throughout its four-year campaign, Tsingtao saw its market share in China rise from 12.9 percent in 2006 to 13.4 percent in 2009.[46] Its brand value rose from $2.9 billion in 2005, to $3.7 billion in 2007, to $7.92 billion in 2011.[47] Perhaps most importantly to Tsingtao, after the Beijing Olympics, data showed that consumers willing to buy Tsingtao rose 74 percent, with young consumers accounting for 14 percent of that total.[48] Despite the completion of the Beijing Olympics, Tsingtao continues to participate in international sports sponsorship with good results. Tsingtao signed a partnership deal in 2011 with the Miami Heat that sent several members of Tsingtao's prestigious dance team, the Passion Dancers, to dance with the Miami Heat dancers, in effect mixing two of the most marketable dance teams in the world.[49] The Passion Dancers are chosen from a national search in China that draws over 100 000 aspirants and is the highest rated show on television in China.[50] In 2011, Tsingtao built China's first overseas factory in Thailand.[51] Tsingtao's sales continue to rise as a result of its expansion overseas. In 2011, Tsingtao sold more than 7 million kiloliters of beer, up from 5 million kiloliters in 2007.[52] That same year, their profits rose to over $278 million, up 14.3 percent from 2010.[53]

**CASE STUDY** *(continued)*

 **QUESTIONS**

1   Despite this impressive growth, Tsingtao still does not have the largest market share of breweries in China. What other ways could Tsingtao develop its reach?

2   Must the company continue to look outside Chinese borders? Or should it begin to focus more in China, where both a sports culture and beer drinking culture are growing?

3   Is penetration in the United States the only way to truly be an international success? If so, what ways can Tsingtao do better business in the United States?

**NOTES**

1   'FIFA and Sony to launch first ever global 3D experience of the FIFA World Cup™' (2010).
2   'Coke going to 100% HFC-free vending machines, coolers' (2009).
3   'Coca-Cola introduces HFC-free vending to the House of Representatives' (2010).
4   Martinez (2012).
5   'Sponsorships' (n.d.).
6   Davis (2010, pp. 140–42).
7   Ibid., pp. 131–5.
8   'Emirates sponsorships' (n.d.).
9   Davis (2010, p. 142).
10   Ibid., pp. 130–31.
11   Love (2011).
12   'Sachin Tendulkar' (n.d.).
13   Nathan (2012).
14   Davis (2010, p. 141).
15   Ibid., pp. 135–40.
16   Delo (2012).
17   Murphy (2011).
18   Lehmberg et al. (2009).
19   Badenhausen (2012).
20   Long (2012).
21   Lobdell (2012).
22   Davis (2010, p. 142).
23   Ibid., Chapter 6.
24   Ibid., pp. 149–52.
25   Ibid.
26   Bhattacharjee (2012).
27   'Marketing – adidas' (n.d.).
28   'History of FIFA – the first FIFA World Cup™' (n.d.).
29   Davis (2010, pp. 152–7).
30   'Sponsorship guide' (n.d.); Sherman (2012); 'Williams seeks new title sponsor' (2012).
31   Davis (2010, pp. 157–64).
32   Ibid., p. 162.
33   Ibid., pp. 164–6.
34   'History' (n.d.).
35   'Brand Olympics underway' (2008).

36  Ibid.
37  Ibid.
38  'Tsingtao Beer becomes sponsor of Beijing 2008 games' (2005).
39  'Brand Olympics underway' (2008).
40  'Cheers, China! Tsingtao gears up for "Beijing 2008"' (2008).
41  Ibid.
42  Ibid.
43  Ibid.
44  Ibid.
45  Ibid.
46  'Beer industry in China' (2010).
47  Jixin (2012).
48  Ibid.
49  'Heat inks deal with Tsingtao' (2011).
50  Ibid.
51  Jixin (2012).
52  Ibid. See also 'Brand Olympics underway' (2008).
53  Jixin (2012).

## REFERENCES

Badenhausen, Kurt (2010), 'How Usain Bolt earns $20 million a year', Forbes.com, 4 August 2012, accessed 5 August 2012 at http://www.forbes.com/sites/kurtbadenhausen/2012/08/04/how-usain-bolt-earns-20-million-a-year/.

'Beer industry in China' (2010), MyDeckerCapital.com, December 2010, accessed 1 September 2012 at http://www.mydeckercapital.com/research.asp.

Bhattacharjee, Nivedita (2012), 'Soccer stakes rise as Nike presses on Adidas' turf', Reuters, 8 June 2012, accessed 19 June 2012 at http://www.reuters.com/article/2012/06/08/us-nike-soccer-idUSBRE8571BD20120608.

'Brand Olympics underway' (2008), Bjinvest.com, August 2008, accessed 1 September 2012 at http://www.bjinvest.gov.cn/english/bn/200808/t266132.htm.

'Cheers, China! Tsingtao gears up for "Beijing 2008"' (2008), PRNewswire.com, 18 April 2008, accessed 1 September 2012 at http://www.prnewswire.com/news-releases/cheers-china----tsingtao-gears-up-for-beijing-2008-57458442.html.

'Coca-Cola introduces HFC-free vending to the House of Representatives' (2010), 28 April 2010, accessed 21 May 2013 at http://www.examiner.com/article/coca-cola-introduces-hfc-free-vending-to-senators-and-congressmen.

'Coke going to 100% HFC-free vending machines, coolers' (2009), Environmental Leader, 3 December 2009, accessed 11 March 2011 at http://www.environmentalleader.com/2009/12/03/coke-going-to-100-hfc-free-vending-machines-coolers/.

Davis, John A. (2010), *Competitive Success – How Branding Adds Value*, New York: John Wiley & Sons.

Delo, Cotton (2012), 'P&G marketing chief touts role of Facebook, Yahoo in 'Thank You, Mom' campaign', Advertising Age, 9 August 2012, accessed 11 August 2012 at http://adage.com/article/digital/p-g-s-pritchard-touts-digital-social-olympics-push/236590/.

'Emirates sponsorships' (n.d.), Emirates.com, accessed 23 July 2012 at http://www.emirates.com/english/about/emirates-sponsorships/sponsorships.aspx.

'FIFA and Sony to launch first ever global 3D experience of the FIFA World Cup(TM)' (2010), PRNewswire, 8 April 2010, accessed 3 November 2011 at http://www.prnewswire.com/news-releases/fifa-and-sony-to-launch-first-ever-global-3d-experience-of-the-fifa-world-cuptm-90201092.html.

'Heat inks deal with Tsingtao' (2011), NBA.com, 19 December 2011, accessed September 2012 at http://www.nba.com/heat/news/heat_inks_deal_with_tsingtao_111219.html.

'History' (n.d.), TsingtaoBeer.com, accessed 1 September 2012 at http://www.tsingtaobeer.com/tsingtao_history_puredraft.php.

'History of FIFA – the first FIFA World Cup™' (n.d.), FIFA.com, accessed 9 December at http://www.fifa.com/classicfootball/history/fifa/first-fifa-world-cup.html.

Jixin, Wang (2012), 'System force activating a hundred-year Tsingtao brewery', CNTV.cn, 14 June 2012, accessed 1 September 2012 at http://english.cntv.cn/special/AD/20120614/106546.shtml.

Lehmberg, Derek, Glenn Rowe, John R. Phillips and Roderick E. White (2009), 'General Electric: an outlier in CEO talent development', *Ivey Business Journal*, February 2009, accessed 1 May 2010 at http://www.iveybusinessjournal.com/topics/leadership/general-electric-an-outlier-in-ceo-talent-development#.UNObWYnjkeU.

Lobdell, Josh (2009), 'Why did the XFL fail?', Examiner.com, 10 October 2009, accessed 22 July 2012 at http://www.examiner.com/article/why-did-the-xfl-fail.

Long, Michael (2012), 'Carlsberg: a sponsor's review of Euro 2012', SportsPro, 9 July 2012, accessed 22 July 2012 at http://www.sportspromedia.com/notes_and_insights/carlsberg_a_review_of_euro_2012/.

Love, Tom (2011), 'Hero Honda switches $15m IPL sponsorship to Mumbai', 9 March 2011, accessed 21 May 2011 at http://www.sportspromedia.com/news/hero_honda_switches_us15m_ipl_sponsorship_to_mumbai/.

'Marketing – adidas' (n.d.), FIFA.com, accessed 23 February 2012 at http://www.fifa.com/aboutfifa/organisation/marketing/fifapartners/adidas.html.

Martinez, Shandra (2012), 'Adidas sues West Michigan competitor for allegedly ripping off "famous" three-stripe shoe design', MLive.com, 3 June 2012, accessed 17 June 2012 at http://www.mlive.com/business/west-michigan/index.ssf/2012/06/adidas_sues_west_michigan_comp.html.

Murphy, Richard McGill (2011), 'How do great companies groom talent?', Fortune.CNN, 3 November 2011, accessed 14 July 2012 at http://management.fortune.cnn.com/2011/11/03/top-companies-for-leaders/.

Nathan, Narendra (2012), 'Hero MotoCorp: company's stellar performance and growth make it an attractive stock', 30 January 2012, accessed 3 March 2012 at http://articles.economictimes.indiatimes.com/2012-01-30/news/31005802_1_export-growth-profit-growth-average-growth.

'Sachin Tendulkar' (n.d.), Indian Premier League.com, accessed 3 August 2012 at http://iplt20.com/teams/mumbai-indians/squad/97/Sachin-Tendulkar/.

Sherman, Freddy (2012), 'Williams Formula 1 team ends AT&T sponsorship deal: fan's view', 5 January 2012, accessed 1 February 2012 at http://news.yahoo.com/williams-formula-1-team-ends-t-sponsorship-deal-075300123.html.

'Sponsorship guide' (n.d.), BBC.com, accessed 23 May 2012 at http://news.bbc.co.uk/sport2/hi/motorsport/formula_one/sponsorship_guide/default.stm.

'Sponsorships' (n.d.), Coca-Cola, accessed 3 June 2011 at http://www.coca-cola.com/content-store/en_CY/pages/Sponsorships.html.

'Tsingtao Beer becomes sponsor of Beijing 2008 games' (2005), China.org.cn, 11 August 2005, accessed 1 September 2012 at http://www.china.org.cn/english/olympic/138617.htm.

'Williams seeks new title sponsor' (2012), ESPNF1 Staff, 4 January 2012, accessed 1 February 2012 at http://en.espnf1.com/williams/motorsport/story/67363.html.

# 8

# The sports marketing fusion

**CHAPTER OVERVIEW**

In this chapter we will focus on a concept called the *sports marketing fusion*, which describes how sports marketers seeking to use sports to communicate their company's offerings to the market must first consider five complements to the marketing mix (the 5 Ps) discussed in Chapter 1: prestige, performance, projection, power, and preference, and represented by Figure 8.1.

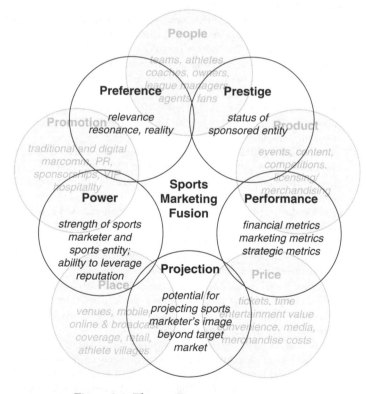

**Figure 8.1** The new Ps

The sports marketing fusion overlays the marketing mix to illustrate the interdependencies among all ten elements. The reason is that each of the fusion's five elements helps marketers assess how important a sports entity will be to their sports marketing activities and, ultimately, in enhancing their company's reputation and performance. We will now turn our attention to each of the sports marketing fusion elements. These are vital for marketers to understand and include in their strategic planning because they provide a clear sense of direction, focusing the marketer's planning on what they intend to gain from the sports marketing investment. In later chapters we will discuss the marketing tactics companies can employ to realize their strategic objectives.

## 8.1  Prestige

The status of the sponsored entity impacts the cost/value of that entity and the potential for the sports marketer to garner association benefits. Luxury brands, such as LVMH, Mercedes, Patek Philippe watches, and Four Seasons Hotels, are recognized by consumers as prestigious and, as a consequence, are able to command premium prices for their offerings. Similarly, luxury brands are perceived as higher quality, more reliable, and aspirational. Prestige suggests the entity has attained the highest levels of status and recognition by the marketplace and marketers covet being associated with prestige brands because the perceived benefits include an enhanced reputation for their company and its offerings.

Marketers generally make their planning decisions based on the potential for the marketing investment to yield positive returns, both financially and in terms of reputation. When considering a sports entity as worthy of a marketing investment, the entity's status as a 'gold plated' event is an important factor. There is no singular best ranking of the most *prestigious* sports entities. Rankings tend to be based more on numerical attributes, such as market size, financial success, market value, and the number of championships. The closest analog to prestige relates to measures of financial wealth, and even these are imperfect, and capturing only a narrow subset of characteristics often associated with prestige. In May 2012 *Forbes Magazine* rated the richest sporting events in the world as determined by reviewing the winner's prize money, but not the event's total prize money. Forbes also did not consider sports that do not have a season-ending play-off. The top ten richest sports events are:[1]

1.  UEFA Champions League (football [soccer]);
2.  UEFA European Football Championship (football [soccer]);

3. FIFA World Cup (football [soccer]);
4. Super Bowl (American football);
5. World Series (baseball);
6. FedEx Cup (golf);
7. Dubai World Cup Night (horse racing);
8. UEFA Europa League (football [soccer]);
9. World Series of Poker;
10. ICC Cricket World Cup.

Soccer has four of the top ten spots, indicative of the popularity of 'the beautiful game' outside of the United States. This list may be interesting and even surprising to review, but it should also provoke readers to ask what criteria are used to determine luxury/prestige/status. After all, if this list were expanded, where do many other acknowledged prestige events rank, such as The America's Cup, F1, horse racing's Triple Crown, golf's Four Majors, and tennis's Grand Slam? Furthermore, how should marketers determine a sports entity's level of prestige? This is a complicated question given that prestige is based on perceptions of quality and achievements. While luxury brands, and premium brands, are not perfect substitutes for prestige, there are luxury brand frameworks that can help marketers gain a deeper understanding of why a sports event is prestigious and, therefore, whether marketing dollars should be invested in it. In their 2009 article 'Aesthetics and Ephemerality: Observing and Preserving the Luxury Brand' for *California Management Review*, authors Pierre Berthon et al. present a useful set of criteria for assessing the qualities and characteristics of a luxury brand. The luxury brand criteria are:[2]

- *Functional*. This describes what the offering *does*. Mercedes is known for building superbly engineered luxury cars that also drive well. The Samsung Diamond League is a series of 14 annual track and field events, sanctioned by the IAAF (International Association of Athletics Federations). Athletes compete for points, with the end of season winner determined by the total number of points earned. Points are awarded based on finishing in the top three of each event. By its design, the Samsung Diamond League incentivizes track athletes to compete in each event, ensuring that fans will see the world's best each time.[3]
- *Experiential*. This refers to consumer tastes and the individual subjective appeal they find in an offering. Works of art are an example of experiential appeal. So, too, are fine wines. Arguably, the individual sports fan's interest in America's Cup sailing is partly based on their individual sense of status associated with this sport.[4]
- *Symbolic*. This describes the value as perceived by society overall. The

brands mentioned earlier in this section are each highly symbolic, almost universally recognized for their unique and distinctive offerings and elevated status. The Forbes list, while insufficient in representing a broader definition of prestige, provides one example of valuable sports entities with well-regarded reputations. The Olympic Games also have a well-known reputation as being an event that represents the very best in sports. Being an Olympian has significant meaning across cultures, describing the very best athletes in their respective sports. With teams from 205 countries and territories, the Olympics can convincingly argue that they truly attract the best athletes in the world and that the top performers really are the elite in their sports.[5]

Keep in mind that prestige does not have to relate only to large, global sports events; it can be specific to local markets where the event has important meaning for local citizens and can be a valuable sports marketing opportunity even though it is not globally recognized. The Beanpot Tournament in Boston each winter is an example of an event with a high degree of local prestige, or bragging rights, for the winner. Comprised of the hockey teams from four Boston area universities (Boston University, Boston College, Harvard University, Northeastern University), the Beanpot has been a fixture for Boston sports fans for 60 years. Boston sports fans have argued for years that this event would benefit from stronger sponsor support and national media coverage, but there is no question that within its local market, the Beanpot is an event filled with tradition and prestige.[6]

Another lens for viewing and assessing a sports event's prestige pertains to its status as a premium offering. Table 8.1 provides marketers with the characteristics premium, non-premium, and even non-competitive brands to determine if the sports entity has the premium qualities desired:

In Table 8.1 the vertical axis describes the sports marketer's point of view as it relates to their customers, their company's market position, and the company's performance characteristics. Let's look at some examples:

## Premium

Premium events are exclusive, special, and even limited. They are less frequent (i.e., league championships are once per year, the Olympics and FIFA World Cup are every four years etc.). Thus, the sports' championships, plus the acknowledged major events, discussed earlier are considered premium events. The sports marketer's customers are likely to perceive the event as prestigious, and attending the event, or even watching it on TV, confers a

**Table 8.1** Sports event reputation/image

|  |  | Premium | Non-premium |
|---|---|---|---|
| Prestige Criteria | Customer | Will the sports event appeal to the sports marketer's customer's sense of: social status (is it prestigious?); self-image (is it unique?) | Will the sports event appeal to the sports marketer's customer's: social community (is it inclusive?); practical interests (i.e., is it accessible?) |
|  | Company positioning | Can the sports event help the sports marketer develop a premium reputation? Does the sports event have an image of exclusivity? | Can the sports event help the sports marketer reaffirm quality; reinforce that their offerings are at least at parity with the competitions; remind the market that they exist and have interesting products? |
|  | Company performance | Is the sports marketer likely to see a performance gain: high margins; premium prices; increased credibility? | Is the sports marketer likely to see a performance gain: revenues; profits; market share; reduced costs? |

Source: Adapted from Davis (2010, p. 269).

bit of prestige on the customer as well. The event's reputation and market position could have association benefits for the sports marketer's company, known also as the halo effect (since the event's reputation casts a positive glow across those connected to it). Over time, if the company continues to use the event as a key part of its marketing, then the potential for improving financial performance also exists.

## Non-premium

A regular season game or contest in any league would be the equivalent of a non-premium event. While the teams competing may well be the premier, or elite teams of the league (a reputation typically resulting from years of consistent success), the individual game itself is one of dozens or even hundreds of games over the course of the season when all teams and their schedules are taken into account. Sports marketers will certainly benefit from sheer repetition if they sponsor a team for an entire season. EMC, the global IT and cloud storage company, has been a sponsor of the Boston Red Sox for many years. Its logo has been on player uniforms and the company also sponsors the EMC Club, an exclusive premium seating area and upscale restaurant in the team's famed Fenway Park stadium. The Boston Red Sox have been one of the elite teams in baseball for years, particularly since they won the World Series in 2004 and 2007. But the prestige from the end of season championships is saved only for that season's top teams, and most teams do not make it. As a result, the price and perceived differences from a regular season game and a season-ending championship are understandably significant.[7]

Aside from premier sports events, as the preceding section suggests, prestige is also associated with those sports entities that have had enduring success. Most sports have a few teams that have risen well above their competitors to have enjoyed success for years, even decades. They may not always be in the season-ending championships, but they are almost invariably among the top teams each year, often reaching the play-offs even if they don't play for the title. Among the most recognized sports entities that have garnered accolades for years are:

- New York Yankees: 27 World Series titles and 40 American League pennants;[8]
- Manchester United: 19 Premier League titles, 11 FA Cups, 4 League Cups, 19 FA Community Shields;[9]
- Real Madrid: 32 La Liga titles, 18 Copas del Rey titles, 9 Supercopas de España, 9 European/UEFA Champions League titles;[10]
- Ferrari F1: 16 Constructor's Championships and 15 Driver's Championships, plus 219 total race victories.[11]

It is worth noting that each of these sports organizations benefits from competitive imbalance in their respective leagues. In essence, as these teams continue to perform well, they reap significant financial gains that are then reinvested in making the club even stronger. The New York Yankees have the highest payroll in MLB, and have for years.[12] Major League Baseball does levy a luxury tax on teams that exceed each year's payroll limits, the tax does not deter teams. Most MLB teams stay within the salary guidelines, but the New York Yankees have paid this penalty numerous times.[13] Barclay's Premier League actually rewards the best-performing teams by allowing them more lucrative TV and merchandise deals, creating additional distance between the haves and have nots.[14] The disparity among F1 teams is also dramatic, with budgets for the lower end teams between $60 and 70 million, whereas the elite teams have budgets in excess of $400 million.[15] The NFL has trumpeted efforts to create parity in the league by sharing the revenue from the league's broadcast deals with all teams. Revenue is also shared from merchandise and licensing deals. Home and away teams split the ticket revenues 66/34 respectively as well, unless the games reach an agreed upon threshold for ticket sales, in which case the revenue split is 50/50. The revenue sharing has helped small market teams that otherwise would not be able to generate the revenues required to support a modern sports franchise and, on occasion, has helped them win the Super Bowl (i.e., the Green Bay Packers, Indianapolis Colts etc.). At the same time, traditional big market teams have also done well. Since 2001, the New England Patriots have been to the Super Bowl five times, winning three. The NFL's efforts to establish parity have not been perfect, although one could argue that the absence of revenue sharing might have created large market dynasties.[16]

For marketers, the choice of sports entity will be affected by the marketer's need. One may wish to work with the New York Yankees, but the cost would be significantly higher versus marketing through small salary clubs, like Oakland Athletics, thereby generating frequency.

## 8.2    Performance

The marketer must select a sports entity that helps, as much as can be anticipated, the company to achieve its strategic and marketing/financial objectives. These expectations are not unfamiliar. Indeed, any marketing investment must contribute toward company objectives. But given that sports marketing investments face greater uncertainty (will the event, team or player do well?), higher risk is typically associated with these investments. As a result, sports marketing activities are most effective when incorporated into the company's long-term plans, and not merely as a promotional, one-time event to generate immediate sales increases. Below are examples of performance objectives that can and should be measured by marketers.

### Strategic

Since marketing activities are intended to generate interest and then stimulate purchase from target customers, marketers must review the sports entity's potential for appealing to the marketplace. Companies will, of course, have different strategic objectives, but it is reasonable to assume that a sports marketing investment is not designed to shrink the company's financial performance or create a negative reputation. Instead, marketers must focus on how the sports marketing opportunity can help expand awareness about the company and create a recognized position based on distinction and differentiation of its offerings. The sports marketing investments do not have to solve each of these strategic objectives unilaterally. Instead, the sports marketing efforts must work in concert with other marketing and corporate growth activities, the combination of which gives the company a greater chance of success than it otherwise would have had had it not used sports marketing as one of its strategic tools. Samsung became an Olympic TOP Sponsor in 1997. Among its initial strategic objectives was the desire to raise awareness about the company as a leader in consumer products. Samsung senior management had also set a goal to overtake Sony, which was the market leader at the time. Both objectives, as well as others, were achieved and company statements reinforce that their Olympic marketing investments were a key reason for the company's impressive growth from 1997 through 2012.[17]

## Marketing/Financial

There are as many ways to measure marketing performance as there are tools and tactics. They encompass the well-known areas of marketing, from marketing communications (traditional and new/social media) to sales management to product launches, and more. Ultimately, marketing activities need to lead to increased sales and market share if they are to be supported in future years. Twenty years or more ago marketers could have a reasonably successful career emphasizing clever advertising and promotions, but this is no longer true. Senior management expects and demands that marketers are held accountable for their plans, so marketing has evolved into far more of a science than ever before. At the same time, the growth of social media means that people everywhere have greater control and are less influenced by company-directed marketing. As a consequence, an emphasis on increasing market share and revenues must be tied to specific marketing activities that keep the company's offerings fresh and interesting to keep the buzz alive. The sense of anticipation that consumers have before the launch of a new Apple product is palpable, yet the company releases no information, nor confirms any rumors, until the day of the new product announcement. This has remained true in both the Steve Jobs and post-Steve Jobs eras, and this heightened sense of expectation is generated by consumers directly. Sports are a natural vehicle for fostering a similar sense of loyalty with target audiences, so marketers must plan how to use the sports marketing activities in a way that is perceived as genuine, and not corporate or slick, since authenticity is a critical need for more consumers today. As the sports marketer's efforts gain favor, then increased sales and market share are far more likely to follow. Standard Chartered Bank, headquartered in the UK, is the title sponsor of the Barclay's Premier League team Liverpool FC. Its sponsorship is a four-year deal with an estimated value of $132 million that began in 2010. At the same time, Standard Chartered is also actively involved in sponsoring marathons, youth sports, and 'inspiring individuals' – people who have overcome significant challenges to achieve their ambitions. The common denominator is Standard Chartered's 100+ year tradition of supporting sports activities around the world. Without question, its Liverpool FC sponsorship creates added awareness, and it also generates substantial goodwill amongst football fans, creating an intangible gain that can also positively influence the company's reputation, revenues, and market share. In mid-2012 money laundering allegations against Standard Chartered erased £10 billion of value from the company, risking its sponsorship of Liverpool.[18]

## 8.3    Projection

While a critical need marketers have is to successfully reach their target audiences, one of the foremost desires for marketers is to successfully project their company's image and reputation not just to their target audiences, but well beyond to a larger market in a way that fosters long-term awareness, thereby helping the company leverage its limited marketing budget investments more effectively. Projection is not meant to suggest that marketers be overly general in their marketing appeals, nor should they try to be all things to all audiences. Instead, successful projection means that because the target audience finds the company's offerings so compelling that they often act as a gateway, or conduit, to other markets by spreading the company's information virally. At the same time the company's image, message, and offerings must relate well to multiple audiences for the viral effect to spread quickly. By studying market conditions and overall environmental factors (political, economic, socio-cultural and technological) marketers will gain a deep appreciation for the dynamics of the marketplace, such as shifting business and consumer preferences, interest rate changes, business investment shifts, and regulatory changes and how to begin tailoring their plans based on market conditions at the time of planning.

Surprises occur constantly in the market just as they do in sports, from political challenges (uncertain election year outcomes) to economic performance (financial shocks like the 2008 meltdown) to cultural (the Arab Spring) to technological (advances in social media). Often these events are interdependent, as the world has seen with social media conveying the images of the Syrian conflict between government forces and rebels, mixing the political with cultural. In the summer of 2012 during the London Olympics, Syrian athletes were the focus of media scrutiny. The athletes demonstrated a remarkable calm and objectivity, stating they wanted to stay out of the political discussions to focus on their competitions and, more generally, their enjoyment of participating in the Olympics (there were even images broadcast via social media of Syrian athletes wearing English Beefeater apparel).[19] Clearly, digital media enable companies and individuals to communicate a wider variety of messages with a wider variety of marketing tools to a wider variety of audiences than ever before. The risk of over-communication exists with the many new media channels, but an even bigger risk relates to poor communication, so when analyzing the potential for projection to enhance their sports marketing activities, marketers must account for the many different ways their messages will be conveyed and interpreted. This means that marketers must try to anticipate how their sports marketing investment might create a domino effect by having their target audience become informal marketers, or even 'evangelists', of their companies. This is not easy to do, and readers should not infer that marketers must be gifted with clairvoyance. Instead, just as start-up companies must prepare for the potential that their innovation may quickly take off by being able to meet demand, marketers must consider how to respond if word of mouth about their marketing activities spreads quickly.

We have already seen that sports can be a tremendous catalyst for improving a company's reputation, and that certain sports have larger, more diverse audiences than others (the Olympics, and association football, for example) and even specific teams within different sports (Manchester United, Dallas Cowboys, New Zealand All Blacks) have broader and more widespread appeal than their competitors. Marketers might logically conclude that they must tie their sports marketing investments to one of these higher profile leagues or teams to be successful. However, major sports entities in the twenty-first century do not operate in a vacuum, isolated from all others. As such, even smaller market clubs, or lesser-known sports leagues, represent good business potential for intelligent marketers with a thoughtful strategic plan for utilizing their sports investment. For example, the bottom four to five teams in the Barclay's Premier League play the top four to five teams each season, gaining a boost from the better teams' fans and larger TV viewership.[20] In 2012 Air Asia signed a one-year deal, with an option for a one-year extension, to have its logo on the home, away, and third Queens Park Rangers (QPR) shirt. QPR struggled for years, moving from Football League Division One, a lower division in English Football, up to one of the 20 Premier League clubs. Air Asia's deal expands on a previous sponsorship in which the company sponsored QPR's 'away' jerseys. QPR's move up into the Premier League, although not among the very top few clubs, highlights the uncertainty and potential for surprising gain from sports sponsorships and by playing other top Barclay's Premier League clubs. QPR illustrates the potential for projection beyond a core target audience.[21]

Evaluating projection potential requires marketers to carefully consider how they must use their sports marketing vehicle to position their company and its offerings. Here, classic marketing positioning guidelines remain as relevant today as they have over time: Marketers must determine their customer value proposition by understanding and outlining the characteristics of their offering that are *expected* and common, known as points of parity, and the characteristics that *distinguish* and differentiate their offerings from others, known as points of difference. Consumers purchase items they know more than those they don't know. These types of purchase decisions are based on familiar frames of reference in which the consumer is easily able to see how the offering fits within the overall product category. Points of parity create standards for product categories that competitors must match to be worthy of consideration. The marketer's task is to then combine the known and familiar with those aspects that are unique, creating a perceived value-added difference, thereby helping the offering own more of a specialty position in the market. These planning activities create the customer value proposition and they are essential to building a strong brand. In the context of sports marketing the marketer can use the association benefits from the sports entity to accentuate those points of difference and thereby help their offerings stand apart from their competitors.

## 8.4  Power

Power describes the strength and resiliency of the sports entity, which is keenly important to marketers since power acts as a key intangible factor in building overall confidence that the entity will be able to reliably deliver a memorable sports experience. Power is represented by having a recognized reputation for long-standing excellence, having consistent and growing financial value, and the ability to influence events, sometimes disproportionately. Power is most often reported through rankings, such as 2012 Power 100, which ranks the most powerful athletes in sports (the first 30 are shown below), and the 'World's Most Valuable Sports Franchises' (in Chapter 1).

Top 30 of the 2012 Power 100 (based on on-field and off-field attributes):[22]

1.  Drew Brees (NFL – American football);
2.  Aaron Rodgers (NFL – American football);
3.  Tom Brady (NFL – American football);
4.  LeBron James (NBA – basketball);
5.  Rafael Nadal (tennis);
6.  Roger Federer (tennis);
7.  Shaquille O'Neal (NBA – retired);
8.  Shaun White (snowboarding);

9. Novak Djokovic (tennis);

10. Calvin Johnson (NFL – American football);

11. Luke Donald (golf);

12. Tiger Woods (golf);

13. Kobe Bryant (NBA);

14. Dwight Howard (NBA);

15. Eli Manning (NFL – American football);

16. Dwayne Wade (NBA);

17. Kevin Durant (NBA);
18. Phil Mickelson (golf);
19. Lee Westwood (golf);

20. Troy Polamalu (NFL – American football);

21. Rory McIlroy (golf);

22. Dale Earnhardt Jr. (American auto racing);

23. Arian Foster (NFL – American football);

24. Dirk Nowitzki (NBA);

25. Serena Williams (tennis);

26. Albert Pujols (Major League Baseball);

27. Adrian Peterson (NFL – American Football);

28. Manny Pacquiao (boxing);
29. Jeff Gordon (auto racing);
30. Derrick Rose (NBA).

Interested readers are encouraged to read the entire list, and the ranking methodology at http://www.businessweek.com/finance/power-100-methodology-01252012.html.

Sports entities know that they have to offer value to companies considering a sports marketing relationship. Having a loyal fan base is among the qualities sought by sports marketers, as is the size of the fan base. In addition, as discussed earlier in the section on projection, the sports entity's potential for reaching beyond its core audience can add intangible value for the marketer. At the same time, marketers want the confidence that the sports property is a skilled operator with the ability to manage its complex, dynamic business and will protect the interests of its various stakeholders. There are three factors that can help marketers evaluate the power potential of the sports entity under consideration:

## Ability to influence

Is the sports entity an opinion leader and/or trendsetter in its sport? This can be determined by evaluating the entity's innovations and creativity. For example, in the NFL the Dallas Cowboys have not won a Super Bowl title since 1996 yet the team is the most valuable franchise in the NFL, with a $2.1 billion valuation, and second in the world in value to Manchester

United. The Cowboys' owner, Jerry Jones, has transformed the team into a marketing juggernaut, generating more than $500 million in annual revenues through creative merchandising, licensing, stadium monetizing, and even the development of TV shows featuring the team. For sports marketers, the Dallas Cowboys are an interesting example of how to look beyond league parity and focus on points of difference to create unique value for sports fans.[23]

## Negotiation strength of the entity

Is the sports entity capable of skillfully negotiating agreements with other parties that are win-win? Negotiation is among the most difficult and contentious areas of the sports business since opponents will perceive a sports entity as selfish and the sports entity will perceive itself as providing a social good through its economic and entertainment value. Whether the negotiation is over athletes' rights, or the development of a new sports complex, the challenge for sports marketers is in determining if the sports entity appears to have the interest of all parties at stake, and not just their own. The International Olympic Committee (IOC) works with large global companies regularly to attract them as TOP (The Olympic Partners) sponsors. These are not simple or easy negotiations, and a great deal of money is at stake. The IOC must convince companies that their sponsorship investment will not only be protected, but return significant long-term value. Companies seek the confidence that the IOC's administration and supervision of global sponsorship rights is of the highest integrity. With TOP sponsors paying an average of roughly $90 million each just for the right to be associated with the Olympics (as of the 2009–12 Olympics quadrennial),[24] one can understand why companies want assurance that the IOC is going to responsibly negotiate protections in each Olympic Host City that not only favors the TOP sponsors, but also does not detract from the Olympics by making them appear overly commercial.

## Potential for leverage

Does the sports entity have residual appeal beyond its core audience? Marketers want to spend their money as efficiently as possible, so the opportunity to leverage an investment into an even greater return is a vital part of their decision calculus. A sports entity that appeals to a narrow target audience may be a perfect marketing vehicle for a company seeking to reach the unique characteristics of that audience, but if the potential spillover gain of that initial investment ends up appealing to a wider audience, then the sports marketer will undoubtedly find the opportunity far more appealing.

Leveraging has many different forms, but a common example in sports marketing is when two or more corporate sponsors collaborate during a sports event. Samsung and Visa, both Olympic TOP sponsors, collaborated during the London 2012 Olympics by developing a new mobile payments platform that came loaded on a limited edition Samsung Galaxy phone. Users could wave the device at any of hundreds of retail outlets in London and make purchases quickly and easily. The IOC provided the platform (the Olympics) for this kind of partnership to be leveraged beyond the core markets each company pursued separately.[25]

## 8.5 Preference

In Chapter 3 we discussed segmentation and targeting and in Chapter 5 we introduced the concept of awareness. Earlier in this chapter we discussed positioning. Segmentation, targeting and positioning are known collectively as STP and they are fundamental to building a financially viable customer base. Each of these concepts will appear in subsequent chapters once our analysis turns toward the specifics of developing sports marketing communication campaigns and new offerings. At this point it is important to recognize that creating awareness is one of several important steps in developing customers *in general*. To develop customers that increase *sales*, marketers must convert awareness to preference, meaning that the interest created from awareness development must turn into a purchase. Turning customers from being merely aware into active purchasers is the core of every marketer's responsibilities, and the range of tactics that can be used is vast. We will discuss specific marketing tactics in later chapters. For now, marketers must consider the larger overall objectives in attempting to convert customers into purchasers. Customer audiences are adept at detecting and separating marketing hype from authentic value and any marketing messages that appear disingenuous (humor can be used to create affinity with customers who might then forgive the extreme messages if they perceive that they are 'in on the joke') will turn customers off. Three ingredients are needed in marketing communication to convert customers to purchasers: relevance; resonance; and reality (believability). They are described further below:

### Relevance

The offering and the message must be useful to the customer. In other words, customers will ask 'How will this help me?' or 'How can I use this?' If the offering is not useful, then it is not relevant and customers will turn away.

## Resonance

Getting past the relevance test is just the first step in converting custom-ers to purchasers. The next step is to have the offering resonate with them. This means that beyond the practical relevance, the offering must connect to them at an emotional level. This does not mean that the offering must inspire deep, burning passion or desire, but it must capture at least a basic level of customer appreciation. If the offering lacks any emotional appeal at all, then the chance of inspiring purchase diminishes significantly.

## Reality (believability)

Finally, the offering and the message must be real and believable. This require-ment might strike some readers as an impossible standard, particularly when humor is used to communicate appeal. But customers are intelligent, capable of recognizing value in humorous and non-humorous appeals alike. The chal-lenge is conveying a sense of authenticity. Rarely are marketers working with utterly unknown new offerings devoid of context (i.e., pure, surprising inno-vations), so marketers need to tap into what customers do know and then try to create a memorable approach that strikes customers as plausible and interesting. If an offer is characterized by over-the-top appeals and extreme promises, then consumers are likely to perceive this as nonsense and avoid it.

When marketers think strategically about their offer through the lens of rel-evance, resonance, and reality, then using sports marketing activities to com-municate it to the market can become a powerful and memorable means to grow the business. Adidas created a memorable video campaign based on its 2012 London Olympics sponsorship. The video featured Team Great Britain's athletes (a nice homage to the home country's athletic stars) in humorous and endearing settings lip-synching to the band Queen's song 'Don't Stop Me Now'. The video captures each of the three requirements, being relevant (the timeliness of the London Olympics coupled with the implication that adidas's athletic products create successful performances), resonating with consumers (the imagery was playful and the song evokes pow-erful emotional memories), and real (the athletes are shown). The video can be seen at this link: http://www.youtube.com/watch?v=ERgU551NFeY.

## 8.6 Chapter summary

The traditional marketing mix of product, price, place, promotion and people has been a useful organisational framework helping marketers develop offerings and determine customer and market outreach. The new Ps are useful for helping marketers evaluate that a sports entity will align with their sports marketing activities while also contributing to the growth of measurable value and an enhanced reputation. Each of the new Ps, prestige, performance, projection, power and preference, are designed to stimulate a deeper analysis of the sports marketer's marketing investment in the sports entity and accompanying programs. Ideally, companies and sports entities should have reasonable consistent objectives and alignment for a longer-term marketing relationship to bear positive results.

**CASE STUDY**

# BP sustainability

On 20 April 2010, an explosion on the oil rig Deepwater Horizon in the Gulf of Mexico initiated what would become worst oil spill in the history of the United States.[26] At the time, the rig was being leased by British Petroleum (BP), and so the British company received the brunt of the blame for the disaster. The incident was incredibly damaging to BP. As of August 2012, BP had spent $38 billion in fixing the damage of the oil spill.[27] In addition to the enormous sums of money the company was paying out, profits had taken a significant hit as well. BP's share value dropped from around $10.39 before the spill, to $4.82 just eight weeks after the spill.[28] BP needed something to repair its image and to show the world that it wanted to make a positive impact on the world in the wake of this terrible tragedy.

Luckily for BP, it had already signed sponsorship deals that would align it with arguably the most glorified sports property in the world: the Olympic Games. In a lavish ceremony in July 2008, BP inked a deal to sponsor the London Olympics as the official oil and gas partner of London 2012.[29] The deal would include providing fuel for the 5000 official Olympic vehicles, and would support the 'Cultural Olympiad', a program designed to ensure that the impact of the Olympic Games would reach the entire country.[30] Initially, BP viewed the sponsorship as a unique way to engage with not only their global customers, but also with its own employees on its home turf.[31] Just two months before the 2010 Deepwater Horizon spill, BP had also signed a deal to become a sponsor of the United States Olympic Committee (USOC).[32] The London 2012 deal was reportedly worth $58 million while the USOC deal's value hovered somewhere between $10 million and $15 million.[33]

After the oil spill, BP had to adjust its sponsorship objectives. While BP had always intended to use the Olympic platform to tout its own sustainability initiatives, leveraging the positive halo effect from the Olympics became a core focus after the spill. BP used the global stage, first and foremost, to promote its commitment to 'Fuelling the Future'.[34] As part of this program, BP made limited quantities of biofuel blends made from sugar cane available prior to commercial launch at select retail sites in London, most notably BP's largest in London at Hammersmith Flyover.[35] BP's showcase at Hammersmith Flyover had biofuel information displays, a futuristic gas pump that detected the car pulling up and sensed what type of gasoline it would need, and of course, the chance for drivers to experience these new products.[36] In the Olympic Park, BP created a 360° rotating cyclorama of images showing the process that energy goes through before it reaches the consumer.[37] The exhibit was designed to illustrate the parallel between Olympic and Paralympic athletes challenging themselves every day to do their best, and how the ordinary consumer can challenge him or herself to achieve their personal best in reducing their carbon footprint at the Games.[38]

Also, as part of its sustainability partner efforts, BP created a BP Target Neutral program 'aimed at encouraging individuals to reduce, replace or neutralize (offset) their carbon

**CASE STUDY** *(continued)*

emissions from travel'.[39] The company encouraged all ticketed Olympic spectators to register on its website, and BP offered to pay to offset all carbon emissions from each spectator's journey to London. More than 476 000 journeys were offset as a result of this program.[40] BP also extended this offer for its athlete ambassadors in their travel to competitions and training prior to the Games.[41] In sum, as an 'Official Sustainability Partner' BP attempted to project itself as providing the 'most efficient and progressive solutions for today and the next 10 to 15 years' through its various programs and activations in and around the London Olympics.[42]

To better capture the positive effects of the Olympic halo, BP sponsored nine national Olympic committees (NOCs) and dozens of individual athletes from these NOCs.[43] BP also made waves by sponsoring a nearly equal number of Olympic athletes as Paralympic athletes.[44] In addition to the Cultural Olympiad, which had exhibitions, performances, and educational opportunities for young people, BP also had a promotion for those who worked behind the scenes to make the Olympic Games a possibility. The initiative was called 'Here's to the Home Team' and BP gave away tickets to the Olympics to those with the best stories.[45] As part of the campaign, applicants uploaded pictures to BP's Facebook page, and some of those pictures were selected to appear in outdoor ads around London.[46] All of BP's Olympic sponsorship activations were combined on its own London 2012 website, BPLondon2012.com, which was designed to highlight and collect all of its initiatives in one place.

BP's Olympic sponsorships were not always greeted with open arms, however. Countless letters on behalf of environmental organizations called for BP to step down, or the IOC and LOCOG to drop it as a sponsor. One open letter to the IOC, which had 34 signatories including Greenpeace UK and London mayoral candidate Jenny Jones, called BP 'one of the least sustainable companies on earth'.[47] Greenpeace's Senior Climate Advisor Charlie Kronick was quoted as saying 'If BP wants to trial advanced biofuels they've got thousands of petrol stations around the country. They're taking advantage of the highest-profile event in the country to blow the trumpet for something that's a tiny part of their business'.[48] Many called BP's title as an 'Official Sustainability Partner' a joke. Evan Morgenstein, an agent who represents several Olympic swimmers, noted that he had received phone calls from several of his athletes expressing concern about BP's connections to the USOC.[49] Nevertheless, both LOCOG and BP stood fast in their decisions and BP was permitted to execute its activation strategies without much interruption. It's unclear just how positively the Olympics have affected this British company's troubled brand. What is clear is that BP spent millions and millions of dollars on one event attempting to fix a brand that has already cost them billions of dollars of repair.

**? QUESTIONS**

1   Is sports sponsorship a good way for companies to repair an image if it has been damaged? Why or why not?

**CASE STUDY** *(continued)*

2   Did it make sense for BP to continue its sponsorship after the oil spill? Should it have backed down and focused its efforts on the cleanup in the Gulf?

3   In a report released by Havas Sports & Entertainment, 38 percent of 3192 adults polled in an online survey believed that BP had been getting better at working towards a cleaner planet. Is this result significant? Should BP be content with that result? Does that mean that its sponsorship of London 2012 was successful?

**NOTES**

1   Burke (2012).
2   Berthon et al. (2009).
3   Samsung Diamond League (n.d.); Diamondleague.com (n.d.).
4   Fisher (2012).
5   Davis (2012, Chapter 1); Mooney (2012).
6   'Tradition' (2001).
7   Davis (2010, pp. 107–10).
8   'WorldSeries.com' (n.d.).
9   'The Club' (n.d.).
10  'History' (n.d.).
11  'Ferrari Formula 1 Team' (n.d.).
12  'New York Yankees salary/payroll Information – 2012' (2011).
13  Waldstein, David (2012).
14  SportsMail Reporter (2010).
15  Benson (2012); 'Mercedes will increase budget for its F1 team by 30%, $56m for '13 campaign' (2012).
16  Dosh (2012); Rovell (2012).
17  Davis (2012, pp. 227–33).
18  Love (2011); Mirror Football (2012).
19  'Syrian athletes arrive in London for Olympics' (2012).
20  Head (2012).
21  Elliot (2012).
22  Newman (2012).
23  Ozanian (2012).
24  Davis (2012, pp. 202–3).
25  Alugbue (2012).
26  'Obama, in Gulf, pledges to push on stopping leak' (2010).
27  Milmo (2012).
28  Brant (2011).
29  Arnott (2008).
30  Ibid.
31  Ibid.
32  'USOC says BP sponsorship still solid' (2010).
33  Ibid.
34  'Fuelling the Games' (n.d.).
35  Ibid.
36  'Olympic Park' (n.d.); Lane (2012).
37  Ibid.
38  Ibid.
39  'Fuelling the Games' (n.d.).

40  'Offset your travel carbon footprint for free' (n.d.).
41  'Fuelling the Games' (n.d.).
42  Ibid.
43  'Supporting athletes' (n.d.).
44  Mickle (2012, p. 4).
45  McCabe (2012).
46  bid.
47  Vidal (2012).
48  Lundgren (2012).
49  'USOC says BP sponsorship still solid' (2010).

 **REFERENCES**

Alugbue, Roy (2012), 'Samsung and Visa announce mobile payments collaboration for Summer Olympic Games', Talk Android, 10 May 2012, accessed 12 May 2012 at http://www.talkandroid.com/110963-samsung-and-visa-announce-mobile-payment-collaboration-for-summer-olympic-games/.

Arnott, Sarah (2008), 'BP aims to win more than plaudits from £50m Olympic sponsorship', *The Independent*, 4 July 2008, accessed 5 September 2012 at http://www.independent.co.uk/news/business/news/bp-aims-to-win-more-than-plaudits-from-16350m-olympic-sponsorship-860060.html.

Associated Press, 'USOC Says BP sponsorship still solid'. June 6, 2010. ESPN Olympic Sports. Retrieved August 7, 2012 from http://sports.espn.go.com/oly/news/story?id=525759.

Benson, Andrew (2012), 'Martin Whitmarsh says a budget cap in Formula 1 is unrealistic', BBC.com, 28 October 2012, accessed 28 October 2012 at http://www.bbc.co.uk/sport/0/formula1/20110248.

Berthon, Pierre, Leyland Pitt, Michael Parent and Jean-Paul Berthon (2009), 'Aesthetics and ephemerality: observing and preserving the luxury brand,' *California Management Review*, **52**(1), 47–50.

Brant, Ben (2011), 'Deepwater Horizon and the Gulf oil spill – the key questions answered', *The Guardian*, 20 April 2011, accessed 4 September 2012 at http://www.guardian.co.uk/environment/2011/apr/20/deepwater-horizon-key-questions-answered.

Burke, Monte (2012), 'The ten richest sporting events in the world', Forbes.com, 24 May 2012, accessed 7 July 2012 at http://www.forbes.com/sites/monteburke/2012/05/24/the-ten-richest-sporting-events-in-the-world/.

Davis, John A. (2010), *Competitive Success – How Branding Adds Value*, New York: John Wiley & Sons.

Davis, John A. (2012), *The Olympic Games Effect – How Sports Marketing Builds Strong Brands*, New York: John Wiley & Sons, Chapter 1.

Diamondleague.com (n.d.), accessed 3 June 2012 at http://www.diamondleague.com/.

Dosh, Kristi (2012), 'NHL seeks revenue-sharing a la NBA, NFL', ESPN.com, 10 August 2012, accessed 11 August 2012 at http://espn.go.com/blog/playbook/dollars/post/_/id/897/nhl-seeks-revenue-sharing-a-la-nba-nfl.

Elliot, Mark (2012), 'AirAsia extends QPR sponsorship', TravelDailyMedia.com, 20 May 2012, accessed 3 July 2012 at http://www.traveldailymedia.com/125827/airasia-extends-qpr-sponsorship.

'Ferrari Formula 1 Team' (n.d.), 4mula1.ro, accessed 9 August 2012 at http://www.4mula1.ro/history/team/Ferrari.

Fisher, Adam (2012), 'Inside Larry Ellison's insane plan to turn America's Cup into a TV spectacle', Wired.com, 20 August 2012, accessed 21 August 2012 at http://www.wired.com/playbook/2012/08/ff_americascup_ellison/all/.

'Fuelling the Games' (n.d.), BP.com, accessed 5 September 2012 at http://www.bp.com/section-genericarticle.do?categoryId=9036378&contentId=7067213.

Head, Simon (2012), 'Getting stuffed this Christmas? Reading's turkeys facing Premier League axe', Mirror.com, 19 December 2012, accessed 19 December 2012 at http://www.mirror.co.uk/sport/football/news/readings-turkeys-facing-premier-league-1497119.

'History' (n.d.), RealMadrid.com, accessed 3 May 2012 at http://www.realmadrid.com/cs/Satellite/en/1193041516534/Historia/Club.htm.

Lane, Jim (2012), 'The 2012 London Olympics, biofuels-style: BP to showcase its three most advanced biofuels', BiofuelsDigest.com, 23 July 2012, accessed 5 September 2012 at http://www.biofuelsdigest.com/bdigest/2012/07/23/the-2012-london-olympics-biofuels-style-bp-to-showcase-its-three-most-advanced-biofuels/.

Love, Tom (2011), '$132 million sponsor expands Liverpool Football Club's presence in Asia', SportsPro, 31 January 2011, accessed 14 June 2012 at http://www.sportspromedia.com/notes_and_insights/132_million_sponsor_expands_liverpool_football_clubs_presence_in_asia/.

Lundgren, Kari (2012), 'Olympic sponsors BP, EDF to restore confidence', Bloomberg.com, 8 May 2012, accessed 5 September 2012 at http://www.bloomberg.com/news/2012-05-08/olympic-sponsors-bp-edf-to-restore-confidence.html.

McCabe, Maisie (2012), 'BP to run user-generated ads in Home Team campaign' (2012), Campaignlive.co.uk, 30 July 2012, accessed 5 September 2012 at http://www.campaignlive.co.uk/news/1143312/.

'Mercedes will increase budget for its F1 team by 30%, $56m for' 13 campaign' (2012), *Sports Business Daily*, 5 November 2012, accessed 8 November 2012 at http://www.sportsbusinessdaily.com/Global/Issues/2012/11/05/Finance/Mercedes-F1.aspx.

Mickle, Tripp (2012), 'Value, inspiration drive Paralympic appeal', *Sports Business Journal*, 16 April 2012, 4.

Milmo, Dan (2012), 'BP's Deepwater Horizon costs rise $847m', *The Guardian*, 31 July 2012, accessed 4 September 2012 at http://www.guardian.co.uk/business/2012/jul/31/bp-deepwater-horizon-costs.

Mirror Football (2012), 'In the red: £10 billion wiped off value of Liverpool sponsors after money laundering allegations', Mirror.com, 7 August 2012, accessed 8 August 2012 at http://www.mirror.co.uk/sport/football/news/10-billion-wiped-off-value-of-liverpool-1231146.

Mooney, Andrew (2012), 'The five most dominant Olympians of all time', Bostonglobe.com, 12 August 2012, accessed 14 August 2012 at http://www.boston.com/sports/blogs/statsdriven/2012/08/the_five_most_dominant_olympia.html.

Newman, David (2012), 'Power 100: methodology', BloombergBusinessweek.com, 25 January 2012, accessed 22 March 2012 at http://www.businessweek.com/finance/power-100-methodology-01252012.html.

'New York Yankees salary/payroll Information – 2012' (2011), ESPN.com, accessed 21 October 2012 at http://espn.go.com/mlb/team/salaries/_/name/nyy/new-york-yankees.

'Obama, in Gulf, pledges to push on stopping leak' (2010), USAToday.com, 28 May 2010, accessed 4 September 2012 at http://www.usatoday.com/news/nation/2010-05-27-oil-spill-news_N.htm?csp=34news.

'Offset your travel carbon footprint for free' (n.d.), SpectatorTargetNeutral.BP.com, accessed 5 September 2012 at https://spectatortargetneutral.bp.com/tag/start.

'Olympic Park' (n.d.), London2012.com, accessed 5 September 2012 at http://www.london2012.com/spectators/venues/olympic-park/partner-showcases.

Ozanian, Mike (2012), 'Dallas Cowboys lead NFL with $2.1 billion valuation', Forbes.

com, 5 September 2012, accessed 7 September 2012 at http://www.forbes.com/sites/mikeozanian/2012/09/05/dallas-cowboys-lead-nfl-with-2-1-billion-valuation/.

Rovell, Darren (2012), 'Package renewals hit 90.6 percent', ESPN.com, 17 August 2012, accessed 24 August 2012 at http://espn.go.com/nfl/story/_/id/8278246/nfl-season-ticket-renewals-league-says.

Samsung Diamond League (n.d.), IAAF.com, accessed 3 June 2012 at http://www.iaaf.org/competitions/samsung-diamond-league.

SportsMail Reporter (2010), 'Premier League prize money up to £800k per place but Manchester United and Chelsea dwarf the rest with £50m cash jackpot', Mailonline, 7 May 2010, accessed 22 November 2011 at http://www.dailymail.co.uk/sport/football/article-1274698/Premier-League-prize-money-800k-place-Manchester-United-Chelsea-dwarf-rest-50m-cash-jackpot.html.

'Supporting athletes' (n.d.), BPLondon2012.com, accessed 5 September 2012 at http://www.bp.com/sectiongenericarticle.do?categoryId=9036380&contentId=7067221.

'Syrian athletes arrive in London for Olympics' (2012), Reuters, 23 July 2012, accessed 13 August 2012 at http://sports.nationalpost.com/2012/07/23/syrian-athletes-arrive-in-london-for-olympics/.

'The Club' (n.d.), Manutd.com, accessed 3 May 2012 at http://www.manutd.com/en/Club.aspx.

'Tradition' (2001), Beanpot.com, 27 December 2001, accessed 3 August 2012 at http://www.beanpothockey.com/tradition.html.

Vidal, John (2012), 'Olympics Games organisers face protests over BP sponsorship deal', *The Guardian*, 16 February 2012, accessed 5 September 2012 at http://www.guardian.co.uk/business/2012/feb/17/olympic-games-protest-bp-sponsorship.

Waldstein, David (2012), 'New plan: Yankees look to cut payroll', *New York Times*, 1 March 2012, accessed 11 March 2012 at http://www.nytimes.com/2012/03/02/sports/baseball/yankees-want-to-cut-payroll-to-189-million-by-2014.html?_r=0.

'WorldSeries.com' (n.d.), MLB.com, accessed 7 May 2012 at http://mlb.mlb.com/mlb/history/postseason/mlb_ws.jsp?feature=club_champs.

# 9

# Sports marketing touchpoints and customer journeys

**CHAPTER OVERVIEW**

The 2000s have seen the development of many of the most advanced marketing techniques ever. This is true not just for products, but for strategic marketing planning, data mining, and marketing communications. With respect to the latter, whereas marketing was once a one-way discipline defined by delayed communication from company to customer, the introduction and rapid growth of two-way social and digital communication has fostered a true conversational dynamic between the company and the marketplace, more often than not controlled by the marketplace itself, with the company's role as both an influencer and listener rather than as a creator and manipulator of messages. We will discuss integrated marketing communications later on, but the importance of this shift directly affects how marketers understand their own company and also how they evaluate their sports marketing opportunities. In this chapter we will look at a technique called 'touchpoint identification and development', which will help sports marketers identify the qualities and characteristics of their own organization, and those of the sports entity, so that they can determine the ways in which their company can align with the sports property.

## 9.1    Touchpoint identification and development

### Mapping

Maps serve many useful purposes. Over the centuries maps have helped people navigate from one geographic location to another. Genetic mapping helped scientists identify the more than 20 000 genes in human DNA, completing the human genome project in 2003, with the resulting insights leading to breakthroughs in medical science and research.[1] NASA has used infrared mapping to complete an atlas of the infrared universe in 2012, showing more than 560 million objects, many of which were previously unseen using normal light, helping scientists gain greater knowledge about the origins of the universe, and even more 'local' findings like the discovery of asteroids near earth.[2] Maps essentially help us learn more about the world around us, whether earthly or otherworldly. Mapping, or more specifically identifying an organization's 'touchpoints', is also useful to help organizations understand the many variables that affect the direction of their company and to also assess potential partner organizations, such as sports properties, for their potential attractiveness as marketing vehicles.

In a business and sports marketing context, mapping is an exercise conducted by management that visually depicts an organization's attributes, their interdependencies, and their relationships to stakeholders (employees, customers, shareholders, suppliers, analysts etc.). Mapping offers the company numerous benefits related to a deeper and more detailed understanding of the many different factors that affect their reputation. Mapping helps the mappers see the world as their stakeholders see it, through the specific points of contact for that stakeholder, creating a visual map that shows the relationships between the departments and services inside the company, and the marketplace.

Two techniques will be discussed in this chapter: the 'brand touchpoints map' and the 'customer experience journey'. While each can be used separately to uncover detailed information about company attributes, when used together a helpful approach is to begin by mapping the touchpoints first, then the customer experience journey because the same touchpoints often show up in both maps. The brand touchpoints map, when fully developed, shows a wide variety of factors, many of which might be surprising to management, and all of which have an impact ultimately on the company's reputation, whether major or minor, providing essential and strategic detail that can then shed light on the customer journey experience. The techniques have been tested regularly with companies around the world through executive education programs and consulting, helping them discover opportunities and potential problem areas that otherwise go unnoticed. For marketing purposes, the two techniques can ensure that a sports marketing investment is more effectively planned and ultimately implemented.

There are several steps to follow in creating both the brand touchpoints map and the customer experience journey. Companies have discovered that both techniques yield the best results when conducted off-site, away from the corporate office and therefore free from normal office distractions. Many managers have asked their participants to shut off their phones and pagers to eliminate the temptation to review email or send text messages.

A distraction-free environment is also ideal to maximize the learning. People should take breaks after each step is completed, which can include an unrelated team exercise, food break, or brief sports activity, to keep people engaged with each other and avoiding fatigue with the mapping exercise.

## Brand touchpoints map[3]

Touchpoints take both tangible and intangible forms. Most touchpoints trigger a range of associations, from emotional to social to intellectual, which help anchor it in the stakeholder's mind. Every organization is different and the number of touchpoints that are mapped will vary as well. As the brand touchpoints map is developed, users will quickly see why touchpoints can and do vary and what makes their organization unique as a result, since many are not always obvious in the course of daily activities. Interrelationships among touchpoints are important for management to see since many strategic and financial resources are shared across the organization and a visual understanding of the relationships will illuminate resource constraints. Furthermore, by thinking through the complexity of their organization's touchpoints, marketers will be more effective at understanding the importance of a touchpoint to the company and to the stakeholder. Differences of opinion inevitably arise between what marketers perceive as critical to their success yet customers will see it as less vital or will even be indifferent. When perception gaps like this arise, the task for marketers is to determine the importance of these perception gaps and then decide whether they should be addressed and, if so, how.

## Developing a touchpoints map

There are six steps in creating a brand touchpoints map:

### Step 1: Brainstorm

The organization begins by brainstorming every conceivable touchpoint related to the organization. This will understandably become complicated as flip charts and white boards are filled with each person's suggestions. To minimize contention, participants need to agree up front that there will be no judgment during this discovery stage. Instead, participants must feel uninhibited in offering their points of view since every person views the organization through a different lens, influenced by their own experiences and biases. Had artificial constraints been set, such as guidelines that describe what is considered a quality contribution, then the participants would understandably focus only on those areas within the constraints. The constraints, or rather the streamlining of the ideas into a manageable set, occurs in later steps. The brand touchpoints mapping exercise is most useful and effective when participants are able to devote significant time. Abbreviated, rushed approaches eliminate many of the key benefits that otherwise come from a rigorous discussion and listing of the organization's innumerable attributes with multiple people from different areas contributing. Once Step 1 is completed, the participants can turn their attention to evaluating the results in the subsequent steps.

## Step 2: Organize

Step 2 is not the stage for eliminating touchpoints. It is used to simply organize them. Step 2 is also time consuming and vigorous discussion will ensue, but as the participants talk through the results from Step 1, common themes and characteristics will emerge that will assist in organizing the many touchpoints. Inevitably there will be overlap among some touchpoints that can be placed into more than one category. When this occurs, then put these touchpoints into each relevant category. Striving for rigid perfection is not helpful here. Instead, developing a clearer sense of the common themes is.

## Step 3: Prune

After the common themes from Step 2 are identified, the participants move on to Step 3, which emphasizes pruning the lists. As years of experience have shown, Step 3 is often when the most vibrant and even emotional discussions occur since participants will seek to persuade others about their points of view. Pruning is quite hard to do. Like gardeners tending their plants know, aggressive pruning can do more harm than good. There is no ideal number of touchpoints. Indeed, striving for this is nonsensical and irrelevant. As the participants evaluate the touchpoints, the most egregious and outlandish will quickly be eliminated, but even some of those will elicit vigorous discussion about their impact on the organization and its stakeholders. These discussions are critical to successfully creating a brand touchpoints map because this is where often unseen and even unpopular touchpoints can emerge that are revealed as more important than previously considered. As with Step 2, the goal here is not to seek perfection, but to have an open dialog and honest appraisal of the organization. Touchpoints that are negative or disagreeable may be uncomfortable, but listing them will be instrumental in helping the organization improve. Less pruning is typically better than more, because as the brand touchpoints map is created in Step 4, participants often reintroduce removed touchpoints or even add new ones that were missed in the first three steps.

## Step 4: Create map

The brand touchpoints map begins with the organization being discussed circled at the center of a board or flip chart, as illustrated here.

Each of the main categories from Step 3 is then added outside the main circle, drawing smaller circles around each theme. Solid connecting lines are then drawn between the main organization and the surrounding themes (Figure 9.1a).

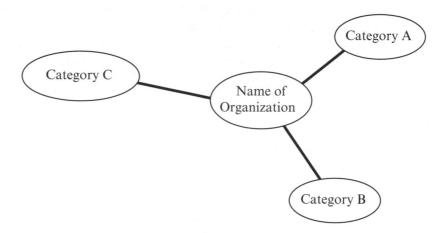

**Figure 9.1a** Creating the map

Extending from each category are additional connections to the individual touchpoints from Step 3, with even smaller circles drawn around them (Figure 9.1b).

As the mapping exercise unfolds the interrelationships between themes and touchpoints are exposed. Additional layers and levels of touchpoints, and sub-touchpoints are often added as the visual cues spark additional insights (Figure 9.1c). Because the brand touchpoints map frees participants from the conventional silos and organization charts that too often make product lines and categories appear as discreet, self-contained units, new and/or previously unrecognized relationships among touchpoints emerge. Dotted lines to the newly revealed dependencies stemming from the categories deline-

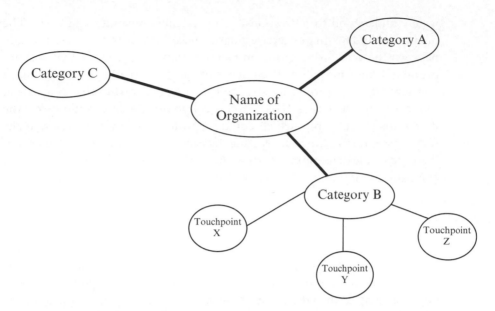

**Figure 9.1b** Creating the map

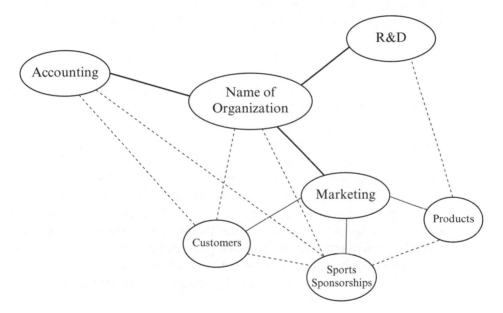

**Figure 9.1c** Creating the map

ate them from the direct, solid line connections, indicating they are indirectly related, often a relationship not previously recognized. These dotted line indirect relationships can be very important in helping the company improve operations. For example, a company's accounting department is widely understood to be responsible for tracking revenues and costs. The brand touchpoints map exercise might reveal that an indirect relationship between the accounting group and sports sponsorships exists that was not previously known, such as the impact of sports marketing decisions made that govern affect promotions related to the sponsorship that might lead to increase product sales. The brand touchpoints exercise would reveal the dotted line relationship, which could help the company's marketers make more cost-effective sports marketing decisions in the future when determining how to create a more informed information network inside their own company about the expectations and implications of the sports sponsorship.

## Step 5: Score each touchpoint

Once Step 4 is completed, the participants will have developed an informative visual map of the organization and gain an approximate idea of how the different touchpoints influence each other. The brand touchpoints maps will be more complex than the examples shown here and may even appear somewhat chaotic, leaving participants to wonder what meaning they can derive from it. At this point a useful device is to score each of the touchpoints from two different perspectives: the company's and the customer's:

*Company perspective*: Importance of the touchpoint to the brand (1 to 5 scale; 1 = low 5 = high)
*Customer perspective*: Ability of the brand to provide/deliver the touchpoint successfully (1 to 5 scale; 1 = low 5 = high)

Many companies have research describing the market's perception of the brand and, conceivably (or perhaps by implication), the importance of the various touchpoints. The data may be hard to gather for some companies, particularly if the brand touchpoints exercise is being conducted for the first time. Therefore an alternative research approach would be to invite a representative selection of customers into the mapping session to spend a day with the group discussing and evaluating the validity of the touchpoints. The least attractive alternative is to have the participants assume the customer's point of view and score accordingly. This latter option is less desirable since bias is more likely to occur.

## Step 6: Discuss and address gaps

The final step is to review the completed brand touchpoints map, discuss the findings and identify problems to address and opportunities to pursue. Reviewing the most extreme pairs of scores is a good way to start, for example: (1, 5), (5, 1), (2, 5), (4, 1). The participants must consider why the discrepancies exist and if fixing them is important to succeeding with the sports marketing investment and eventually increasing brand value. As with any meaningful business exercise, the discussion must lead to concrete plans for addressing changes, with each discrepancy recorded and responsibility for fixing it assigned, along with a detailed timeline for progress updates, task completion, and review.

The brand touchpoints exercise is an extended effort, often taking several hours or days to properly capture the sports marketer's myriad touchpoints. But the results provide an in-depth visual understanding of the company's touchpoints, the associated areas of strength versus weakness, providing a reasonable guideline of areas where the company can improve in its efforts to implement a successful sports marketing plan. The brand touchpoints exercise is not a one-time effort, but a regular activity that should be updated each year as the company's fortunes and competitive situation change.

A completed brand touchpoints map will look complicated as Figure 9.2 shows, as well it should, given that each company is comprised of innumerable points of contact with customers and the market, each of which affects perceptions and, eventually, brand value.

## 9.2    Customer experience journey[4]

The customer experience journey helps sports marketers evaluate the composite customer relationship with their company by mapping the sequence of interactions between the customer and the company before, during, and after their experience. By conducting this exercise the company is able to more clearly understand the interaction dynamic with their customers at multiple points in the relationship, from pre-purchase to post-purchase support and follow up.

### Creating a customer experience journey map

The following six steps describe the customer experience journey exercise:

#### Step 1: Identify customer needs

Identify what the customer needs are and what is driving them. This information will come from market research, and past experience. Each need must be written directly on the customer experience journey map.

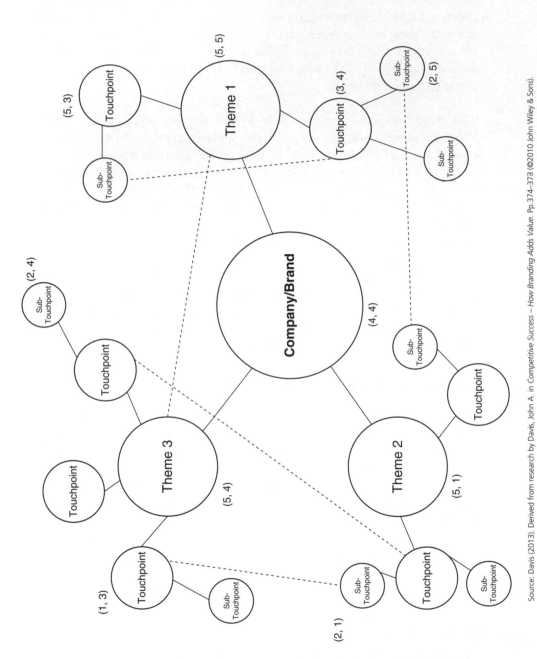

Source: Davis (2013). Derived from research by Davis, John A. in *Competitive Success – How Branding Adds Value*. Pp.374–373 (©2010 John Wiley & Sons).

**Figure 9.2** Brand touchpoints map

## Step 2: Determine your company's response to each need

Every customer's expressed need will generate a corresponding response from the sports marketer's company. The challenge is determining what the response level should be, since every need is different in its intensity, and how to respond accordingly. Sports marketers should also identify who is responsible for addressing each need, including which resources are required, and their corresponding touchpoints. These responses should be added to the customer experience map.

## Step 3: Score each response

Each response is to be score using two measurement scales: (1) competitor comparison; (2) customer assessment. Competitor comparisons are based on existing data, market knowledge, and customer feedback. The following scale (Figure 9.3) is useful, but you are welcome to develop your own scale.

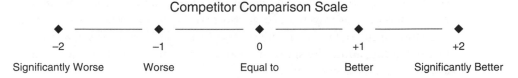

### Competitor Comparison Scale

| −2 | −1 | 0 | +1 | +2 |
|---|---|---|---|---|
| Significantly Worse | Worse | Equal to | Better | Significantly Better |

Source:  Davis (2013). Derived from research by Davis, John A. in *Competitive Success – How Branding Adds Value*. Pp.374–378 (©2010 John Wiley & Sons).

**Figure 9.3**  Competitor comparison scale

Customer assessments are derived from market research surveys that examine customer satisfaction. Each need and response on the customer experience journey map should be a catalyst for management to discuss where the company is doing well versus areas in need of improvement. There will inevitably be customer needs requiring multiple simultaneous responses from the sports marketer's company. Each response needs to be scored individually since this will provide a clearer and more accurate picture of the firm's ability to completely satisfy customer needs.

The following customer assessment scale (Figure 9.4) is one possible approach to evaluating customer satisfaction. This scale scores the customer's perceived satisfaction to the sports marketer's company's response on a 1 to 5 scale (1 = poor 5 = excellent).

Sports marketers will note that there will likely be some overlap between the touchpoints from the brand touchpoints map and the responses in the customer experience journey. The touchpoint scores from the brand

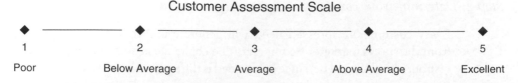

Customer Assessment Scale

| 1 | 2 | 3 | 4 | 5 |
|---|---|---|---|---|
| Poor | Below Average | Average | Above Average | Excellent |

Source: Davis (2013). Derived from research by Davis, John A. in *Competitive Success – How Branding Adds Value*. Pp.374–378 (©2010 John Wiley & Sons).

**Figure 9.4** Customer assessment scale

touchpoints map should be consistent with how the customers perceive the company's response at each stage of the customer experience journey.

## Step 4: Identify gaps, problems, and opportunities

Based on the need/response scores at each stage along the customer experience journey, it is helpful to add another score based on perceptions of how the closest competitor(s) would handle each need. While imperfect without rigorous data, a reasonable understanding of the market would suggest that sports marketers are aware of competitor strengths and weaknesses and can therefore approximate competitor responses. This will reveal additional understanding about the sports marketer's company versus the competitors as it relates to customer satisfaction.

## Step 5: Determine plan of action

After the customer experience journey has been mapped, responsibility for changes in how the company responds should be assigned and scheduled, with periodic measurement and review stages included, to ensure that needed adjustments can be made.

## Step 6: Review

A final review at the end of each sports marketing campaign is necessary to assess results once the sports marketing activities have been completed and market results have been gathered.

Figure 9.5 shows a hypothetical customer experience journey, divided into three phases: pre, during, and post. The pre-phase describes how customers first gain knowledge of the sports marketer's company and also how the relationship between the company and the customer begins. As the customer makes inquiries, the company responds, and each response influences whether and how the customer chooses to continue, or end, the relation-

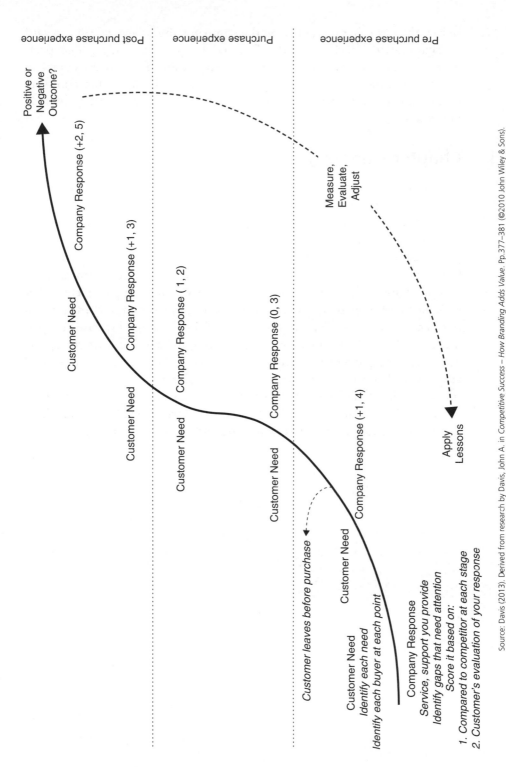

Post purchase experience      Purchase experience      Pre purchase experience

Positive or Negative Outcome?

Company Response (+2, 5)

Customer Need

Company Response (+1, 3)

Company Response ( 1, 2)

Customer Need

Measure, Evaluate, Adjust

Customer Need

Company Response (0, 3)

Customer Need

Apply Lessons

Customer Need

Company Response (+1, 4)

Customer leaves before purchase

Customer Need      Customer Need

Identify each need

Identify each buyer at each point

Company Response

Service, support you provide

Identify gaps that need attention

Score it based on:

1. Compared to competitor at each stage

2. Customer's evaluation of your response

Source: Davis (2013). Derived from research by Davis, John A. in *Competitive Success – How Branding Adds Value*. Pp.377–381 (©2010 John Wiley & Sons).

**Figure 9.5** Hypothetical customer experience journey

ship. If the customer remains with the company, then they will shift toward purchase-related decisions, identified by the purchase stage. The post-purchase stage describes the customers' expectations for how the company should continue to service and support their needs, while the company is focusing on relationship development to encourage more profitable purchases.

## 9.3 Chapter summary

Sports marketers are investing considerable sums of money in associating with a given sports entity. As with any corporate activity, the results will be dependent on the skills the company has within, coupled with satisfying customer needs externally. To assess the skills within, the brand touchpoints exercise is an important tool for gaining a detailed understanding of the company's many points of interaction with the market, both tangible and intangible. The resulting insights will reveal the complex factors that influence customer perceptions and identify gaps where the company can fine-tune its activities. The customer experience journey exercise complements the brand touchpoints map by showing the specific ways the sports marketer's company responds to customer needs. The two exercises should also reveal that areas of research findings overlap where the brand touchpoints results should be consistent with the customer experience journey responses. The knowledge gained from these exercises will be invaluable in finalizing decisions on how to create a successful sports marketing plan.

**CASE STUDY 1**

# Manchester United

Often when we hear the word power, we think of dollar signs. The sports world is no different. There are few sports franchises with truly global power, and perhaps the most well-known example of a sports powerhouse is Manchester United Football Club of the English Premier League (EPL). Manchester United, or ManU, has been around since 1878, was started by railway workers, and has grown into the largest sports franchise in the world.[5] The team went from a locally oriented soccer team, to a global soccer enterprise worth $2.23 billion in 2012.[6] There are an estimated 659 million Manchester United fans in the world, all of whom contribute to the team's continued success.[7] During the 2011 season, the club generated a cumulative audience reach of over 4 billion viewers across 211 countries.[8] Per game, it drew an average live cumulative audience reach of 49 million in 2011.[9] United's fan base is so diverse that its website is published in seven languages.[10] Its fan support is also evidenced on Facebook with 26.5 million likes and 477 500 followers on Twitter (the club's official Twitter account was launched in late 2012). Fans purchased over 5 million items of Manchester United branded licensed products in 2011, which includes over 2 million jerseys.[11] Manchester United branded products are sold through over 200 licensees in over 130 countries.[12]

Much of ManU's financial success stems from the fact that it has had great success on the pitch. In the club's history, it has won 20 championships and has a long history of attracting the world's biggest football stars.[13] In 2012, the club won its most recent English Premier League championship.[14] Somewhat surprisingly, Manchester United has seen significant success on the field without paying the highest wages in the Premier League. Though ManU spent £153 million in wages in 2011, it was topped by Chelsea (£191 million) and Manchester City (£174 million).[15]

The Red Devils, according to Forbes, are also dwarfing their competition in terms of overall franchise value. On Forbes' list, the next largest sports franchise is Real Madrid, coming in at a value of $1.88 billion, an astounding 19 percent lower than Manchester United.[16] As a base for comparison, the Dallas Cowboys and New York Yankees are tied for number three on Forbes's list of the most valuable sports teams at $1.85 billion.[17] During 2011, ManU raked in €367 million in overall revenues, up from €349.8 in 2010.[18]

Manchester United is also part of a growing trend of foreign-owned clubs. In 2005, the Glazer family (who also own the NFL's Tampa Bay Buccaneers) bought the club for $1.45 billion and took it off the London Stock Exchange.[19] Prior to its August 2012 IPO, the company had spent 14 years in the public's hands. The latest IPO was a $663 million IPO, the largest of any sports team in history.

Sponsorships have also proven to be incredibly lucrative for Manchester United, with sponsorship accounting for $133 million in 2011.[20] While jersey sponsorships are quite common in football, Manchester United has found unique ways to boost its astounding revenues through its current game jersey deal with Aon worth $31 million annually, its

**CASE STUDY 1** *(continued)*

practice jersey deal with DHL worth $62 million over four years, and its merchandise and sales agreement with Nike worth another $39 million annually.[21] The Red Devils can also look forward to its next jersey deal, set to begin in 2014 with General Motors, which is worth up to $80 million a year and one of the richest deals in football history.[22]

Ticket revenues are also high for Manchester United, as all Premier League games have sold out since the 1997–98 season.[23] In 2011, the club sold out all 52 000 of its season tickets.[24] Season tickets retail for between $900 and $1550, and the cheapest tickets at the club's Old Trafford stadium cost $46 in 2011.[25] Total match day revenues for the club were €120.3 million in 2011, with average revenue falling at the €4.1 million per home match.[26] Finally, broadcast revenues are also soaring to record highs. In 2011, as part of a newly signed EPL collective broadcast rights deal, Manchester United earned €66.9 million, which boosted its overall broadcast revenues to €132.3 million that year.[27]

Manchester United isn't just earning lots of money on its home turf. In addition to playing in the EPL and various UEFA (Union of European Football Associations) events, Manchester United is a popular choice for exhibition matches all over the globe. The team has done several tours that have included stops in the United States, Canada, China, Malaysia and South Africa among others over the past ten years. While the opponents vary between friendly matches with professional teams in whichever country they are visiting to exhibitions with other major European soccer clubs, the common thread is that these matches are growing in popularity and financial success.

All of this financial clout that the club has means it constantly attracts international attention. In September 2012, Olympic gold medalist, and the fastest man in the world, Usain Bolt said he would like to tryout for ManU.[28] Bolt exchanged tweets with player Rio Ferdinand and told a British newspaper that he was open to having a tryout. A spokesman for the United was quoted saying 'as the fastest man on Earth, he would undoubtedly add speed to the team'.[29] In addition to positive attention garnered by athletes such as Bolt, some negative attention follows the Red Devils. Liverpool striker Luis Suarez blamed Manchester United for his eight-game ban following a supposed racially charged incident with Patrice Evra.[30] He charged Manchester United with framing the incident incorrectly because they wanted to stop Liverpool from winning.[31]

Based on these astounding statistics, one could make a pretty convincing argument that football is a truly global language and Manchester United is as fundamental to this language as learning the alphabet. For over 100 years, fans have shown their loyalty to Manchester United to the extent that companies are now paying millions of dollars to leverage this fervent support.

**? QUESTIONS**

1  Identify Manchester United's brand touchpoints, and create a hypothetical customer experience journey map based on the club's fan membership activities.

**CASE STUDY 1** *(continued)*

2   What are some ways that Manchester United can continue to grow their global following? Is their success truly about on-field football performance? Or have United simply built a strong brand?

3   Now that Manchester United are a public company, shareholder interests can often be of greater importance than fan interests. How should United balance these interests, which could potentially be at odds with one another?

## CASE STUDY 2

# Penn State scandal

Scandals are nothing new in sports. As previously described in this chapter, since the days of Ancient Greece, athletes and coaches have been meddling with pure competition. While many of the scandals over the years have directly influenced the outcome of competition, perhaps no scandal has been as affective to an entire institution as the scandal at Pennsylvania State University that broke on 5 November 2011 with the arrest of former football coach Jerry Sandusky and subsequent arraignment on 48 criminal counts.[32] The arrest came after allegations from a teenage boy that he had been inappropriately touched by Sandusky years earlier during his involvement with Sandusky's charity, The Second Mile. Sandusky would later be convicted on 45 of 48 counts of sexual abuse, with several victims involved.[33]

The reach of the sex abuse scandal rapidly increased in the coming weeks as numerous officials at Penn State were drawn into its maelstrom. Athletic director Tim Curley and University Vice President for Finance and Business stepped down immediately after Sandusky was arrested, with allegations that they failed to inform police of their knowledge of the incidents.[34] University president Graham Spanier and legendary head football coach Joe Paterno were fired on 9 November.[35] And more than anything, the small township of University Park, Pennsylvania was thrust into the international spotlight as the entire university seemed to be caught in a scandal showing a complete institutional lack of control.

In addition to the cultural sanctions slammed against the university, the National Collegiate Athletic Association (NCAA) came down heavy with its own athletics-aimed sanctions. In addition to a $60 million fine (to be paid over five years) and a four-year post-season bowl ban, the NCAA forced Penn State to give up ten of its football scholarships and held them to only 65 of a possible 85 scholarship players on the roster for four years.[36] The university was also placed on probation for five years.[37] In effect, the school will be unable to field a full scholarship roster till 2020.[38] Perhaps the most lasting impact of NCAA sanctions on Penn State was that the university was forced to vacate all of its victories from 1998 to 2011, thus dashing away Joe Paterno's title as the major-college career leader in football wins.[39] Current players on the team were given the option to transfer schools without penalty.[40] The Big-10 Conference also fined Penn State $13 million over four years, which was the equivalent of what the team would have ordinarily earned in post-season bowl revenue.[41]

The athletic department was also forced to lower donation levels for its 'Seat Transfer and Equity Plan (STEP)'.[42] Despite projected higher donation levels to the booster Nittany Lion Club of $17.5 million in 2012, attendance levels are down at football games.[43] At the beginning of the 2012 season, attendance levels were hovering around 91 percent of capacity compared to 97–98 percent in typical years.[44] To combat the decreased attendance, the athletic department lowered donation levels for about 11 500 seats at the 106 572-seat Beaver Stadium.[45] For about 6000 seats, the donation level will fall to $200 from $400 and for the other 5500 seats, the donation level will be $400 down from $600.[46]

**CASE STUDY 2** *(continued)*

The university also announced that there will be no increases in ticket prices for the 2013 season, nor will there be necessary donation level increases for season tickets.[47]

The Nittany Lion Club (NCL) also announced a 'One Team Commitment' campaign to help encourage Penn State fans to donate. For the first time ever, NLC members can earn bonus points, which can then be applied towards priority status for football and basketball games, for demonstrating long-term support of the athletic department.[48] NLC members commit to giving over a five-year period and, in making this commitment, they lock in the 2013 donation level for five years.[49]

During the 2011–12 fiscal year, the university reported donations of $208.7 million, the second highest annual amount in school history.[50] Donors that year also set school records in number of donors (191 712) and total gifts (323 271).[51] In the wake of the scandal, only four of Penn State's multi-year pledges backed out of their commitments, while 15 of roughly 1800 bequests pulled Penn State from their wills.[52] These numbers, however, don't show the entire story. Total commitments, which include pledges and outright gifts were down to $223.7 million from $353 in 2010–11, and $273 in 2009–10.[53] The giving total commitments from 2011–12 are the lowest since 2005–06.[54] The self-supporting athletic department is projected to take in $108 million in the 2012–13 fiscal year, with about 60 percent of that coming from football. And with a normal operating budget in the mid-$80 million range, it will be difficult for Penn State athletics to continue to grow given that they have to pay a $60 million fine over several years. The school has promised not to use donation dollars to pay the fine, and must continue to find new ways to earn money.[55]

Penn State has also made a concerted effort to right the wrongs of former coach Jerry Sandusky. The $60 million fine levied by the NCAA will 'go into an endowment to fund programs for the detection, prevention and treatment of child abuse'.[56] In addition, Penn State donated $1.5 million from its 2011 bowl proceeds to the Pennsylvania Coalition Against Rape and another $1.1 million of bowl earnings went to a new child abuse research and treatment center at Penn State.[57] Penn State alumni have also rallied around the cause and raised $540 000 for the Rape, Abuse, and Incest National Network.[58]

While the immediate impact of the Jerry Sandusky scandal has been seen, it's unclear what will transpire in the coming years for Penn State.

 **QUESTIONS**

1 How might the scandal affect Penn State's brand touchpoints? Give examples and hypothetical scores. How would you address the concerns?

2 What are some ways that the Penn State athletic department can continue to encourage donations?

3 How can Penn State repair its image as a football program fuelled by honor and integrity?

4 How should Penn State approach potential sponsors in the wake of this incident? Should Penn State have appealed the NCAA's sanctions?

## NOTES

1 'The Human Genome Project' (2008).
2 'NASA releases new WISE mission catalog of entire infrared sky' (2012).
3 Davis (2010, pp. 374–7).
4 Ibid., pp. 377–82.
5 De La Merced (2012).
6 Badenhausen (2012).
7 Ibid.
8 'About Manchester United' (n.d.).
9 Ibid.
10 Ibid.
11 Ibid.
12 Ibid.
13 Badenhausen (2012).
14 Ibid.
15 'Annual review of football finance – 2012 highlights' (2012).
16 Badenhausen (2012).
17 Ibid.
18 Jones, Dan (2012).
19 De La Merced (2012).
20 Mickle (2011, p. 1).
21 Badenhausen (2012).
22 Mamudi (2012).
23 'About Manchester United' (n.d.).
24 'Key business issues facing EPL franchises' (2011).
25 Ibid.
26 Jones, Dan (2012).
27 Ibid.
28 'Report: Usain Bolt eyes ManU' (2012).
29 Ibid.
30 'Suarez blames ban on Man Utd "power"' (2012).
31 Ibid.
32 'Sandusky, Penn State case timeline' (2011).
33 Gallman (2012).
34 'Sandusky, Penn State case timeline' (2011).
35 Ibid.
36 Thamel, Pete (2012).
37 Ibid.
38 Ibid.
39 Ibid.
40 Ibid.
41 Ibid.
42 Smith (2012).
43 Ibid.
44 Ibid.
45 Ibid.
46 Ibid.
47 Jones, Ben (2012).
48 'Nittany Lion Club unveils 'One Team Commitment' and additional seating options for 2013 Season' (2012).
49 Ibid.
50 Gallman (2012).
51 Smith (2012).

52  Ibid.
53  Ibid.
54  Ibid.
55  Gallman (2012).
56  Levy and Rubinkam (2012).
57  Ibid.
58  Jones, Ben (2012).

 **REFERENCES**

'About Manchester United' (n.d.), ManUtd.com, accessed 8 September 2012 at http://www. manutd.com/.

'Annual review of football finance – 2012 highlights' (2012), Deloitte LLP, 31 May 2012, 10.

Badenhausen, Kurt (2012), 'Manchester United tops the world's 50 most valuable sports teams', Forbes.com, 16 July 2012, accessed 8 September 2012 at http://www.forbes.com/sites/kurt badenhausen/2012/07/16/manchester-united-tops-the-worlds-50-most-valuable-sports-teams/.

Davis, John A. (2010), *Competitive Success – How Branding Adds Value*, New York: John Wiley & Sons.

De La Merced, Michael (2012), 'Manchester United prices IPO at $14 a share', *The New York Times*, 9 August 2012, accessed 8 September 2012 at http://dealbook.nytimes. com/2012/08/09/manchester-united-prices-i-p-o-at-14-a-share/.

Gallman, Stephanie (2012), 'Despite Sandusky scandal, Penn State draws $208.7 million in donations', CNN.com, 9 July 2012, accessed 6 October 2012 at http://www.cnn. com/2012/07/09/us/pennsylvania-penn-state-donations/index.html.

Jones, Ben (2012), 'Penn State football: Nittany Lion Club to alter STEP program', StateCollege. com, 4 October 2012, accessed 6 October 2012, http://www.statecollege.com/news/ local-news/penn-state-football-nittany-lion-club-to-alter-step-program-1147269/.

Jones, Dan (2012), 'Football money league – 2012', Deloitte LLP, February 2012, 7.

'Key business issues facing EPL franchises' (2011), *Sports Business Journal*, 15 August 2011, 35.

Levy, Marc and Michael Rubinkam (2012), 'Record Penn State fine to help abused kids', Sports. Yahoo.com, 25 July 2012, accessed 6 October 2012 at http://finance.yahoo.com/news/ record-penn-state-fine-help-abused-kids-063528182--spt.html.

Mamudi, Sam (2012), 'Manchester United is "biggest sports business in the world" CEO crows', *The Wall Street Journal*, 10 August 2012, accessed 8 September 2012 at http://blogs.marketwatch.com/thetell/2012/08/10/manchester-united-is-biggest-sports-business-in-the-world-ceo-crows/.

'NASA releases new WISE mission catalog of entire infrared sky' (2012), 14 March 2012, accessed 21 March 2012 at http://www.nasa.gov/mission_pages/WISE/news/wise20120314.html.

'Nittany Lion Club unveils "One Team Commitment" and additional seating options for 2013 season' (2012), GoPSUSports.com, 3 October 2012, accessed 6 October 2012, http://www. gopsusports.com/sports/m-footbl/spec-rel/100312aac.html.

Mickle, Tripp (2011), 'U.S. sports executives who run Arsenal see slow gains, intense scrutiny', *Sports Business Journal*, 15 August 2011, 1.

'Report: Usain Bolt eyes ManU' (2012), ESPN.com, 7 August 2012, accessed 8 September 2012 at http://espn.go.com/olympics/summer/2012/trackandfield/story/_/id/8242606/2012-london-olympics-usain-bolt-wants-manchester-united-tryout-report-says.

'Sandusky, Penn State case timeline' (2011), ESPN.com, 9 November 2011, accessed 3 October 2012 at http://espn.go.com/college-football/story/_/id/7212054/key-dates-penn-state-sex-abuse-case.

Smith, Chris (2012), 'Did the Jerry Sandusky scandal help Penn State make more money?', Forbes.com, 10 July 2012, accessed 6 October 2012 at http://www.forbes.com/sites/chris smith/2012/07/10/did-the-jerry-sandusky-scandal-help-penn-state-make-more-money/.

'Suarez blames ban on Man Utd "power"' (2012), Soccernet.ESPN.com, 18 July 2012, accessed 8 September 2012 at http://soccernet.espn.go.com/news/story/_/id/1125313/ luis-suarez-blames-ban-on-manchester-united-%27political-power%27.

Thamel, Pete (2012), 'Sanctions decimate Nittany Lions now and for years to come' (2012), *The New York Times*, 23 July 2012, accessed 6 October 2012 at http://www.nytimes. com/2012/07/24/sports/ncaafootball/penn-state-penalties-include-60-million-fine-and- bowl-ban.html?pagewanted=all&_.

'The Human Genome Project' (2008), *Stanford Encyclopedia of Philosophy*, 26 November 2008, accessed 1 May 2011 at http://plato.stanford.edu/entries/human-genome/.

# 10

# Sports marketing – leadership and organizations

 **CHAPTER OVERVIEW**

Thus far we have discussed the overall environment for sports marketing planning and decisions. By examining the sports marketing value chain and context, we gained insight into the factors that shape sports marketing decisions. Next, the discussions about sports history and sports fans described the characteristics of fans and the factors that make sports appealing to them. These topics led us to a better understanding of the potential benefits companies derive from their sports marketing investments. As we learned, sports marketers must be accountable for their decisions, so we explored relevant measures that, in turn, reinforced the importance of how sports marketing can create value, both tangible and intangible. An important complement to and by-product of successful value creation is an improved reputation. Of course, an improved reputation is caused by more than merely investing money and clever positioning. The details include understanding the touchpoints and mapping a customer journey sequence that reveals the strengths and weaknesses of the sports marketer's firm and where improvements can be made to sustain long-term value creation. In this chapter we explain key management roles and the marketing function's responsibilities in implementing the sports marketing plan.

## 10.1 Organizational roles and responsibilities in brand planning

As sports marketing has grown in popularity as an area for marketing investment designed to enhance a company's reputation and foster growth, so too has the importance of having a talented management team leading the marketing effort. Marketing organizational structures and the roles within vary depending on the company and its unique characteristics, but there are responsibilities and activities common to most marketing organizations, even if the titles and individual people responsible change.

Brands have evolved from decades of practice that once defined them prima-rily as products, particularly in the consumer world, into strategic assets that contribute significant value to the total enterprise. As strategic assets, brands can even be defined as the entire company. By implication, the responsibil-ity for brand building extends beyond the responsibility of one department. Arguably, this suggests that every department and each person plays a role in developing the brand, which loosely ties people in the company to market-ing even if they don't have a formal marketing title or they perform tradition-ally defined non-marketing activities like human resources, accounting, or shipping and receiving. But how do companies effectively organize them-selves to support this broader brand-oriented emphasis? A brand-oriented company is one that has achieved a certain amount of recognition and stature in the marketplace. In this regard, companies do not start out as brands. Instead, they evolve into brands based on the collective experiences of the company's many stakeholders, whose relationship with the company and its products have helped build an understanding of the company with each interaction. These interactions become part of the company's story, as told by its users, and over time the company develops iconic characteristics that become embedded in society, reinforcing the company's image and reputation.

By using sports to burnish their brand image, companies are attempting to link the sports property's qualities with their company. This linkage is harder to achieve than just advertising alongside the sports property's name or hanging banners around venues. Making meaningful associations that increase brand awareness, attracts new customers, grows revenues, and increases brand value requires a well-structured sports marketing game plan supported by an organizational plan where roles and responsibilities are clearly understood by each member of the sports marketing team.

## Senior management

Company strategy drives decisions, growth-oriented activities, departmen-tal plans, and individual behaviors throughout the organization and every location. As we have discussed throughout this book, brand value is an important and measurable strategic asset whose value is a significant con-tributor to total market capitalization. Increases in brand value are the result of a company having a strong and positive brand reputation, part of which is achieved by creating superb customer experiences anywhere and everywhere they interact with the brand. Since customer experiences are connected to a wide range of the company's operations, as we learned from the brand touch-points and customer experience journey exercises in Chapter 9, responsibility for managing the brand image extends to every area of the company. Proper expectations and guidelines must be established by senior management that describe the role each area of the organization plays in enhancing the company brand. CEO support, followed by support from senior management, demonstrates that brand building is a major objective of the company. Without overt CEO and senior management support for developing a strong brand reputation, the likelihood of increasing brand value that enhances total market capitalization is remote.

## Marketing

Support for marketing must flow from the very top, at the CEO level, if a company and its marketing efforts are to be perceived as important by the rest of the organization. At the same time, the importance of having the right marketing organization to support the company's brand and sports marketing needs is paramount. In fact, more than just a marketing or brand management activity, brand leadership involves influencing the company's many touchpoints so that company practices work in concert to support a consistent image and reputation. Brand image is not a superficial façade, nor is it a creative advertising campaign. It is the brand as seen through the eyes of the company's stakeholders, which means both individual and collective experiences directly shape the market's understanding of the company. Therefore, understanding the company's marketing needs evolves from marketers knowing their firm's strategic objectives and will help them develop their marketing organization so that it is effective in the development, management, and measurement of its sports marketing activities. In other words, the marketing department is a vital driver of a larger cross-organizational effort to use sports marketing activities to enhance brand value. Marketing still owns the responsibility for product decisions, marketing communications campaigns, market research, and customer relationship development, but its expertise also includes an ongoing collaboration and interaction with other departments in a collaborative effort to manage the company's overall brand reputation.

Management cannot reasonably expect every brand touchpoint to be perfectly controlled and managed, but planning activities need to account for the broader organizational mandate implied by emphasizing brand as a strategic asset for the company, and sports properties as a key investment in building the brand. In this regard, the marketing group has a direct role to play in leading the brand development effort since its expertise is in understanding customers, competitors, and market conditions. Brand teams are a logical supporter of brand development efforts especially when senior management mandates brand value and leadership as critical strategic needs. Brand teams spend their sports marketing planning identifying the brand touchpoints impacted by the sports marketing activities, as revealed from the brand touchpoints exercises discussed in Chapter 9. Customer perceptions of the brand and its touchpoints, based on the company's customer research, are then factored into the planning. The marketing team must have expertise in the following:

## Business/brand strategy

Developing the brand strategy is done by a brand strategist using the corporate strategy to provide overall direction. If the company has a Chief Marketing Officer (CMO), then this person leads the planning effort. Brand managers with corporate-level responsibility may be responsible for this as well, and in larger companies their responsibilities are likely to include leadership of multiple brands and product categories. Since the brand strategist dictates the direction and objectives in building the brand, they lead the brand planning effort and have final responsibility for authoring the plan and leading the implementation of the strategy. As a member of senior management the brand strategist is the primary conduit between the rest of the marketing team, and perhaps indirectly, the rest of the organization, and senior management. In the latter capacity, the brand strategist must work collaboratively with his or her counterparts in senior management and their organizations to coordinate brand development activities and manage the many different brand touchpoints. With a sports marketing investment that includes a sophisticated activation plan, the brand strategist has a unique addition to his or her other marketing responsibilities since sports properties have demanding and complex implementation needs of their own, any one of which can become an obstacle to the sports marketer's success if execution is poor. Brand strategists work with the field sales force, make presentations about the brand strategy at company-wide events, plus they may also talk to the analyst community as well as the broader range of value chain members, such as suppliers and distributors. Since the brand is a strategic asset, its value is tracked through budgeting, market surveys, brand value calculations (including discounted cash flow), as well as unit sales and profit and loss responsibilities for all product categories in the company. GE's (General Electric's) Christopher Katsuleres is the company's Director of Olympic and Sport Marketing, playing a vital role in ensuring proper alignment between GE's corporate goals and its sports marketing investments. Prior to this role at GE, Katsuleres held similar positions at Visa and Intel, giving him a thorough understanding of how sports marketing can be used to enhance a company's brand.[1]

## Category management

Category managers are responsible for managing all brands within an entire category of products, not just individual products. Their role is to develop business plans that strengthen the company's position in their category, including merchandising plans. Category managers are responsible for their category's profit and loss performance. Category management's interests are often seen in sports sponsorships, such as the Olympics' TOP (The Olympic Partners) program, which grants sponsors exclusive worldwide rights in their product category to be associated with the Olympics,[2] and FIFA World Cup's three sponsorship tiers, which provide exclusive product category rights to sponsors on a global scale (the FIFA Partners program, the highest sponsorship level, gives sponsors exclusive rights with FIFA and all FIFA events worldwide), FIFA World Cup Sponsors (providing sponsors exclusive rights with FIFA Federations Cup and FIFA World Cup), and FIFA Supporters (providing host country sponsors with rights in their domestic market).[3] Note that being a sponsor is one of many sports marketing choices available to companies. Product categories can also simply be advertised during a major event, such as the MLB World Series, or even a regular season game in almost any league. Viewership levels are lower than for the larger, season-ending championships and mega-sports events like the FIFA World Cup, but the marketing activities can still produce positive results for the sports marketer depending on their objectives and implementation strategy.

## Marketing communications

Marketing communications describes a key role often mistakenly viewed as the *only* activity in marketing. The people responsible for marketing communications work on the communications message, tactics, and media strategy, using traditional and digital/social marketing tools. Larger companies will usually outsource the major advertising activities to a third party advertising agency, public relations, and/or marketing communications firm. If this occurs, then the company's internal marketing communications team work in collaboration with the external agency, conveying the wishes of marketing and senior management. Marketing communications managers are usually responsible for any budget items related to advertising and media expenditures. They write the marketing communications briefs that inform company management and the external agency about what their communications strategy is expected to accomplish. As consumers, particularly in North America, we see the finished product anytime we watch a TV ad or hear a radio promotion during a sports event, such as the Super Bowl, the NBA Finals, or almost any weekend sports programming.

## Marketing research

Market researchers are experts in surveying techniques, statistical analysis, data mining, and sometimes even consumer behavior. Market research findings are more than just pages of numbers and statistical data, they are *insights* into customers, their purchase patterns and preferences, and even their more general shopping and social behaviors. Market researchers will often hire third party market research/consulting firms to gather the research, allowing the company's marketing team to focus on implementing the product and communications decisions related to the sports marketing activities.

## Product management

Product managers in marketing, also known as product line managers, are responsible for planning product lines and the individual products within, including any individually branded products. Product managers work cross-functionally with managers in design, development, and engineering, usually leading the business planning for their product lines. The business planning includes explaining target customer needs, product direction, and pricing while also working collaboratively with the product team's other members to identify materials suppliers and production locations. Product managers work within larger product categories, which might have several product managers. Product managers may also work with partner companies to co-develop offerings for a specific market. Visa and Samsung did this for the 2012 Summer Olympic Games in London when they collaborated on a new mobile payments platform using Visa's financial services expertise and Samsung's mobile device technology.[4]

## Creative management

The creative team is briefed by product management about the customer needs for new editions of the product and the role of the product in the sports marketing plan. The creative team then works on new designs that are subsequently presented to the rest of the product management team, sometimes leading to debate about the preliminary designs versus the stated objectives. Design refinements are made while development and engineering work on finding ways to produce the designs cost effectively.

## Business development

Business development is responsible for developing and managing strategic partnerships and alliances with suppliers, distributors, and outsourcing partners. Depending on the structure and associated responsibilities of the company's sales force, the business development managers might also be responsible for selling and managing key strategic customers. The afore-mentioned collaboration between Visa and Samsung is an example of a partnership where business development played a vital role.

## 10.2 Principles of brand and sports marketing planning

Research into the practices about leading brands around the world showed the broad principles they follow in their brand-building efforts:[5]

1. *The brand's traditions are honored and respected.* Leading brands, whether globally recognized or regional favorites, honor their traditions, crea-tively incorporate historical success and recognized achievements to communicate the brand's story to the market. These efforts serve to inspire generations of employees and reinforce known strengths to cus-tomers and helps management evolve their brand reputations in a way that stays true to society's understanding of the brand while also staying relevant to the times. Nike reinforces its traditions from the moment new employees go through orientation. New hires learn about Nike's athletic heritage during a multi-day orientation. Employees are immersed in a corporate office with visual reminders of the company's innovative prod-ucts and great athletes everywhere, from iconic images of past athletes to current advertising, from buildings named after famous Nike athletes to fitness facilities for employees that are unrivalled in the corporate world.[6]

2. *Strong values guide behavior and actions.* The company's values are known and regularly articulated across the organization, reminding employees of what the company stands for and how it expects everyone to behave. Values differ widely depending on the company. The important point is that the values should be broad guides to the company's expected behav-ior and to have those values communicated, understood, embedded, and lived by everyone in the company. Adidas values emphasize innovation, collaborative work, superior performance and corporate responsibil-ity. Like Nike, adidas embeds its values into new employees from the moment they are hired, and the values also serve to guide the company's business practices around the world.[7]

3. *They are brutally honest about their capabilities.* Most well-run companies are quite clear about their expertise and competencies. Dishonesty does not serve anyone well, especially as it relates to promises to the market about a company's products and reputation. Knowing the company's capabilities assists the process of identifying brand-building opportunities

that offer the best potential. Furthermore, this self-knowledge positively impacts relationships with other businesses in the brand's value chain because management is motivated to find complementary skills that enhance the overall product offered. Sports marketing can be a powerful vehicle for conveying and reinforcing the company's reputation because the imagery and emotions are so well understood across cultures and markets.

4. *They focus on fulfilling needs distinctively to create strategic benefits.* Leading brands become recognized as having a strong reputation because over time the marketplace has gained important experiences interacting with the brand, creating a clear understanding of the company's distinctive capabilities. Distinction is a quality recognized by customers because the company has met their needs uniquely well. Focusing on the company's distinctive capabilities is an important consideration when developing sports marketing plans.

5. *Their plans encompass pre/during/post-plan activities and follow-up.* Successful planning involves descriptions of what is to be done, assigning responsibility, setting deadlines and expected deliverables, determining measures of progress, and preparing options for fine-tuning tactics along the way. Professional athletes are not likely to last long if they are unprepared mentally or physically for the upcoming season. Their success is predicated on rigorous training before the season, tailoring training based on the demands of the competitive playing schedule, and preparing for the next season as well. Leading brands describe clear expectations about long-term objectives, the activities to be implemented designed to move the company closer to the objectives, and adjustments made along the way based on market conditions.

6. *They are flexible but core principles are never compromised.* Leading brands operated by a simple principle: if an activity is illegal, unethical, immoral, or simply against the organization's core values, then don't do it, no matter how attractive and tempting the short-term benefits might be. Ethical compromises immediately and directly impact the company negatively, and can be devastating for the long-term reputation. Once Lance Armstrong gave up his efforts to fight doping allegations and when coupled with a devastating set of findings from the US Anti-Doping Agency in 2012, the evidence appeared overwhelmingly negative for him and his sponsors. Armstrong's former sponsors Nike, Anheuser-Busch, Oakley, Trek Bicycles, and FRS (energy drink maker) all dropped him as a result.[8] *They have a palpable commitment to authenticity and excellence.* Brand success occurs when every brand touchpoint is supported by a commitment from senior management on down to authenticity in the company's products and communications, and excellence in quality and operations.

## 10.3    The sports promotion mix

Knowing the marketing team's responsibilities and their company's values enables the development of a sports promotion mix that is consistent with the company's strategy and reputation. The sports promotion mix is similar to its non-sports counterpart, although tailored to the range of products associated with sports properties. The components are: advertising; promotions; sponsorship; licensing; public relations; community relations; social responsibility; and experiences.

### Advertising

Sports advertising is when a company attempts to attract the marketplace to its products through sports-related print, broadcast, cable, or new media appeals. The range of advertising choices encompasses traditional and new media and will be discussed further in Chapters 11 and 12. Examples of sports advertising abound from sports product companies advertising their offerings (Under Armour, adidas, Reebok, PowerBar, Babolat, Specialized Bicycles etc.) to sports properties advertising their upcoming contests (professional tennis tournaments, NFL teams, F1 racing, Rugby 7s tournaments etc.).

### Promotions

Sports promotions are inducements or incentives, often in the form of discounts or special offers. They are used to generate quick, short bursts of increased consumer interest that can lead to temporary increases in sales and market share. Examples include advance purchase ticket plans, special game day promotions, and limited time offers to encourage the sale of select items (food, merchandise). Chapters 11 and 12 will provide descriptions and examples of both traditional and social/digital marketing.

### Sponsorship

Sports sponsorship is defined as gaining the rights to associate with a sports property by exchanging cash or in-kind value. Sponsorships can also include event management activities and naming rights for venues or landmarks in or near sports properties. Examples of sponsorship include the Olympic TOP program and the FIFA Partners program. Examples of event management activities include the planning and operational control of single game events or multi-day mega-sports events like the Olympics. Examples of naming rights are evident in most sports, from Major League Baseball's AT&T Park (named for the US telecommunications firm) where the San Francisco Giants baseball team plays to Etihad Stadium (named for the Abu Dhabi airline) where the English Premier League's Manchester City football club plays. Chapter 14 will discuss this in detail.

## Licensing

Sports licensing is legal agreements allowing use of sports entities' trademarks by paying a royalty or similar fee. Most often the licensee uses the trademarks on merchandise they manufacture directly or contract indirectly, including apparel, trinkets, beverage containers, linens, toys, and more. Fans buy licensed merchandise to show their support of the team or athlete, and license agreements are tightly controlled and regulated by each of the world's major sports leagues. Chapter 15 explores licensing and merchandising further.

## Public relations

Sports public relations is described as management's efforts to foster long-term goodwill and understanding with the public. Public relations includes several activities, such as press releases, news conferences, crisis communications, and ongoing media relations. Post-game press conferences with coaches and/or players, as seen in the English Premier League (EPL), National Football League (NFL), National Basketball Association (NBA) and Professional Golfers' Association (PGA), are a common and expected activity that allows the media to gain access to the sport's key people of the day. Sports product companies illustrate public relations through announcements of new product launches, press conferences about their latest sports sponsorship, and similar activities. Chapter 11 describes more about public relations.

## Community relations

Whereas public relations are geared toward a broad audience, community relations are interactions between the organization and people in a particular area, usually the sports entity's hometown, although community relations can occur on behalf of the sports property in any focused community location. The premise of community relations is to break down barriers between the sports entity and the community it serves by making it more human, accessible, and approachable. The NFL's Green Bay Packers have invested years of effort in getting children in the local community more involved with sports, from their 'Fit Kids' program designed to address childhood obesity, to their 'Coats for Kids' campaign that seeks donations of warm outerwear for poor children in the community.[9]

## Social responsibility

In sports marketing, social responsibility refers to an organization's efforts to add lasting value to society at large through activities that get the organization directly involved in important causes. The NBA established the 'NBA Cares' program, which actively involves teams and players in outreach efforts in communities across the United States and around the world. The outreach activities vary depending on the community's needs, but much of the emphasis is on providing safe, modern places where kids can 'live, learn, and play'. Internationally, NBA Cares partners with organizations to improve the life of youths in three areas: education; youth and family development; and health-related causes.[10]

## Experiences

Sports experiences are defined as the combination of tangible and intangible interactions that affect market perceptions of the organization through its sports activities, such as a sports event and/or sports products. Each city in which an F1 race is held becomes a multi-day entertainment event, including the warm ups two to three days before, when F1 teams can test their cars on the race course, fans can attend live music shows and vendor trade shows, and a wide range of parties are held.[11]

## 10.4 Chapter summary

The success of any sports marketing plan will depend on the organizational support and the talent of the individuals responsible for implementation. While every company has characteristics that are unique from every other firm, there are also common roles and responsibilities. Most marketing organizations in large companies are staffed with experienced professionals that have the support of senior management. This level of support is crucial to gaining company-wide support as well. Within marketing, there are several needs that are typically addressed by specific roles, including brand strategy, product management, marketing communications, marketing research, creative management, and business development. There are also seven principles practiced by leading brands, and understanding them is vital to successfully implementing sports marketing plans. We also learned about the general components of the sports promotion mix that will be explored in depth in the remaining chapters.

**CASE STUDY 1**

# NFL China

Introducing a sports property to a new market can be a daunting task. Introducing a sports property to a new market that has a very limited sports culture in society can be an overwhelming task. Yet that is exactly what the National Football League (NFL) is attempting in China. This expansion branch has set out to not only bring the NFL to China, but also to introduce the game of American football to that culture, which has a long history of favoring individual-focused sports. NFL China began in 2007 when the league realized that the Chinese market was simply too alluring to ignore.[12] With a total population of around 1.3 billion people and a rapidly growing middle class, many American sports leagues are increasing operations in the world's biggest country to create truly global sports properties. NFL China has one simple goal: to make American football a top ten sport for males in China's Tier 1 cities by 2020.[13] Currently, the league sits at twentieth on the list.[14] While the total billion-strong market is an extremely attractive target, NFL China has focused its target market on the 39 million males between the ages of 15 and 54 living in Tier 1 cities.[15]

To date, NFL China has seen strong reach in China. Despite airing early on Monday and Tuesday mornings in China, the league reaches 335 million homes via television.[16] NFL China's real growth has been online, which is a dominant medium in the Tier 1 cities the league is targeting. Online, the league has a reach of 680 million people, which includes 280 million via social media.[17] NFL China currently offers an app called NFL Game Pass for purchase that enables fans in China to see every NFL game.[18] Within 20 minutes of every game's conclusion, the app allows fans in distant lands to watch a distilled highlight version of the game that's about 40 minutes long.[19]

To better introduce the people of China to the game of American football, NFL China holds a traveling event called the NFL Experience. This event brings NFL players and cheerleaders, equipment, and the chance for kids to throw, kick, and run with a football. As part of the NFL Experience, both flag football and tackle football games are played.[20] Former NFL quarterback Kordell Stewart took part in the first NFL Experience, which attracted 4000 attendees on 8 September 2012.[21] The NFL Experience will also visit Shanghai and Guangzhou during the fall of 2012.[22]

Another growing successful venture that NFL China has produced is a university flag football league. The season, which stretches between September and November, culminates in the University Bowl.[23] In its fifth year, the university league has 36 participating universities throughout the largest cities in China.[24] The season-long competition in 2011 drew over 1000 athletes, with 1500 spectators showing up at the University Bowl match to cheer on their respective teams.[25] In the cities of Beijing, Shanghai, and Guangzhou, there are 12 000 flag football fans.[26]

One potential weakness that the NFL has seen in China stems from the lack of international infrastructure for the game of American football. The game of basketball has seen tremendous success in the Chinese market partially due to FIBA (the International Basketball

**CASE STUDY 1** *(continued)*

Federation), the global governing body for the sport.[27] American football's equivalent, Paris-based IFAF (International Federation of American Football), does not have the same strength or power and thus, American football has not seen the strong international growth that basketball has.[28] Still, in 2012, youth tackle football leagues popped up in Guangzhou, Tianjin, Hong Kong, and Zhuhai.[29] The Beijing Guardians, another youth tackle football team also practices at the brand new Tongzhou American Football Center, a facility built recently to meet demand for American football.[30] The facility boasts an 8000-seat mini stadium and is the only field lined for American football in China.[31]

Creating a sports culture in China has also proven to be a worthy challenge for NFL China as it meanders through the process of conducting business in China. In a country that faces heavy government regulation of sport, very little attention is paid to changing the culture of sport in the country. Children are selected for their athletic talent and potential from a young age and follow a separate educational track from their peers who display less potential.[32] Those who don't fall into the sports track very often have little opportunity to play organized team sports. In order to truly take hold and become a top ten sport in popularity, NFL China realizes that a fundamental shift in the entire educational process will play a role in meeting its goal.[33] Furthermore, NFL China faces resistance in broadcasting NFL games because the television channels in the country are also government-censored and controlled.[34]

Still, there are many proponents of the NFL in China outside of NFL China. There are approximately 72 000 American ex-patriots living in China who have familiarity with the league that has produced some of the most-watched sports programs in the world.[35] At the United States Embassy in China, ambassadors happily give out American footballs with the embassy seal on them.[36] These footballs have proven to be the embassy's most popular premium gift.[37] In addition to the youth leagues popping up in the world's biggest country, some Chinese players are knocking on the door of the NFL. Long Ding, a native of Qing Dao, China got a tryout with the Jacksonville Jaguars in 2012.[38] In addition, Ed Wang, the son of 1984 Chinese Olympians Nancy and Robert Wang and the first Chinese player in the NFL, was drafted in 2010 by the Buffalo Bills.[39] He sat out the 2012 season with a shoulder injury for the Oakland Raiders.[40] Perhaps a Chinese success story, like Yao Ming in the NBA, is just what the NFL needs for the sport to take hold in China.

 **QUESTIONS**

1 What are some ways that NFL China can connect with people in China?

2 Should it focus on the expatriate community to grow the sport? Or should it target its efforts towards native Chinese citizens?

3 Where should NFL's priorities lie – in growing the sport of football or increasing the popularity of the league?

**CASE STUDY 2**

# Mark Cuban

Team ownership structure varies widely in the world of professional sports. While some owners opt to take a 'hands off' approach, other owners play an active role in shaping the successes and failures of their team. Some owners, however, have reached iconic status for the personal brand they have built for themselves. One of those owners is Mark Cuban, owner of the Dallas Mavericks since 14 January 2000.[41]

Cuban made his billions as a serial entrepreneur, but has arguably risen to fame due to his tenure as the Mavs' outspoken owner. And from the moment Cuban's tenure began, the entire atmosphere of Dallas Mavericks' games began to change. Games became a full entertainment experience with his push for the return of the 'Reunion Rowdies', a spirited group of fans named for the then-called Reunion Arena (the name of the group has since changed to the Maverick ManiAACs to reflect the arena's new name, the American Airlines Center).[42] Cuban has, and continues, to go to great lengths to make himself available to Mavericks fans by posting his email address on the Mavericks' webpage and personally answering hundreds of emails per week.[43] He calls himself a 'fan-owner' and rather than sit in a box, separated from fans, Cuban's seats are a few rows back from the Mavericks bench.[44]

Despite his enthusiasm, his emotions often get the best of him and he has found himself getting his wrist slapped by the media and the NBA. In 2006, Cuban made history when the NBA fined him $25 000 for comments he made about the officiating during a 2006 play-off game.[45] He became the first person ever to be fined by a professional sports league due to comments made on Twitter.[46] Despite that first fine, Cuban didn't stop his rants on officials. After Game 5 of the NBA Finals, Cuban stormed the floor, went on a profane rant to the officials' faces, and stared down NBA Commissioner David Stern as he walked off the floor.[47] That stunt cost him $250 000 and in total, Cuban racked up nearly $500 000 in fines throughout the 2006 NBA play-offs alone.[48] To date, Cuban has accumulated close to $2 million total in fines from the NBA.[49]

Still, in some ways, Cuban has seemingly changed the Dallas Mavericks organization for the better. In his tenure, the Mavs have improved their regular-season winning percentage from 40 to 69 percent.[50] In addition, the team has been to the play-offs every year he has been there and won the NBA Finals in 2011.[51] Despite his heavy fines, Cuban has pledged to donate an equal amount to various charities.[52] Cuban has also significantly raised the visibility of the organization due to the media frequently seeking him out for quotes because he is so candid in his comments. The jury is still out, however, in some ways regarding Cuban's overall impact.

**?  QUESTIONS**

1   Is Cuban really a good owner? Or is he just a passionate person? What are the characteristics of a 'good' owner?

---

**CASE STUDY 2** *(continued)*

2   What role should an owner play in team operations?
3   Is it fair to attribute a team's success with the ownership? How should the
    owner relate to his/her management team?
4   How does an owner affect sports marketing decisions for the sports property?
5   How does an owner affect the sports marketing investment decisions for a
    company considering sponsorship?

**NOTES**

1   'General Electric director joins Olympic debate at deaders in sponsorship' (2012).
2   Olympics.org website (n.d.).
3   FIFA website (n.d.).
4   'Samsung, Visa partner on m-payments for London 2012 Olympics' (2012).
5   Davis (2010, pp. 369–70).
6   Ransdell (1999).
7   'Vision and values' (n.d.).
8   'Factbox: sponsors drop Lance Armstrong' (2012); Rovell (2012).
9   'Fit Kids' (n.d.)
10  'The NBA Cares commitment' (n.d.); Bee (2012).
11  'France, Turkey and now Austria could fill in 2013 calendar gap' (n.d.).
12  Zhe (2012).
13  Young (2012).
14  Ibid.
15  Ibid.
16  Ibid.
17  Ibid.
18  Ibid.
19  Ibid.
20  Ibid.
21  Zhe (2012).
22  Ibid.
23  Young (2012).
24  Ibid.
25  Ibid.
26  Ibid.
27  Ibid.
28  Ibid.
29  Zhe (2012).
30  Crayon (2012).
31  MacLeod (2011).
32  Young (2012).
33  Ibid.
34  Ibid.
35  MacLeod (2011).
36  Young (2012).
37  Ibid.
38  Mihoces (2012).
39  Dyer (2010).
40  Williamson (2012).

41  'Mark Cuban biography' (n.d.).
42  Young (2011).
43  'E-mail Mark Cuban' (n.d.).
44  Yaeger (2011).
45  Abrams (2011).
46  Ibid.
47  Preston (2012).
48  Ibid.
49  Ibid.
50  Yaeger (2011).
51  Ibid.
52  Ibid.

## REFERENCES

Abrams, Jonathan (2011), 'With Dallas leading, outspoken owner lowers the volume', *The New York Times*, 6 May 2011, accessed 31 October 2012 at http://www.nytimes.com/2011/05/07/sports/basketball/07mavericks.html?_r=0.

Bee, Trisha (2012), 'Packers' Coats for Kids collection set for Oct. 28', Fox6Now.com, 23 October 2012, accessed 26 October 2012 at http://fox6now.com/2012/10/23/packers-coats-for-kids-collection-set-for-oct-28/.

Crayon, Lance (2012), 'NFL gradually tackles the Chinese sports market', GlobalTimes.cn, 2 August 2012, accessed 23 September 2012 at http://www.globaltimes.cn/content/724861.shtml.

Davis, John A. (2010), *Competitive Success – How Branding Adds Value*, New York: John Wiley & Sons.

Dyer, Kristian (2010), 'Next year's role model', Scout.com, 11 May 2010, accessed 23 September, 2012 at http://profootball.scout.com/2/969396.html.

'E-mail Mark Cuban' (n.d.), DallasMavericks.com, accessed 31 October 2012 at http://www.nba.com/mavericks/mailbox/email_mark.html.

'Factbox: sponsors drop Lance Armstrong' (2012), Reuters, 22 October 2012, accessed 22 May 2013 at http://www.reuters.com/article/2012/10/22/us-cycling-armstrong-sponsorship-idUSBRE89L0WY20121022.

FIFA website (n.d.), accessed 3 May 2012 at http://www.fifa.com/aboutfifa/organisation/marketing/sponsorship/strategy.html.

'Fit Kids' (n.d.), Packers.com, accessed 30 August 2012 at http://www.packers.com/community/community-programs/fit-kids.html.

'France, Turkey and now Austria could fill in 2013 calendar gap' (n.d.), F1 Cities.com, accessed 26 October 2012 at http://www.f1cities.com/France-Turkey-and-now-Austria-2013-calender.

'General Electric Director joins Olympic debate at Leaders in Sponsorship' (2012), Leaders in Sponsorship, 14 August 2012, accessed 27 August 2012 at http://www.leadersinsponsorship.com/news/general-electric-director-joins-olympic-debate-at-leaders-in-sponsorship/.

MacLeod, Craig (2011), 'U.S. expatriates pursue American dream in China', USAToday.com, 12 July 2011, accessed 23 September 2012 at http://www.usatoday.com/news/world/2011-07-12-Americans-China-dreams-transplants_n.htm.

'Mark Cuban biography' (n.d.), NBA.com, accessed 26 October 2012 at http://www.nba.com/mavericks/news/cuban_bio000329.html.

Mihoces, Gary (2012), 'NFL Jaguars giving Long Ding of China a tryout', USAToday.com, 1 May 2012, accessed 23 September 2012 at http://content.usatoday.com/communities/thehuddle/post/2012/05/NFL-Jaguars-giving-placekicker-Long-Ding-of-China-a-tryout-685310/1#.UF9raEQ6-Kw.

Olympics.org website (n.d.), accessed 3 May 2012 at http://www.olympic.org/sponsors.

Preston, Michael (2012), 'Mark Cuban: "won't be the same when David Stern retires"', SB Nation, 25 October 2012, accessed 31 October 2012, http://dallas.sbnation.com/2012/10/25/3555722/david-stern-retirement-mark-cuban-comments.

Ransdell, Eric (1999), 'The Nike story? Just tell it!', Fast Company.com, 31 December 1999, accessed 27 October 2010 at http://www.fastcompany.com/38979/nike-story-just-tell-it.

Rovell, Darren (2012), 'Oakley drops Lance Armstrong', ESPN.com, 22 October 2012, accessed 22 October 2012 at http://espn.go.com/olympics/cycling/story/_/id/8536558/oakley-drops-lance-armstrong-sponsorship.

'Samsung, Visa partner on m-payments for London 2012 Olympics' (2012), Telecompaper, 4 June 2012, accessed 23 June 2012 at http://www.telecompaper.com/news/samsung-visa-partner-on-m-payments-for-london-2012-olympics--876876.

'The NBA Cares commitment' (n.d.), NBC.com, accessed 11 April 2012 at http://www.nba.com/nba_cares/keyissues.html.

'Vision and values' (n.d.), Adidas Group.com, accessed 29 July 2011 at http://www.adidas-group.com/en/SER2007/b/b_1.asp.

Williamson, Bill (2012), 'Raiders make roster moves', ESPN.com, 29 August 2012, accessed 23 September 2012 at http://espn.go.com/blog/afcwest/post/_/id/47528/raiders-make-roster-moves.

Yaeger, Don (2011), 'The ultimate maverick', *Success Magazine*, 10 October 2011, accessed 31 October 2012 at http://www.success.com/articles/1573-the-ultimate-maverick.

Young, Michael (2011), '"Reunion Rowdies" were there at the start for Mavs; "We've Got That Feeling Again"', 16 June 2011, 31 October 2012 at http://www.dallasnews.com/sports/dallas-mavericks/headlines/20110616-reunion-rowdies_were-there-at-the-start-for-mavs-weve-got-that-feeling-again_.ece?ssimg=206539.

Young, Richard (2012), 'NFL China', NFL China, 17 September 2012, Guest Lecture, Park Plaza Hotel, Beijing, People's Republic of China.

Zhe, Tang (2012), 'A lot to tackle', ChinaDaily.com, 13 September 2012, accessed 23 September 2012 at http://www.chinadaily.com.cn/sports/2012-09/23/content_15775934.htm.

# 11

# Traditional advertising

 **CHAPTER OVERVIEW**

As this book has discussed to this point, sports marketing involves a wider range of activities beyond the conventional notions of marketing as being primarily a set of communications and advertising activities. Successful sports marketing integrates industry and market dynamics with the needs of sports fans, sponsors and product manufacturers, and sports entities (athletes, coaches, teams, governing bodies), using a myriad of tactics and touchpoints that are organized and deployed based on a cohesive strategy and implementation plan to create sustained value for the sports marketer and the target marketplace. Marketing as a communications vehicle is introduced in this and subsequent chapters as this is central to developing awareness of and preference for the sports marketer's offerings. A vital component of a successful sports marketing plan is traditional advertising. We will discuss non-traditional advertising in subsequent chapters, but the impact traditional advertising has on helping companies position and communicate the core messages of their offering(s) remains an important factor in their sports marketing success since most sports fans continue to use traditional media for following their favorite sports and athletes.

## 11.1 The role of traditional advertising

Traditional advertising is defined as television, radio, print, and outdoor advertising. Traditional advertising is one-way communication from company to consumer, and is particularly useful for developing awareness of a company and its products on a mass scale. Since customers cannot interact with traditional advertising beyond passive listening or viewing, it is most useful for conveying a simple message that requires little thinking or involvement on the customer's part.

Traditional advertising was often used as a more tactical, rather than strategic, approach to communicating with consumers about the qualities of the product advertised (the company identifies an opportunity through basic research, develops a product to address it, and designs advertising to create market awareness and inspire buyer purchase). Strategic considerations, such as the potential impact of the new product on the company's overall brand reputation and long-term direction, were secondary because the primary concern was increasing product sales. The term 'brand value' was called goodwill on the balance sheet. The more expansive definition of brand as a strategic asset and as the entire organization as seen through the eyes of stakeholders was virtually non-existent.

Until very recently, traditional advertising was the only means available to companies to present themselves to their target publics. Since the advent of the commercial internet, and the concurrent advancements in software technology, computers, mobile devices, and communications, the range of advertising media companies can use has increased significantly. Today's sports market is more complex than ever, with companies, sports properties, media companies, and fans all interacting through multiple channels. Few companies in any industry, let alone sports, will be successful in growing their businesses if they depend only on traditional advertising. However, traditional advertising is still an important part of a larger marketing communications and overall brand development strategy.

The right traditional advertising approaches in sports marketing are those that are relevant to each target audience, meaning that the advertising used should be tailored to the needs of each customer segment. Sports marketers must rely on their own internal research, plus consider working with external advertising agencies and market research firms to help determine a traditional advertising strategy. Traditional advertising is designed to appeal to customers by describing the sports marketers' products attractively. Successful traditional advertising, like any marketing, depends on accurate market research that identifies target customers, builds detailed profiles of their characteristics, and considers the broader competitive environment. Traditional advertising messages are then either 'pushed' to the market by company-led promotions and/or field sales forces selling directly, or 'pulled' via heavy advertising typically geared for building awareness directly with consumers.

Sports advertising success will be predicated on the following stages. These are designed to focus the advertising campaign on achieving positive results based on clearly set expectations. Figure 11.1 describes this process.

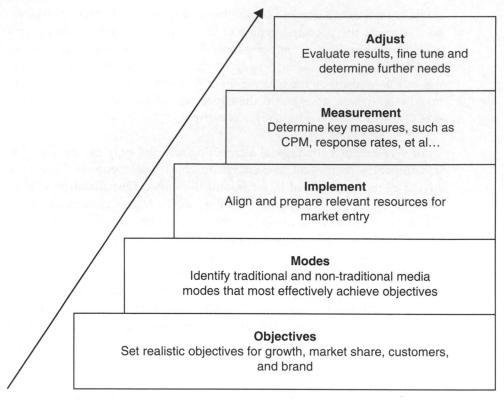

Source: Davis (2013).

**Figure 11.1** Marketing communications key activities

## Objectives

Sports marketers need to be clear on why they are using traditional advertising. An important starting point is to ask, 'What do we hope to accomplish by using traditional advertising?' The answer will affect the traditional advertising media chosen. For example, an objective to raise awareness is quite different from an objective to increase sales by 12 percent, therefore each requires a different advertising message. Sports marketers must also be keenly aware of their total advertising budget so that appropriate budget allocations can be made to traditional advertising.

## Modes, implementation, measurement

Integrated marketing communications (IMC) describes the sports marketer's efforts to seamlessly align their various marketing communications activities (print, radio, TV etc.) to reinforce a cohesive, consistent message.

Traditional advertising campaigns must also be consistent with the company's larger strategic needs, such as brand positioning, customer targeting, product development, and messaging to create a memorable campaign for customers that also reinforces key qualities associated with the company and/or its products. Maximizing brand value is vital to increasing overall company success as measured by market capitalization, and IMC is one of the critical marketing activities in this effort. Each traditional advertising activity should be evaluated based on the potential for the increased value it adds, as well as the actual value added after the campaign has ended, in support of building a consistent and cohesive brand. Therefore, each marketing communications tool must be measured and compared to projections.

## Adjustment

Even when a marketer follows the five stages carefully, there are no guarantees that the traditional advertising approach will work as intended. However, careful consideration must be given to each element of the advertising before deciding to eliminate an advertising approach just because initial results are not as first envisioned. Sports marketers must review the original intent, implementation effort, flaws within each stage, and the potential for improvement or adjusting the campaign.

## 11.2 Traditional advertising tools[1]

The modes shown in 11.2 are an expanded set of traditional marketing tools. Each has been used by companies around the world for decades.

| Traditional Marketing | | |
|---|---|---|
| Television | Sales Promotion | Hospitality/VIP Venues |
| Radio | Outdoor Advertising | Event/Trade Show Booth |
| Print | Team and/or Event Sponsorship | Sales/Business Development |
| Direct Marketing | Public Relations | |

Source: Davis (2013).
**Figure 11.2** Traditional marketing tools

## Television (TV) advertising

TV advertisements are visually descriptive videos with simple dialogs and messaging, ranging in length from 15 seconds to 2 minutes. In the USA,

30-second length advertisements are common on most television networks and cable programming.

*Pros*

TV advertising is used predominately to build awareness and reinforce basic messages. TV has high potential audience reach (defined as the number or percentage of people in the target audience reached by a single exposure ad/commercial in a specified period of time is large).[2] The cost per exposure is relatively low. Since many countries with commercial TV have a wide variety of shows, sports advertisers have many choices for reaching target audience.

*Cons*

The total cost of TV advertising can be quite expensive, particularly if the sports marketer has hired an outside advertising agency to develop the creative message. Furthermore, the cost of media varies depending on the time of day, the popularity of the shows during which the advertising is shown, the frequency (number of times the ad is broadcast), and the length of the actual exposure. Another risk is that viewers may decide to take a short break when the advertisement is shown, eliminating any benefit to the advertiser. TV advertising messages are known as interruption marketing since they intrude on the viewer's involvement in their chosen program, which may lead to negative reaction from viewers. Finally, while general viewing audiences are large, the ideal target audience is small, so effectiveness per exposure can be low.

*Measures*

There are several measures that are useful to sports marketers in evaluating the success of the TV advertising. They are:

- *Reach* (the number or percentage of people in the target audience reached by a single exposure of an advertisement in a specified period of time).
- *Frequency* (the number of times an average member of the target audience is exposed to the same advertisement over a given period of time).[3]
- *GRPs (gross rating points)* (an aggregate measure of the total amount or volume of advertising exposures a media campaign will generate via specified media vehicles during a specific time period – it is the product of reach % x frequency #).[4]
- *Recall* (a test of overall brand awareness or of advertising impact where,

given a product category, a consumer can name [or 'recall'] a brand or advertising campaign without further prompting).[5]

- *Recognition* (it measures if consumers can remember being exposed to a particular advertisement).[6]

# Radio

Radio advertising can be a useful complement or alternative to a TV advertising campaign.

## Pros

Radio advertising is usually far less expensive than TV advertising, although in large metropolitan markets and nationally syndicated radio shows the cost of advertising can be similar to the cost of advertising on TV in local markets. Radio is very effective for messaging tailored to local markets. In the USA many commuters listen to their favorite radio stations during their work commute, so can become a loyal audience that transforms into loyal customers for the sports marketer over time if the company regularly and consistently uses radio tied to the local sports property. Radio compels listeners to visualize the messages, which serves as a particularly memorable way to create a lasting reputation.

## Cons

Listeners may switch radio stations if the programming does not suit their tastes, which means advertisers' promotions may not be heard. As with TV, poorly executed creative advertising can affect the company negatively.

## Measures

Several of the measures used for TV apply to radio as well, including: reach, frequency, and awareness measures. Since many radio stations are online, web-based metrics are also easy to track for sports marketers. Web-based metrics will be discussed in Chapter 12.

# Sales promotion

Sales promotions are defined as a short-term limited edition special offer, such as a price discount or a bundled product offer, designed to temporarily increase demand and sales, with the hope that some of the customers captured remain even after the special promotion has ended.

*Pros*

Sales promotions are quite effective in attracting new customers and/or encouraging existing customers to purchase more products, assuming the sports marketer has designed an appealing and relevant offer. The result of successful promotions is easily measured by increases in revenues, and since most promotions are tied to a specific offer, often with a special code that shows the customer is using the promotion, changes in sales performance (revenues, unit sales, market share) are easy to track. Sales promotions can also stimulate new interest in the company, which can lead to increases in word of mouth recommendations while also increasing awareness of the brand. Short-term increases in market share are probable as well.

*Cons*

While sales promotions may lead to temporary increases in sales, the total volume of units sold must also be large enough to offset the inevitable reduction in margins (which decreases profitability as well). Sales promotions may also educate consumers to wait for the next promotion rather than purchasing during non-promotion periods, increasing sales cycle volatility, which can negatively impact labor costs. Promotions also risk diluting the company's image and reputation (there is a reason why most luxury brands don't discount, and many highly respected non-luxury brands also avoid price discounts).

*Measures*

Sales promotion measures include: markdown goods percentage (amount reduced from the original selling price),[7] transactions per hour,[8] hourly customer traffic,[9] and close-ratio (how many customers convert from shoppers to actual buyers).[10]

## Print

Despite the significant changes to print publications around the world due to the rapid growth of digital books and periodicals, print publications remain an important information source and highly sought medium and cover a wide range of topics.

*Pros*

Print advertising has historically been perceived as highly credible because print publications have generally been associated with quality journalism and analysis. Newspapers offer reasoned insights based on the daily news and have a short shelf life, while magazines offer more in-depth analysis on a less frequent basis with a longer shelf life. Both mediums are effective for sports marketers needing to convey either general or detailed message in their advertising, depending on publication and target audience. Many print publications are now formatted for digital devices, like Apple's iPad, enabling the digital equivalent of print ads in digital form.

## Cons

Whereas newspapers were the go to source for the most recent news, the internet and digital media update stories real time at all hours. The tactile feel that many fans of newspapers love has been disappearing now that iPads and tablets have become the medium of record. Newspapers not only have shorter shelf life, but they are also declining in distribution. Traditional magazines are more expensive, require longer subscription agreements, and are also declining in readership.

## Measures

Print advertising measures include: reach, frequency, awareness, recognition, recall, and impressions (which is the product of reach x frequency).[11]

# Direct marketing

Direct marketing is a form of advertising communications that is addressed directly to target customers and designed to motivate the recipient to reply. Direct marketing is conducted via direct mail, infomercial, telemarketing, or digital offers.

## Pros

Direct marketing messages can be personalized to the specific recipient if the sports marketer's customer database provides deep detail, including name, location, shopping patterns, and favorite brands. Direct marketing is a good medium for short-term promotions or limited time discount offers. A well-constructed direct marketing advertisement can increase short-term sales sharply.

## Cons

Maintaining an up to date customer database is expensive, and while online direct marketing is often less expensive that traditional postal direct marketing, the cost of any high-quality direct mailing/emailing creative design is high, and if the sports marketer relies on third party market research firms for their outreach, then the rental costs of acquiring accurate customer lists is expensive on a per name basis. The cost of traditional telemarketing labor and equipment is expensive, as are the costs of producing infomercials and the corresponding media-buy. Furthermore, fulfillment and associated operating support costs are also expensive. Traditional direct mail is increasingly perceived as environmentally unfriendly, especially when the per-piece costs of design, postage, and follow-up are factored in.

## Measures

Direct marketing measures will vary slightly depending on the medium used (direct mail, infomercial, telemarketing). They include: revenue and profit goals,[12] gross and net profit,[13] response rate (number of people who respond to an offer relative to the number of people who received the offer),[14] conversion rate (percentage of recipients that purchase),[15] and return on investment (ROI).[16]

# Sales/business development

Sales and business development continue to influence customer purchase decisions, particularly in the business-to-business world. Sales people have specialized training and are skilled at increasing sales and developing relationships with new and existing customers. Business development people have similar skills, but they tend to focus more on developing revenue-generating strategic partnerships with other companies in the value chain, gathering competitive intelligence and business planning.

## Pros

Business activities require the interaction between seller and buyers and field sales representatives are an important trust and confidence-building tactic, partly because relationship development is a key aspect of the latter's jobs. Sales professionals gain a thorough understanding of their customers and related issues, shedding light on how customers make decisions and thereby helping the sports marketer tailor their marketing efforts based on this knowledge. The most successful sales people are considered top performers for their companies because they generate significant revenues and profits, serve as brand ambassadors by acting as surrogates for their company's reputation, and generally promote and reinforce a positive image. Sales representatives are selected based on their ability to work with people. At the same time, sales people must run a financially successful business in their territory, so having demonstrated business skills is also an important and necessary skill. Perhaps the biggest challenge in sales is overcoming objections and rejection, and the best ones find sales techniques that increase their chances of success.

## Cons

One of the biggest challenges for companies is designing a compensation program that rewards sales people based on achieving key financial objectives. Sometimes revenues are pushed at the expense of profits, usually based on a belief that it is better to capture a customer's business and then grow the relationship into a profitable one over time, rather than lose a customer to a competitor. The challenge is how to increase profitability when revenues are emphasized over profits. Customers will expect additional value of some kind in exchange for the higher prices. Sales representatives may also give away some products and service/support to secure the customer's business. The unique requirements company management seeks from top sales professionals leads to hiring representatives that are independent and able to work alone in the field. As a consequence, sales people can develop a 'go-it-alone' mentality that may be in conflict at times with the decision-making from company management, fostering impatience. Rather than wait for corporate marketing, sales people might create their own marketing materials, potentially harming their company's brand image.

## Measures

Numerous measures are useful for evaluating the field sales and business development efforts, and the final selection of measures will depend on the company's individual needs. Important measures include: independent sales representative analysis (helps management compare costs between having independent and company sales forces),[17] average sales per call,[18] break-even sales volume,[19] and sales productivity (total revenues per sales person).[20]

## Public relations

Public relations (PR) is responsible for developing relationships between the company and its various publics, from the customer marketplace to the media. One of the primary objectives of PR is to foster a positive image for the company through announcements about new products, minimizing crises, and elevating senior management as authorities in their field and industry. When PR succeeds it is because the information it sends to the media is published in the press, so it does not cost the company as advertising placement would (other than the cost of the PR team's salaries).

### Pros

Since PR is not paid media, unlike advertising, it is perceived as more credible since it is not perceived as company-generated advertising hype. Furthermore, since PR efforts are designed to place information and stories that are 'of interest' to the market, journalists and their editors will often include the information as part of in-depth articles and/or the PR information may inspire editors to learn more to see if a more detailed story can be developed.

### Cons

PR's strengths are also its weaknesses, since coverage is not guaranteed, and even if the information is picked up by the media, there is also no guarantee that the journalist will use it 'as is' without further investigation into seeing the information from different points of view, which might transform what was initially perceived as positive information into a story that mixes in negative elements. PR information is subject to the editorial needs of target media whose editors determine newsworthiness. Another challenge with PR pertains to the company's ability to manage a crisis since poor management can negatively affect the brand.

### Measures

Most companies pay for third party firms known as news clip services (PR agencies do this as well) to track the company's coverage in the media. Relevant PR measures include: the ratio of news stories printed vs sent; the ratio of favorable to unfavorable stories; the total number of news stories featuring the company and its products; and the number of conference speaking engagements secured for key company leaders that are also covered in the media.

## Outdoor advertising

Outdoor advertising describes visible signage such as billboards, wall boards, street placards, banners, sandwich boards, and marquee electronic displays.

*Pros*

Outdoor advertising is effective for simple advertising messages and images since the visibility is high from both ground and high-elevation vantage points. Whether in high-density urban areas or less crowded sub-urban and rural locations, outdoor advertising provides quick and potentially memorable exposure, assuming the message is relatively simple and straightforward. Costs vary based on the location, but on a per person basis the cost of each exposure is relatively low. Evidence exists throughout sports around the world when one sees almost any sports contest (with the exception of Olympic Games venues where no in-venue signage of any kind is allowed).

*Cons*

Since a sizable number of the outdoor advertising displays are in higher density locations (stadiums with tens of thousands of fans, busy freeways where commuters travel, city center locations where people live and work), the message can quickly become tiresome, and even ignored, as people grow used to its presence. Since the medium is most effective when simple messages and imagery are used, the information companies can impart is limited.

*Measures*

Outdoor advertising measures include: awareness (determined by surveying people to see if they even noticed the display),[21] measuring the overall number of people that noticed the display as compared to the total traffic volume, and reference ads (where consumers are asked to refer to the ad when purchasing the advertised product).

## 11.3 Traditional advertising planning

Table 11.1 is an advertising planning template. To illustrate, let's assume a sports marketer has three target audiences (represented by A, B, C). The marketer's research has shown that each of her company's target audiences are most effectively reached using the traditional advertising vehicles shown.

**Table 11.1** Traditional advertising planning template

|  | TV | Radio | Print | Direct Marketing | Outdoor | Sales Promotion |
|---|---|---|---|---|---|---|
| Target audience A | ✓ | ✓ | ✓ |  | ✓ |  |
| Target audience B |  |  |  | ✓ | ✓ |  |
| Target audience C |  | ✓ |  | ✓ |  | ✓ |

Source: Adapted from Davis (2012, p. 316).

In this illustration, the sports marketer's customer research indicates that TV, radio, print and outdoor are the most effective traditional media for reaching target audience A, and target audiences B and C are best reached through other traditional marketing tools. Sports marketers will want to promote a consistent company image overall to each of their three target segments, but the differences in media will allow some variation in how the image is conveyed. The sports marketer will summarize their media plan in a marketing activity worksheet such as that shown in Table 11.2.

Each media tactic is part of a larger sports market whole, described as follows:

### Message

The sports marketer's advertising campaign is based on the message 'Compete or Go Home', using this theme consistently in all the media tactics for each target audience.

### Reach

This measures the number or percentage of people that were exposed to a single ad during a specified period of time. In this example, 1 August is the start date for the TV campaign, and the other media start dates are also shown. Each of those media have their own reach target.

### Frequency

Refers to the number of times the target audience is exposed to the same ad during the specified period of time with each specific media.

### Insertion date

This describes the start date of each media type (i.e., magazine publication date, TV or radio broadcast date etc.).

**Table 11.2** Traditional advertising planning template

| Media Type | Target Audience | Message | Reach | Frequency | Insertion Date | Ad Length or Size | GRP (gross rating points) | Total Cost (creative, media-buy) | Project Outcome |
|---|---|---|---|---|---|---|---|---|---|
| TV | A | 'Compete or Go Home' | 20% | 6x | 1 August | 30 sec. | 225 | $3m | 15%↑ awareness |
| Radio | A, C | ' | 40% | 12x | 1 July | 15–30 sec. | 300 | $300k | ' |
| Print | A | ' | 25% | 8x | 15 June | 1 page | 75 | $225k | ' |
| Outdoor | A, B | ' | | 3-month contract | 1 June | 5 billboards | Unknown | $125000 | ' |
| Direct marketing | B, C | Plus special promotion | 30% | 4 pieces, 1 per week for 1 month | Start date of 15 August | Postcards | Unknown | $100000 | ↑ Short-term sales by 10% |
| Sales Promotion | C | Plus special promotion | ' | ' | ' | ' | ' | Part of direct marketing cost | ' |

Source: Adapted from Davis (2012, p. 316).

## Ad length/size

This refers to the advertisements characteristics (time-length, physical dimensions).

## GRP (gross rating points)

GRPs are calculated by multiplying reach x frequency. GRPs describe the total number of ad exposures of an advertising campaign during a specified period of time.

## Total cost

This is the total cost of the creative effort (producing the creative content either in-house or through an outside ad agency), the cost of each chosen media (fees charged by the media type to place an ad with them in a specified size, location and time slot), and any related-support costs (other professional services hired to facilitate the advertising plan).

## Project outcome

In this example the sports marketer seeks to increase brand awareness 15 percent. This can be measured using different survey techniques before, during, and after the advertising campaign. The technique selected will depend on the research objectives, but there are two primary survey approaches: probabilistic (random sampling of the population, from which the results can be reasonably projected to the rest of the population); non-probabilistic (non-random sample and therefore not likely to represent overall population). Probability surveys approaches include:

- mail (questions mailed to respondents);
- telephone (questions asked via telephone);
- in-person (interviewer-led questioning);
- mixed mode (combination of other modes).

Non-probability surveys are:

- focus groups (facilitated discussion groups);
- location interviews (respondents go to specific location);
- convenience samples (respondents selected from busy areas such as shopping malls).

Measuring results requires that sports marketers collect data from each of the media companies selected and their respective audience characteristics (most media companies produce reports that describe this), and compare it to projections and also historical results. Historical data include past awareness levels of the company and its products, and the objective of any advertising is to improve over past performance. Sports marketers must blend optimism and realism in their projections. If past awareness has grown an average of 3 percent in previous years, then projecting awareness increasing to 80 percent would be unrealistic. Conversely, under-forecasting is a risk as well and targeting awareness improvements to only 4–5 percent suggests a lack of ambition.

## 11.4  Traditional advertising costs

The cost of traditional advertising on TV and radio depends on the size and demographic characteristics of the target audience and the media market in which the sports marketer advertises. In the United States broadcast advertising rates are based on the size of the expected audience and the corresponding time of day. The most expensive advertising on TV is generally at Prime Time, which is between the hours of 7 to 11 pm, when most Americans watch TV.[22] Cable television has grown significantly since the early 1980s, altering viewing habits in the USA significantly. Correspondingly, the traditional big US broadcast networks (ABC, CBS, NBC) have incurred viewership declines. In more recent years, digital video recorders have allowed viewers to skip past advertisements entirely, frustrating the efforts of companies to broadcast their messages and compelling them to use a wider variety of marketing tools to reach their target audiences.[23]

Integrated marketing communications (IMC) is essential to successful advertising campaigns that support the company's business strategy. Traditional advertising remains an important tool in the sports marketer's arsenal of communications tools. However, IMC planning must focus beyond tactical advertising campaigns by including the company's strategic objectives in the development of their image and message campaigns. Understanding the broader corporate strategy will help sports marketers determine which media modes and creative approaches to use. Broadcast television and radio are good media to use for increasing brand awareness in the mass market. Tactical marketing programs, such as direct marketing and sales promotions, are then useful for making limited time offers to specific audiences that inspire purchase and eventually long-term loyalty.

## 11.5 Chapter summary

This chapter discussed the traditional advertising tools used by marketers today, and historically. Whether print, broadcast or relationship based (through business development activities, for example), traditional advertising expenditures are the largest in the world, although their growth rate is lower than newer advertising tools (discussed in Chapter 12). Traditional advertising tends to be most effective for developing and building awareness in the market, helping attract new customers while also reinforcing to existing customers why the company remains an important contributor to their lives. For sports marketers traditional advertising is still popular, with broadcast advertising during major sports events considered an effective way to reach target audiences. One disadvantage to traditional advertising is its one-way communications approach: messages are directed from the sports marketer to the marketplace, but there is no mechanism for an easy, let alone immediate, reply, which is why traditional advertising works better for creating an image for a company. Any advertising campaigns need to be measured, and numerous such measures are referenced within. It is incumbent on marketers to select those measures that are most effective for the advertising media used.

**CASE STUDY**

# Pepsi and Pakistani cricket

Pepsi International is no stranger to sports marketing. The cola giant has been sponsoring sports events and properties for decades. But Pepsi's sponsorship of cricket in Pakistan helped drive the company to hold an 80 percent market share during the late 1990s.[24] Pepsi began its earliest days in Pakistan in the 1970s by sponsoring Imran Khan, the most popular cricketer in the country to date at the time.[25] Through the 1970s and 1980s, Pepsi's ads featured the charismatic athlete and effectively put cans of the cola in hands of Pakistanis of all ages.[26] While Coca-Cola now has reduced Pepsi's market share to around 65 percent within the country, Pepsi's continued sponsorship of cricket continues to be a driving success for the company in Pakistan.[27]

Since 1991, Pepsi has sponsored the Pakistani national cricket team and its logo is featured on the Pakistani jerseys. But many of Pepsi's current advertisements around the sport of cricket happen during the T20 International Cricket Council (ICC) World Cup. During the 2012 World Cup, Pepsi's campaign revolved around the title 'Made for Cricket' with the 'o' in the word 'for' being the Pepsi logo.[28] A series of three popular commercials ran on television throughout the tournament. Each of the commercials had famous Pepsi-sponsored cricketers trying their hand unsuccessfully at other sports. Towards the end of the commercials, the shots switch to the players on the cricket pitch playing the game they do best.[29] Each of the commercials ends with the player shown drinking Pepsi with the 'Made for Cricket' logo.[30] Pepsi also maintained an active Pakistan-specific Facebook page and YouTube account during the 2012 T20 World Cup so as to keep all of its content easily accessible for its fans (almost 202 000 of them on Facebook alone). The videos are available at https://www.youtube.com/user/pepsipakistan?feature=results_main.

 **QUESTIONS**

1   Search the internet for examples of Pepsi's' Made for Cricket' television advertisements. Weigh the pros and cons of these ads.
2   After viewing the Pepsi Cricket TV ads, describe what you think are the characteristics of Pepsi's target audience for these ads. Be specific.
3   What other ways would you recommend Pepsi use traditional media (broadcast and print) in sports marketing? Which sports are best for using traditional media?
4   What factors must Pepsi, or any other sports marketer, consider when deciding how to use traditional advertising?

## NOTES

1  Davis (2010, pp. 290–300).
2  Davis (2013, pp. 163–4).
3  Ibid., pp. 165–6.
4  Ibid., pp. 167–70.
5  Ibid., pp. 157–9.
6  Ibid., pp. 161–3.
7  Ibid., pp. 147–8.
8  Ibid., pp. 229–30.
9  Ibid., p. 237.
10  Ibid., pp. 251–2.
11  Ibid., p. 201.
12  Ibid., pp. 3–4.
13  Ibid., pp. 5–6.
14  Ibid., pp. 173–4.
15  Ibid., pp. 174–6.
16  Ibid., pp. 197–8.
17  Ibid., pp. 273–4.
18  Ibid., pp. 295–6.
19  Ibid., pp. 303–4.
20  Ibid. pp. 305–6.
21  See recall and recognition.
22  Hinckley (2012).
23  Guskin and Rosestiel (n.d.); Gough (2007); Gandosey (2009); Schechner and Dana (2009); *The Economist* (2009).
24  Wright (2010).
25  Rizvi (2011).
26  Ibid.
27  Wright (2010).
28  Mankani (2012).
29  Ibid.
30  Ibid.

## REFERENCES

Davis, John A. (2010), *Competitive Success – How Branding Adds Value*, New York: John Wiley & Sons.

Davis, John A. (2012), *The Olympic Games Effect – How Sports Marketing Builds Strong Brands*, New York: John Wiley & Sons.

Davis, John A. (2013), *Measuring Marketing: 110+ Key Metrics Every Marketer Needs*, Singapore: John Wiley & Sons (Asia) PTE Ltd.

Gandosey, Taylor (2009), 'TV viewing at "all-time high", Nielsen says', CNN.com/entertainment, 24 February 2009, accessed 26 February 2009 at http://edition.cnn.com/2009/SHOWBIZ/TV/02/24/us.video.nielsen/.

Gough, Paul J. (2007), 'The case of the disappearing TV viewers', Reuters, 25 May 2007, accessed 15 November 2008 at http://www.reuters.com/article/entertainmentNews/idUSN2523545420070525.

Guskin, Emily and Tom Rosestiel (n.d.), 'Network: by the numbers', accessed 27 May 2013 at http://stateofthemedia.org/2012/network-news-the-pace-of-change-accelerates/network-by-the-numbers/.

Hinckley, David (2012), 'Network advertising costs depend on the type of audience and buzz, not just total viewers', NYDailyNews.com, 23 October 2012, accessed 23 October 2012 at http://www.nydailynews.com/entertainment/tv-movies/football-packs-top-wallop-tv-ad-dollars-article-1.1189479.

Mankani, Mahjabeen (2012), 'Advertising analysis – Pepsi: made for cricket', Dawn.com, 29 September 2012, accessed 21 October 2012 at http://dawn.com/2012/09/29/advertising-analysis-pepsi-made-for-cricket/.

Rizvi, Basit (2011), 'Tapping into the Pakistani consumer market', PakistanToday.com.pk, 28 September 2011, accessed 21 October 2012 at http://www.pakistantoday.com.pk/2011/09/28/news/profit/tapping-into-the-pakistani-consumer-market/.

Schechner, Sam and Rebecca Dana (2009), 'Local TV stations face a fuzzy future', 10 February 2009, *The Wall Street Journal*, accessed 9 March 2009 at http://online.wsj.com/article/SB123422910357065971.html.

*The Economist* (2009), 'The not-so-big four', 8 April 2009, accessed 10 April 2009 at http://www.economist.com/businessfinance/displaystory.cfm?story_id=13446620.

Wright, Tom (2010), 'Coke gains on Pepsi in Pakistan: 15 bottles per person and counting', *The Wall Street Journal*, 20 July 2010, accessed 17 October 2012 at http://online.wsj.com/article/SB10001424052748704720004575377190499667312.html.

# 12

# Social and digital advertising

**CHAPTER OVERVIEW**

Social and digital media, sometimes called non-traditional (NT) marketing, are a complement to traditional advertising and offer sports marketers many newer media tools for communicating with customers. Unlike traditional advertising, social and digital advertising is a two-way dialog between the company and its customers. As with traditional advertising, sports marketers are able to influence the image of their company through the creative messaging and imagery used, but the key difference is the real-time conversation that occurs with customers. This dialog allows marketers to gather qualitative and quantitative data about their markets. When customers are directly interacting with the company the ensuing conversation tends to reveal a more informal, less 'corporate' side of the company, fostering the potential for a more authentic image to be seen by the market. Customers are the final determinants of a company's reputation and believability, making their purchase decisions based on customer-generated insights and not just company-led messages.

## 12.1  Social and digital advertising characteristics

Social and digital advertising can be a catalyst for affecting customer emotions by using messages that tap into specific customer preferences, reinforce the company's understanding of the customer, foster trust between the company and its customers, while also emphasizing relevant product features and benefits. Previously unknown needs (known as 'latent needs') can be revealed in these discussions when enough information is gathered that uncovers emerging trends. The real-time conversation with customers suggests the company is transparent, further developing trust and encouraging deeper customer loyalty. Since customer decisions are a combination of logic and emotion, authentic conversations give companies a more human quality, affecting the emotional part of the customer's decision-making in favor of the company. Social and digital advertising gives companies a digital footprint of each customer's interaction with the company and its mobile and digital media. Social and digital advertising choices have developed quickly since the mid-2000s due to advances in social media, although digital technology has been a driving contributing to changes in advertising media since the mid-1990s. An important implication of these technological advances is that customers have greater influence and, arguably, control over a company's reputation than even the company itself does. With the concurrent distrust of traditional advertising, the influence and importance of social media in a sports marketer's advertising planning cannot be overstated. Customers can now quickly identify misleading or false claims and spread their discovery rapidly. Companies today must pay ongoing attention to each of their company's touchpoints.

## Johnson & Johnson

Johnson & Johnson's total advertising expenditures decreased 10 percent in 2006 to $1.9 billion. Its traditional advertising expenditures declined 22 percent so that the advertising budget could be shifted toward search engine advertising. Johnson & Johnson's subsidiaries and related healthcare brands moved into online advertising as well. Despite decreased total advertising expenditure, the company's sales grew 6 percent in 2006 to US$53.2 billion, increasing again in 2008 to US$63.7 billion.[1]

In 2011 the company announced it would become a sponsor for the 2014 FIFA World Cup in Rio de Janeiro, Brazil. Its website features a new slogan called 'Care Inspires Care', connected to its supporting of healthy lifestyles.

## 12.2 Social and digital advertising tools[2]

Figure 12.1 shows the various social and digital advertising tools (NT marketing).

| Non-Traditional Marketing | | |
|---|---|---|
| Multimedia | Interstitials | BI |
| Web | Podcasts | Email |
| Search | Mobile | Permission |
| Social Media | Blogs | One to One |
| Banners | CRM | Partnership |

Source: Davis (2013).

**Figure 12.1** Social and digital advertising tools

## Multimedia

Multimedia tools include video, text, photos, slide shows, audio and animation effects, games, and interactive features.

*Pros*

Multimedia engage and entertain users, creating far richer and more visually stimulating advertising that is also 'sticky' – a term that describes the length of time a user spends viewing content. Creating customer experiences is an important aspect of developing a company's reputation and brand image today and multimedia offers dynamic way to do this. Technologies have become increasingly easy for people to use, and less expensive, enabling non-professionals to create their own content, website, music, videos and even ads. Multimedia are used extensively by sports properties (leagues and clubs), sports networks (ESPN, for example) and companies that make sports and non-sports products.

*Cons*

Good, high-quality multimedia are complex to produce, despite the advances in user friendliness. This may require that companies hire outside agencies to develop their multimedia content, increasing the costs. Multimedia can slow down the user's broadband performance and can even be distracting.

*Measures*

Since multimedia have several related tools, the measures vary. Engagement and abandonment, explored in Table 12.2, measure if content is engaging and leads users to purchase.

## Web

The advent of the commercial internet through the World Wide Web ushered in an new era of marketing and advertising communications, enabling organizations to move away from static brochures to dynamic, fast-paced interactive websites that can be updated continuously.

*Pros*

The web offers users a wealth of information, from commercial websites to research on a wide range of topics. Since every action leaves a digital footprint, sports marketers can track the advertising response of their customers far more accurately than with qualitative surveys or passive, one-way advertising that urges action but where the direct connection to purchase is unclear. By regularly updating content and new visual imagery sports marketers are able to appeal directly to the entertainment and information needs of sports fans. Sports teams, from the NFL's New England Patriots, to the EPL's Liverpool FC, use their websites to keep fans informed of the latest result of their team and players, insights about team management decision-making, the newest fan club membership benefits, and information about their team's standing each season. Websites are an essential extension of the sports property's personality. Sports product companies use their websites to convey their brand personality as well, and display the latest product information. Publicly traded companies also have extensive Investor Relations pages where visitors can read the latest financial information, the company's annual report, and even senior management's latest speeches. For non-sports product companies that use sports marketing to elevate their brand reputation, like Barclays, Emirates Airlines, and McDonald's, their company websites are used to primarily promote their products. Visitors interested in their sports marketing support activities will have to dig deeper into the official corporate website to learn about their sports-related activities. Of course, non-sports companies are using multiple advertising media to communicate their sports marketing support.

## Cons

Web content ranges from high-quality, reliable, and properly cited information to random opinions, unsubstantiated facts, and offensive material, so users have to learn from experience, and from recommendations, which websites are useful and insightful. Of course, most users in the second decade of the twenty-first century are adept at searching the web and finding the information they seek, unlike the early days of the web when users were still learning how to search. High-quality websites are expensive to develop and support and require that organizations hire people and technology resources dedicated for this one purpose. Marketers must be careful not to create a web presence that is too busy, replete with multimedia content, confusing colors, multiple columns and links, and advertising.

## Measures

The following web measures are useful: direct URL access; engagement, and abandonment (to be explained following Table 12.2). In addition, entry and exit pages, bounce rates, average sale price, profit margin, conversion rate[3] and total number of unique and repeat visitors (and buyers) are all useful for evaluating website results.

## Search

Search advertising is illustrated by placing ads on search engine results pages.

### Pros

Search advertising locates the sports marketer's advertisements (paid or unpaid) on the user's results pages, shown alongside complementary or compatible products. Since users had a specific search in mind, the ad placement increases the possibility of click-through.

### Cons

Regular users of search engines may find search ads intrusive, interrupting their search efforts.

### Measures

The social and digital measures discussed in this chapter apply to evaluating most search advertising. Key measures include: CPM (cost per mille – cost per thousand visitors), CPA (cost per action),[4] and click-through rates.[5]

## Banner

Banner advertising is used on websites. Most banner ads are small, simple strips ('banners') with an equally simple message designed to inspire users to click on them, linking the user to the sports advertiser's main website or item featured in the ad. Banner ads are either static or dynamic, depending on message and image needs of the sports marketer. Some banner ads allow users to hover over them with their mouse, causing the banner to increase in size and inserting additional content and/or dynamic multimedia to engage the user.

### Pros

Banner ads are an online version of outdoor signage and billboards. Due to their smaller size, detailed content is generally not possible or recommended, requiring sports marketers to simplify their message, which is not always easy when organizations are trying to convey as much information as possible about their products and services, but the effort can often result in more focused messaging. Banner ads are also less expensive to create (note that this is not the same as the cost of placing the ad). Banner ads act as a memorable entry door to the sports marketer's main website.

## Cons

Banner ads can be visually distracting, interrupting the user's experience, which could foster a negative image about the advertiser. Over-reliance on dynamic content can also irritate users. Banner ad cost depends on where they are placed, with less popular websites being cheaper (but also having fewer visitors). Banner ad cost is also affected by user click-throughs' behavior, with costs escalating rapidly when more visitors click, yet ultimately abandon before purchase. This can cause the sports marketer to invest additional budgetary resources in developing a unique website that engages customers and encourages purchase.

## Measures

Banner ads evaluation uses measures that are similar to traditional print ads. In addition, impressions (if web page shows four banner ads, then that equals four impressions), and click-throughs (describes when a user clicks on the banner) are two additional measures used.

# Interstitials

Interstitials (which describes website ads that are 'in-between' user actions) are web pages that appear prior to the main content sought. Interstitials usually show expanded ads or information about the next section of the website.

## Pros

Interstitials are similar to full-page print ads because they provide detailed information and even multimedia designed to enhance the user's experience.

## Cons

Interstitials interrupt the user's experience and may thereby be ignored or, worse, foment a negative reaction to the sports marketer's organization. Since interstitials involve more content and possibly multimedia, they are more expensive to produce.

## *Measures*

The same measures as used to assess banner advertising.

# Blogs

Blogs are online journals and opinion sites that allow visitors to respond with their own comments, creating the potential for sports marketers to develop a community of followers if the content is useful to the marketplace. Blogs are easy to start and maintain, with many blog software providers allowing free or very low cost access.

## *Pros*

Good blogs, like good journalists and columnists, develop large readerships. Blog readers are often broadly representative of society at large, with diverse demographic characteristics and psychographic profiles, although narrowly focused blogs will naturally have an equally narrow audience. Popular blogs have become credible sources of information, such as ESPN's sports writers that blog, helping sports marketers to further reinforce their image and expertise.[6] When blogs are part of a larger integrated marketing effort, engaging customers directly, then the chances of developing customer loyalty increase. The best-known blogs can have hundreds of thousands of followers whose enthusiastic support encourages them to share the blog, creating a viral marketing effect.

## *Cons*

There are millions of blogs worldwide, creating a cluttered blog landscape that makes it hard for bloggers to develop a following. Since blogs are accessible via the web and mobile technology, all opinions spread quickly, including negative ones, placing the sports marketer's organization at risk for being perceived negatively.

## *Measures*

Many of the website measures discussed in this chapter are useful to marketers. In addition, reviewing changes to the number of RSS feed subscribers (RSS is an abbreviation for Really Simple Syndication, a form of digital notification to users about content changes to their favorite blogs and websites), the number of RSS to email subscribers, top posts, top feed readers, trackbacks, and replies.

## Podcasts

Podcasts are digital web and mobile programs, often featuring content similar to broadcast TV and radio. With millions of podcasts worldwide, users have a wide variety of topics to choose. Sports marketers with clever programming ideas can develop a follower fan base.

*Pros*

Podcasts can help the sports marketer's brand positioning and even offer followers another dimension of their organization's personality. Sports marketers can also advertise on their own podcasts.

*Cons*

While there are millions of podcasts, very few have a large and loyal fan following, so most simply add to the clutter, and conceivably, user confusion (or disinterest). Just as with creators of broadcast programming, developing successful podcast content consistently requires financial investment that can be quite expensive.

*Measures*

Measures of total subscribers are the most commonly used.

## Social media

Social media describe online social networking communities, such as Facebook, Twitter, Instagram, YouTube, and Foursquare. Users meet online socially, share opinions, collaborate, and even track their usage timelines.

*Pros*

Social media's massive and rapid growth means there is a huge global audience. Users gain enjoyment from discussing their lives and learning about those of their friends, while sports marketers gain first-hand insights about their customers and their interests and behaviors.

*Cons*

Social media sites are not typically reviewed or vetted by impartial news editors, so users are encouraged to police themselves and not engage in illegal or immoral activities. Beyond that, the content is often profane and inane. At the same time, social media users put up pages about organizations (companies, sports properties, and more etc.), offering a wide range of opinions, many of which are unflattering and negative. Exaggeration is common, as is the use of emotion, and accuracy is less important. Consequently, quality varies. Viral marketing can spread any and all messages quickly, hampering the company's control of its own image.

## Measures

Most social media hosts provide usage statistics and reviewer ratings systems. This data, along with the other social and digital media discussed in this chapter, are helpful in assessing social media contribution to a sports marketer's overall branding effort.

# Mobile

Mobile advertising refers to placing ads on the software and hardware associated with computer, online, and digital communications. Smart phones and tablets have transformed how people interact with others, search for information and entertain themselves and they offer sports marketers yet another invaluable potential medium for reaching customers.

## Pros

There are several billion mobile phone users around the world,[7] which means sports marketers can directly reach people anywhere and everywhere, or target individual users for advertising and promotions. Marketing programs can be easily tracked, due to the digital footprint users leave. For loyal customers, such as those of a favorite sports property, thoughtful targeted mobile advertising can complement their enjoyment of their sport.

## Cons

Advertising to consumers on their mobile devices is another form of interruption and distraction that can create a negative impression with consumers.

## Measures

Measures include: tracking download activity; customer response; customer conversion; comparing usage of cost-plus content (priced just above the cost to produce the content, such as ringtones) to premium fee-based charges (higher prices for better content); ratio of longer-term subscribers to one-time users; download activity; visitors; hits; page views; engagement; and abandonment.

# CRM

CRM means customer relationship management, which refers to software systems that track information about customers, thereby adding detail to the sports marketer's profile of each customer. This information includes purchase history, order statistics, financing requirements, interactions with service and support.

## Pros

CRM software provides sports marketers with comprehensive, central-ized, and easy to access customer profiles. When a sizable database is developed, then planning forecasts can be more confidently developed since trends may become evident. This information can assist sports mar-keters to manage customers more effectively (this is especially true for business-to-business situations), facilitate new customer development, influence product development, and shape the marketing communica-tions used.

## Cons

CRM software is expensive. Installation and implementation is complicated, can take months, and may require users to change the way they do their jobs. Companies must be realistic about what they want their CRM system to do for their marketing activities before deciding which system they will purchase.

## Measures

CRM integrates data from marketing, finance, operations, support and logis-tics systems, so measures will depend on the needs of the user. But the clear by-product is knowing that the data directly affects financial and marketing program performance. The more data gathered, the greater the chance that the sports marketer will be able to use the information to develop creative and effective marketing plans.

## Business intelligence/analytics (BI)

BI is software that is complementary to the CRM system, organizing data it into common themes and distilling the most relevant information to help marketers evaluate emerging trends and opportunities.

### Pros

BI information helps evaluate the sports marketer's marketing mix activities, including pricing, promotion, and direct response campaigns.

### Cons

Expense is a primary con, although sports marketers can readily justify the expense if they can show that the resulting data will improve marketing effectiveness.

### Measures

In addition to CRM's measures, BI can be assessed on the usefulness, accuracy, and accessibility of the data used for forecasting.

## Personalization[8]

Personalization describes personalized messages and content directed to users.

### Pros

Personalization helps users feel that the company understands them. CRM and BI software are important tools used in successful personalization. Users experience personalization whenever they return to a favorite website and see new recommendations for them from the company.

### Cons

Personalization software, like CRM and BI software, is complex and expensive. Personalization is an operating philosophy that requires an intensive, company-wide commitment to ensuring a seamless experience for users, from their first visit to the website to accurately receiving products they purchased on a timely basis.

*Measures*

Measures include: share of wallet (percentage of the customer's spending the company receives), engagement (see Table 12.2), and conversion rates.

## Email marketing

Email marketing is the electronic equivalent of direct mail (physical mailers sent via postal services). Email marketing is useful for delivering surveys to customers to understand their awareness of the brand, levels of customer satisfaction, and competitor comparisons.

*Pros*

When sports marketers have detailed customer profiles then messages can be tailored automatically to the recipient. Like other forms of advertising, email marketing is designed to inform customers about the organization's latest offerings.

*Cons*

Email marketing can be perceived as intrusive, which might upset recipients and undermine the organization's brand reputation. When email marketing is overdone recipients perceive it as spam (email messages that are designed to inundate the recipient's inbox with advertising and promotional messages) and even if the message is useful, it is disregarded. Viruses have also been sent using false email marketing disguised as legitimate sources. The viruses are typically activated when the user clicks on the message. The end result has fostered customer suspicions about almost any message received, even if from a known and trusted source.

*Measures*

Email marketing measures include: response rates, conversion, click-through, purchase volume, and amount.

## Permission marketing[9]

Permission marketing is the practice of asking customers if they would like to be contacted or receive information about the sports marketer's company and its offerings. Customer can accept or reject these requests. Email marketing success is usually predicated on customers being asked their permission about receiving future communications from the company.

## Pros

When customers grant permission to companies, they are signaling their interest in learning more about the company and their willingness to receive regular communications about the latest news. Sports marketers can then shift their marketing efforts toward further developing the relationship since the customer has now indicated their preference for the company. This increases the chances of developing a longer-term profitable relationship

## Cons

As with email marketing, permission marketing can be abused and lead target customers to perceive the communications as spam if the sports marketer over-communicates. Sports marketers have to maintain a consistent image and message across every marketing medium used, and when multiple permission marketing messages are sent, the risk of message quality erosion increases.

## Measures[10]

Permission marketing measures are similar to those with email, as well as: delivery rate (measures the number of emails sent minus those that bounced or were rejected, divided by total emails sent); unsubscribe rate (percentage of customers that unsubscribe from permission request); open rate (percentage of emails opened after delivery); and click-throughs.

# Partnerships

Partnerships marketing describes the collaborative relationships between two or more companies in pursuit of a new market opportunity.

## Pros

Partnerships provide each company with added credibility since the relationship suggests that each firm sees actual value in the offerings of their partners, signaling confidence to the market. The marketing and advertising costs, and possibly non-marketing costs as well (support, operations, logistics, design, distribution), are shared by the partners, thereby decreasing each firm's respective investment that they would otherwise have to spend individually to pursue the same opportunity. Partnering firms also gain new customers from each other. The expanded market opportunity of new customers and new locations increases each firm's knowledge of the marketplace and can conceivably spur innovation to address emerging needs.

## Cons

Each firm brings its own cultural and operating biases to the partnership, creating the potential for disagreement if clear expectations are not reviewed in detail at the outset of the partnership. At the same time, ensuring every detailed is covered through advanced agreement may be unreasonable given the limited time most market opportunities have. It is incumbent on each partner to outline their respective expectations, including objectives, benefits, concerns, and even 'walk-away' provisions. The challenge is that partnering firms may be reluctant to share too much information, hindering progress.

## Measures

While partnerships are characterized by complexity and dependent on the details of the opportunity each firm is pursuing, the following measures are helpful: cost take-outs (for redundant activities), new customers, increased sales, units sold, revenues and profits, market share increases, brand image improvements, and awareness increases.

## 12.3  Social and digital advertising planning

The advertising planning template in Table 12.1 shows three hypothetical target audiences X, Y, Z and the corresponding advertising media that most effectively reaches them.

**Table 12.1**  Social and digital advertising planning template

|  | Multimedia | Web | Banners | Blogs | Podcasts | Social Media | Mobile |
|---|---|---|---|---|---|---|---|
| Target audience X | ✓ | ✓ | ✓ | ✓ | | | |
| Target audience Y | | ✓ | | ✓ | ✓ | ✓ | |
| Target audience Z | | ✓ | | | | | ✓ |

Source: Adapted from Davis (2012, p. 322).

A social and digital advertising worksheet for the web is shown in Table 12.2.

The sports marketer's message continues the 'Compete or Go Home' theme introduced in Chapter 11. Select web metrics shown are:

**Table 12.2** Social and digital advertising worksheet

| | Target Audience | Message | Direct URL Access | Engagement | Abandonment | Cost | Purchase Goals |
|---|---|---|---|---|---|---|---|
| Web | X | 'Compete or Go Home' | 5k↑ per week | 20%↑ in time spent on site | 15%↓ in shopping cart abandonment | $250k | 15%↑ in purchases |

Source: Adapted from Davis (2012, p. 322).

- *Direct URL access.* As implied, direct URL access describes the number of customers entering the site by directly entering the URL address (in contrast to gaining access from linking to it from another site). This metric is a reasonable approximation of the user's awareness and knowledge of the sports marketer's offerings. In this illustration, the sports marketer hopes to increase the number of people who visit the site using direct URL access by 5000 per week.
- *Engagement.* Engagement is the length of *active* time a user spends on a website (in contrast to idle time, when the user leaves a page open and unattended). The sports marketer seeks to increase engagement 20 percent, which means part of their marketing emphasis will likely include making their website experience as engaging as possible.
- *Abandonment.* This refers to an incomplete or abandoned website visit, such as stopping a purchase before completion.[11] In this example the sports marketer has improved the shopping cart's ease of use by improving its design, so she seeks a 15 percent decrease in shopping cart abandonment.
- *Cost.* The total cost of developing the website.
- *Purchase goals.* Purchase goals are the new sales targets for the sports marketer, based on the website's characteristics (design, ease of use, quality of content).

## 12.4 Social and digital advertising costs

Social and digital marketing costs can be lower than those for traditional marketing. However, achieving lower advertising costs through social and digital tools depends on the design of the advertising, its location and timing (similar to traditional advertising), and the size of the target audience. It is quite possible that a sports marketer may see an increase in costs if their digital and social ads capture the market's imagination, inspiring respondents to click-through (if it is a web-based advertisement). At the same time, many blog and podcast applications are either free or inexpensive, allowing sports marketers the possibility of lower advertising costs than with traditional advertising. There is a trade-off, however, since these two media require greater resource inputs (people with expertise in design, programming, content, writing etc.). Social and digital advertising has transferred some of the control of company images to consumers, through the use of blogs, podcasts, Twitter, Facebook, and similar digital tools. The good news for sports marketers is that social and digital advertising have spawned a new interactive social world where qualitative insights about customers are plentiful. Social and digital advertising gives sports marketers an invaluable vehicle for real-time interaction with customers anywhere, offering an authentic antidote to the increasing distrust of traditional marketing. Social and digital marketing offers sports marketers the potential for their message to grow and spread rapidly through viral marketing. Professor John Deighton of Harvard Business School, a marketing expert who has written extensively on new media, suggests that today's business world requires that marketers must become comfortable with suggesting topics for consumer discussion, rather than directly dictating a one-way message, encouraging customers to respond. He says: 'When a brand adopts a point of view, rather than simply making a claim for softer skin, for instance, it can become a lightning rod for discourse. You have to be confident that your message can withstand reinterpretation'.[12]

Sports marketers must be confident in their company's ability to listen to, withstand and respond to instant customer feedback, and even altering the message, as it spreads.

## Mobile

According to Juniper Research, mobile entertainment will grow from $36.5 billion in 2011 to $65 billion in 2016. This increase is spurred by the rapid growth of the tablet market.[13] Developing marketing programs that work effectively in mobile entertainment, including games, videos, and real-time sports updates, will help marketers leverage their sports marketing investment.[14]

## Blogs

In 2012 there were 210 million blogs in the world.[15] 2 million blog postings are added each day, and the majority of Fortune 500 corporations have blogs.[16] When sports marketers build a readership through their blogs, they develop credibility for themselves and their organizations, while also encouraging input from their readers.[17]

# Podcasts

Podcasting, at one time a new media being rapidly adopted by the public, has seen slower growth since 2010, but the numbers of podcasts worldwide still hover over 260 million. In the USA, awareness of podcasting has remained at 45–46 percent since 2010, but is up significantly from 2006 when awareness was only 22 percent. In 2012, 26 percent of all Americans had listened to or viewed a podcast at some point in their lives since podcasting first become a phenomenon. Fifty-four percent of podcast consumers in the USA were male in 2012, 46 percent female, and 50 percent of podcast consumers are between the ages of 12 and 34. Forty percent of podcast consumers have a household income of $75 000 or more.[18] Overall podcast ad spending world-wide grew from an estimated US$240 million in 2008 to US$435 million in 2012,[19] and some of that is invested in sports marketing. It would appear that these are important consumers for sports marketers to reach.

## Social media

Companies in this space have grown dramatically since 2006. YouTube had more than 1 trillion views in 2011, and more than 800 million unique visitors per month in 2012, up from 100 million visitors per month in 2009. YouTube is now localized in 43 countries and 60 languages. YouTube offers visitors access to a wide array of sports content, from informal fan videos to official sports and league channels from the NFL, NBA, MLB, NHL, EPL, FIFA, IRB Rugby, AFL (Australian Football League), and the Olympics, among others.[20]

In 2012 Twitter had grown to over 465 million accounts, with more than 175 million tweets being sent every day. Eleven new Twitter accounts are created every second and 1 million accounts are added every day. Twitter saw total minutes spent 'tweeting' increase 3712 percent from April 2008 to April 2009 alone.[21] In 2012 Twitter's ad revenue was approximately $260 million and is projected to grow to $540 million by 2014. Worldwide in 2012, the USA had nearly 108 million Twitter users, Brazil had 33.3 million users, Japan had 30 million users, the UK had nearly 24 million users, Indonesia had 19.5 million users, and India had over 13 million users. US sports fans use Twitter constantly. During the 2012 Super Bowl Football game, 10 245 Tweets per second were sent in the final minutes, and during the Denver Broncos' win streak in 2011 when quarterback Tim Tebow was the starter, fans tweeted 9420 times per second.[22]

Facebook grew from 50 million users in 2007 to 1 billion users in 2012, adding millions of new users every week. More than 80 percent of Facebook's users are outside the USA and Canada, signaling a very strong international user base. In addition, more than 580 million users are active on Facebook every day and 600 million+ monthly users use the company's mobile products. Over 40 percent of Facebook's customers are 35+ (their fastest-growing demographic), college educated, white-collar professionals. The average length of each visit in 2012 is 23 minutes, up from 20 minutes in 2010, and the average user visits the site at least 40 times per month[23] indicating that the social commitment level is high. Facebook has over 550 000 applications deployed, of which many are suggested by users and designed to make the site even more useful and customized. Sports marketers will find thousands of sports-related fan pages and official sport pages on Facebook, connecting with the company's enormous, diverse, and growing social community.

According to the 2011 Social Media Examiner report (a summary of selected findings is shown in Table 12.3), marketers are using social media as an important, if not dominant, part of their overall marketing investment.

**Table 12.3** Social media as percentage of total marketing investment

|  | % |
| --- | --- |
| Social media is important to my business | 83% |
| Marketers using social media for 6+ hours weekly | 59% |
| Marketers using social media for 11+ hours weekly | 33% |
| Marketers using social media for 20+ hours weekly | 15% |
| Social media increased my exposure | 85% |
| Social media increased my traffic | 69% |
| Lead generation from social media | 58% |
| Those who invested in social media for 6 or more months gained new business partnerships | 44% |
| B2C companies were much more likely to develop a loyal fan base through social media | 63% |
| YouTube is the top area where marketers plan to increase social media efforts | 76% |

Source: Stelzner (2012).

## 12.5 Trends in integrated marketing communications (IMC)

IMC describes the efforts companies undertake to integrate their myriad communications activities and channels to convey with clarity a consistent and compelling message to the marketplace. Tables 12.4 to 12.7 summarize the trends in expenditures by region and medium, and share of ad

**Table 12.4** Ad expenditures by region – major media (newspapers, magazines, TV, radio, cinema)

|  | 2011 | 2012 | 2013 | 2014 | 2015 |
|---|---|---|---|---|---|
| North America | 165086 | 171937 | 177897 | 185779 | 194666 |
| Western Europe | 109244 | 106815 | 107066 | 109126 | 111549 |
| Asia Pacific | 132131 | 140151 | 147912 | 156713 | 167410 |
| Central & Eastern Europe | 26153 | 26716 | 28367 | 30449 | 32858 |
| Latin America | 35282 | 37991 | 41780 | 45549 | 49835 |
| Middle East & North Africa | 4155 | 4198 | 4313 | 4412 | 4521 |
| Rest of World | 9508 | 9505 | 10332 | 11422 | 12848 |
| World | 481560 | 497312 | 517668 | 543450 | 573686 |

Source: 'ZenithOptimedia forecasts 4.1 percent growth in global adspend in 2013' (2012).

**Table 12.5** Global advertising spending by medium

|  | 2011 | 2012 | 2013 | 2014 | 2015 |
|---|---|---|---|---|---|
| Newspapers | 96688 | 93176 | 91320 | 90263 | 90076 |
| Magazines | 44990 | 43234 | 42341 | 41833 | 41599 |
| Television | 190064 | 197645 | 205505 | 215280 | 226450 |
| Radio | 33741 | 34296 | 35246 | 36187 | 37138 |
| Cinema | 2495 | 2746 | 2769 | 2962 | 3144 |
| Outdoor | 31712 | 32288 | 33325 | 34533 | 35948 |
| Internet | 76906 | 88573 | 101468 | 116090 | 132402 |
| World | 476595 | 491958 | 511882 | 537148 | 566757 |

Source: 'ZenithOptimedia forecasts 4.1 percent growth in global adspend in 2013' (2012).

**Table 12.6** Internet advertising by type

|  | 2011 | 2012 | 2013 | 2014 | 2015 |
|---|---|---|---|---|---|
| Display | 28221 | 33249 | 39826 | 47691 | 57207 |
| Classified | 11313 | 12129 | 12831 | 13434 | 14138 |
| Paid search | 37372 | 43195 | 48812 | 54965 | 61057 |
| Total | 76906 | 88573 | 101468 | 116090 | 132402 |

Note: Figures shown above in Tables 12.4, 12.5, and 12.6 are in millions US$ using 2011 currency average rates The totals here are lower than the totals in the previous table of ad expenditures by region, since that table includes total ad spend figures for a few countries for which spend is not itemized by medium. That table also excludes some advertising that does not fit into the above media categories.

Source: 'ZenithOptimedia forecasts 4.1 percent growth in global adspend in 2013' (2012).

**Table 12.7** Share of total spend by medium (%)

|            | 2011 | 2012 | 2013 | 2014 | 2015 |
|------------|------|------|------|------|------|
| Newspapers | 20.3 | 18.9 | 17.8 | 16.8 | 15.9 |
| Magazines  | 9.4  | 8.8  | 8.3  | 7.8  | 7.3  |
| Television | 39.9 | 40.2 | 40.1 | 40.1 | 40.0 |
| Radio      | 7.1  | 7.0  | 6.9  | 6.7  | 6.6  |
| Cinema     | 0.5  | 0.6  | 0.5  | 0.6  | 0.6  |
| Outdoor    | 6.7  | 6.6  | 6.5  | 6.4  | 6.3  |
| Internet   | 16.1 | 18.0 | 19.8 | 21.6 | 23.4 |

Source: 'ZenithOptimedia forecasts 4.1 percent growth in global adspend in 2013' (2012).

spend by medium, indicating where companies are focusing their advertising spending priorities. For sports marketers these trends provide important context for any sports marketing investments being made, by region and medium.

## Top sports advertising corporate spenders

Chapter 11 and and this chapter have given insight into both traditional and social/digital advertising choices for sports marketers. Table 12.8 shows the top 25 corporate sports advertisers in 2011 in the USA, which combines their spending in traditional and social/digital advertising. A notable insight is that the proportion of their total budget committed to sports represents a substantial portion of their total ad spending, indicating the important of sports marketing to companies as they seek ways to enhance their image, boost their reputation, increase customer loyalty, and improve their overall financial performance. Given its importance in the overall marketing budget, sports advertising can be reasonably considered a strategic marketing investment in that its usage is intended to position companies for the long term by associating with the qualities and characteristics of sports since those are considered to be generally positive. For marketers, their ongoing challenge is how to use sports marketing to convey a trustworthy image that is believable and authentic. This is not meant to suggest that sports marketing advertising campaigns can't be humorous or whimsical to be taken seriously or to convey credibility. Indeed, humor and unusual creativity in the advertising work particularly when consumers are 'in on the joke'. Instead, authenticity is relative to the market's perception of the brand and if the message is 'in character' with the brand, then consumers will consider it consistent with their own understanding.

**Table 12.8** Top 25 sports advertisers in the USA – 2011

| 2011 Rank (2010 Rank) | Company/Brand | 2011 Sports Ad Spending | 2011 Total Ad Spending | Percentage of Ad Spending Devoted to Sports | Change in Sports Spending vs 2010 | Change in Sports Spending vs 2009 |
|---|---|---|---|---|---|---|
| 1(3) | Verizon | $345 438 719 | $1 523 982 375 | 22.7% | +1.4% | +40.1% |
| 2(2) | Anheuser-Busch | $299 721 969 | $456 239 625 | 65.7% | −15.9% | −3.8% |
| 3(1) | AT&T Mobility | $296 940 250 | $1 310 781 500 | 22.7% | −18.9% | +64.4% |
| 4(4) | Ford | $263 507 645 | $1 371 668 594 | 19.2% | −13.6% | +6.0% |
| 5(6) | Chevrolet | $249 866 151 | $1 029 529 844 | 24.3% | +4.6% | +49.9% |
| 6(5) | Toyota | $218 603 617 | $1 067 944 875 | 20.5% | −8.9% | +7.5% |
| 7(8) | MillerCoors | $203 025 062 | $360 294 438 | 56.3% | −5.3% | −10.4% |
| 8(10) | Sprint | $171 090 500 | $558 439 000 | 30.6% | −4.5% | −14.6% |
| 9(15) | Southwest Airlines | $165 499 688 | $240 861 062 | 68.7% | +26.0% | +28.6% |
| 10(7) | Geico Direct | $163 494 641 | $766 306 750 | 21.3% | −24.6% | −4.1% |
| 11(12) | Nissan | $153 167 485 | $577 850 691 | 26.5% | −4.9% | +96.9% |
| 12(11) | DirecTV | $137 980 781 | $356 739 531 | 38.7% | −21.3% | −18.1% |
| 13(9) | McDonald's | $127 131 258 | $996 054 375 | 12.8% | −37.3% | −18.4% |
| 14(16) | State Farm | $125 383 266 | $523 524 906 | 23.9% | −3.1% | +7.7% |
| 15(14) | Warner Bros. Ent | $123 810 031 | $652 460 688 | 19.0% | −10.7% | +11.9& |
| 16(19) | Lexus | $120 587 471 | $323 716 125 | 37.3% | −3.5% | NA |
| 17(25) | Mercedes Benz | $101 405 853 | $287 888 226 | 35.2% | −6.9% | +56.1% |
| 18(NR) | Chrysler | $96 888 814 | $405 599 655 | 23.9% | NA | NA |
| 19(18) | Subway | $96 174 164 | $513 575 031 | 18.7% | −23.3% | −2.8% |
| 20(23) | Apple | $95 068 961 | $338 849 031 | 28.1% | −14.0% | +0.6% |
| 21(29) | Honda | $94 147 979 | $630 150 868 | 14.9% | −5.8% | +30.4% |
| 22(41) | Volkswagen | $93 320 194 | $387 565 754 | 24.1% | +29.5% | +81.9% |
| 23(28) | Hyundai | $88 229 366 | $517 189 031 | 17.1% | −12.5% | +3.3% |
| 24(13) | Coca-Cola | $86 550 656 | $239 212 750 | 36.2% | −40.2% | +6.4% |
| 25(38) | Capital One Bank | $85 617 227 | $339 769 281 | 25.2% | +9.7% | +92.1% |

Source: Broughton (2012).

## 12.6 Chapter summary

Social and digital advertising tools have transformed marketing communications over the past several years. Whereas traditional advertising is a one-way marketing communications approach from company to customers, social and digital advertising allows two-way, simultaneous and direct engagement between companies and customers. There are numerous benefits, and risks, with social and digital advertising tools. Benefits include interacting directly with customers and the ability to respond to their needs immediately. In addition, if customers favor the sports marketer's company, then there is a good chance that a positive viral marketing response will follow, quickly building awareness for the company. Of course, the risks include the downside to viral marketing – if customers find your company lacking in almost any area, word will spread equally quickly and potentially overwhelm the company's ability to respond effectively. As companies are experiencing today, while it takes years and even decades to build a lasting brand reputation, it takes only a few hours or days to unravel and even irreparably harm a company's image. Furthermore, even relatively minor incidents can be overblown. As with the brand touchpoints and customer experience journey exercises in Chapter 9, both traditional and social/digital advertising must be thoughtfully planned and measured, and the implications of any message campaign must be known well before it is launched, lest the company find itself unable to respond to expectations built from the advertising.

**CASE STUDY 1**

# Adidas FIFA 2010 activation

In 2005, adidas signed a deal worth $351 million to extend its partnership as an official sponsor at the FIFA World Cups.[24] The deal would extend adidas's relationship with the tournament, which began in 1970, through the 2014 World Cup.[25] As part of its deal, adidas was the official supplier of all referee uniforms, match balls, and sports product category-related advertising. But adidas's activation of its sponsorship of the 2010 World Cup held in South Africa beyond this scope was particularly popular. The world's second-largest sportswear company viewed the event as a premier platform to increase its market share and position itself as the football market leader.[26] In addition, adidas used the event to promote new products that it launched in 2009.[27] Adidas outfitted more than 200 players and 12 teams at the 2010 World Cup, including Spain, the champion of the tournament.[28]

Adidas's integrated campaign at the 2010 World Cup was called 'The Quest' and featured 32 players from the 32 federations playing in the tournament.[29] It was a multilevel campaign that culminated in a social media hub where fans could interact on adidas's 'The Quest' Facebook page.[30] 'The Quest' featured numerous YouTube videos, each in the company's 'Every Team Needs' brand strategy.[31] The idea behind the campaign was to give sponsored players superhero powers that would combine to create the ultimate team.[32] Every day, sponsored players were 'matched up' against one another on the Facebook page and squared off in skill and statistical analysis. Those fans who correctly predicted the victors would accumulate points, which in turn could earn them prizes.[33]

Another key part of 'The Quest' campaign included a collaboration between adidas and George Lucas's seminal film *Star Wars*. As part of this effort, adidas shot several videos, which were used as advertisements featuring the athletes' part of their 'The Quest' campaign, as well as original footage from the film. In conjunction with this campaign, adidas released special edition *Star* Wars apparel and footwear for its Spring/Summer 2010 line.[34] To date, the adidas Originals 'Star Wars Cantina 2010' video featuring original footage from *Star Wars*, Snoop Dogg, and David Beckham has amassed over six million views.[35] The *Star Wars* collaboration was so successful that adidas released a second line of *Star Wars*-inspired apparel and footwear the following year outside the scope of its FIFA sponsorship.[36]

Adidas also engaged with its own brand battle with Nike throughout the 2010 World Cup. While Nike was not an official sponsor of the tournament, it engaged in some heavy ambush marketing that adidas had to compete against. Nike's largely digital campaign was called 'Write the Future'[37] and featured several Nike-clad football players imagining what their future would be like had crucial events in their careers turned out differently.[38] Nike's interactive campaign also allowed Nike fans to 'Write the Headline', a tactic in which fans could post short 'grabber' phrases on Twitter and Facebook.[39] Many of these phrases were then scrolled across the side of a massive LED display on the fourth largest building in

**CASE STUDY 1** *(continued)*

Johannesburg, which Nike rented.[40] In addition, Nike supplanted the campaign with more traditional print and television ads (none of which could have aired during World Cup matches due to adidas's category ownership).[41]

The ongoing battle between the world's first and second biggest sportswear companies generated nearly as much buzz as the individual campaigns. As a result of its efforts, adidas sold 6.5 million soccer jerseys, more than double what it sold at the 2006 FIFA World Cup in Germany.[42] In addition, adidas ended up generating the highest percentage of online world cup buzz after the first two weeks at 25.1 percent.[43] It seemed, however, that Nike had done something to peak the interest of the world's soccer fans as Nike's three-minute version of its 'Write the Future' campaign generated more than 20 million views after just five weeks.[44]

 **QUESTIONS**

1   Evaluate adidas's 'Quest' campaign. Does it fit with the company's image? Why or why not?

2   Should adidas be worried about Nike's ongoing success with its ambush marketing activities? Explain.

3   Compare and contrast the two companies' uses of social media? What are the key lessons from each company?

**CASE STUDY 2**

# Portland Timbers' social media

The Portland Timbers became the 18th team to join Major League Soccer (MLS) in 2011. Though three other different iterations of the Portland Timbers have existed in other soccer leagues in Portland in the past (North American Soccer League, Western Soccer League, and United Soccer League – First Division) the current iteration of the Timbers is the first to be a part of the MLS.[45]

Portland as a market for professional sports team is often viewed as a second-tier market as the 29th most populous city in the United States. In addition to the Timbers, the Portland Trail Blazers are currently the only other professional team competing in a major American sport. Founded in 1970, the Trail Blazers have won only one NBA Championship during the 1976–77 season. The city also has a major junior league hockey team called the Portland Winterhawks, which competes in the Western Hockey League (WHL). Portland's track record with sports teams has not always been successful as many sports franchises have failed in the city of Portland. In the past, the Portland Beavers (minor league Triple-A baseball),[46] the Portland Fire (Women's National Basketball Association),[47] and the Portland LumberJax (National Lacrosse League),[48] have all come and gone.

In its inaugural season, the Portland Timbers were fairly successful on the field. The team finished in sixth place in the Western Conference and just barely missed qualifying for the MLS Cup play-offs.[49] However, the club became well known around the league for its enthusiastic fan base, which was anchored by the Timbers Army. Every single game sold out in 2011 during the Timbers' first season and all season tickets for the 2012 season sold out months before it began.[50]

The Timbers adopted a few unique ways of integrating themselves into the Portland community. One particularly successful way the Timbers became a part of Portland was through their social media communications. Currently, the Portland Timbers operate official accounts on Facebook, Twitter, Instagram, YouTube, and Foursquare.[51] However their fans and followers have dedicated followings to the Timbers on other social media platforms, thus increasing the social media reach of the Timbers.

Through various successful marketing campaigns, the Timbers have effectively leveraged their social media presence. Before the inaugural season began in 2011, billboards of Portlanders holding an axe began popping up all over the city. The billboards fell under the 'We Are Timbers' campaign, which sought to increase the appeal of the new sports team to everyone in the community.[52] As such, the people depicted in these billboards came from many walks of life and portrayed a diverse Timbers fan base. After the success of the billboards, through social media, the Timbers solicited their fans to come to their downtown store on a January day prior to their inaugural season to have their own picture taken with the axe. The club anticipated only a few hundred fans showing up, and were flabbergasted when nearly 1500 fans came to have their picture taken and show their support for the

**CASE STUDY 2** *(continued)*

new team.[53] The club posted many of these photos on its Facebook page. As a result of the thousands of photos taken, the Timbers staged a social media contest for their fans to vote for their favorite photos to be featured on the next round of billboards around the city.[54]

The club also has a strong emphasis on the team as the focal point of its social media communications. It often features exclusive video content of the players through its '90 With' video spots in which it asks players as many questions as possible in 90 seconds.[55] This platform has also allowed the club to engage with its Spanish-speaking fans as it occasionally captures these segments entirely in Spanish. On Twitter, the club employs several exclusive hashtags including #Timbers and #RCTID, an acronym that stands for Rose City 'Til I Die (an homage to one of Portland's nicknames).

While social media has proven to be successful for the Timbers in that it has engaged with many different fans, a successful social media presence is nothing without proven returns down the sports marketing value chain. The Timbers have completed some promotions with great success – can this continue?

 **QUESTIONS**

1 What roles can social media play in the sports marketing value chain?
2 As the initial excitement that comes with an expansion team begins to wear off, how can the Timbers continue to generate buzz around their social media platforms?
3 What are some other marketing tactics the Timbers can use to continue leveraging their social media relationships to generate continued ticket and merchandise sales?

**NOTES**

1 Research projects conducted by students at Singapore Management University for term projects in their Strategic Brand Management Course between 2004 and 2008. Annual reports supplied through investor relations and Yahoo! Finance for publicly traded companies; Chen et al. (2007); Depuy Orthopaedics, Inc. (2007); Ethicon, Inc. (2007); Leggatt (2007).
2 Davis (2010, pp. 302–20).
3 Davis (2013, pp. 163–4).
4 Ibid., p. 211.
5 Ibid., pp. 207–8.
6 'Blogs' (n.d.), ESPN.com, accessed 17 July 2012 at http://espn.go.com/espn/blogs.
7 'Worldwide mobile cellular subscribers to reach 4 billion mark in late 2008' (2008).
8 Peppers and Rogers (2005). Return on Customer[sm] and ROC[sm] are registered service marks of Peppers and Rogers Group, a division of Carlson Marketing Group, Inc. Readers who are interested in a more comprehensive treatment of ROC[sm] are encouraged to review Peppers and Rogers' book. Furthermore, their websites, www.peppersandrogers.com and www.1to1.com/ provide additional information about personalization.
9 Godin (1999).
10 Ibid. In addition, 'E-mail permission marketing fundamentals' (2009).
11 Davis (2012, p. 322).

12 Hanna (2007).
13 Holman (2012).
14 'Mobile music, games and TV to generate $34 billion by 2010' (2008); 'Mobile entertainment markets: opportunities & forecasts 2007–12' (2008).
15 Prayiush (2012a).
16 Digital Buzz Blog (n.d.), 'Infographic: 24 hours on the internet', accessed 23 July 2012 at http://www.digitalbuzzblog.com/infographic-24-hours-on-the-internet/.
17 Data from speech made by Mitch Joel, CEO of Twist Image and 6 Pixels of Separation, in a July 2007 presentation made to Singapore Management University's conference called PodCamp 2007. Cited source was Arbitron & Edison Media Research (2007).
18 'The podcast consumer 2012' (2012).
19 Verna (2008).
20 'Statistics' (n.d.), YouTube.com, accessed 28 August 2012 at http://www.youtube.com/t/press_statistics.
21 Schroeder (2009).
22 Prayiush (2012b).
23 Burbary (2011).
24 'World Cup runneth over: adidas signs $351m pact with FIFA' (2005).
25 Ibid.
26 Mickle (2009), 'Coke, McDonald's adidas built global plans around event' (2009).
27 Ibid.
28 'Adidas Group annual report 2010' (2011, p. 7).
29 Ibid.
30 'Adidas Originals – Star Wars Cantina' and 'Adidas/The Quest' (2010).
31 Ibid.
32 Ibid.
33 Ibid.
34 Ruano (2009).
35 'Adidas Originals – Star Wars Cantina' and 'Adidas/The Quest' (2010).
36 Kan (2011).
37 Ofek (2010).
38 Ibid.
39 Ibid.
40 Ibid.
41 Ibid.
42 Thomaselli (2010).
43 'World Cup sponsors recover from competitor ambushes' (2010).
44 Ofek (2010).
45 'Timbers soccer history' (n.d.).
46 Fentress (2010).
47 'Portland Fire' (n.d.).
48 Fentress (2009).
49 'Portland Timbers 2011' (n.d.).
50 Ibid.
51 'Timbers social media' (n.d.).
52 Crane (2012).
53 'We are Timbers' (n.d.).
54 Crane (2012).
55 '90 With' video spots.

 **REFERENCES**

'Adidas Group annual report 2010' (2011), adidas AG.
'Adidas Originals – Star Wars Cantina 2010' and 'Adidas/The Quest' (2010), *Contagious*

*Magazine*, 9 June 2010, accessed 8 October 2012 at http://www.contagiousmagazine.com/2010/06/adidas_21.php.

Broughton, David (2012), 'Verizon tops among ad spenders', 4 June 2012, *Sports Business Journal*, accessed 29 September 2012 at http://www.sportsbusinessdaily.com/Journal/Issues/2012/06/04/Research-and-Ratings/Ad-spending.aspx.

Burbary, Ken (2011), 'Facebook demographics revisted – 2011 statistics', 7 March 2011, accessed 27 May 2013 at http://socialmediatoday.com/kenburbary/276356/facebook-demographics-revisited-2011-statistics.

Chen, Yixiao, Yinghao Lan, Yuan Shan Lee, Yiling Eileen Leo, Hongxi Loo and Han Xian Wong, under supervision of John A. Davis (2007), 'Johnson & Johnson: a case study', November 2007, updated July 2008.

Crane, William (2012), 'How the Portland Timbers have scored big with social media', Bonfire Social Media, 14 June 2012, accessed 5 July 2012, http://bonfiresocialmedia.com/how-the-portland-timbers-have-scored-big-with-social-media/.

Davis, John A. (2010), *Competitive Success – How Branding Adds Value*, New York: John Wiley & Sons.

Davis, John A. (2012), *The Olympic Games Effect – How Sports Marketing Builds Strong Brands*, New York: John Wiley & Sons, p. 322.

Davis, John A. (2013), *Measuring Marketing: 110+ Key Metrics Every Marketer Needs*, Singapore: John Wiley & Sons (Asia) PTE Ltd.

Depuy Orthopaedics, Inc. (2007), AllAboutArthritis.com, DePuy website within Johnson & Johnson, accessed 11 May 2009 at http://www.allaboutarthritis.com/portal/DPUY/AAA.

Digital Buzz Blog (n.d.), 'Infographic: 24 hours on the Internet', accessed 23 July 2012 at http://www.digitalbuzzblog.com/infographic-24-hours-on-the-internet/.

'E-mail permission marketing fundamentals' (2009), idaconcpts.com, 2 March 2009, accessed 5 March 2009 at http://idaconcpts.com/2009/03/02/e-mail-permission-marketing-fundamentals/.

Ethicon, Inc. (2007), Allaboutmyheart.com, accessed 11 May 2009 at http://www.allaboutmy-heart.com/.

Fentress, Aaron (2009), 'LumberJax done in Portland, team announces', *The Oregonian*, 4 May 2009, accessed 5 July 2012 at http://www.oregonlive.com/lumberjax/index.ssf/2009/05/lumberjax_done_in_portland_tea.html.

Fentress, Aaron (2010), 'Portland Beavers to be sold, likely moved to escondido, CA', *The Oregonian*, 14 October 2010, accessed 5 July 2012 at http://www.oregonlive.com/pbeavers/index.ssf/2010/10/portland_beavers_to_be_sold_mo.html.

Godin, Seth (1999), *Permission Marketing: Turning Strangers into Friends, and Friends into Customers*, New York: Simon & Schuster.

Hanna, Julia (2007), 'Authenticity over exaggeration: the new rule in advertising', 3 December 2007, Harvard Business School Working Knowledge, accessed 12 January 2009 from http://hbswk.hbs.edu/item/5812.html.

Holman, Rebecca (2012), 'Press release: games and infotainment to drive mobile entertainment revenues to $65bn by 2016', Juniper Research, 13 June 2012, accessed 23 July 2012 at http://www.juniperresearch.com/viewpressrelease.php?pr=318.

Kan, Eugene (2011), 'Star Wars x Adidas Originals 2011 Fall/Winter Collection', Hypebeast.com, 2 July 2011, accessed 9 October 2012 at http://hypebeast.com/2011/07/star-wars-x-adidas-originals-2011-fallwinter-collection/.

Leggatt, Helen (2007), 'J&J reallocates budgeting in favor of online marketing', accessed 2 July 2008 at http://www.bizreport.com/2007/03/more_indications_of_budget_shifts_for_large_firms.html.

Mickle, Tripp (2009), 'Coke, McDonald's Adidas built global plans around event' (2009), *Sports Business Journal*, 15 June 2009, accessed 8 October 2012 at http://www.sportsbusinessdaily.com/Journal/Issues/2009/06/20090615/This-Weeks-News/Coke-Mcdonalds-Adidas-Build-Global-Plans-Around-Event.aspx?hl=adidas%20fifa%202010&sc=0.

'Mobile entertainment markets: opportunities & forecasts (2nd edition) 2007–12' (2008), Juniper Research, 22 January 2008, accessed 11 April 2008 at http://www.juniperresearch.com/reports.php?id=99.

'Mobile music, games and TV to generate $34 billion by 2010' (2008), Juniper Research, March 2008, accessed 11 April 2008 at http://www.cellular-news.com/story/29857.php.

Ofek, Elie (2010), 'The World Cup brand winner: Adidas or Nike?' (2010), blogs, *Harvard Business Review*, 9 July 2010, accessed 9 October 2012 at http://blogs.hbr.org/hbsfaculty/2010/07/the-world-cup-winner-adidas-or.html.

Peppers, D. and M. Rogers (2005), Chapter 1, 'An open letter to Wall Street', in *Return on Customer: Creating Maximum Value From Your Scarcest Resource*, New York: Doubleday, pp. 16–18.

'Portland Fire' (n.d.), Hoopedia.nba.com, accessed 5 July 2012 at http://hoopedia.nba.com/index.php?title=Portland_Fire.

'Portland Timbers 2011' (n.d.), MLSSoccer.com, accessed 5 July 2012 at http://www.mlssoccer.com/history/club/portland/2011.

Prayiush (2012a), 'Number of blogs up from 35 million in 2006 to 181 million by the end of 2011', 10 March 2012, accessed 3 June 2012 at http://www.dazeinfo.com/2012/03/10/number-of-blogs-up-from-35-million-in-2006-to-181-million-by-the-end-of-2011/#ixzz2BJlJ2gz4.

Prayiush (2012b), 'Twitter statistics, facts and figures from 2006–2012', 27 February 2012, accessed 3 April 2012 at http://www.dazeinfo.com/2012/02/27/twitter-statistics-facts-and-figures-from-2006-2012-infographic/.

Ruano, L. (2009), 'Adidas Originals 2010 spring/summer Star Wars collection preview', Hypebeast.com, 20 November 2009, accessed 9 October 2012 at http://hypebeast.com/2009/11/adidas-originals-2010-springsummer-star-wars-collection-preview/.

Schroeder, Stan (2009), 'The web in numbers: Twitter's phenomenal growth suddenly stops', Mashable – The Social Media Guide, 9 June 2009, accessed 10 June 2009 from http://mashable.com/2009/06/09/web-in-numbers-may/.

'Statistics', (n.d.), YouTube.com, accessed 28 August 2012 at http://www.youtube.com/t/press_statistics.

Stelzner, Michael A. (2012), *2012 Social Media Marketing Industry Report*, accessed 12 May 2012 at http://www.socialmediaexaminer.com/SocialMediaMarketingIndustryReport2012.pdf.

'The podcast consumer 2012', Edison Research and Arbitron, 29 May 2012, accessed 31 July 2012 at http://www.slideshare.net/webby2001/the-podcast-consumer-2012.

Thomaselli, Rick (2010), 'Official sponsors score with World Cup', AdAge.com, 26 July 2010, accessed 8 October 2012 at http://adage.com/article/special-report-sports-marketing-2010/marketing-official-sponsors-score-world-cup/145067/.

'Timbers soccer history' (n.d.), PortlandTimbers.com, accessed 5 July 2012 at http://www.portlandtimbers.com/timbers-soccer-history.

'Timbers social media' (n.d.), PortlandTimbers.com, accessed 5 July 2012 http://www.portlandtimbers.com/news/social-media.

Verna, Paul (2008), 'Podcast advertising: seeking riches in niches', January 2008, accessed 23 March 2008 at http://www.onlinemarketing5.com/item/Podcast-Advertising-Seeking-Riches-in-Niches-6150.

'We are Timbers' (n.d.), PortlandTimbers.com, accessed 5 July 2012 at http://www.portlandtimbers.com/promotions/we-are-timbers.

'World Cup runneth over: adidas signs $351m pact with FIFA' (2005), *Sports Business Daily*, 19 January 2005, accessed 9 October 2012 at http://www.sportsbusinessdaily.com/Daily/Issues/2005/01/Issue-82/Sponsorships-Advertising-Marketing/World-Cup-Runneth-Over-Adidas-Signs-$351M-Pact-With-FIFA.aspx?hl=FIFA%20World%20Cup&sc=0.

'World Cup sponsors recover from competitor ambushes', Nielsen.com, 2 July 2010, accessed 8 October 2012 at http://blog.nielsen.com/nielsenwire/online_mobile/world-cup-sponsors-recover-from-competitor-ambushes/.

'Worldwide mobile cellular subscribers to reach 4 billion mark in late 2008' (2008), ITU – International Telecommunications Union website, 25 September 2008, accessed 6 November at http://www.itu.int/newsroom/press_releases/2008/29.html.

'ZenithOptimedia forecasts 4.1 percent growth in global adspend in 2013' (2012), ZenithOptimedia, accessed 3 December 2012 at http://www.zenithoptimedia.com/zenith/zenithoptimedia-forecasts-4-1-growth-in-global-adspend-in-2013/.

# 13

# Sports marketing revenues

 **CHAPTER OVERVIEW**

Marketing strategy is comprised of several components, each focusing on different and important knowledge areas designed to illuminate the overall market situation in which the company competes, thereby helping the marketer develop more effective plans. At a general level, we have learned about leading sports leagues around the world, creating an introductory understanding of each league's unique characteristics. This knowledge helps marketers understand the qualities that are attractive to sports fans and, thereby, is useful in crafting sports marketing activities that are also attractive to those same fans. We have also gained a firmer understanding of the role segmentation and targeting play in revealing market attractiveness, as well as the importance of converting awareness into preference since the latter indicates the customer's interest has been confirmed with a purchase. In this chapter we dig deeper into the revenue sources for different sports leagues, providing more information about the key contributors to their respective financial success. The composition of revenues reveals insights that will help marketers understand where the leagues focus their own business development efforts and shed light on those activities that fit best given each league's operating approach. Specifically, sponsorships are the most visible sports marketing activity that contributes revenues and are introduced here among other revenue sources, with additional insight in Chapter 14, when we discuss sponsorships in conjunction with event management. Here, we discuss sponsorships and major sports leagues and events.

## 13.1 NFL

The National Football League's (NFL's) total league revenues were nearly $10 billion in 2011. Under a 2011 collective bargaining agreement (CBA), the NFL owners and players' union agreed to split the revenues 53/47 (owners/players), meaning that the owners' share of total league revenues must average 53 percent and the players' share must average at least 47 percent for the ten years of the agreement's life. In other words, an average of 47 percent of league revenues each year must be spent on player salaries.[1]

This agreement was an important milestone for the league as disparities were growing between the large and small market clubs. The objective of the agreement was to set more rigorous salary caps and floors on what teams could spend on player salaries. By sharing revenues, the league is better able to balance out the disparities, enabling all teams to compete for talent on a relatively 'level playing economic field'. Sponsorship revenues contributed $946 million in 2011.[2] Total advertising revenues were $3 billion in 2011 during the regular season, and an additional $900+ million was generated in the post-season.[3] Merchandise revenues added another $2.5 billion in 2011,[4] and broadcast revenues were about $1.9 billion.[5] Ticket revenues (gate receipts) were approximately $1.2 billion in 2011.[6] Broadcast revenues are contracted to increase 7 percent annually, up to a maximum of $3.1 billion per year until 2022.[7]

In a 2011 Harris poll, 36 percent of the respondents rated pro football as the most popular sport in the USA. Baseball and college football were next, tied at 13 percent each. Auto racing followed at 8 percent, then professional and college basketball with 5 percent each.[8]

Marketers can infer that the NFL's efforts to reinforce parity across the league is intended to not only give more teams a chance to succeed, but also to provide media companies and sponsors with a wider range of sports marketing opportunities. In the years ahead, league revenues will certainly increase from all sources, giving sports marketers a bigger audience and additional avenues for marketing their companies.

## League sponsors

As of 2012, NFL sponsors included: Visa, Pepsi (PepsiCo), Nike, Lenovo, Verizon Wireless, Tide (P&G), Duracell (P&G), GMC Trucks, Gatorade (PepsiCo), Frito Lay, Tropicana, Anheuser-Busch (BudLight) and Quaker Oats (PepsiCo). The average 30-second TV commercial cost $545k. Official figures are not released, but the estimated cost of an NFL sponsorship is approximately $40–50 million per year,[9] but the figures vary depending on the length of the deal and the depth of the commitment. Anheuser-Busch paid $1.2 billion for its six-year sponsorship agreement. Nike paid a reported $1.1 billion to become the NFL's official apparel sponsor in 2012. VerizonWireless invested $720 million for a four-year deal. PepsiCo spent $560 million for the eight-year sponsorship from 2004 to 2012.[10] In 2012 PepsiCo and the NFL announced a new ten-year sponsorship agreement valued at $2.3 billion. Sponsors pay a premium for their NFL sponsorship because the league's fan base and viewership are growing, as is the league's popularity. In 2011, the NFL had 23 of the 25 top-rated shows, and the NFL has 144 percent more viewers than the average network television show. The average number of viewers per game in 2011 was 17.5 million, the highest since 1989. NBC's *Sunday Night Football* was the number one Sunday show in 2011, with nearly 21 million viewers per game. It is also number one among adults and men ages 18–54, a prime demographic for companies, and it was also the number four show for women ages 18–49.[11] According to a 2012 study[12] NFL sponsorships are successful in appealing to fans and changing attitudes required in determining purchase decision choices. Conducted from 2008 to 2010 by surveying 16 000 consumers, the study focused on five official NFL sponsors, and three primary competitors in each official sponsor's business categories (15 competitors overall). The official sponsors were in their fourth year (or more) of their sponsorship. Passionate fans (a category we describe as 'intense enthusiasts' in Chapter 3), had higher positive opinions of NFL sponsors than those fans that were less intense (this category of fans are termed 'casual enthusiasts'). The four-year+ tenure of the sponsors studies was important as well – by focusing on their sponsorship as a strategic, long-term investment, and not a short-term one-time deal, they were able to improve their brand positioning as compared to their primary competitors.

### Sponsor snapshot – PepsiCo and Gatorade

After announcing its new $2.3 billion ten-year sponsorship deal with the NFL in 2012, Pepsi presented its 2012 NFL marketing campaign, known as 'Power of One', which will be on over 25 000 NFL-related displays, including in-store display racks. Point-of-purchase displays are among the most effective mechanisms for inspiring purchase and Pepsi's own research indicated that when consumers see NFL messages on Pepsi displays it induces purchase. Gatorade, one of the many PepsiCo brands, was founded in 1965 and in 1967 it became the official beverage of the NFL. Since that time Gatorade has consistently advertised its beverages during NFL games, and also uses football imagery during off-season advertising. The brand is closely associated with many sports because of its qualities to help athletes rehydrate, particularly in hot weather and in the course of water loss during physical exertion. Gatorade has a 56.7 percent recognition among all fans as the brand they most closely associate with the NFL, the highest among all sponsors.[13]

## 13.2  EPL

Total English Premier League (EPL) revenues in 2010–11 were €2.5 billion (approximately $3.2 billion in 2012 dollars). The league distributes 50 percent of domestic TV revenues, 25 percent of which is based on how the team is ranked at the end of the season and the other 25 percent is based on how frequently a team's matches are broadcast. International TV rights are shared equally. Sponsorship revenues totaled $229 million. Shirt sponsorships alone for the 2012 season were estimated at $128 million. Total advertising revenues were $155 million, and total merchandise revenues were $220 million. Broadcast revenues were approximately $1.54 billion. Ticket revenues were approximately $690 million.[14]

The EPL has faced ongoing debt problems over the years. In 2009–11, 16 of the 20 teams lost money, even though revenues league-wide increased. Servicing the debt significantly reduced profitability, fomenting the losses. Player costs have soared, accounting for much of the debt. In comparison to all European football clubs, the EPL remains the richest league in Europe. While only 2 percent of the top clubs in Europe play in the EPL, they account for 56 percent of total debt for all European clubs. In contrast to the NFL, more than 70 percent of club revenues in the EPL go to player salaries. Over the past 20 years salaries for EPL players in the top clubs have increased over 1500 percent, demonstrating the source of the debt problem.[15] The challenge for these clubs is clear: how to reduce player costs as a percentage of total club revenues while also increasing revenues, primarily from sponsors and merchandise sales since broadcast revenues are contractually locked in and ticket prices are already expensive, frustrating fans. This is not an easy task since fans want their clubs to recruit the best talent.

Despite the EPL's financial challenges, sports marketers continue to find the league an attractive investment. As the most popular and visible sports league in Europe in both fan attendance and TV viewership, and with many of the most storied clubs, the EPL remains a magnet for sports marketing.

## League sponsors

In 2012 EPL sponsors were listed as: Barclays (league title sponsor), EASports (official partner), Nike (official partner), Topps (official licensee), Lucozade (official supplier), SkySPORTS (broadcast partner), ESPN (broadcast partner), BBCSport (broadcast partner), Yahoo! (broadcast partner), BBC Radio 5 live (radio broadcast partner), talkSPORT (radio broadcast partner), Absolute Radio extra (radio broadcast partner), and sportingiD (official licensee). Barclays announced that it agreed to a new three-year title sponsor deal with the EPL in 2012, spending $61.7 million per season. The new agreement cost 50 percent more than its previous EPL title sponsorship. SkySPORTS also announced a new three-year, $4.6 billion broadcast deal, representing a 70 percent increase over the league's prior broadcast deal.[16] In September 2012, the EPL announced that Nike would be the new kit supplier through 2018, supplanting Umbro, a former Nike subsidiary, which had been supplying kits to the Football Association since 1952. While the amount of the Nike relationship was not disclosed, the value of the previous Umbro agreement was $31.6 million per year, so the Nike agreement was undoubtedly significantly larger.[17]

### Sponsor snapshot – Barclays

Barclays in the UK's third largest bank and has been the title sponsor of the EPL since 2001. In 2012 Barclays was embroiled in a scandal over fixing market interest rates, known as LIBOR (London Interbank Offered Rate, which is the interest London banks are charged when borrowing from other banks; the rate is published each day) and was fined over $400 million by regulators in both the USA and UK, and its CEO was also forced to resign.[18] The title sponsorship offers significant potential benefits to Barclays. The EPL reaches a global audience of 640 million people in 240 different markets around the world. As title sponsor, Barclays receives exclusive worldwide marketing, branding, and product rights, including having the Barclays name used in all league-related branding globally. Like other sports sponsorships, Barclays receives tickets and hospitality rights. In addition, the company also gets title sponsorship of the Barclays Asia Trophy and serves as key match sponsor for one out of every 20 matches each season. As Barclays sees it, the title sponsorship continues a 100-year relationship with the Football Association and, in the age of digital communications and mass media, extends the brand around the world, raising the company's profile and associating it with the sport's ongoing popularity.[19]

## 13.3 MLB

Major League Baseball (MLB) revenues were $7.5 billion in 2012.[20] Each of the league's 30 teams pay 31 percent of local revenues into a central pool, and then this amount is redistributed equally back to all 30 teams.[21] The league also has a central fund, including TV revenues, a portion of which is distributed back to the teams as well. Low revenue teams receive the largest percentage of the distribution. In addition, MLB has a luxury tax that penalizes teams based on the amount they exceed each season's maximum team salary, with the proceeds benefitting the lowest payroll teams. While reliable figures were not available for 2012, sponsorship revenues in 2011 were

$585 million.[22] Post-season 2011 advertising revenues were $452 million and merchandise revenues $2.82 billion in 2010, increasing 10 percent in 2011 to over $3 billion.[23]

Broadcast revenues average approximately $701 million per year from national agreements.[24] Total ticket revenues were not reported, but MLB enjoyed the fifth highest attendance in its history in 2011, with 73 425 568 fans attending all games. This was the highest attendance since 2008, particularly interesting given the economic challenges the USA, and much of the world, continued to confront in 2011.[25]

Baseball is unique among professional sports because of the number of games each team plays (162), giving companies an important sponsorship and marketing opportunity. While pro football has emerged in recent years as more popular, baseball remains the national pastime, with rich traditions and rivalries going back to its founding in 1869.

## League sponsors

MLB has a wide range of sponsors, organized into two groups: Official Sponsors of MLB Advanced Media; and Official Sponsors of MLP Properties. The Official Sponsors of MLB Advanced Media are: Anheuser-Busch, Bank of America, Bayer (One a Day and Advanced Aspirin), Captain Morgan, Citi, Firestone, Frito-Lay, Gatorade, General Motors (Chevrolet), Intel, InterContinental Hotels Group (Holiday Inn), MasterCard International, Nike, Pepsi-Cola, Scotts, Sprint, State Farm Insurance, and the US Army. The Official Sponsors of MLP Properties are: Anheuser-Busch, Bank of America, Bayer (One a Day and Advanced Aspirin), Citi, Firestone, Frito-Lay, Gatorade, General Motors (Chevrolet), InterContinental Hotels Group (Holiday Inn), MasterCard International, Nike, P&G (Gillette, Head & Shoulders), Pepsi-Cola, Scotts, SIRIUS XM, State Farm Insurance, and Taco Bell.[26]

Few specifics are available about the cost of MLB sponsorships, but the 2012 Anheuser-Busch six-year sponsorship of MLB was estimated by IEG to be valued at $20 million per year and another $20 million in promotional commitments.[27] Separate from MLB league sponsorship are the individual sponsors each club secures. One example is stadium-naming rights, which are discussed in detail in Chapter 14. Twenty companies have stadium sponsorship rights for various MLB clubs. These sponsorship arrangements vary significantly in the length of the agreement, as do the associated costs. Minute Maid sponsors the Houston Astros stadium. The value of its deal was $170 million over 28 years.[28] Overstock.com signed a six-year, $7.2 million agreement for the Oakland A's ballpark.[29] Comerica signed a 30-year, $66 million stadium naming rights deal with the Detroit Tigers.[30]

*Sponsor snapshot – Anheuser-Busch*

Anheuser-Busch and MLB announced a new six-year sponsorship deal in 2012 that allows the company to be the official beer sponsor of MLB, as well as the presenting sponsor of each season's opening week and end of season wildcard play-off games. The agreement, which continues the company's 33-year relationship with the sport, also allows the company to be the sponsor of the Player of the Month awards, the MLB Fan Cave, and the MLBFanCave.com Concert Series. The company will have exclusive rights in the malt beverage category, including use of all official MLB trademarks and logos. Budweiser also sponsors 23 of the league's 30 teams. After the deal was announced, Anheuser-Busch blanketed the market with messages about the new MLB sponsorship that said 'America's Pastime and America's Beer. The Celebration Continues',[31] Part of the company's rationale relates to increasing consumer preference for micro/craft brews and decreasing interest in beer consumption with young adult consumers. In addition, Anheuser-Busch faced increased competition from Coors Light, which had seen sales increase 5.3 percent in 2011, whereas Budweiser sales declined 0.8 percent.[32]

## 13.4  NBA

Not all figures for 2011 were available due to data inconsistencies from the 2011 lockout, which delayed the start of the 2011–12 season by over a month, reducing the total number of games from the normal 82 to 66. The National Basketball Association (NBA) had total revenues of $4.3 billion in 2011. The NBA requires all teams to contribute approximately 50 percent of their total annual revenue, less arena operating costs and related expenses, into a common fund. The revenues are then redistributed back to the teams in an amount equivalent to the average payroll per team. Teams with revenue contributions to the pool that are less than the average team payroll for the league receive the redistributed revenue. In 2010 league sponsorship revenues were $572 million, and in 2012 the NBA was seriously considering allowing advertising on player jerseys, projected to add another $100 million in annual revenue. In 2011–12, post-season advertising was $448.5 million. Merchandise revenues in 2009–10 were $1.8 billion, and broadcast revenues for the league are $900 million annually. Ticket sales were $1.1 billion in the 2010–11 season.[33]

The NBA is considered to be the most exciting professional sport in the USA, and has the greatest potential for global expansion, particularly given the growth of international teams and leagues (playing under FIBA [International Basketball Federation] rules), and the sport's inclusion in the Olympics. Any given NBA game features amazing feats of athletic prowess and physical agility, creating a virtually limitless supply of highlight videos that travel quickly through the digital world, making an appealing sports marketing package for corporate marketers.

## League sponsors

The NBA had 14 sponsors in 2012, including: Sprint, Taco Bell, Sprite (Coca-Cola), Anheuser-Busch (Budweiser), Gatorade (PepsiCo), Kia, Under Armour, AutoTrader.com, BBVA, and Bacardi, among others.[34]

Bloomberg, the global financial information firm, tracks the returns of sponsor portfolios of each of the US sports leagues. Its report is called the 'Bloomberg Riskless Return Ranking', and in 2012 the NBA's sponsor portfolio performed best, with a risk-adjusted return of 2.5 percent. MLB had a return of 1.4 percent and the NFL's return was approximately 1.2 percent. The study suggests that the NBA works with the strongest and most consistent consumer brands as its corporate sponsors. For sponsors, this report provides a beneficial notoriety above and beyond the benefits of being associated with the NBA in general.[35]

Sprint secured a four-year, $45 million sponsorship agreement in 2011,[36] and BBVA, a financial firm from Spain, signed a four-year sponsorship deal with the NBA, WNBA (Women's National Basketball Association) and the NBA Development League in 2010 valued at over $100 million. Also in 2010, Kia Motors renewed its sponsorship with the NBA. While specific figures for the NBA sponsorship were not stated, in 2010 the company had a sponsorship budget of $15–20 million, allocated to the NBA, 13 NBA teams, the LPGA (Ladies Professional Golf Association), the Kia Classic LPGA tournament, and professional golfer Michelle Wie.[37]

### *Sponsor snapshot – BBVA*

BBVA and its US subsidiary, BBVA Compass, represent the first time a bank has sponsored the NBA. The NBA's global expansion ambitions, plus the more than 20 percent of NBA players that are from overseas, are key reasons why the league decided to go with an international bank.[38] BBVA has more than 700 branches in the USA and, coupled with the bank's sponsorship of

La Liga, helps it build a reputation as the 'Bank of Sports'. Each year the NBA plays a few games overseas in Europe and Asia, and the global appeal of basketball, particularly NBA players remains strong, giving both the NBA and BBVA better exposure to new markets.[39]

## 13.5 NHL

Total revenues were $3.3 billion in 2011–12, the seventh consecutive year of revenue growth.[40] A 2005 collective bargaining agreement that expired in September 2012 allocated 57 percent of league revenues to the players, higher than the NFL's 47 percent but lower than the EPL's 70 percent. The National Hockey League (NHL) sought to reduce the players' share to less than 50 percent.[41] Revenues from sponsors totaled $356 million in 2010, and for the 2011 Stanley Cup play-offs sponsorship revenues increased 40 percent over 2010, and 2010 was up 160 percent over 2009.[42] While total advertising revenues were not disclosed, merchandise revenues were $750 million in 2009 and between 2010 and 2011 these increased another 15 percent. In 2011 a new, ten-year broadcast agreement was signed, valued at $2 billion. Total ticket revenues in 2011 were $1.2 billion.[43] While the league confronts labor issues with the players' union about revenue allocations, and despite uneven TV viewership, the sport has displayed a strong overall growth trajectory. Fan attendance has steadily increased, with teams playing to 95.6 percent capacity in 2011–12.

Hockey is more of a niche sport in the United States, partly due to the strong fan following for the NFL, MLB, and NBA, but its fans are recognized for their loyalty and passion for their teams and the sport. Just north, hockey is the national pastime in Canada and Canadian teams are among the NHL's best financial performers.

## League sponsors

The NHL's sponsors are divided into three categories: North America, USA, and Canada:[44]

- North American sponsors: Cisco, Compuware, EA Sports, Enterprise, OnlyVegas, Reebok, SiriusXM, Westin, *The Hockey News*, Coors Light, G Series (PepsiCo), PepsiMax (PepsiCo), Lay (PepsiCo), Panini, Upper Deck, Ticketmaster, Molson Canadian and Bridgestone;
- Canadian Sponsors: Bell, Canadian Tire, Kraft, Tim Hortons, Scotiabank, Hershey's, and Visa;
- US sponsors: GEICO, Discover, Verizon Wireless, McDonald's, and Honda.[45]

MolsonCanadian's sponsorship was valued at $400 million for its seven year agreement.[46] In 2010 Canadian Tire signed a five-year sponsorship valued at $20 million.[47] ScotiaBank signed a five-year sponsorship agreement in 2007, valued at a reported $50 million. The bank renewed its sponsorship in 2012 for an undisclosed sum.

*Sponsor snapshot – Canadian Tire*

Canadian Tire has decades of experience in hockey. It is one of Canada's largest retailers, offering a wide range of goods, from tools, to automotives, to sports and recreation. Canadian Tire has been the place many families purchase their first hockey equipment for their children when they are first starting out. In addition, the company sponsors the Canadian Tire Hockey School as well as NHL players like Jonathan Toews of the Chicago Blackhawks. The scope of the sponsorship includes being an official partner of the NHL Heritage Classic, the NHL All-Star Game, the Stanley Cup Playoffs and Final, and the NHL Face-Off. Each of these events have huge and loyal fan followings, making the five-year deal signed in 2010 appear to be a sensible sports marketing opportunity in a country where hockey is the main sport, followed by most Canadians.[48]

## 13.6 Bundesliga

The German football league had revenues of $2.55 billion in 2011.[49] The league's teams have a unique ownership structure, with each team 50 percent+ owned by members of the club (members are fans).[50] All television revenues are shared equally across the league, and there are strict budget guidelines that all teams must follow. In 2012, shirt sponsorship revenues were $162.6 million,[51] and revenues from advertising totaled $686 million.[52] In 2011, league merchandise revenues totaled $104 million, broadcast revenues were $682 million, and ticket sales were $540 million.[53] Bayern Munich is also among the world's highest-ranked sports clubs in terms of brand value, second in 2012 to Manchester United.[54] The Bundesliga is notable as compared to the other leading European leagues – EPL (UK), La Liga (Spain), and Serie A (Italy) – because of the unique academy structure it has created to develop young football talent in Germany. The German Football Association and the Bundesliga agreed in 2002 that all teams in the league must operate regulated academies before they are allowed to play in the league.[55] Players from age 12 that display high potential are taken into the academies and roughly 5000 are under development at a time. A critical operating rule requires that each new entering class must have at least 12 players capable of playing for Germany. The results since 2002 have shown favorable trends, with the percentage of qualified players from Germany increasing from 56 percent in 2003 to 62 percent in 2002.[56] The average age of the German national team, comprised predominantly of players coming through the academies since 2002, has decreased as well, with an average age of 24.7 in 2010 when the German team finished third in the South Africa FIFA World Cup, suggesting that future World Cup teams will be even stronger as the younger players gain experience. Equally important, the Bundesliga academies will continue to develop new talent that should maintain the German team with an ongoing, deep selection of high-caliber players. In addition, the league has a rule preventing any individual or organization from owning more than 49 percent of any Bundesliga club. This rule was designed to prevent foreign owners from dominating the clubs, and thus preventing these owners from paying for talent from anywhere just to win titles, irrespective of whether their players are qualified to play on the national team. The end result has been a strong and positive collaborative relationship between Bundesliga clubs and the Football Association, with each focused on how develop youth talent.[57]

## League sponsors

The Bundesliga has six main sponsors: adidas, Sky, Grundig, Krombacher, Topps, and EASports. Grundig signed a two-year sponsorship agreement in 2011 for approximately $3.2 million per year.[58] Krombacher renewed a two-year sponsorship deal in 2011 valued at $7.4 million annually.[59] Sky Deutschland signed a five-year broadcast partnership agreement in 2012 valued at $634 million.[60] EA Sports agreed to a one-year sponsorship in 2011 valued at approximately $285 000.[61]

The 18 teams in the Bundesliga earned a combined $173 million in shirt sponsorship agreements. Bayern Munich, the top team in the league, has the richest shirt sponsorship deal with Deutsche Telekom, valued at $30.3 million per year.[62]

### Sponsor snapshot – Krombacher

Krombacher is a well-known German beer maker, based in the North Rhine-Wesphalia region of Germany. Krombacher will benefit from the Bundesliga's owned media assets, including regular exposure on the Bundesliga television show and the league website. The company will also gain ticket promotions and advertising rights within Germany for all broadcast Bundesliga matches.[63] The company also decided to sponsor Bundesliga relegation play-offs, which determine which clubs will either move up or drop down a division. The relegation matches are do or die, creating an intense and exciting atmosphere. Krombacher hoped that the added interest from German football fans would foster memorable recall of Krombacher's sponsorship.[64] In July 2012 the Bundesliga club Eintracht Frankfurt announced that Krombacher agreed to be the club's title sponsor, signing a six-year deal valued at $6.7 million.[65]

# 13.7 F1

Revenues were between $1.5 billion and $2 billion in 2011.[66] Revenue allocations and general team guidelines are governed by the Concorde Agreement. As with the EPL and other European football leagues, the best teams are rewarded, leading to significant differences in team budgets between the top and bottom teams.

Sponsorship revenues were nearly $890 million in 2011, merchandise revenues were $104 million, and broadcast revenues were $682 million.[67]

## League sponsors[68]

F1 sponsors vary each year slightly. Listed here are the 2012 team sponsors: Lotus-Renault, STR-Ferrari, McLaren Mercedes, Caterham-Renault, Mercedes, Sauber-Ferrari, Red Bull Racing-Renault, Marussia-Cosworth, Ferrari, Force India-Mercedes, Williams-Renault, and HRT Cosworth. The following companies were sponsors of the various teams: Altria (Marlboro), Benetton Group, Beta Tools, Brembo, British American Tobacco (Lucky Strike), Brooke Bond Oxo, Candy, Ceramiche Ragno, Champion, Compaq, Computer Associates, Copersucar, Credit Suisse, DHL, Eifelland, Essex Petroleum, Federal Express, First National Bank, Fondmetal SpA, Foster's, Gallaher (Benson & Hedges), Hewlett-Packard, Hong Kong & Shanghai Bank, Hugo Boss, Imperial Tobacco (Embassy), Imperial Tobacco (Gold Leaf), Imperial Tobacco (JPS), Japan Tobacco (Mild Seven), Martini & Rossi, Orange, Parmalat, PlayStation (Sony), Politoys, Red Bull, Reemtsma (West), Saudia Airlines, SEITA (Gitanes & Gauloises), Siemens, Skol, Sonax, STP Corporation, TAG-Heuer, Tissot, Unipart, UOP, Valvoline, Villiger (Tabatip), Vodafone, Warsteiner Brauerei and Yardley.

The cost for being a team title sponsor ranges from $30 million to $60 million and the agreements are generally for five years or more. Title sponsors gain significant exposure through F1's many media and marketing platforms plus being directly part of their team's logos. Below title sponsors are official partners, which cost companies from $1.5 million to $25 million each per year.[69] The cost depends on the location of the sponsor's name/logo on the car and/or driver's suit. Official partners that spend approximately $7 million or more per year are granted additional benefits and access to exclusive F1 activities. The next tier are official suppliers and promotional partners, costing between $500 000 and $1 million per year. These sponsors do not get their name on the cars or driver's apparel, but they are featured in their team's garage and various hospitality activities.[70]

### Sponsor snapshot – Red Bull

Founded in 1984 in Austria, Red Bull has become the global market leader in energy drinks. In 2011 the company grew 11.4 percent to approximately $5.6 billion in revenues on the sale of 4.6 billion units (cans).[71] In 2010 the company had grown 15.8 percent, to revenues of nearly $5 billion and approximately 4 billion units. Global profits are not disclosed but in 2011 they were estimated to be near $1.6 billion, and its UK profits were approximately $14.1 million.[72] Red Bull Racing, a subsidiary of Red Bull, Inc., had profits of approximately $4.5 million in 2011, 75 percent of which are attributed to its F1 sponsorship. Red Bull became an F1 team owner in 2004 after purchasing from Ford. The company's stated intent with its F1, and other sport sponsorships, is to associate the company with extreme sports. The company contributes just under 50 percent of the Red Bull Racing Team's $220 million+ annual budget. The advertising equivalent value for this investment was $356 million, indicating a strong return for the company's sports marketing investment, at least in terms of media exposure. The Red Bull Racing Team (RBR-Renault) won the team championship in 2010 and 2011 and was on its way to another championship in 2012.[73]

## 13.8 Non-league sports events

### Olympic Games

The Olympic Games comprise Winter and Summer editions, with season-specific Games held every four years and two-year interval between each Winter and Summer edition. Revenues for the Olympics come from five sources:[74]

- broadcast/media agreements;
- TOP (The Olympic Partner program) sponsorships (the highest sponsorship tier giving companies exclusive worldwide rights in their product category to be associated with the Olympics);

- domestic sponsors, given sponsorship rights within the host country only;
- ticketing;
- merchandise.

The two sponsorship categories, the TOP program and domestic, generated nearly $1 billion and $1.7 billion respectively for the 2009–12 Olympic quadrennial period[75] (each quadrennial consists of one Winter and one Summer Games). The TOP sponsors are: Coca-Cola, Visa, Samsung, P&G, GE, Acer, Atos Origin, Panasonic, DOW, McDonald's and Omega.[76] The domestic sponsorship programs are controlled by each host city's OCOG (Organizing Committee for the Olympic Games). The 2010 Vancouver Winter Olympics had 57 domestic sponsors[77] and the 2012 London Summer Olympics had 42.[78]

## FIFA World Cup

The FIFA World Cup is held in a different country every four years. In 2010 it was held in South Africa. Revenues are from the following sources:[79]

- television rights;
- marketing rights (sponsorships);
- hospitality rights;
- licensing rights.

Marketing/sponsorship revenues in 2010 were $1.072 billion.[80] Sponsors are divided into three categories: FIFA Partners; FIFA World Cup Sponsors; and National Supporters. In 2010 the FIFA Partners were: adidas, Coca-Cola, Emirates, Hyundai/KIA Motors, Sony, and Visa. FIFA World Cup Sponsors were: Budweiser, Castrol, Continental, McDonald's, MTN, Mahindra Satyam, Seara, and Yingli Solar. National Supporters were: Ultimate, Neo Africa, Aggreko, FNB, Prasa, and Telkom.[81]

The Olympic Games and the FIFA World Cup are the two largest mega-sports events in the world with decades-long fan interest and sophisticated operating structures. They both have audiences in the billions, with hundreds of teams and thousands of athletes competing. The Olympics have a nearly 3000-year tradition related to athletic competition as a virtue, with Olympians representing the best of the best. The FIFA World Cup brings together the very best national teams from around the world in the world's most popular sport. The marketing opportunities for companies that sponsor these events have significant potential, assuming the sports marketer undertakes a detailed multi-year approach to activating their sponsorship. As both of these mega-sports events and the leading leagues discussed earlier, marketers have a diverse array of sports platforms to enhance their company's brand reputation.

## 13.9 Chapter summary

In this chapter we learned about the significant financial gains generated by sports marketing, from sponsorships to merchandise sales to ticketing/gate receipts. The leagues discussed, from the NFL to the Bundesliga to F1 and more, offer their fans a unique sports experience and corporate sponsors understand this. With increased viewership and growing fan bases companies are eager to link their brands to the major sports leagues in order to gain the halo affect cast by each sport and its corresponding reputation and values. As discussed, the revenue sources are varied and sophisticated, enabling leagues and sports events to generate funding through multiple marketing mechanisms. An interesting implication is the symbiotic nature of the sport entity/company/fan relationship: by attracting well-known companies as sponsors, sports leagues enhance their own authenticity and validity; by being associated with major sports, companies enhance their credibility; and by following these sports and availing themselves of the various ways to interact with their favorite sport, fans are enhancing their enjoyment of the sport experience.

# San Francisco Giants' dynamic ticket pricing

In 2008, the San Francisco Giants, as a franchise, had an exciting season. It was their 50th anniversary in San Francisco (its golden season), and pitcher Tim Lincecum was the National League's Cy Young Award.[82] Their team on-field performance was not spectacular. They finished 72–90 for the season, which was good enough for fourth in the NL West Division.[83] But despite the positives of 2008, their games weren't selling out. Their average attendance in 2008 was 35 356, or approximately 85.1 percent of capacity.[84] While many teams would have been ecstatic at those figures, the ball club wanted more.

For the following 2009 season, the ball club decided to experiment with single-game dynamic ticket pricing, which is a pricing scheme in which prices of single-game tickets can change any moment with a single click.[85] Dynamic pricing is also purported to accurately reflect the real-time value of a ticket.[86] Initially, the team only wanted to experiment with 2000 upper deck seats (these seats are traditionally more difficult to sell).[87] They signed a one-year contract with a software company called Qcue that enabled the club to change prices. Qcue uses an algorithm that takes factors such as team performance, opponent, starting pitchers, gate giveaways, and even weather to determine the right price for seats.[88] Prices between games could vary significantly for these seats, selling for as much as $45 on Opening Day and as little as $5 for a Monday night game.[89] However, on any given day, the price of a single-game ticket would fluctuate up or down between $0.25 and $2.[90] The 2009 season was slightly better for the Giants on the field. They finished 88–74 and third in the NL West Division.[91] While the team's on-field results were better, the club was blown away by the results of their dynamic ticketing experiment. After the 2009 season, in which average attendance figures were slightly lower than the year before (35 322 or 85 percent full), the club realized an additional $500 000 in incremental ticket revenue.[92]

By the end of October 2009, the Giants had already signed another contract with Qcue and had plans to roll out dynamic ticket pricing for all of AT&T Park's 41 914 seats. 2010 turned out to be a blockbuster year for the San Francisco Giants. The team rallied behind players like Buster Posey, Tim Lincecum, and Brian Wilson and won the World Series title. Ticket revenues for the year went up more than 7 percent for the 2010 season. Also during the 2010 season, San Francisco saw their average attendance rise to 37 499 per game (90.1 percent of capacity) and up again in 2011 to 41 818 per game, or 99.8 percent full.[93] Since making the switch to dynamic pricing, ticket revenues have climbed every year for the Giants.[94] As of 6 August 2012, the San Francisco Giants had sold out 140 straight games and average attendance hovered around 99.6 percent.[95]

While members of the ball club's executive team were celebrating the additional income they were earning from dynamic ticket pricing, they were also biting their nails in fear of backlash of season ticket holders and single-game ticket purchasers. The San Francisco Giants' season ticket base is one of the largest in Major League Baseball. In 2011, the club capped season ticket sales at 27 700.[96] Since 2008, the team is one of just seven teams to

**CASE STUDY 1** *(continued)*

post attendance figures exceeding 3 million.[97] The Giants executive team would need to strike a balance. They needed to make sincere efforts to convince season ticket holders that they weren't going to get ripped off by investing in season tickets. At the same time, they needed to inform single-game ticket purchasers that 75 percent of seats during the 2010 season were cheaper than during the 2009 season, so the new dynamic ticket pricing system wouldn't automatically raise prices for all seats.[98] What the Giants quickly found out was that because of the already existent secondary ticket market, fans were already familiar with fluctuating ticket prices.[99] Moreover, those factors that affected ticket prices, such as starting pitcher, opponent, and weather, often dictated ticket prices on the secondary ticket market.[100]

News of the Giants' ticket revenue successes quickly spread throughout major professional sports in the United States and they are now known as pioneers of the scheme. As of August 2012, more than 30 teams currently employ Qcue's services, which are altered depending on the sport, local community, and players involved.[101] The University of California at Berkeley will become the first university to use a dynamic ticket pricing scheme during the 2012–13 school year.[102] In its first experiment, the school will roll out the program with its football and men's basketball teams.[103] It makes sense that now universities are beginning to take a look at this model. Those properties who used Qcue's dynamic pricing software in 2011 saw an average increase of $1.55 per ticket.[104] Of the tickets that went up in price, on average they increased by $3.63.[105] Some properties, however, did see an average decrease in price. That average was $13.63.[106]

As more and more teams and properties adopt dynamic ticket pricing, it's clear that further innovation will ensue. As CEO of Qcue Barry Kahn said, 'It is not just about how teams price tickets but how they get those to the fans'.[107]

 **QUESTIONS**

1   Do you think that some day all teams will have dynamic ticket pricing?
2   Why or why not?
3   What other potential innovations in ticketing could come as a result of Qcue's technology?

**CASE STUDY 2**

# Chinese Basketball Association (CBA)

While professional leagues in the USA are often emulated, they are rarely replicated. The same has held true for the 17-team Chinese Basketball Association (CBA), the premier professional basketball league in China labeled as 'basketball with Chinese characteristics'.[108] Founded in 1995, the league attracts the best players from China.[109] It has also built itself as a potential outlet for players who are either not quite good enough to play in the NBA in the United States, or those in other countries looking to take a step up from competition in their respective countries. Yet until quite recently, the CBA has struggled to gain traction in a country where basketball was declared the national pastime in 1935.[110]

With a fan base of 450 million, basketball is the most popular sport in China.[111] Part of the reason that basketball is so popular in China stems from the NBA's initial deal in 1987 with CCTV, the government-controlled media company, to offer rights for NBA games essentially free of charge.[112] Before the CBA became a professional league in 1995, the sport of basketball was hindered in growth due to limited government funding for the sport. Even today, the CBA is controlled by the government in China, which acts as a further limiting factor in its growth.[113] Still, the CBA is nowhere near as popular as the NBA and as recently as the 2008–09 season, the league incurred losses of nearly $17 million.[114]

From its inception, the CBA was modeled after the NBA. Each of the teams in the CBA, has a differing ownership structure much like in the NBA. Some are owned privately, others are owned by sports bureaus or local governments.[115] Some of the teams that are privately owned are in Tier 3 cities simply because that is where their owners want them to be located.[116] Because there exists a wide disparity of income amongst the teams, the CBA will seek to enforce a stricter salary cap during the 2012–13 season.[117] In 2009, a salary cap of $44000 per season for Chinese players and $60000 per season for foreign-born players was created, but was not well enforced due to the lack of a luxury tax like the NBA enforces.[118]

One of the CBA's biggest competitors is the NBA. Chinese fans find the NBA style of play more athletic, fast-paced, and therefore, more exciting.[119] In addition, facilities are lacking in China. In order to attract top-notch talent across the globe, NBA Commissioner David Stern and the Chinese government realize that they will need to build facilities capable of attracting international talent and publicity.[120] The government has built 800000 basketball courts in the country, but they are still a far cry from the facilities that will attract top talent globally.[121] In 2011, the CBA shot itself in the foot with the impending NBA lockout by banning opt-out clauses in all contracts signed by NBA players.[122] Though the Chinese market is extremely attractive to US-based players for potential merchandise and other consumer products endorsements, the CBA has been evidently clear that it doesn't want the CBA to be a 'quick buck scheme' for foreign players, but rather, it wants to build China into a global basketball power.[123]

**CASE STUDY 2** *(continued)*

Over 200 international players have played in the CBA throughout its history from countries including the United States, Israel, Turkey, and throughout Europe.[124] Many foreign players, especially those who have played in the NBA, have increased the viability of the league. During the 2011–12 season, Stephon Marbury led the Beijing Ducks to their first-ever league championship and has admitted that playing in China has changed him for the better.[125] Because of league rules, Marbury is ineligible to be named league or all-star game MVP, but a petition circulated and collected over a million votes to commemorate Marbury's triumphs in the form of a bronze statue.[126]

Foreign-born players don't always work out as well as planned, however. In 2011, when the NBA was looking like it was heading towards a full season lockout, Kenyon Martin signed a one-year contract with the Xinjian Flying Tigers for $2.7 million.[127] The deal was the most lucrative in CBA history but quickly turned sour when the NBA ended the lockout and Martin pulled out of the China deal to come back to the USA.[128] The three-time runner-up Flying Tigers were left mired in chaos and finished fourth during the 2011–12 season.[129] There is often ill will towards foreign players in the CBA because of the distinct lifestyles they lead. While Chinese professional players often live together in drab dormitories and earn lower salaries, foreign players often stay in cushy hotels with nice amenities.[130] Furthermore, despite limitations on playing time for foreign players, they often earn reputations of being ball hogs and can build resentment from their teammates.[131]

Perhaps the biggest problem facing the CBA is that it is unable to produce world-class players. In China, children are identified at a young age for their basketball potential (in many cases this simply means they are projected to be tall based on x-rays).[132] These kids are then funneled into schools that focus heavily on sport.[133] Due to the alluring nature of a professional athletic career, many of the kids who are funneled into this athletic track are the children of members of the government, thus further tightening the state's hold on the sport.[134] Because there isn't a robust university league system in China like there is in the USA, players don't develop in the same way.[135] Above all, sports are of secondary importance to academics, so resources devoted to sports are very limited for those who aren't in the sports funnel.[136]

Sponsorship is already a key part of the CBA, but it hasn't quite reached the levels of success necessary to take the league to the next level. Anta Sports Products, an athletic footwear company based in China, had a sponsorship deal reportedly worth $9.4 million over three years, or $3.14 million per year, which ended in 2012.[137] But Anta, adidas and Nike all backed out of the official apparel sponsor bidding war when the value of the five-year deal peaked over $39.3 million.[138] Li Ning ended up winning the bidding war by signing a five-year $314 million deal and set a new record for sports sponsorship in China.[139] As a base of comparison, Nike paid $2.5 million to outfit the eight-team league over its first four years beginning in 1995.[140]

Yao Ming, the CBA-bred NBA superstar, to date has been the only player to truly bridge the gap between China and the USA. Even now, with Yao Ming having retired from the

## CASE STUDY 2 *(continued)*

NBA and moved back in Shanghai as an owner of the Shanghai Sharks, the team struggles to sell tickets.[141] The NBA had expressed a willingness to co-brand a new league as recently as 2008 but the proposal was rejected.[142] The NBA has stated that it is still willing to consider the possibility of a co-branded league, but it won't move forward with that venture unless the CBA cooperates.[143]

In some ways, the inability of the world's biggest country to field competitive teams befuddles those in basketball circles. In other ways, it's not surprising that the government's tight hold on the sport's development has slowed forward progress.

 **QUESTIONS**

1 Is it the role of the CBA to develop more widespread talent throughout China? Or is it the role of companies like Nike and Li Ning (who arguably have an equal if not greater influence) to encourage increased basketball participation?
2 How can the CBA become a more attractive sponsorship option to both Chinese and multi-national companies alike?
3 Is the CBA's best shot at becoming a powerhouse league relinquishment of government control?

### NOTES

1  'Deal summary of NFL Players Association' (2011, pp. 5–7).
2  'Major pro sponsorships to total $2.46 billion in 2011' (2011).
3  Thomaselli (2011).
4  'Away from the noise of the NFL, Dreams Inc. is having another very good year' (2011); Roberts (2011).
5  Futterman et al. (2011).
6  Ibid.
7  Ibid.
8  'Poll shows popularity of pro football growing while baseball slides' (2012). Harris Poll conducted 5–12 December 2011, 2237 adults 18 years and older. At least 1466 respondents followed one or more sports.
9  Pietz (2012).
10  'Inside the NFL's $9.3 billion money machine' (n.d.).
11  Nielsen data via NFL (2012).
12  Wakefield and Rivers (2012).
13  Broughton (2012a).
14  'Premier League club accounts: how in debt are they?' (2011).
15  Baxter (2012).
16  'Barclays officially extends sponsorship deal with EPL through '16' (2012).
17  'Football Association announces new England kit supplier from 2013' (2012).
18  'Barclays renews title sponsorship of Premier League' (2012).
19  'Barclays extends Barclays Premier League sponsorship' (n.d.).
20  Snyder (2012).
21  Jacobson (2008).

22  'Inside baseball: teams experience healthy growth; other sponsorship trends' (2012).
23  Mamudi (2012b).
24  Snyder (2012).
25  'Attendance up by under 1 percent' (2011).
26  'Official info' (n.d.).
27  Mamudi (2012a).
28  'Quirkiest stadium naming rights deals' (2002).
29  'Overstock.com lands naming rights to Oakland Coliseum' (2011).
30  Shea (2012).
31  Crupi (2012).
32  Rovell (2012).
33  Soshnick and Levinson (2011).
34  Broughton (2012b).
35  Kuriloff (2012).
36  Gelles (2011).
37  'IEG sponsorship report' (2012).
38  Belson (2010).
39  'BBVA Group signs multi-year marketing partnership with NBA' (2010).
40  Klein (2012).
41  'Collective bargaining agreement FAQs' (n.d.).
42  'Major pro sponsorships to total $2.46 billion in 2011' (2011).
43  Westhead (2012).
44  'Spons-o-Meter: NHL boasts 23 official corporate sponsors this season' (2012).
45  Broughton (2012c).
46  Korn (2011).
47  Love (2010).
48  Ibid.
49  'Bundesliga on the move – another successful season' (2012).
50  Conn (2012).
51  'Premier League tops shirt sponsorships; Bundesliga gets more per team' (2012).
52  'Bundesliga revenue stream' (2012, p. 8).
53  Ibid.
54  'The Brand Finance® sporting brands 2012' (2012).
55  Jackson (2010).
56  Ibid.
57  Ibid.
58  Long (2011a).
59  Long (2011b).
60  'Sponsorship – new deals for Bordeaux, Leyton Orient; Sky Deutschland buys Bundesliga rights' (2012).
61  Connolly (2011).
62  'German Bundesliga clubs earn $173m from shirt sponsorship deals' (2012).
63  Dickens (2011).
64  Connolly (2010).
65  'Bundesliga champion Borussia Dortmund partners with German automaker Opel' (2012).
66  Barreto (2012a).
67  Barreto (2012b).
68  'Sponsors' (n.d.); Sherman (2012).
69  Wood (2008); Mickle (2012).
70  Heikkila (2011).
71  Redbull.com (n.d).
72  Quinn (2011).
73  Syit and Reid (2011).
74  'Olympic marketing revenue generation' (2012, p. 6).

75  Ibid.
76  Ibid., p. 13.
77  'International Olympic Committee market report Vancouver 2010' (2010).
78  Goldsmith (2012).
79  'Income (n.d.).
80  'Mihir Bose: FIFA may lack the power to reform itself' (2011).
81  'Marketing affiliates' (n.d.).
82  'Wall of fame' (n.d.); Schulman (2008).
83  'Standings – September 30 2008'.
84  'MLB attendance report – 2008' (n.d.).
85  Rishe (2012).
86  Ibid.
87  Branch (2008).
88  Muret (2009).
89  Ibid.
90  Branch (2008).
91  'Standings – October 6, 2009'.
92  'MLB attendance report – 2009' (n.d.).
93  'MLB attendance report –2010' (n.d.); 'MLB attendance report – 2011' (n.d.).
94  Dunne (2012).
95  Schectman (2012); 'MLB attendance report – 2012' (n.d.).
96  'San Francisco Giants' (2012).
97  Ibid.
98  Brustein (2010).
99  Rishe (2012).
100  Ibid.
101  Schectman (2012).
102  Young (2012).
103  Ibid.
104  Dunne (2012).
105  Ibid.
106  Ibid.
107  '40 under forty Barry Kahn' (2011).
108  Bou et al. (2011).
109  Li (2012).
110  Ibid.
111  Ibid.
112  Ibid.
113  Bou et al. (2011).
114  Epstein (2011).
115  Yardley (2012).
116  Zengerle (2012).
117  Xiaochen (2011).
118  Ibid.
119  Bou et al. (2011).
120  Ibid.
121  Ibid.
122  Epstein (2011).
123  Ibid.
124  Li (2012).
125  Tower (2011).
126  Clayton (2011).
127  Xiaochen (2011).
128  Ibid.

129  'Xinjiang Flying Tigers' (n.d.).
130  Yardley (2012).
131  Ibid.
132  Bou et al. (2011).
133  Ibid.
134  Ibid.
135  Yardley (2012).
136  Bou et al. (2011).
137  'Li Ning bets $314m on basketball turnaround' (2012).
138  Ibid.
139  Ibid.
140  Bou et al. (2011).
141  Yardley (2012).
142  Ibid.
143  Ibid.

## REFERENCES

Associated Press, 'Barclays renews title sponsorship of Premier League'. July 12, 2012. CBCSports/ Soccer. Retrieved July 12, 2012 from http://www.cbc.ca/sports/soccer/story/2012/07/12/ sp-barclays-pays-more-for-premieship-rights.html.

'Attendance up by under 1 percent' (2011), ESPN MLB.com, 29 September 2011, accessed 12 January 2012 http://espn.go.com/mlb/story/_/id/7035729/major-league-baseball-attendance-1-percent.

'Away from the noise of the NFL, Dreams Inc. is having another very good year' (2011), Proactive Investor's Instablog, 2 August 2011, accessed 1 October 2011 at http://seekingalpha.com/ instablog/485861-proactive-investor/200941-away-from-the-noise-of-the-nfl-dreams-inc-is-having-another-very-good-year.

'Barclays extends Barclays Premier League sponsorship' (n.d.), Barclays Football Club, accessed 27 May 2013 at http://www.premierleague.com/en-gb/news/news/2012-13/jul/barclays-extends-sponsorship-of-the-premier-league.html.

'Barclays officially extends sponsorship deal with EPL through '16' (2012), Sports Business Daily, 13 July 2012, accessed 20 July 2012 at http://www.sportsbusinessdaily.com/Global/ Issues/2012/07/13/Marketing-and-Sponsorship/Barclays.aspx.

Barreto, Elzio (2012a), 'Revenue seen rising to $2.37 billion in 2016 from $1.52 billion in 2011', Reuters, 30 May 2012, accessed 11 July 2012 at http://www.reuters.com/article/2012/05/30/ formulaone-ipo-idUSL4E8GU36L20120530.

Barreto, Elzio (2012b), 'UPDATE 1 – F1 revenues to grow nearly double digits till 2016: UBS', Reuters, 30 May 2012, accessed 23 June 2012 at http://www.reuters.com/ article/2012/05/30/formulaone-ipo-idUSL4E8GU36L20120530.

Baxter, Kevin (2012), 'More debt than goals in European football', The Los Angeles Times, 24 August 2012, accessed 3 September 2012 at http://articles.latimes.com/2012/aug/25/ sports/la-sp-baxter-soccer-20120826.

'BBVA Group signs multi-year marketing partnership with NBA' (2010), NBA.com, 13 September 2010, accessed 7 July 2011 at http://www.nba.com/2010/news/09/13/bbva-nba-partnership/index.html.

Belson, Ken (2010), 'NBA has sponsorship deal with global bank', The New York Times, 12 September 2010, accessed 3 July 2011 at http://www.nytimes.com/2010/09/13/sports/ basketball/13nba.html.

Bou, Fay et al. (2011), 'Beyond Yao: the future of Chinese basketball', Knowledge@Wharton,

University of Pennsylvania, 26 January 2011, accessed 7 October 2012 at http://knowledge.
wharton.upenn.edu/article.cfm?articleid=2689.

Branch Jr., Alfred (2008), 'San Francisco Giants to introduce dynamic pricing for some 2009 tickets',
TicketNews.com, 5 December 2008, accessed 3 September 2012 at http://www.ticketnews.
com/news/San-Francisco-Giants-to-introduce-dynamic-pricing-for-some-tickets12855.

Broughton, David (2012a), 'Avid fans know their NFL sponsors', *Sports Business Journal*, 20
February 2012, accessed 22 February 2012 at http://www.sportsbusinessdaily.com/Journal/
Issues/2012/02/20/Research-and-Ratings/NFL-Sponsor-Loyalty.aspx.

Broughton, David (2012b), 'Sprite finally wins fan vote as NBA's soft drink', *Sports Business
Journal*, 16 July 2012, accessed 16 July 2012 at http://www.sportsbusinessdaily.com/Journal/
Issues/2012/07/16/Research-and-Ratings/NBA-Sponsor-Loyalty.aspx.

Broughton, David (2012c), 'NHL sponsor loyalty numbers move to top tier', *Sports Business
Daily*, 18 June 2012, accessed 24 June 2012 at http://www.sportsbusinessdaily.com/Journal/
Issues/2012/06/18/Research-and-Ratings/NHL-Sponsor-Loyalty.aspx

Brustein, Joshua (2010), 'Star pitchers in a duel? Tickets will cost more', *New York Times*,
27 June 2010, accessed 3 September 2012 at http://www.nytimes.com/2010/06/28/
technology/28tickets.html.

'Bundesliga champion Borussia Dortmund partners with German automaker Opel'
(2012), *Sports Business Daily*, 20 July 2012, accessed 23 July 2012 at http://www.sportsbusi-
nessdaily.com/Global/Issues/2012/07/20/Marketing-and-Sponsorship/Opel.aspx.

'Bundesliga on the move – another successful season' (2012), Bundesliga Football, 14 May
2012, accessed 23 May 2012 at http://bundesligafootball.co.uk/2012/05/bundesliga-on-
the-move-a-recap-of-another-successful-season/.

'Bundesliga revenue stream' (2012), accessed 22 August 2012 at http://static.bundesliga.com/
media/native/autosync/dfl_bl_wirtschaftssituation_2012_01-12_gb_72dpi.pdf.

Clayton, Andy (2011), 'Chinese fans campaign for a Marbury statue', NYDailyNews.com, 11
April 2012, accessed 7 October 2012 at http://articles.nydailynews.com/2012-04-11/
news/31326900_1_bronze-statue-cba-stephon-marbury.

CNNMoney, 'Inside the NFL's $9.3 billion money machine.' n.d. Retrieved July 29, 2012 from
http://money.cnn.com/galleries/2011/news/1103/gallery.nfl_total_value.fortune/index.
html.

'Collective Bargaining Agreement FAQs' (n.d.), NHL.com, accessed 2 March 2012 at http://
www.nhl.com/ice/page.htm?id=26366.

Conn, David (2012), 'Democratic Germany leads free-market England in football's recovery', *The
Guardian*, 21 September 2012, accessed 21 September 2012 at http://www.guardian.co.uk/
world/2012/sep/21/german-english-football-recovery.

Connolly, Eoin (2010), 'Krombacher to sponsor Bundesliga relgation play-off', SportsPro,
4 March 2010, accessed 21 March 2012 at http://www.sportspromedia.com/news/
krombacher_to_sponsor_bundesliga_relegation_play-off/.

Connolly, Eoin (2011), 'Bundesliga champions secure EA Sports support', SportsPro, 28 July
2011, accessed 22 March 2012 at http://www.sportspromedia.com/news/bundesliga_
champions_secure_ea_sports_support/.

Crupi, Anthony (2012), 'Major League Baseball and Anheuser-Busch renew sponsorship pact',
22 August 2012, ADWEEK, accessed 22 August 2012 at http://www.adweek.com/news/
advertising-branding/major-league-baseball-and-anheuser-busch-renew-sponsorship-
pact-143054.

'Deal summary of NFL Players Association' (2011), NFL Players Association.com, 25 July 2011,
accessed 23 October 2011 at http://ht.cdn.turner.com/si/images/2011/07/25/New_2011_
Deal_Summary_7.pdf.

Dickens, Chris (2011), 'Krombacher extend Bundesliga partnership', SportsPro, May, 2011, accessed 22 March 2012 at http://www.sportspromedia.com/news/krombacher_extend_bundesliga_partnership/.

Dunne, Patrick (2012), 'Dynamic pricing trend sweeps across major league baseball', TicketNews.com, 22 February 2012, accessed 4 September 2012 at http://www.ticketnews.com/news/Dynamic-pricing-trend-sweeps-across-Major-League-Baseball021222303.

Epstein, Eli (2011), 'Pro basketball hits a wall in China (2011)', Fortune.com, 17 August 2011, accessed 7 October 2012 at http://features.blogs.fortune.cnn.com/2011/08/17/pro-basketball-hits-a-wall-in-china/.

'Football Association announces new England kit supplier from 2013' (2012), BBCSport, 3 September 2012, accessed 4 September 2012 at http://www.bbc.co.uk/sport/0/football/19464718.

'40 under forty Barry Kahn' (2011), Sports Business Journal, 21 March 2011, 37A.

Futterman, Matthew, Sam Schechner and Suzanne Vranica (2011), 'NFL: the league that runs TV', The Wall Street Journal, 15 December 2011, accessed 16 December 2011 at http://online.wsj.com/article/SB10001424052970204026804577098774037075832.html.

Gelles, David (2011), 'Sponsors strike fresh deals with revived NBA' (2011), 14 December 2011, Financial Times, accessed 5 January 2012 at http://www.ft.com/cms/s/0/e88a7054-25c9-11e1-9c76-00144feabdc0.html#axzz26ffVPQWs.

'German Bundesliga clubs earn $173m from shirt sponsorship deals' (2012), Sports Business Daily, 26 July 2012, accessed 30 July 2012 at http://www.sportsbusinessdaily.com/Global/Issues/2012/07/26/Marketing-and-Sponsorship/Shirt-Sponsor.aspx.

Goldsmith, Belinda (2012), 'Pssst...want to buy some chewing gum?' (2012), Reuters, 31 July 2012, accessed 27 May at http://www.reuters.com/article/2012/07/31/oly-branding-day-idUSL4E8IV11B20120731.

Heikkila, Pia (2011), 'India keen to draw F1's power' (2011), 31 October 2011, accessed 27 May 2013 at http://callcenterinfo.tmcnet.com/news/2011/10/31/5893834.htm.

'IEG sponsorship report' (2012), 30 January 2012, accessed 19 February 2012 at http://www.sponsorship.com/IEG/files/5c/5c6bf99a-fb01-4dfe-86ad-d88be0137433.pdf.

'Income' (n.d.), FIFA.com, accessed 17 June 2012 at http://www.fifa.com/aboutfifa/finances/income.html.

'Inside baseball: teams experience healthy growth; other sponsorship trends', IEG Sponsorship Report, 3 December 2012, accessed 3 December 2012 at http://www.sponsorship.com/IEGSR/2012/12/3/Inside-Baseball--Teams-Experience-Healthy-Growth;.aspx.

'International Olympic Committee market report Vancouver 2010' (2010), accessed 30 July 2012 at http://www.olympic.org/Documents/IOC_Marketing/Marketing_Report_Vancouver_2010_eng.pdf, 85–99.

Jackson, Jamie (2010), 'Germany provide the blueprint for England's academy system', The Guardian, 3 July 2010, accessed 10 January 2012 at http://www.guardian.co.uk/football/2010/jul/04/germany-youth-development-england.

Jacobson, David (2008), 'MLB's revenue-sharing formula', CBS MoneyWatch, 14 July 2008, accessed 22 July 2012 at http://www.cbsnews.com/8301-505125_162-51210897/mlbs-revenue-sharing-formula/.

Klein, Jeff Z. (2012), 'N.H.L. to resume labor talks as preseason is canceled', The New York Times, 27 September 2012, accessed 27 September 2012 at http://www.nytimes.com/2012/09/28/sports/hockey/nhl-labor-talks-to-resume-friday.html?_r=0.

Korn, Melissa (2011), 'Court upholds Molson's NHL deal', The Wall Street Journal, 11 July 2011, accessed 23 August 2011 at http://online.wsj.com/article/SB100014240527023036787045764441892568419536.html.

Kuriloff, Aro (2012), 'NBA sponsors Stellar like LeBron James: riskless return', Bloomberg, 19 June 2012, accessed 18 July 2012 at http://www.bloomberg.com/news/2012-06-20/nba-sponsors-stellar-like-lebron-james-riskless-return.html.

'Li Ning bets $314m on basketball turnaround' (2012), WantChinaTimes.com, 12 August 2012, accessed 7 October 2012 at http://www.wantchinatimes.com/news-subclass-cnt.aspx?id=20120812000029&cid=1206.

Li, Zhenyu (2012), 'Basketball in China Part II: the evolution', BleacherReport.com, 25 July 2012, accessed 7 October 2012 at http://bleacherreport.com/articles/1271992-basketball-in-china-part-ii-the-evolution.

Long, Michael (2011a), 'Grundig to partner German soccer', SportsPro, 7 July 2011, accessed 21 March 2012 at http://www.sportspromedia.com/news/grundig_to_partner_german_soccer/.

Long, Michael (2011b), 'Krombacher extend Bundesliga partnership', SportsPro, 5 May 2011, accessed 21 March 2012 at http://www.sportspromedia.com/news/krombacher_extend_bundesliga_partnership/.

Love, Tom, 'Canadian Tire announces comprehensive NHL partnership.' August 23, 2010. SportsPro. Retrieved March 3, 2012 from http://www.sportspromedia.com/news/canadian_tire_announces_comprehensive_nhl_partnership/.

'Major pro sponsorships to total $2.46 billion in 2011' (2011), IEG Sponsorship Report, 26 September 2011, accessed 1 October 2011 at http://www.sponsorship.com/IEG/files/41/410d14a3-e499-4635-9d61-7a0f74fdf4ed.pdf.

'MLB attendance report – 2008' (n.d.), ESPN.com, accessed 3 September 2012 at http://espn.go.com/mlb/attendance/_/year/2008.

Mamudi, Sam (2012a), 'MLB, Anheuser-Busch extend Bud pact', MarketWatch, 22 August 2012, accessed 24 August 2012 at http://articles.marketwatch.com/2012-08-22/general/33304013_1_wild-card-games-wild-card-budweiser.

Mamudi, Sam (2012b), 'MLB heads for record merchandise sales', MarketWatch.com, 4 April 2012, accessed 7 April 2012 at http://articles.marketwatch.com/2012-04-04/industries/31285326_1_sales-fanatics-new-logo.

'Marketing affiliates' (n.d.), FIFA.com, accessed 17 June 2012 at http://www.fifa.com/worldcup/organisation/partners/index.html.

Mickle, Tripp (2012), 'New York F1 race makes plans for ticket prices', Sports Business Journal, 26 March 2012, accessed 23 June 2012 at http://www.sportsbusinessdaily.com/Journal/Issues/2012/03/26/Events-and-Attractions/Formula-One-NY.aspx.

'Mihir Bose: FIFA may lack the power to reform itself' (2011), Inside the Games, 29 May 2011, accessed 17 June 2012 at http://www.insidethegames.biz/blogs/13106.

'MLB attendance report – 2008' (n.d.), ESPN.com, accessed 3 September 2012 at http://espn.go.com/mlb/attendance/_/year/2008.

'MLB attendance report – 2009' (n.d.), ESPN.com, accessed 3 September 2012 at http://espn.go.com/mlb/attendance/_/year/2009.

'MLB attendance report – 2010' (n.d.), ESPN.com, accessed 3 September 2012 at http://espn.go.com/mlb/attendance/_/year/2010.

'MLB attendance report – 2011' (n.d.), ESPN.com, accessed 3 September 2012 at http://espn.go.com/mlb/attendance/_/year/2011.

'MLB attendance report – 2012' (n.d.), ESPN.com, accessed 3 September 2012 at http://espn.go.com/mlb/attendance.

Muret, Don (2009), 'Giants consider dynamic pricing for all of AT&T Park' (2009), Sports Business Daily, 5 October 2009, accessed 3 June 2013 at http://www.sportsbusinessdaily.com/Journal/Issues/2009/10/20091005/This-Weeks-News/Giants-Consider-Dynamic-

Pricing-For-All-Of-ATT-Park.aspx?hl=san percent20francisco percent20giants percent20dynamic percent20ticket&sc=0.

Nielsen Data Via NFL (2012), broadcast 5 September 2012 on FoxBusiness with sports reporter Dennis Kneale, accessed 14 September 2012 at http://video.foxbusiness.com/v/1824640678001/sponsors-shell-out-big-bucks-for-nfl-kickoff/.

'Official info', (n.d.), MLB.com, accessed 20 July 2012 at http://mlb.mlb.com/mlb/official_info/official_sponsors.jsp.

'Olympic marketing revenue generation' (2012), Olympic Marketing Fact File 2012 Edition, accessed 29 July 2012 at http://www.olympic.org/Documents/IOC_Marketing/OLYMPIC-MARKETING-FACT-FILE-2012.pdf, 6.

'Overstock.com lands naming rights to Oakland Coliseum' (2011), CBS SFBayArea.com, 27 April 2011, accessed 4 March 2012 at http://sanfrancisco.cbslocal.com/2011/04/27/overstock-com-lands-naming-rights-to-oakland-coliseum/.

Pietz, John (2012), 'Motorola ends heasdet sponsorship with NFL', ChicagoBusiness.com, 17 April 2012, accessed 23 April 2012 at http://www.chicagobusiness.com/article/20120417/NEWS07/120419838/motorola-ends-headset-sponsorship-with-nfl.

'Poll shows popularity of pro football growing while baseball slides' (2012), Sports Business Daily, 26 January 2012, accessed 24 February 2012 at http://www.sportsbusinessdaily.com/Daily/Issues/2012/01/26/Research-and-Ratings/Harris-Poll.aspx.

'Premier League club accounts: how in debt are they?' (2011), The Guardian, 19 May 2011, accessed 17 July 2011 at http://www.guardian.co.uk/news/datablog/2011/may/19/football-club-accounts-debt.

'Premier League tops shirt sponsorships; Bundesliga gets more per team' (2012), Sports Business Daily, 21 June 2012, accessed 14 July 2012 at http://www.sportsbusinessdaily.com/Global/Issues/2012/06/21/Marketing-and-Sponsorship/Shirts-Europe.aspx.

Quinn, Ian (2011), 'Red Bull profits take a pit stop as sales lose momentum', The Grocer, 24 June 2011, accessed 23 July 2011 at http://www.thegrocer.co.uk/fmcg/red-bull-profits-take-a-pit-stop-as-sales-lose-momentum/219069.article#.

'Quirkiest stadium naming rights deals' (2002), BloombergBusinessWeek, 6 June 2002, accessed 29 July 2011 at http://images.businessweek.com/ss/09/10/1027_quirkiest_stadium_naming_rights_deals/13.htm.

Redbull.com (n.d), accessed 14 July 2012 at http://www.redbull.com/cs/Satellite/en_INT/Company-figures/001242939605518?pcs_c=PCS_Article&pcs_cid=1242937556133.

Rishe, Patrick (2012), 'Dynamic pricing: the future of ticket pricing in sports', Forbes.com, 6 January 2012, accessed 4 September 2012 at http://www.forbes.com/sites/prishe/2012/01/06/dynamic-pricing-the-future-of-ticket-pricing-in-sports/.

Roberts, Daniel (2011), 'The biggest losers in an NFL lockout? Everyone', CNNMoney, 4 March 2011, accessed 1 October 2011 at http://money.cnn.com/2011/03/03/news/companies/nfl_lockout_losers_labor.fortune/index.htm

Rovell, Darren (2012), 'Anheuser-Busch extends MLB deal', ESPNMLB.com, 22 August 2012, accessed 30 August 2012 at http://espn.go.com/mlb/story/_/id/8291880/anheuser-busch-extends-mlb-deal-2018.

'San Francisco Giants' (2012), Forbes.com, March 2012, accessed 3 September 2012 at http://www.forbes.com/teams/san-francisco-giants/.

Schectman, Joel (2012), 'San Francisco Giants CIO says dynamic ticket pricing helped pack the stadium', CIO Blog, The Wall Street Journal, 6 August 2012, accessed 4 September 2012 at http://blogs.wsj.com/cio/2012/08/06/san-francisco-giants-cio-says-dynamic-ticket-pricing-helped-pack-the-stadium/.

Schulman, Henry (2008), 'Giants' Lincecum wins Cy Young Award', SFGate.com, San Francisco

*Chronicle*, 12 November 2008, accessed 3 September 2012 at http://www.sfgate.com/sports/article/Giants-Lincecum-wins-Cy-Young-Award-3185797.php#page-1.

Shea, Bill (2012), 'Detroit misses out on estimated $17m due to shortened play-offs, World Series', Crain's Detroit Business, 29 October 2012, accessed 29 October 2012 at http://www.crainsdetroit.com/article/20121029/FREE/121029861/detroit-misses-out-on-estimated-17m-due-to-shortened-playoffs-world-series.

Sherman, Freddy (2012), 'Formula 1 Grand Prix race sponsors: fan's view', Yahoo!Sports, 3 March 2012, accessed 23 June 2012 at http://sports.yahoo.com/f1/news?slug=ycn-11045692.

Snyder, Matt (2012), 'Report: MLB revenues in 2012 were $7.5 billion', CBSSports.com, 9 December 2012, accessed 9 December 2012 at http://articles.marketwatch.com/2012-04-04/industries/31285326_1_sales-fanatics-new-logo.

Soshnick, Scott and Mason Levinson (2011), 'NBA lockout seen costing $1 billion as darkened arenas become black holes', Bloomberg, 23 August 2011, accessed 9 November 2011 at http://www.bloomberg.com/news/2011-08-24/nba-lockout-may-cost-1-billion-in-tickets-as-arenas-sit-dark.html.

'Spons-o-Meter: NHL boasts 23 official corporate sponsors this season', *Sports Business Daily*, 11 April 2012, accessed 6 July 2012 at http://www.sportsbusinessdaily.com/Daily/Issues/2012/04/11/Marketing-and-Sponsorship/NHL-sponsometer.aspx.

'Sponsors' (n.d.), Formula 1-Sporting99.com, accessed 23 June 2012 at http://formula1.sporting99.com/about-formula-one/sponsors.html.

'Sponsorship – new deals for Bordeaux, Leyton Orient; Sky Deutschland buys Bundesliga rights' (2012), World Football Insider, 20 April 2012, accessed 30 July 2012 at http://www.worldfootballinsider.com/Story.aspx?id=35082.

'Standings – September 30 2008' (2008), MLB.com, accessed 3 September 2012 at http://sanfrancisco.giants.mlb.com/mlb/standings/?ymd=20120903#20080930.

'Standings – October 6, 2009' (2009), MLB.com, accessed 3 September 2012 at http://sanfrancisco.giants.mlb.com/mlb/standings/?ymd=20120903-20091006.

Syit, Christian and Caroline Reid (2011), 'Formula one success revs up Red Bull Racing's profits', *The Guardian*, 26 September 2011, accessed 3 February 2012 at http://www.guardian.co.uk/business/2011/sep/26/red-bull-racing-formula-one-profits.

'The Brand Finance° sporting brands 2012' (2012), BrandFinance.com, accessed 28 October 2012 at http://brandirectory.com/league_tables/table/sports-250-2012.

Thomaselli, Rich (2011), 'Over $12b at stake if NFL lockout prevents 2011 season' (2011), Advertising Age, 10 January 2011, accessed 1 October 2011 at http://adage.com/article/news/12b-stake-nfl-lockout-prevents-2011-season/148093/.

Tower, Wells (2011), 'Welcome to the Far Eastern Conference', GQ.com, May 2011, accessed 7 October 2012 at http://www.gq.com/sports/profiles/201105/stephon-marbury-china-basketball?currentPage=1.

Wakefield, Kirk and Anne Rivers (2012), 'The effect of fan passion and official league sponsorship on brand metrics: a longitudinal study of official NFL sponsors and ROO', 5 March 2012. Presented at the MIT Sloan Sports Analytics Conference on Fan Passion and League Sponsorship, accessed 22 May 2012 at http://www.baylor.edu/mediacommunications/news.php?action=story&story=110752.

'Wall of fame' (n.d.), SanFranscicoGiants.mlb.com, accessed 3 September 2012 at http://sanfrancisco.giants.mlb.com/sf/ballpark/attractions/index.jsp?content=wall_fame.

Westhead, Rick (2012), 'For NHL, the cash is in Canada', thestar.com, 1 January 2012, accessed 29 April 2012 at http://www.thestar.com/sports/hockey/nhl/article/1109400--for-nhl-the-cash-is-in-canada.

Wood, Ryan (2008), 'Formula One information guide part 2: money, money, money (making a profit)', BleacherReport.com, 27 July 2008, accessed 23 June 2012 at http://bleacherreport.com/articles/41459-formula-one-information-guide-part-2-money-money-money-making-a-profit.

Xiaochen, Sun (2011), 'CBA wants to cap salaries – and soon', *China Daily*, 5 September 2011, accessed, 7 October 2012 at http://www.chinadaily.com.cn/cndy/2012-09/05/content_15734131.htm.

'Xinjiang Flying Tigers' (n.d.), Asia-Basket.com, 7 October 2012 at http://www.asia-basket.com/team.asp?Cntry=CHN&Team=4369.

Yardley, Jim (2012), 'The N.B.A. is missing its shots in China', *The New York Times*, 1 February 2012, accessed 7 October 2012 at http://www.nytimes.com/2012/02/05/magazine/NBA-in-China.html?pagewanted=all.

Young, Eric (2012), 'Cal to use dynamic prices for football, men's basketball tickets', *San Francisco Business Times*, 3 August 2012, accessed 4 September 2012 at http://www.bizjournals.com/sanfrancisco/blog/2012/08/cal-to-use-dynamic-prices-for.html.

Zengerle, Jason (2012), 'Chian's basketball culture', *The New York Times*, 24 February 2012, accessed 7 October 2012 at http://www.nytimes.com/2012/02/26/books/review/brave-dragons-by-jim-yardley.html.

# 14

# Sponsorship and event management

 **CHAPTER OVERVIEW**

Each of the marketing topics discussed throughout this book are understandably important factors in developing success with sports marketing investments. More recently, companies have taken their relationship with sports entities to a deeper and more sophisticated level by using sponsorships and event management to create much stronger associations between the company and the sports entity. When these associations are positively recognized by the public at large, thereby demonstrating how companies benefit from the sports entity's best qualities, then companies are also in a better position to leverage sponsorship and event management investments to generate profits and maximize returns.

## 14.1  Sports sponsorship of an entity

Sports sponsorship describes the marketing activity by a company that invests cash and in-kind exchanges in a sports entity (team, player, league, event) or naming rights (for a sports venue/facility), for the purpose of convincing fans and viewers of a positive connection between the sponsor and the sponsored entity. At a strategic level, companies seek closer associations with sports entities because of the potential for the positive values and attributes of that sports entity casting a halo over the sponsor, supporting the sponsor's longer-term brand position and reputation objectives. Sports sponsorship has become a significant strategic marketing activity involving sophisticated communication and management efforts designed to align the company with its chosen sports properties and, as a result, gain association benefits from the sponsored entity. At a more personal level, companies seek to develop deeper relationships with their own customers, much like sports entities have with their fans, therefore the investment in sponsorships is often focused on this goal. The by-product of these sponsoring efforts is expected to be any or all of the following: an increase and improvement of the company's brand awareness, brand value, brand position, engagement

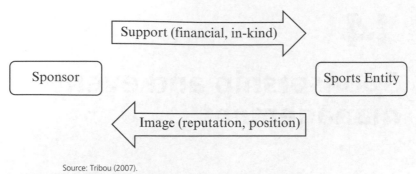

Source: Tribou (2007).

**Figure 14.1** The sports sponsor/entity relationship

with customers, and overall financial performance. The sponsor and sports entity relationship is shown in Figure 14.1.

## 14.2 Global sports sponsorship growth

According to data from PwC, sports sponsorship revenues (Tables 14.1 and 14.2) are nearly 30 percent of total revenues from sports (sponsorships, gate receipts, merchandising, media rights), representing a significant portion of the market.

**Table 14.1** Global sports market revenues 2006–15 (US$ millions)

|  | 2006 | 2007 | 2008 | 2009 | 2010 | 2011 | 2012 | 2013 | 2014 | 2015 | CAGR 2011–15 |
|---|---|---|---|---|---|---|---|---|---|---|---|
| Global revenues | 107516 | 113934 | 120760 | 112489 | 121391 | 118690 | 129929 | 130164 | 146469 | 145341 | |
| Percentage change | 12.1 | 4.1 | 7.9 | (6.8) | 7.9 | (2.2) | 9.5 | 0.2 | 12.5 | (0.8) | 3.7 |

Source: PwC (2011, p. 18).

From 2006 to 2012 sports sponsorship global revenues grew 50 percent from $26.7 billion to $39.2 billion. Between 2012 and 2015 revenues from sports sponsorships are expected to grow another 13 percent to $45.3 billion.

## 14.3 Sports event sponsorship

Sports event sponsorships, such as companies sponsoring the Olympic Games, FIFA World Cup, or the National Football League's Super Bowl,

**Table 14.2** Sponsorship revenues 2006–15 (US$ millions)

| | 2006 | 2007 | 2008 | 2009 | 2010p | 2011 | 2012 | 2013 | 2014 | 2015 | CAGR 2011–15 |
|---|---|---|---|---|---|---|---|---|---|---|---|
| Sponsorships revenues | 26749 | 29273 | 32494 | 31467 | 34972 | 35132 | 39173 | 40236 | 45559 | 42281 | |
| Percentage change | 14.2 | 9.4 | 11.0 | (3.2) | 11.1 | 0.5 | 11.5 | 2.7 | 13.2 | (0.6) | 5.3 |

Source: PwC (2011, p. 18).

provide a unique showcase to associate sponsoring companies with the premier events in sports. For sports marketers, the attraction of sports event sponsorship is partly due to the sizable TV audiences. TV viewership for the top sports events are shown in Table 14.3.

**Table 14.3** TV viewership

| Sports Event | TV Viewing Audience |
|---|---|
| Summer Olympic Games | 4.8 billion viewers worldwide (London 2012)[a] |
| IRB Rugby World Cup | 4 billion viewers worldwide (New Zealand 2011)[b] |
| FIFA World Cup | 3.2 billion viewers worldwide (South Africa 2010)[c] |
| Winter Olympic Games | 1.8 billion viewers worldwide (Vancouver 2010)[d] |
| NFL Super Bowl | 111 million viewers in U.S. (Indianapolis 2012)[e] |
| NHL Stanley Cup Finals | 3.01 million viewers in U.S. (Average over series)[f] |

Sources:
a. 'Cumulative TV viewership of the Olympic Summer Games worldwide 1996–2012' (n.d.).
b. 'Record TV audience tunes in to RWC 2011' (2011).
c. 'Almost half the world tuned in at home to watch the 2010 FIFA World Cup South Africa™' (2011).
d. '100 years of Olympic marketing' (n.d.).
e. 'Super Bowl TV audience reaches record 111.3 million' (2012).
f. Gorman (2012).

This list is by no means exhaustive. The NBA Championship, Major League Baseball's World Series, the Cricket World Cup, the four Tennis Grand Slam tournaments (Australian Open, French Open, Wimbledon, US Open), golf's four majors (Masters, British Open, US Open, PGA Championship), NCAA basketball's March Madness, NCAA football's Bowl Championship Series (BCS) and the other bowl games, as well as the Commonwealth Games and even the individual games in each sport's annual schedule, constitute potentially valuable sports event sponsorship opportunities for companies. Arguably, the major global sports events like the Olympics and FIFA World Cup, may not offer sponsors the most effective sponsorship investment opportunity since these events occur once every four years. However, their infrequency is an important part of their appeal and a reason why their viewership numbers are substantially higher than other annual championships, perhaps offsetting some of the negative assumptions of a once-in-four-years sponsorship exposure.

## 14.4 Sports athlete sponsorship

Companies that sponsor athletes are linking the reputation of the athlete to their firm, with the hope that the most memorable and positive characteristics of the athlete are linked to their brand. Some athletes have controversial reputations so sponsors are risking part of their own reputation by trying to create a memorable linkage with the athlete. However, if the athlete succeeds then the sponsor is banking on the athlete's winning qualities being the primary associations. By sponsoring athletes sponsors also risk that the athlete may be injured, preventing them from playing and thereby reducing their media exposure while they are recovering. Athletes that engage in immoral, unethical, and even illegal activities may find their sponsorship deals with sponsors at risk of financial penalties, including immediate termination, depending on the severity of the transgression. Sponsors may also see their reputations tarnished by the bad behavior of their athletes. In 2012 *Forbes Magazine* published its annual list of 'The World's 100 Highest Paid Athletes'. The top 26 are shown Table 14.4. It is interesting to note that the highest-paid female athlete, Maria Sharapova, enters the list at #26, although if the rankings used only endorsements and sponsorships as the criteria, she would be ranked #10 out of the top 100.

**Table 14.4** The world's 26 highest-paid athletes

| Athlete | Total Earnings | Salary/ Winnings | Endorsements & Sponsorships | Sponsors |
| --- | --- | --- | --- | --- |
| 1 Floyd Mayweather | $85 million | $85 million | $0 | |
| 2 Manny Pacquiao | $62 million | $56 million | $6 million | Monster Energy, Hennessy, Nike and HP |
| 3 Tiger Woods | $59.4 million | $4.4 million | $55 million | EA Sports, Fuse Science, Kowa, NetJets, Nike, Tatweer, TLC, Upper Deck |
| 4 LeBron James | $53 million | $13 million | $40 million | Nike, McDonald's, Coca-Cola, State Farm, Dunkin' Donuts, Baskin Robbins |

**Table 14.4** (continued)

| Athlete | Total Earnings | Salary/ Winnings | Endorsements & Sponsorships | Sponsors |
|---|---|---|---|---|
| 5 Roger Federer | $52.7 million | $7.7 million | $45 million | Nike, Rolex, Wilson, Credit Suisse |
| 6 Kobe Bryant | $52.3 million | $20.3 million | $32 million | Nike, Nubeo, Turkish Airlines, Coca-Cola's Energy Brands, Guitar Hero, Call of Duty |
| 7 Phil Mickelson | $47.8 million | $4.8 million | $43 million | Callaway, Barclay's, KPMG, Exxon, Rolex, Amgen/Pfizer |
| 8 David Beckham | $46 million | $9 million | $37 million | Samsung, adidas, Burger King, Armani, Sainsbury's, H&M |
| 9 Cristiano Ronaldo | $42.5 million | $20.5 million | $22 million | Nike, Castrol, Konami, Banco Espirito Santo |
| 10 Peyton Manning | $42.4 million | $32.4 million | $10 million | Reebok, Sony, Wheatires, DirecTV, Gatorae, Papa John's |
| 11 Lionel Messi | $39 million | $20 million | $19 million | Adidas, Pepsi, Cherry, Herbalife, EA Sports, Audemars Piguet, Dolce & Gabbana |
| 12 Haloti Ngata | $37.3 million | $37.1 million | $200 000 | |
| 13 Larry Fitzgerald | $36.8 million | $35.3 million | $1.5 million | Nike, EAS, University of Phoenix, AT&T |
| 14 Ndamukong Suh | $36 million | $35.5 million | $500 000 | Omaha Steaks |
| 15 Charles Johnson | $34.4 million | $34.3 million | $100 000 | |
| 16 Rafael Nadal | $33.2 million | $8.2 million | $25 million | Nike, Babolat, Kia Motors, Richard Mille, Bacardi |
| 17 Mario Williams | $33.2 million | $32.9 million | $250 000 | MuscleTech |
| 18 Alex Rodriguez | $33 million | $31 million | $2 million | Nike, Rawlings, Topps, Vita Coco |
| 19 Fernando Alonso | $32 million | $29 million | $3 million | Puma, Tag Heuer, Santander |
| 20 Valentino Rossi | $30 million | $17 million | $13 million | Monster Energy |
| 21 Michael Schumacher | $30 million | $20 million | $10 million | Jet Set, Navyboot, Audemars Piguet |
| 22 Darrelle Revis | $28.3 million | $27 million | $1.3 million | Nike, Range Rover |

**Table 14.4** (continued)

| Athlete | Total Earnings | Salary/ Winnings | Endorsements & Sponsorships | Sponsors |
|---|---|---|---|---|
| 23 Dale Earnhardt Jr. | $28.2 million | $13.2 million | $15 million | Mountain Dew, National Guard, AMP, Wrangler, Hellmann's, GoDaddy.com |
| 24 Wadimir Klitschko | $28 million | $24 million | $4 million | |
| 25 Lewis Hamilton | $28 million | $25 million | $3 million | Reebok |
| 26 Maria Sharapova | $27.9 million | $5.9 million | $22 million | Nike, Cole Haan, Evian, Head, Samsung, Tag Heuer |

Source: Badenhausen (2012).

## 14.5 Sports team sponsorship

Companies sponsor teams and clubs for many of the same reasons athletes and events are sponsored: to be linked to the qualities of the team, providing association benefits for the sponsor. Team sponsorship once benefitted primarily local companies since they were the most obvious connection for the local fans and community. Each sport has witnessed the rise of particularly successful and often dynastic teams. Table 14.5 highlights examples of well known teams in key major sports around the world.

**Table 14.5** League/organizing body examples of prominent teams

| League or Organizing Body | Top Team(s) |
|---|---|
| Barclay's Premier League | Manchester United, Liverpool, Chelsea, Arsenal |
| National Football League | New England Patriots, Green Bay Packers, Dallas Cowboys, New York Giants |
| Major League Baseball | New York Yankees, Boston Red Sox, San Francisco Giants |
| IRB Rugby | New Zealand All-Blacks, South Africa Springboks |
| National Hockey League | Detroit Red Wings, Boston Bruins |
| National Basketball Association | Los Angeles Lakers, San Antonio Spurs, Boston Celtics, Miami Heat |
| F1 | Renault, Ferrari, Mercedes |
| La Liga | Real Madrid, Barcelona |
| Bundesliga | Bayern Munich, Borussia Dortmund |
| Serie A | Juventus, Internazionale Milan |
| Ligue 1 | Marseille, Lyon |

**Table 14.6** Examples of prominent team sponsorships

| Sponsor | Team | Value | Date(s) |
|---|---|---|---|
| Nike | French national football (soccer) team[a] | $400 million | 2011–18 |
| General Motors | Manchester United[b] | $559 million | 2014–21 |
| Etihad Airways | Manchester City[c] | $645 million | Ten years, signed in 2012 |
| Deutsche Telekom | Bayern Munich[d] | $150 million | 2013–17 |
| Samsung | Chelsea[e] | $29 million/season | 2012–15 |
| Qatar Airways | Barcelona[f] | $210 million | One year 2013/14 |
| Vodafone | McClaren F1[g] | Est. $75 million/year | 2010–13 |
| AIG | New Zealand All Blacks[h] | TBD | Five and a half years announced in 2012 |
| Wonga.com | Newcastle United[i] | $6.5 to $13 million/year | Four-year deal, commences in 2013 |

Sources:
a.  Pfanner (2011).
b.  'Chelsea and Samsung agree new shirt sponsorship deal' (2012).
c.  Taylor (2011).
d.  'Bayern Munich extends sponsorship deal with Deutsche Telekom through '17' (2012).
e.  'Soccer – Samsung renews shirt sponsorship deal with Chelsea' (2012).
f.  'Qatar Airways becomes Barcelona's shirt sponsors instead of Qatar Foundation' (2012).
g.  Thomas (2012).
h.  'AIG finally unveiled as All Blacks shirt sponsor' (n.d.).
i.  'Magpies in the money with Wonga.com' (n.d.).

There are several examples of prominent teams and their main corporate sponsors in Table 14.6.

Given this, plus the growth of sports beyond national boundaries to other countries around the world, companies from beyond the team's local market have invested in sponsoring as well, as part of their effort to grow into new markets and extend their reputation. A strong company sponsorship is ideally one that focuses on achieving strategic objectives, such as raising awareness and brand preference, and also growing sales over time, while also benefitting the team by providing a stable source of support for the long term (often several years). Top teams that have succeeded in attracting sponsors from beyond their local market exist in every major sport. The following list is not comprehensive, but it does highlight those teams and clubs that have had particularly successful efforts both on the field and in business attracting sponsors from other markets.

The UAE airline Emirates sponsors clubs in association football (soccer), cricket, and Australian Rules Football (aka the Australian Football League –

AFL, formerly known as the Victorian Football League – VFL until 1989). Emirates has been a premier partner of the AFL's Collingwood Magpies since 1999. Collingwood has a rich and storied legacy. The club was founded in 1892 and since then has contested 43 Grand Finals, more than any other VFL/AFL club, winning 15 VFL/AFL Championships. An average of 70 000 fans attend each of Collingwood's games. Emirates renewed its sponsorship for five more years in 2010 for a reported $5.5 million.[1]

Sports products companies such as Nike and Adidas sponsor many of the world's leading professional sports clubs. These companies also sponsor amateur teams, including many of the collegiate teams across multiple sports in the United States. For example, Table 14.7 shows the 2012 NCAA Women's Basketball tournament and the participating schools and their respective shoe/apparel sponsors.

**Table 14.7** Team sponsorships 2012 women's NCAA basketball tournament

| TEAM | SHOE/JERSEY | TEAM | SHOE/JERSEY |
|---|---|---|---|
| *Des Moines Region* | | *Fresno Region* | |
| 1 Baylor | Nike/Nike | 1 Stanford | Nike/Nike |
| 2 Tennessee | adidas/adidas | 2 Duke | Nike/Nike |
| 3 Delaware | Nike/Nike | 3 St. John's | Nike/Nike |
| 4 Georgia Tech | Nike/Russell | 4 Purdue | Nike/Nike |
| 5 Georgetown | Nike/Nike | 5 South Carolina | Under Armour/Under Armour |
| 6 Nebraska | adidas/adidas | 6 Oklahoma | Nike/Nike |
| 7 DePaul | Nike/Nike | 7 Vanderbilt | Nike/Nike |
| 8 Ohio State | Nike/Nike | 8 WVU | Nike/Nike |
| 9 Florida | Nike/Nike | 9 Texas | Nike/Nike |
| 10 BYU | Nike/Nike | 10 Middle Tenn State | Nike/Nike |
| 11 Kansas | adidas/adidas | 11 Michigan | adidas/adidas |
| 12 Fresno State | Nike/Nike | 12 E. Michigan | adidas/adidas |
| 13 Sacred Heart | adidas/adidas | 13 South Dakota State | Nike/Nike |
| 14 Arkansas-Little Rock | Nike/Nike | 14 Creighton | Nike/Nike |
| 15 Tennessee-Martin | adidas/adidas | 15 Samford | Nike/Russell |
| 16 UC Santa Barbara | Nike/Nike | 16 Hampton | Nike/Russell |
| *Raleigh Region* | | *Kingston Region* | |
| 1 Notre Dame | adidas/adidas | 1 UConn | Nike/Nike |
| 2 Maryland | Under Armour/ Under Armour | 2 Kentucky | Nike/Nike |
| 3 Texas A&M | adidas/adidas | 3 Univ. of Miami | Nike/Nike |
| 4 Georgia | Nike/Nike | 4 Penn State | Nike/Nike |
| 5 St. Bonaventure | adidas/adidas | 5 LSU | Nike/Nike |

**Table 14.7** (continued)

| TEAM | SHOE/JERSEY | TEAM | SHOE/JERSEY |
|---|---|---|---|
| *Raleigh Region* | | *Kingston Region* | |
| 6 Arkansas | Nike/Nike | 6 Rutgers | Nike/Nike |
| 7 Louisville | adidas/adidas | 7 Green Bay | Nike/Nike |
| 8 California | Nike/Nike | 8 Kansas State | Nike/Nike |
| 9 Iowa | Nike/Nike | 9 Princeton | Nike/Nike |
| 10 Michigan State | Nike/Nike | 10 Iowa State | Nike/Nike |
| 11 Dayton | Nike/Nike | 11 Gonzaga | Nike/Nike |
| 12 Florida Gulf Coast | Nike/Nike | 12 San Diego State | Nike/Nike |
| 13 Marist | Nike/Nike | 13 UTEP | adidas/adidas |
| 14 Albany | Nike/Jordan | 14 Idaho State | Nike/Nike |
| 15 Navy | Nike/Nike | 15 McNeese State | Nike/Nike |
| 16 Liberty | Nike/Nike | 16 Prairie View | Nike/Russell |

Source: 'Nike once again the predominant shoe sponsor of NCAA women's tournament teams' (2012).

Why do companies sponsor amateur teams? The reasons are similar to why companies sponsor major events and professional clubs: to connect their company to the team for the purpose of improving brand image, brand value, connections to fans, and overall financial gain. The collegiate sports market in the United States has been well developed for over 100 years, with colleges and universities across the country competing in dozens of men's and women's sports. Many well-known rivalries have decades-long traditions. Alumni follow their school's sports teams for years, often for the rest of their lives, as a part of their ongoing support for collegiate athletics. The biggest sports include football (American), basketball, baseball, swimming, volleyball, and soccer, but many schools have teams in smaller sports as well, such as gymnastics, fencing, rowing/crew, lacrosse and more. College football has the largest fan base of the collegiate sports, with a fan base estimated to be 54 percent of the US population, and 22 percent of the US population follow games regularly.[2] As with professional sports, the size of the television viewing audience is important to corporate sponsors of collegiate athletics, particularly football. Table 14.8 shows the best television markets for college football.

The number of fans in these markets explains only part of the attraction for sponsors. Another important ingredient is the appeal of the team across markets, such as teams whose popularity is not limited to their local geography, much like professional clubs that have global fan followings. The New York market is the largest metropolitan market in the USA as Table 14.9 shows. Interestingly, college football fans in New York follow local, as well as non-local teams.

**Table 14.8** Top television markets for college football (USA)

| Television Market | Population | Share of Population that Follows College Football | College Football Fans |
|---|---|---|---|
| New York | 20235243 | 14% | 2911514 |
| Atlanta | 6481132 | 41% | 2633017 |
| Los Angeles | 15258292 | 17% | 2582840 |
| Dallas-Ft. Worth | 6986116 | 27% | 1892114 |
| Chicago | 9430878 | 19% | 1756048 |
| Birmingham | 2011831 | 85% | 1702758 |
| Philadelphia | 8120182 | 20% | 1649448 |
| Houston | 5862228 | 28% | 1637337 |
| Tampa-St. Petersburg | 4833628 | 30% | 1431867 |
| Detroit | 5072294 | 26% | 1330846 |

Source: Silver (2011).

**Table 14.9** Most popular college football teams in New York City TV market

| School | Fans | Share of Market | Share of Population |
|---|---|---|---|
| Rutgers | 607157 | 20.9% | 3.0% |
| Notre Dame | 266935 | 9.2% | 1.3% |
| Penn State | 186410 | 6.4% | 0.9% |
| Connecticut | 150150 | 5.2% | 0.7% |
| Michigan | 144231 | 5.0% | 0.7% |
| Syracuse | 133900 | 4.6% | 0.7% |
| Miami (FL) | 77497 | 2.7% | 0.4% |
| Army | 75345 | 2.6% | 0.4% |
| Ohio State | 64581 | 2.2% | 0.3% |
| Boston College | 61042 | 2.1% | 0.3% |

Source: Silver (2011).

This pattern of fan following where non-local teams are also followed is seen in most major markets across the USA. Part of this is due to the decades-long reputations that a few college football teams have built, adding to their popularity and transcending geographic boundaries. Notre Dame is arguably the best example. Located in South Bend, Indiana (more than 700 miles from New York City), their football program is legendary in the USA, with storied traditions of success and a long list of athletes whose athletic prowess and exploits have elevated them to iconic status. Notre Dame inspires intense passions in sports fans; people either love the team or hate them. There is

**Table 14.10** Top TV markets for Notre Dame football

| City/TV Market | Number of Fans |
| --- | --- |
| New York | 304 535 |
| Chicago | 244 684 |
| Boston | 127 026 |
| South Bend | 120 604 |
| Philadelphia | 108 288 |
| Los Angeles | 75 389 |
| Washington | 57 482 |
| Indianapolis | 53 934 |
| St. Louis | 53 356 |
| Detroit | 44 426 |

Source: Silver (2011).

little gray area in between. Notre Dame football fans are located across the USA and even the world. The top TV markets for Notre Dame football are shown in Table 14.10.

Notre Dame's brand is well known, synonymous with excellence in academics and athletics, and the university has attracted companies from across the USA as sponsors. The university has several sponsorship tiers:[3]

1. *Team Notre Dame.* This is the highest level of sponsorship and is a national program that grants sponsors exclusive category rights, among other benefits. Sponsors at this level are: adidas, Coca-Cola, Xerox, Gatorade, McDonald's and Sprint.
2. *Regional marketing partners.* Sponsors receive regional promotional rights, exposure on Notre Dame sports broadcasts, plus some print advertising and hospitality benefits. Regional marketing partners are: Meijer, Bank of America, SiriusXM, Comcast, UPS, CBTS, and Ford.
3. *Local promotion partners.* Local sponsors receive local promotion rights, plus tickets and hospitality at Notre Dame men's basketball games, among other local benefits. Local promotion partners are: O'Rourke's and Boling Vision Center.

Another reason for this cross-market fan support is due to the mobility of the US population: alumni may not, and often do not, remain in the city or town where they went to college, taking jobs in other markets depending on their skills and the opportunities offered. But their time as a college student is infused with loyalty-building experiences, instilling a sense of commitment and support for their alma mater that often lasts for the rest of their lives, even if they never return to the area where the college is located.

## 14.6 Sports venue sponsorship

Sports venue sponsorships are also known as naming rights, and they have become an important area of sponsorship growth. Sports venue sponsorships are designed to be long-term agreements, with the intent that sponsors' gain nearly permanent association with the venue being sponsored. Some venues have especially rich, decades-long legacies as iconic fan favorites that do not easily lend themselves to corporate sponsor renaming (or at all). Fenway Park in Boston, home of the famed Boston Red Sox; Wrigley Field in Chicago, home of the Chicago Cubs; Lambeau Field, home of the Green Bay Packers; and Bernabéu Stadium in Madrid, home of Real Madrid, are each examples of venues whose names are deeply entrenched in the psyches of fans and are highly unlikely to have fans accept a corporate sponsor as a new name.

*Example: NFL stadium naming rights*

The NFL has 32 teams, 22 of which are named for companies. More than $2 billion is invested in these 22 stadiums, a sizable sum that the companies with these naming rights (Table 14.11) not just hope, but *expect*, to translate to long-term goodwill for their firms.

**Table 14.11** NFL stadiums with naming rights

| Company | Stadium/Team | Value | Date(s) |
|---|---|---|---|
| Bank of America | Bank of American Stadium/Carolina Panthers | $140 million | 2004–24 |
| CenturyLink | CenturyLinkField/Seattle Seahawks | $75 million | 2012–27 |
| EdwardJones | EdwardJonesDome/St. Louis Rams | $31.8 million | 2002–14 |
| EverBank | EverBank Field/Jacksonville Jaguars | $16.6 million | 2012–17 |
| Farmers | Farmers Field/Los Angeles (no team, stadium is proposed) | $700 million | 30 years |
| FedEx | FedEx Field/Washington Redskins | $205 million | 1999–2026 |
| Ford | Ford Field/Detroit Lions | $40 million | 1999–2019 |
| Gillette | Gillette Stadium/New England Patriots | $105 million | 2017–31 |
| Heinz | Heinz Field/Pittsburgh Steelers | $57 million | 2001–21 |
| Lincoln Financial | Lincoln Financial Field/Philadelphia Eagles | $139 million | 2002–23 |
| Louisiana Pacific | LP Field/Tennessee Titans | $30 million | 2006–16 |
| Lucas Oil | Lucas Oil Stadium/Indianapolis Colts | $122 million | 2006–26 |
| M&T Bank | M&T Bank Stadium/Baltimore Ravens | $75 million | 2003–18 |

**Table 14.11** (continued)

| Company | Stadium/Team | Value | Date(s) |
|---|---|---|---|
| Mall of America | Mall of America Field at the Hubert H. Humphrey Metrodome/Minnesota Vikings | $6 million | 2010–13 |
| MetLife | MetLife Stadium/New York Giants, New York Jets | $400 million | 2009–34 |
| Overstock.com | O.co Coliseum/Oakland Raiders | $7.2 million | 2011–17 |
| Qualcomm | Qualcomm Stadium/San Diego Chargers | $18 million | 1997–2017 |
| Raymond James | Raymond James Stadium/Tampa Bay Buccaneers | $32.5 million | 1999–2015 |
| RRI Energy | Reliant Stadium/Houston Texans | $320 million | 2000–32 |
| Sports Authority | Sports Authority/Denver Broncos | $150 million | 2012–26 |
| Sun Life | Sun Life Stadium/Miami Dolphins | $37.5 million | 2010–15 |
| University of Phoenix | University of Phoenix Stadium/Arizona Cardinals | $154 million | 2006–32 |

Source: Finkel (2011).

Companies are also buying naming rights for areas within stadiums. Technology companies SAP and EMC signed an agreement in 2012 to co-sponsor a corner of the MetLife Stadium, paying $7–8 million each for ten years. Such naming rights for limited areas of major sports venues are still evolving, and represent a possible new area of revenue growth for teams, owners, and leagues, assuming the stadium sponsor is in agreement.[4]

## Example: NBA Barclays Center

The Brooklyn Nets (formerly the New Jersey Nets) of the NBA moved to a new arena in Brooklyn in 2012. Barclays, from the UK, paid $400 million for 20 years for the naming rights.[5]

## Example: Old Trafford's naming rights potential

English football clubs have been reluctant to sell their naming rights, primarily for reasons of tradition, with a few notable exceptions (Arsenal sold their stadium naming rights to Emirates in 2006 and Manchester City's stadium became Etihad Stadium in 2011). Manchester United's stadium, Old Trafford, is perhaps the best-known venue in English football. While no official agreement is in place, estimates project a naming rights value of $1 billion+ over 20 years, an amount that would make investors undoubtedly pleased for the club, which made its IPO in 2012 to underwhelming support. However, would English football fans support such a deal? Time will tell.[6]

*Example: Risks of naming rights*

It is clear that naming rights afford select companies with increased, repetitive exposure by having their name on sports venues for extended agreement periods (usually several years). As we have seen, the value of these can be in the several hundred million dollar range. Herein lies the risk as well. If the associated team or team owner were to run afoul of the law, or the team or company holding the naming rights underperformed, or even some of the athletes had engaged in illegal activity, then the naming rights holder would possible damage to their reputation. Chesapeake Energy Arena paid for the naming rights for the arena where the NBA's Oklahoma City Thunder play, paying $3 million annually. Unfortunately, Chesapeake Energy saw its share price decline dramatically due to the declining price of natural gas and, at the same time, the misconduct of its CEO, who was discovered to have used his ownership stake in well drilling to borrow more than $1 billion.[7] PSINet was a pioneer in the early days of internet service providers in 1999, and it secured naming rights to NFL's Baltimore Ravens' stadium for $5.3 million per year. In the early 2000s, PSINet went bankrupt and the naming rights were subsequently taken on by M&T Bank.[8] TWA (Trans World Airlines) paid for the naming rights for the St. Louis Rams in the mid-1990s after the team moved from Los Angeles for $1.3 million per year. However, the airline's struggles eventually led to bankruptcy and was subsequently acquired by American Airlines (although American chose not to acquire the naming rights).[9]

The risks affect all parties involved: venue owners, team owners, shareholders, and naming rights acquirer, serving to hamper their reputation and/or become the butt of jokes in the sports world.

## 14.7 Sport governing body sponsorship

Since governing bodies oversee most, if not all, aspects of competition in their respective sports, companies find them attractive as highly visible properties to sponsor. Sports governing body sponsorships are similar to event sponsorships – the governing bodies tend to attract larger companies with the financial wherewithal to afford a sustained commitment to supporting them. Governing bodies often have sponsorship tiers to reflect the differing commitments and benefits sponsors receive based on the amount of their investment.

*Example: Pepsi sponsorship of IPL*

Pepsi secured the title sponsor rights to the Indian Premier League (IPL) in November 2012, paying nearly $72 million for a five-year period. The bid size was more than twice the size of the prior title sponsor's bid, DLF, the inaugural sponsor when the league first began in 2008. This was the most Pepsi has invested in cricket. As discussed earlier in this book, the IPL is the newest professional sports league in the world and enjoys a loyal fan following already, despite its relative youth. With the IPL based in India, in the center of the country with the world's second largest population, and as being a significant offshoot of India's national pastime (cricket), plus the ties to Bollywood, the title sponsorship represents a significant exposure opportunity for Pepsi.[10]

### Example: SAP sponsors NFL

SAP is a field cornerstone co-sponsor of MetLife Stadium in New York, where both the New York Jets and New York Giants play. The company is also a founding sponsor for a new stadium for the San Francisco 49ers. Late in 2012 SAP also agreed to become an NFL sponsor, as the Official Cloud Software Solutions, Business Software and Business Analytics Software Sponsor.[11]

### Example: Aon sponsors NFL

Like SAP, Aon became an NFL sponsor, but specifically to promote the NFL's games played in the UK. The specific choice of location for Aon coincides with the company's move of its headquarters to London, creating a unique double publicity benefit for both Aon and the NFL. Aon will also sponsor football clinics in the UK in an effort to increase awareness about American football in the UK. Aon's sponsorship deal was for 2012–13.[12]

### Example: Hermes sponsors Bundesliga

Hermes, the German logistics service provider, became a premium partner for Germany's Bundesliga in 2012 in an agreement lasting four and a half years as the official logistics company for the league. Part of the sponsorship agreement included a trophy tour through many of Germany's largest cities. The company's logo will be shown on sleeves of teams in both the Bundesliga and Bundesliga 2 (lower division).[13]

## 14.8 Chapter summary

With the enormous popularity of sports worldwide, it is no wonder that sports sponsorships are a significant portion of sports marketing activities. Very few 'regular' marketing activities are able to deliver the level of customer/fan intensity, diversity, and passion that sports can. Sports sponsorships can been negotiated for a number of different sports entity types: sports events (Olympics, FIFA World Cup, F1 events, NCAA Basketball's March Madness and Final Four, and the Super Bowl, among others); sports governing bodies (EPL, NFL, Bundesliga, NHL, MLB etc.); sports venues (MetLife Stadium, Emirates Stadium, CitiLink Field etc.); and athletes (almost any known athlete, but notables include Usain Bolt, Roger Federer, Rory Gallagher, LeBron James, Fernando Alonso, Lionel Messi etc.). Each of these sports entities provides potentially significant brand reputation benefits for their sponsoring companies and, as has been described, some companies sponsor multiple sports-related entities. The bottom line is that sports afford companies a distinctive way to generate exposure, reach fans, and change perceptions.

**CASE STUDY 1**

# Matthias Steiner

On 25 August 1982, Matthias Steiner was born in Vienna, Austria. His father, Friedrich Steiner, is the all-time leader on the International Weightlifting Federation Hall of Fame points list.[14] Matthias always dreamed of becoming a weightlifter, but he had a problem. He suffered from intense thirst, lost a ton of weight, and then his eyesight began to deteriorate. When he finally went to see a doctor at age 18 he was told that he had diabetes.[15] It didn't stop Matthias from chasing his dream to become a weightlifter, however.

Steiner participated in the European Junior Championships in 1998 and 1999, and in 2000 participated in the World Junior Championships. It wasn't until 2001 until Matthias began to win medals, taking home the bronze in 2001 and 2002 at the European Junior Championships. In 2003 and 2004 he won the Australian national championships and would compete for his home country at the Athens Olympic Games in 2004. At Athens, he finished in seventh place in the 105 kg category lifting 405 kg.[16]

He would continue to succeed at the Austrian national level in 2005, taking home another championship. However, later in 2005, the Austrian national team coach was replaced against Matthias's will and put his relationship with the national weightlifting federation under stress. At the 2005 European championships, Matthias and the Austrian team coach disagreed over which weight he should start at, too much time elapsed, and he missed his first attempt.[17] Later, the federation would accuse him of deliberate failure, which was the last straw for Steiner. He left the Austrian federation in 2005 and would start elsewhere.

A year before, a young German woman named Susann would see Matthias competing on TV. She bothered Eurosport commentators for his email so she could meet him and they finally consented.[18] Shortly thereafter they married. When Matthias ended his relationship with the Austrian weightlifting federation, Susann and Matthias moved to Germany and he applied for German citizenship. While he was applying for German citizenship, Matthias was not allowed to participate in any international competition. He did stay in shape, however, and was ready to jump back into international competition when he received his German citizenship in early 2008.[19]

Tragedy struck before the Beijing Olympic Games in 2007 when Susann was killed in a car accident. Matthias swore to her as she lay dying in the hospital he would realize their dream of his return to the Olympics.[20] The road to Beijing was not easy for Matthias, however. He lost 18 lbs, his diabetes flared up, and he battled depression.[21]

At the Beijing Games, it seemed as if Matthias used his grief to fuel him through the competition. And when it looked like Matthias would be out of contention to win a medal by missing his first two attempts at 248 kg, he increased his weight by 10 kg and won the gold medal at 258 kg. One of the more touching moments of the entire Beijing Games occurred when Steiner was on the medal stand wiping tears from his eyes as he clutched a photo of his late wife.[22]

**CASE STUDY 1** *(continued)*

After his victory in Beijing, Matthias took off for superstardom. He was on the cover of numerous magazines, approached for countless interviews, and participated as a commentator for several weightlifting competitions. He signed sponsorship deals with several companies and was closely followed by cameras at consequent weightlifting in the months following his gold medal.[23] He wrote a book, married a German former television host, and is now a father.[24]

He soon met more adversity, however. He had inguinal hernia surgery in January 2009[25] and then tore a tendon in his knee in 2011, which had him off his feet for weeks. The severity of his knee surgery even had analysts worried that he wouldn't qualify for the 2012 London Olympic Games. In April 2012, Steiner qualified for the Olympics and once again represented Germany in his third Olympic appearance.

 **QUESTIONS**

1 What is so interesting about Matthias's story?
2 If you are Matthias Steiner's agent, what types of endorsement deals would you seek?
3 If you were a sponsor, would you invest in sponsoring Matthias Steiner? Why or why not?

**CASE STUDY 2**

# Hot Wheels and extreme sports

What started as a modest gathering of 'extreme sports' athletes and enthusiasts in 1995 in Newport, Rhode Island for the inaugural Extreme Games has grown into one of the largest alternative sports events in the world. And because of the tremendous growth of what is now known as the X Games, major sponsors are lining up to take part in this event that occurs every winter and spring in the United States. To launch a new marketing strategy for the 18–34 age demographic that the X Games attracts, Mattel signed up as an 'event partner' in 2012, the second tier of its three-tiered sponsorship system.[26] The goal was for the toy company to re-engage men with the brand who played with the toy cars as kids in hopes that they would collect the toys again, or that they would play with them with their own kids.[27]

How would Hot Wheels achieve this formidable goal? By bringing its brand to life by creating a life-size re-enactment of one of its best-selling toys. Hot Wheels built a six-story double loop in which two cars (with real drivers) would race through the loop at 52 mph.[28] The stunt, which took place at the 2012 Summer X Games in Los Angeles was to break a world record of having two cars mounted on a vertical loop at once, which it did. In addition, the stunt attracted international media attention as the cars completed the loop-the-loop.[29] While not all sports sponsorship activations are as aggressive and extreme as Hot Wheels', it seems its venue choice was appropriate in the X Games to align with its new brand marketing strategy.

**NOTES**

1 Fraser, Adam (2011).
2 '10/1: majority of U.S. residents college football fans. . .nearly half watch NFL & college ball' (2010).
3 'Sponsorship opportunities' (n.d.).
4 Long (2012).
5 Anderson (2012).
6 Ozanian (2012).
7 Noble (2012).
8 Ibid.
9 Ibid.
10 Krishna (2012).
11 'NFL seals sponsorship at home and abroad' (n.d.); Cushman (2012).
12 Ibid.
13 'DFL announce Hermes as new premium partner' (2012); 'Hermes becomes Bundesliga's premium partner' (2012).
14 'Men's Hall of Fame points list' (2012).
15 'Steiner lifts weights with diabetes' (2009).
16 'Biography: sporting successes' (n.d.).
17 'No Austria comeback by Olympic champ Steiner' (2009).
18 Voight (2008).
19 'Steiner steals gold for Germany (2008).
20 Hardach (2008).
21 'Steiner steals gold for Germany (2008).

22  Hardach (2008).
23  'Partners and sponsors' (n.d.).
24  Reinke (2012).
25  Strossen (2009).
26  Mickle (2012b).
27  Mickle (2012a).
28  Mickle (2012b).
29  Ibid; see also Carter (2012).

 **REFERENCES**

'AIG finally unveiled as All Blacks shirt sponsor' (n.d.), Sports Marketing Frontiers, accessed 12 November 2012 at http://frontiers.sportbusiness.com/frontloaded/deal-tracker/aig-finally-unveiled-all-blacks-shirt-sponsor.

'Almost half the world tuned in at home to watch the 2010 FIFA World Cup South Africa[tm]' (2011), FIFA.com, 11 July 2011, accessed 7 April 2012 at http://www.fifa.com/worldcup/archive/southafrica2010/organisation/media/newsid=1473143/index.html.

Anderson, L.V. (2012), 'Why Barclays Center? Why not Nets Center?', Slate.com, 28 September 2012, accessed 29 September 2012 at http://www.slate.com/articles/sports/explainer/2012/09/barclays_center_how_corporate_naming_rights_work_and_why_stadiums_are_hardly_ever_named_after_teams_anymore_.html.

Badenhausen, Kurt (2012), 'The world's 100 highest paid athletes', Forbes Magazine, 11 July 2012, accessed 3 August 2012 at http://www.forbes.com/pictures/mli45igdi/1-floyd-mayweather/.

'Bayern Munich extends sponsorship deal with Deutsche Telekom through '17' (2012), Sports Business Global, 23 August 2012, accessed 27 August 2012 at http://www.sportsbusinessdaily.com/Global/Issues/2012/08/23/Marketing-and-Sponsorship/Bayern-Munich.aspx.

'Biography: sporting successes' (n.d.), Matthias Steiner, accessed 14 July 2012 at http://www.matthiassteiner.com/.

Carter, Beth (2012), 'Giant Hot Wheels track with double vertical loop and real race car drivers? Check', Wired.com, 20 June 2012, accessed 16 October 2012 at http://www.wired.com/playbook/2012/06/playbook_0620_jump/.

'Chelsea and Samsung agree new shirt sponsorship deal' (2012), BBCNews.com, 7 September 2012, accessed 8 September 2012 at http://www.bbc.co.uk/news/business-19522787.

'Cumulative TV viewership of the Olympic Summer Games worldwide 1996–2012' (n.d.), Statista.com, accessed 23 November 2012 at http://www.statista.com/statistics/236692/total-number-of-tv-viewers-of-olympic-summer-games-worldwide/.

Cushman, David (2012), 'SAP becomes sponsor of NFL; will deploy cloud solutions', SportsPro, 24 October 2012, accessed 24 October 2012 at http://www.sportspromedia.com/news/sap_becomes_sponsor_of_nfl_will_deploy_cloud_solutions/.

'DFL announce Hermes as new premium partner' (2012), Bundesliga, 15 October 2012, accessed 20 October 2012 at http://www.bundesliga.com/en/liga/news/2012/0000226505.php.

Finkel, Brian (2011), 'NFL stadiums with the most-expensive naming rights', 23 August 2011, BloombergBusinessweek, accessed 11 November 2011 at http://images.businessweek.com/slideshows/20110822/nfl-stadiums-with-the-most-expensive-naming-rights.

Fraser, Adam (2011), 'Collingwood AFL team handed double boost', 16 March 2010, accessed 22 November 2011 at http://www.sportspromedia.com/news/collingwood_afl_team_handed_double-boost/.

Gorman, Bill (2012), '2012 Stanley Cup final averages 3.01 million viewers, down 34% vs. last year', 13 June 2012, accessed 21 June 2012 at http://tvbythenumbers.zap2it.com/2012/06/13/2012-stanley-cup-final-averages-3-01-million-viewers-down-34-vs-last-year/18091/.

Hardach, Sophie (2008), 'Weightlifting – grieving Steiner wins gold', Reuters, 19 August 2008, accessed 14 July 2012 from http://www.reuters.com/article/2008/08/19/idININdia-35083120080819.

'Hermes becomes Bundesliga's premium partner' (2012), Hermes World, 15 October 2012, accessed 20 October 2012 at https://www.hermesworld.com/int/press/press_releases/pm-detail-all-companies_13888.html.

'100 years of Olympic marketing' (n.d.), Olympics.org, accessed 3 June 2010 at http://www.olympic.org/sponsors/100-years-of-olympic-marketing.

Krishna, R. Jai (2012), 'Pepsi pays $72 million to sponsor Indian cricket tournament', *The Wall Street Journal*, 21 November 2012, accessed 21 November 2012 at http://online.wsj.com/article/SB10001424127887324352004578132633409993830.html.

Long, Michael (2012), 'SAP and EMC complete MetLife stadium line up', SportsProMedia, 18 October 2012, accessed 19 October 2012 at http://www.sportspromedia.com/news/sap_and_emc_complete_metlife_stadium_sponsorship_line_up/.

'Magpies in the money with Wonga.com' (n.d.), Sports Marketing Frontiers, accessed 12 November 2012 at http://frontiers.sportbusiness.com/frontloaded/deal-tracker/magpies-money-wongacom.

'Men's Hall of Fame points list' (2012), IWF-Masters Weightlifting, accessed 14 July 2012 at http://www.iwfmasters.net/.

Mickle, Tripp (2012a), 'Mattel bringing Hot Wheels stunt to X Games', *Sports Business Journal*, 9 April 2012, 5.

Mickle, Tripp (2012b), 'X Games sells 11 sponsorships, meets goals', *Sports Business Journal*, 25 June 2012, 11.

'NFL seals sponsorship at home and abroad' (n.d.), Frontiers Sports Marketing, accessed 27 October 2012 at http://frontiers.sportbusiness.com/frontloaded/deal-tracker/nfl-seals-sponsorship-home-and-abroad.

'Nike once again the predominant shoe sponsor of NCAA women's tournament teams' (2012), *Sports Business Daily*, 16 March 2012, accessed 30 March 2012 at http://www.sportsbusiness-daily.com/Daily/Issues/2012/03/16/Marketing-and-Sponsorship/Womens-Shoe-Jerseys.aspx.

'No Austria comeback by Olympic champ Steiner' (2009), *Austrian Times*, 11 June 2009, accessed 14 July 2012 at http://www.iwf.net/2009/06/11/no-austria-comeback-by-olympic-champ-steiner/.

Noble, Jason (2012), '10 disasters in stadium naming rights', The Street.com, 16 May 2012, accessed 17 May 2012 at http://www.thestreet.com/story/11536541/1/10-disasters-in-stadium-naming-rights.html.

Ozanian, Mike (2012), 'Old Trafford's naming rights could fetch $1 billion for Manchester United's shareholders', Forbes.com, 11 August 2012, accessed 11 August 2012 at http://www.forbes.com/sites/mikeozanian/2012/08/11/old-traffords-naming-rights-could-fetch-1-billion-for-manchester-uniteds-shareholders/.

'Partners and sponsors' (n.d.), Matthias Steiner, accessed 14 July 2012 at http://www.matthiassteiner.com/.

Pfanner, Eric (2011), 'Nike introduces new look for French soccer team', *The New York Times*, 18 January 2011, accessed 23 July 2011 at http://www.nytimes.com/2011/01/19/business/global/19nike.html.

PwC (2011), 'Changing the game: outlook for the global sports market to 2015', December 2011, retrieved 17 February 2012 at http://www.pwc.com/en_GX/gx/hospitality-leisure/pdf/changing-the-game-outlook-for-the-global-sports-market-to-2015.pdf.

'Qatar Airways becomes Barcelona's shirt sponsors instead of Qatar Foundation' (2012),

Albawaba.com, 17 November 2012, accessed 17 November 2012 at http://www.albawaba.com/sport/qatar-airways-barcelona-shirt-sponsors-foundation-451255.

'Record TV audience tunes in to RWC 2011' (2011), IRB, 19 October 2011, accessed 11 December 2011 at http://www.rugbyworldcup.com/home/news/newsid=2059514.html.

Reinke, Emanuel (2012), 'Matthias Steiner: my little son fondles my leg', International Weightlifting Federation, 20 January 2012, accessed 14 July 2012 at http://www.iwf.net/2012/01/20/moment-matthias-steiner/.

Silver, Nate (2011), 'The geography of college football fans (and realignment chaos)', *The New York Times* 19 September 2011, accessed 2 February 2012 at http://thequad.blogs.nytimes.com/2011/09/19/the-geography-of-college-football-fans-and-realignment-chaos/.

'Soccer – Samsung renews shirt sponsorship deal with Chelsea' (2012), Reuters, 7 September 2012, accessed 9 September 2012 at http://www.reuters.com/article/2012/09/07/samsung-chelsea-idUSL6E8K7ATZ20120907.

'Sponsorship opportunities' (n.d.), UND.com, accessed 22 August 2012 at http://www.und.com/sponsorship/nd-corporate-sponsors-opportunities.html.

'Steiner lifts weights with diabetes' (2009), *Diabetes Parents Journal*, February 2009, accessed 14 July 2012 at http://www.diabetes parents-journal.com/english/archive/archiv-022009/steiner-lifts-weights-with-diabetes.html.

'Steiner steals gold for Germany (2008), Associated Press, 19 August 2008, accessed 14 July 2012 at http://www.2008.nbcolympics.com/weightlifting/news/newsid=235388.html.

Strossen, Randall, J. (2009), 'German superstar weightlifter Matthias Steiner has just undergone surgery', International Weightlifting Federation 4 February 2009, accessed 14 July 2012 at http://www.iwf.net/2009/02/04/german-superstar-weightlifter-matthias-steiner-has-just-undergone-surgery/.

'Super Bowl TV audience reaches record 111.3 million' (2012), Reuters.com, 6 February 2012, accessed 23 April 2012 at http://www.reuters.com/article/2012/02/06/us-superbowl-tv-idUSTRE8151Q020120206.

Taylor, Daniel (2011), 'Manchester City bank record £400m sponsorship deal with Etihad Airways', *The Guardian*, 8 July 2011, accessed 3 September 2011 at http://www.guardian.co.uk/football/2011/jul/08/manchester-city-deal-etihad-airways.

'10/1: majority of U.S. residents college football fans. . .nearly half watch NFL & college ball' (2010), Maristpoll.com, 1 October 2010, accessed 28 June 2012 at http://maristpoll.marist.edu/101-majority-of-u-s-residents-college-football-fans-%E2%80%A6-nearly-half-watch-nfl-college-ball/.

Thomas, Daniel (2012), 'Vodafone renews its sports sponsorship' FT.com. 1 July 2012, accessed 11 July 2012 at http://www.ft.com/intl/cms/s/0/612a9420-c373-11e1-966e-00144feabdc0.html#axzz2ErTMFdek.

Tribou, G. (2007), *Sponsoring sportif*, 3rd edition, Paris: Economica.

Voight, Benedikt (2008), 'Matthias Steiner lifts gold – for Germany and his late wife', *Der Tagesspiegel*, 19 August 2008, accessed 13 July 2012 from http://www.tagesspiegel.de/sport/starker-mann-matthias-steiner-hebt-gold-fuer-deutschland-und-seine-verstorbene-frau/1305502.html.

# 15
# Licensing and merchandising

**CHAPTER OVERVIEW**

As we have learned, sports marketing comprises a wide range of strategies and tactics designed to lead to increases in financial performance and improved brand reputation and image for the company. At the strategic planning level, financial improvements and reputational gains are the result of a sustained, dedicated commitment to position the sports marketer as a quality, differentiated firm, using the association with the sports entity to bolster the firm's credibility and awareness in the marketplace, ultimately influencing consumer preference for the sports marketer's company over its competitors. The intended financial gains come from increased revenues and/or profits from several areas: product sales, service and support, ticket sales, and licensing and merchandising. This chapter discusses the latter components of licensing and merchandising, bringing to conclusion the strategies and tools available to companies as they pursue their sports marketing activities.

## 15.1 Licensing

The global sports licensing market is $21.7 billion overall,[1] and sports-licensed merchandise is a large part of the total licensing market:

- Sports merchandising is 13.5 percent of the total licensing market in the United States.[2]
- Retail sales of professional sports licensed merchandise was $12.8 billion in the USA and Canada in 2011, up 5.3 percent from $12.15 billion in 2010.[3]
- Retail sales of collegiate licensed merchandise grew 5.1 percent to $3.3 billion in 2011.[4]
- In the USA in 2011, Major League Baseball (MLB) and the National Football League (NFL) each had approximately 25 percent market share, and the two leagues led the licensed merchandise sales for the sports market with growth rates of 5.5 percent (MLB, with $3.1 billion in revenues) and 5.3 percent (NFL, with $3 billion in revenues). Major

League Soccer (MLS) saw a 25 percent increase in merchandise sales to $394 million. The National Basketball Association (NBA) had an increase of 2.1 percent to $2 billion, and the National Hockey League (NHL) increased 5.8 percent with sales of $887 million.[5]

Licensing is in a legal area of sports marketing also known as intellectual property which describes the ownership of ideas and related intangible assets.[6] The concept of an intangible asset contrasts with a tangible asset in a important way: intangible assets, such as trademarks, lack physical characteristics so they literally cannot be touched or held; whereas tangible assets, such as computers, desks and chairs, can. This contrast is important to understanding one of the drivers of brand value, which comprises both tangible and intangible assets.

A license is an agreement that governs how a licensee (a person or business) is allowed to legally use a protected piece of intellectual property from a licensor (the entity that owns or represents the property) for use in a product or service, most commonly sold as licensed merchandise, typically in the form of apparel, sporting goods, video games, collectible cards, and accessories.[7] The range of products and services allowed can certainly be broader than this, but the final items are governed by the license agreements in an effort to ensure that a given sports entity's intellectual property is used only on approved and acceptable types of merchandise (this prevents using the IP on unacceptable items, such as socially and ethically inappropriate or questionable items).

Owners of intellectual property, such as governing bodies like the IOC (International Olympic Committee) or the NFL (National Football League), and athletes themselves, typically grant license agreements to official sponsors and suppliers, who then have the right to use the legally protected trademarks of these sports entities in the merchandise they develop and sell. The process usually begins with the licensee making an upfront payment, with subsequent payments called royalties paid to the licensor.[8] Royalties typically range from 5 percent to 10 percent for sports marketing products, with the specific rate determined based on a combination of factors, including: the licensee's industry, the needs of the licensor and licensee, and the conventional practice for royalty rates based on product type. In some cases, companies might agree to cross-license arrangements wherein the firms exchange licenses in lieu of payment.

The concept of intellectual property (IP) and intangible assets merits further discussion. Examples include trademarks and copyrights:

- *Trademarks*. Trademarks are symbols and/or words. In sports market-ing, license agreements prescribe the specific allowable usage of the trademark in merchandise by the seller.[9] Government authorities, such as the United States Patent and Trademark Office, typically grant trade-marks and, in the case of the USA, trademarks can be valid indefinitely so long as timely paperwork is filed with the USPTO every few years to keep the trademark current.
- *Copyrights*. A copyright protects works of authorship, such as writings, music, and works of art that have been tangibly expressed.[10]

IP can also include symbols (a graphic/image only), logos (generally defined as a graphic/image plus script or writing), likenesses (photo, image, paint-ing, drawing etc. of a person), names (organization or person), and slogans (concisely worded descriptor).

As briefly mentioned at this beginning of the chapter, sports licensing contributes value in several important ways:[11]

- *Revenue*. Licensing is a potentially lucrative means for generating revenue for both the licensor and licensee.
- *Brand value*. Licensing can contribute to improving the brand value of both licensors and licensees. Licensors want quality, reputable, and appealing products that are accurate representations of their brand; licensees want to align with sports entities that have the potential to enhance their reputation. At the same time, licensees will often empha-size quantity, even over quality, since increased unit sales will likely improve their revenues and increase their profits from the expanded audience purchasing the licensed offerings.
- *Relationships*. Licensing deals can inspire unique business relationships. In turn, these relationships can expand the reach of a particular sports property's reach (e.g., Manchester United and their multiple licensing deals that help the club reach a global audience).
- *Distribution*. Having strong distributions systems will enable both sports properties and their licensees to more effectively meet market demand. In addition, developing multiple channels is often in the best interest of both the sports property and the licensee.
- *Brand protection*. Licensing is a way to extend and expand a brand, both for the licensor and licensee. Give this, in a licensing agreement it is important that the various sports property marks are protected to main-tain the value and integrity of their brand, and it is also important for the licensee to make sure that these marks stay protected so that the authenticity of their merchandise is unquestioned. Counterfeit items are

a significant concern for both sides in a licensing deal, hence the need for brand protection.

As with any other area of sports marketing, licensees can also be subject to successes and failures on and off the field. The NHL lockout in 2012 severely impacted licensees, as well as businesses located around their local team. Fanatics.com reported that NHL merchandise sales were down 14 percent. In the collectable trading card business, where rookie cards drive business, manufacturers were unable to produce rookie cards because they could not access new players in uniform. While the lost NHL business cannot be easily replaced, some licensees can mitigate the damages of one league's lockout by securing deals with other major leagues.[12] Licensees can grow by finding new revenue sources. These include:

- *Diversifying.* Licensees can offer products in new categories not previously offered.
- *Specialized lines.* Licensees can tailor their merchandise selection to specific target audiences such as females, children, and so on.
- *Alternate uniforms/kit.* By offering limited edition and specialty uniforms, teams can increase merchandise revenue (the Oregon Ducks football team wears different uniforms every game; the NHL Winter Classic jerseys are limited edition 'throwbacks'; the Brooklyn Nets debuted a new logo and new jersey).
- *Promotions.* Sports properties can enhance the fan experience by offering discounts, giveaways, or exclusive merchandise for fan clubs.

## 15.2 Merchandising

Merchandising is defined as 'the arrangement of products in a physical or online store to maximize sale'.[13] Determining the appropriate mix of merchandise (in other words, the selection of items, from apparel to accessories bearing the licensed trademarks of the sports entity) must be based on the sports entity's knowledge of its customer base, which includes a detailed profile encompassing demographic (age, income, gender, ethnicity etc.), behavioral (what people do), psychographic (lifestyle) and geographic (location) characteristics. Students of marketing will quickly recognize these characteristics as the familiar components of the segmentation and targeting framework. Developing the merchandise mix incurs costs, including:

- *The purchase of license rights.* Sports properties will usually own their IP and grant permission through agreements to licensees to use the approved trademarks and/or related IP on selected products.

- *The purchase of materials.* Licensees must identify suppliers of materials and negotiate the cost of purchasing those materials and/or manufacturing them. The prices are usually based on volumes purchased, so licensees must be as accurate as possible in forecasting demand.
- *Point-of-purchase displays.* As with almost any consumer product marketing (sports and non-sports), marketers (licensees, in this case) create point-of-purchase displays for highlighted products. The displays are designed to feature the products in a visually compelling way and are intended to inspire purchase. The displays cost money, from design (whether in-house or through an external provider such as a marketing communications firm/advertising agency) to materials development to transportation and set-up.
- *Packaging.* Many products require special packaging to ensure the product is not damaged while being transported and subsequently displayed. Packaging is also useful for providing more written information and insight about the product. As with point-of-purchase displays, the services of design experts and materials providers are required and must be accounted for in the budget.
- *Slotting allowances* These are fees charged by retailers to manufacturers for placing products on their shelves; in effect, the equivalent of shelf space real estate. Suppliers/manufacturers/licensees typically negotiate these directly with distribution partners. The cost of these slotting fees must be added to the cost of marketing and promoting the product, and are usually captured within 'cost of goods sold' in financial statements.
- *Shipping and transportation.* Moving raw materials to manufacturing and, ultimately, to retail distribution locations requires the use of transportation services (air, rail, ship, truck), all of which are also part of 'cost of goods sold' and must be factored in the budget.
- *Credit card transaction fees.* Since most retailers allow credit card purchases, and banks charge retailers fees for using this service, those fees can also be considered part of the marketing budget, reducing the licensee's profits.

To account for these costs the sports marketer must develop a budget that forecasts expected revenues (based on a combination of market trends research, customer expectations, the marketer's own experience and instinct, and the company's realistic financial goals), subtracting these costs to determine the gross profit. The most common method for forecasting revenue from merchandise sales is the sports entity's estimation of average sales per person in attendance. Assuming 100 percent of the event's spectators and/or athletes purchase merchandise is unrealistic, so a reasonable estimate will be something less than 100 percent and will depend on the sports entity's knowledge of the attending customer, the merchandise selection, attractiveness, and uniqueness of the event, event-day surprises (such as a dramatic and unexpected outcome, or an unusual performance from the athletes), and even ancillary factors such as weather conditions (which can affect fan interest in merchandise purchases, particularly for outdoor sports events). Since less than 100 percent of the spectators will be purchasing merchandise, a per person purchase value must also be estimated. An approximate guide to estimating merchandise revenues and profits would look as follows:[14]

$$\text{Profits} = \text{Gross revenue} - \text{Cost of goods sold} \qquad (15.1)$$

Where:
Gross revenue = Per person purchase value x # of spectators expected to purchase;
Cost of goods sold = costs as shown above.

*Example:* assume a sports event has a per person purchase value of $2.10 and the number of spectators expected to purchase is 17 500 (out of a total 50 000); and cost of goods sold is 50 percent of gross revenues. The result is the following:

$$\text{Profits} = \$36\,750 - \$18\,375$$

$$= \$18\,375 \qquad (15.2)$$

The agreement between the merchandise retailer and the sports entity, such as a team or an event, is typically structured on terms favorable to the sports entity to minimize their risk. The reason for this is because the merchandiser is leveraging off the sports entity's established reputation, so the sports entity has the stronger negotiating position. For example, the sports entity will require that the concessionaire provide the merchandise at no cost, with any proceeds from sale give to the merchandiser once the event has ended, plus unsold inventory.

The types of merchandise range from timeless to time sensitive. An example of timeless merchandise would be logo'd apparel with the sports entity's primary insignia, logo, or slogan on it. Time-sensitive merchandise would include event-specific items that include the name and/or date/time of the particular event. Sales of timeless merchandise are easier to forecast since the sports entity's main identities tend to remain stable over time, whereas the time sensitive merchandise expires once the event is over. However, because time-sensitive merchandise is likely to be perceived by consumers as uniquely valuable, memorializing their attendance or viewing of a special event, then its unit sales may be higher than regular licensed merchandise.

Sports entities and their associated merchandisers can encourage more sales by broadening the distribution based beyond concession stands at the event itself and into the local market and selected retailers within. Online merchandise can and should be encouraged as another means for encouraging sales from even more customers, as well as social media campaigns. The sports entity's risk is in over-forecasting demand and having post-event inventory surplus as a result, which can lead to reduced profits if the merchandise has to be discounted to encourage sales of the remaining inventory.

## 15.3 Licensing plan

Details will vary, but a general planning sequence for licensing includes several steps:

1. *Determining the sports property to license.* Most leagues/governing bodies, teams/clubs, venues, and athletes allow the ability to license some or all of their IP. It is important for licensees to consider the relative value of their chosen sports property, how that sports property is perceived/valued in the marketplace, and whether becoming a licensee will enable them to achieve their business and growth targets. Licensors are interested in whether potential licensees are skilled and capable of adding to their revenues without diluting or harming their image.
2. *Negotiating the fee/cost payment terms.* Most licensors will require licensees to pay an upfront royalty, or non-refundable guarantee. In addition, a royalty structure will be negotiated based on the length of the agreement, projected quantities, and changes in the royalty as volumes change.
3. *Develop the agreement parameters.* Agreement parameters typically encompass product type, geographic location, periods of exclusivity, deliverables time frame, and excess inventory returns policy.
4. *Ambush/counterfeit protection terms.* Once a licensee is official, their interest is in ensuring the licensor protects them from ambush marketers and counterfeiters since these kinds of products are illegal and undermine the value of being an approved licensee.
5. *Measurements and reviews.* As with other areas of sports marketing, measurement and review expectations should be included in any agreement. This includes: merchandise product compliance, financial terms adjustments based on performance, marketing and promotion and so on.

*Example: The sports licensing process at Sports Media, Inc.*[15]

Sports Media, Inc. is a firm that specializes in helping companies (merchandisers) legally obtain, use, and distribute licensed properties in the

USA for sports marketing and brand promotion purposes. Its particular expertise is in obtaining past/retired player/athlete images and related assets:

1. Companies must submit the product/concept for approval.
2. If approval is given, then Sports Media will usually request a retainer fee before commencing work on licensed product development.
3. Approved merchandisers will then select the leagues/schools that are allowed to license the merchandiser's product.
4. Sports Media presents the proposed merchandiser's product to the selected leagues/schools for their approval.
5. Once leagues/schools approve the merchandiser's product, then the license fee (royalty) schedule will be finalized, including any advanced royalty payments and agreement duration.
6. The final contract is issued.
7. Sports Media provides the approved licensed content for use by the merchandiser in preparing a product for final approval.
8. Sports Media confirms whether final approval is given.
9. Assuming final approval is given, then product can begin and royalties will become due after the advance royalty has been depleted.

## Example: Football (soccer) licensed replica jerseys and kits

The top-selling club football replica jerseys in the world average 1.4 million jerseys per year. Table 15.1 shows the top ten clubs in the world.

**Table 15.1** Top ten football clubs by # of jerseys sold

| Club | Number of Jerseys Sold (avg. sales per season for the five years 2007–12) | Supplier |
|---|---|---|
| 1 Manchester United | 1.4 million | Nike |
| 2 Real Madrid | 1.4 million | Adidas |
| 3 Barcelona | 1.15 million | Nike |
| 4 Chelsea | 910 000 | adidas |
| 5 Bayern Munich | 880 000 | adidas |
| 6 Liverpool | 810 000 | adidas |
| 7 Arsenal | 800 000 | Nike |
| 8 Juventus | 480 000 | Nike |
| 9 Inter Milan | 425 000 | Nike |
| 10 AC Milan | 350 000 | adidas |

Source: Miller and Harris (2012). Based on research by Dr. Peter Rohlmann.

**Table 15.2** Top ten European football clubs by value of kit deals

| Club | Supplier | Start | End | Value per Year $ millions (revenues) |
|---|---|---|---|---|
| 1 Real Madrid | adidas | 1998 | 2020 | 49 |
| 2 Barcelona | Nike | 1998 | 2018 | 43 |
| 3 Manchester United | Nike | 2002 | 2015 | 41 |
| 4 Liverpool | Warrior | 2012 | 2015 | 40 |
| 5 Chelsea | adidas | 2006 | 2018 | 32 |
| 6 Bayern Munich | adidas | 1966 | 2020 | 26 |
| 7 Inter Milan | Nike | 1998 | 2019 | 24 |
| 8 Manchester City | Nike | 2013 | 2019 | 19 |
| 9 AC Milan | adidas | 1998 | 2017 | 19 |
| 10 Juventus | Nike | 2003 | 2016 | 17 |

Source: Miller and Harris (2012). Based on research by Dr. Peter Rohlmann.

Replica jerseys are part of an overall uniform, or kit, that players wear. In European football, the top ten kit suppliers and the value to the sports clubs are shown in Table 15.2.

## Example: Sports licensing in the National Football League (NFL)

In 2010 the NFL signed new apparel license agreements with Nike and New Era, plus five other suppliers, which commenced in April 2012 at the end of the league's previous agreement with Adidas. While exact figures were not known, industry experts estimated the value of the new agreements at over $1 billion for the NFL. The previous agreement with adidas was a ten-year, $300 million deal that began in 2001. The new agreement stipulates that Nike supplies the uniforms and apparel for the players and coaching staff while New Era supplies the hats.[16]

## Example: Sports licensing in the Indian Premier League (IPL)[17]

Bollywood has been an important entertainment element of India's IPL cricket since the league's inception in 2008. Both are extremely popular in India, creating lucrative and diverse merchandising opportunities. The IPL matches are popular with Bollywood stars and titans of Indian industry, creating events with plenty of celebrities and inspiring heightened fan buzz that is translating to merchandise sales. In 2010, merchandise sales for the top IPL teams averaged over $22 000 per matches, although sales from low-end teams were closer to $2000 sales per team. Since the number of matches has varied a bit over the seasons due to changes in the numbers of teams in the league, the total merchandise sales also vary, but assuming a $10 000 average per team per match, and an 80+ match season, means a reasonable estimate is $800 000 per year in total league merchandise sales.

## Example: FIFA Licensing

FIFA is football's (soccer's) global governing body. FIFA's licensing programs encompass four areas:[18]

- *Brand collaborations.* FIFA brand collaborators are a select group of companies whose reputations for quality help reinforce FIFA's efforts to create memorable experiences and products for fans. Four companies are official brand collaborators: Panini (creates FIFA's World Cup sticker albums); Electronic Arts (produces football video games); Hublot (luxury watchmaker that is also FIFA's official timekeeper); and Louis Vuitton (luxury goods brand that designed FIFA's World Cup Trophy travel case).
- *Print media and publications.* Official print publishers produce and disseminate publications with FIFA branded content, including updates about FIFA football competitions. FIFA also appointed an official, exclusive publisher from Latin America (Editora Abril S.A.). The agreement ensures the editorial independence of Editora Abril. Editora Abril will also produce official licensed publications about the FIFA World Cup in Brazil.
- *Philatelic and numismatic collections.* FIFA's philatelic (stamp) and numismatic (coin/medals/tokens) merchandise has been an important part of FIFA since 2004. The production and distribution of these items are designed to expand awareness about FIFA and its official trademarks worldwide.
- *Consumer retail licensing.* Official FIFA licensed goods are produced through this program, distributed through approved retailers around the world.

FIFA generated $37 million between 2007 and 2010 from its Brand Licensing Program.[19]

## Example: Olympic Games licensing

The Olympics have a licensing program that has grown successfully the past 25 years. The program is controlled by the Organizing Committees of the Olympic Games (OCOGs), which are each host city's main Olympics governing authority. The OCOGs operate under the direction of the International

Olympic Committee (IOC). The program is designed to protect the integrity of Olympic IP and official Olympic licensees through 'trademark legislation, education, monitoring and enforcement'.[20] The Olympics have a nearly 3000-year history of licensing-type programs, although during Ancient Greek times these programs did not have this precise description. As far back as 425 BC tetra drachmas (silver coins) were used to honor the athlete's success.[21] In the modern Olympic era, collectors' coins, as well as commemorate stamps, were the forerunners to today's more sophisticated licensing and merchandising efforts. The revenues generated from the sale of the coins and stamps were used to support the Olympic Games and the participation of Olympic teams from different countries. Table 15.3 shows the number of licensees and corresponding revenues to the IOC from the Summer Olympics.

**Table 15.3**  Summer Olympic Games licensing

| Olympic Games (Summer) | Licensees | Revenue to OCOG (US$ million) |
| --- | --- | --- |
| 1988 Seoul | 62 | 18.8 |
| 1992 Barcelona | 61 | 17.2 |
| 1996 Atlanta | 125 | 91 |
| 2000 Sydney | 100 | 52 |
| 2004 Athens | 23 | 61.5 |
| 2008 Beijing | 68 | 163 |

Source: Olympic Marketing Fact File (2012, p. 31).

Table 15.4 shows the number of licensees and revenue for the Winter Games since 1994.

**Table 15.4**  Winter Olympic Games licensing

| Olympic Games (Winter) | Licensees | Revenue to OCOG (US$ million) |
| --- | --- | --- |
| 1994 Lillehammer | 36 | 24 |
| 1998 Nagano | 190 | 14 |
| 2002 Salt Lake | 70 | 25 |
| 2006 Turin | 32 | 22 |
| 2010 Vancouver | 48 | 51 |

Source: Olympic Marketing Fact File (2012, p. 31).

## 15.4  Chapter summary

Licensing and merchandising investments help sports marketers reinforce their image, extend the brand's reach via the sale of logo'd apparel and accessories, serve as a reminder of the sports entity in general, and can serve as a vehicle for fans to express their loyalty. Official licensed merchandise is also a valuable way for the sports entity to partner with high-quality suppliers. As we have seen, licensed merchandise programs have grown around the world, with most major sports clubs and leagues supporting an active and ongoing assortment of varied items that appeal to fans. Of course, an important by-product of having a robust merchandising program are increased sales, profits, and more customers.

**CASE STUDY**

# Ralph Lauren merchandising

Very often in the sports world, the importance of superior technical aspects of apparel out-weighs the importance of high fashion. More recently, however, high fashion seems to be gaining favor in the world of sports merchandise as American fashion icon Ralph Lauren has taken a deep dive into sports. Though Ralph Lauren has made a name for itself in its partnerships with the USTA and Wimbledon in tennis, and by outfitting the US Olympic Team for the 2008–14 Olympic Opening Ceremonies, its presence in golf has been quite significant.[22]

Ralph Lauren launched its golf line in 1987 under the moniker 'Polo Golf'.[23] Since then, the American-style icon has grown its golf offerings into its other divisions including RLX and Polo Golf, each of which are defined by the words classic, timeless, and quality.[24] Polo has firmly rooted itself in the game of golf with sponsorships of some of the game's most well-known names including Tom Watson, Davis Love III, and Jeff Sluman since 1993.[25] The company also outfitted the US team at the Ryder Cup in 2006.[26] On a more conventional note, the company has made significant investments in more traditional advertising including print ads in *The New York Times* and *Golf Digest* magazine.[27] But perhaps Polo's most indelible and impressive mark on the game of golf is its deal with the US Golf Association (USGA) signed in October 2011 as the official apparel sponsor.

As part of the five-year deal, Polo will be outfitting 5500 volunteers, 300 USGA staffers, and about 1100 USGA committee members at each US Open tournament.[28] Another key tenet of the deal includes the design of the merchandise pavilion that goes up at the tournament every year. In 2011, at the first event part of Polo's official relationship with the USGA, the merchandise pavilion was a massive undertaking. In all, 30 tractor-trailers carried the contents of what would become the 36 000 square foot merchandise pavilion.[29] The pavilion resembled a permanent structure with woodwork and millwork accents that gave the space a distinctly Ralph Lauren feel.[30] Within the store, attendees would complete over 100 000 transactions with the help of 1200 volunteers at 52 terminals.[31] Attendees could also purchase Polo's newest line of exclusive US Open merchandise at the pavilion, with hats tending to be the most popular item sold.[32]

 **QUESTIONS**

1 While Polo's play in the golf merchandise world has certainly been described as 'the most exciting thing [the USGA has done] in merchandising', does bigger always mean better in the merchandising world?
2 With the recent influx of younger, more fashion-forward golfers on the tour, is there room for Polo to further experiment to appeal to all fashion tastes? Or, is golf too traditional a sport without room for innovation in attire?

## NOTES

1 'Sport licensing report 2012' (2012).
2 Miller and Washington (2012).
3 Ibid.
4 Ibid.
5 'Sports on the rebound: retail sales of licensed merchandise based on sports properties rises 5.3 percent in 2011' (2012).
6 Intellectual property' (n.d.).
7 'Introduction to licensing' (n.d.).
8 'What is royalty?' (2012).
9 'Trademark' (n.d.).
10 'Frequently asked questions about trademarks' (n.d.).
11 Linton (n.d.).
12 Lefton (2012, p. 4).
13 Basu (n.d.).
14 Davis (2013, p. 253).
15 'Sports Media product licensing' (n.d.).
16 Klayman (2010).
17 'Mumbai, Bangalore front-runners in IPL 3 merchandise sales' (2010).
18 'Income' (n.d.).
19 Ibid.
20 'Olympic licensing overview' (2012, pp. 31–3).
21 Ibid.
22 Long (2011).
23 Smith (2011).
24 Yasuda (2012).
25 Smith (2011).
26 Ibid.
27 Ibid.
28 Ibid.
29 Ibid.
30 Ibid.
31 Ibid.
32 Ibid.

## REFERENCES

Basu, Chirantan (n.d.), 'The definition of merchandising techniques', *Houston Chronicle*, accessed 14 December 2012 at http://smallbusiness.chron.com/definition-merchandising-techniques-18341.html.

Davis, John (2013), *Measuring Marketing: 110+ Key Metrics Every Marketer Needs*, Singapore: John Wiley & Sons (Asia) PTE Ltd.

'Frequently asked questions about trademarks' (n.d.), United States Patent and Trademark Office, accessed 14 December 2012 at http://www.uspto.gov/faq/trademarks.jsp#_Toc275426672.

'Income' (n.d.), FIFA.com, accessed 13 September 2012 at http://www.fifa.com/aboutfifa/finances/income.html.

'Intellectual property' (n.d.), *Entrepreneur Magazine*, accessed 14 December 2012 at http://www.entrepreneur.com/encyclopedia/term/82302.html#.

'Introduction to licensing' (n.d.), International Licensing Industry Merchandisers' Association, accessed 14 December 2012 at http://www.licensing.org/education/introduction-to-licensing/.

Klayman, Ben (2010), 'NFL signs apparel licenses with Nike, six others', 12 October 2010, Reuters, accessed 3 March 2012 at http://www.reuters.com/article/2010/10/12/us-nfl-apparel-idUSTRE69B4D320101012.

Lefton, Terry (2012), 'Lockout wreaks havoc on NHL consumer products business; licensees circle wagons', *Sports Business Journal*, 26 November 2012.

Linton, Ian (n.d.), 'Main goals and objectives in sports marketing', *Houston Chronicle*, accessed 30 May 2013 at http://smallbusiness.chron.com/main-goals-objectives-sports-licensing-37071.html.

Long, Michael (2011), 'Ralph Lauren named as open patron', SportsProMedia.com, 21 September 2011, accessed 13 October 2012 at http://www.sportspromedia.com/news/ralph_lauren_announced_as_open_patron/.

Miller, Alex and Nick Harris (2012), 'Exclusive: Manchester United and Real Madrid top global shirt sale charts', SportingIntelligence, 8 October 2012, accessed 13 October 2012 at http://www.sportingintelligence.com/2012/10/08/exclusive-manchester-united-and-real-madrid-top-global-shirt-sale-charts-081001/. Based on research by Dr. Peter Rohlmann at http://www.pr-marketing.de.

Miller, Richard and Kelli Washington (2012), *Sports Marketing 2013*, Loganville, GA: Richard K. Miller and Associates, p. 58.

'Mumbai, Bangalore front-runners in IPL 3 merchandise sales' (2010), MSN Sports.com, 4 December 2010, accessed 21 July 2011 at http://sports.in.msn.com/ipl2010/news/article.aspx?cp-documentid=3811321.

Olympic marketing fact file 2012 (2012), accessed 3 August 2012 at http://www.olympic.org/Documents/IOC_Marketing/OLYMPIC-MARKETING-FACT-FILE-2012.pdf.

Smith, Michael (2011), 'Polo dresses up US open merchandise sales', *Sports Business Daily*, 13 June 2011, accessed 14 October 2012 at http://www.sportsbusinessdaily.com/Journal/Issues/2011/06/13/Marketing-and-Sponsorship/Polo-USGA.aspx?hl=merchandising&sc=0.

'Sport licensing report 2012' (2012), EPMCom.com, accessed 14 December 2012 at http://www.epmcom.com/products/item132.cfm.

'Sports Media product licensing' (n.d.), SportsMedia.net, accessed 3 June 2012 at http://www.sportsmedia.net/MediaKit/Collegiate_Licensing/collegiate_licensing.htm.

'Sports on the rebound: retail sales of licensed merchandise based on sports properties rises 5.3 percent in 2011' (2012), EPMcom, 1 June 2012, accessed 11 June 2012 at http://www.epmcom.com/public/Sports_On_The_Rebound_Retail_Sales_Of_Licensed_Merchandise_Based_On_Sports_Properties_Rises_53_in_2011.cfm.

'Trademark' (n.d.), *The Merriam-Webster Dictionary*, accessed 14 December 2012 at http://www.merriam-webster.com/dictionary/trademark.

'What is Royalty?' *Blacks Law Dictionary*. 2nd. Ed. Web. 14 Dec 2012.

Yasuda, Gene (2012), 'Polo to branch out', GolfWeek.com, 29 February 2012, accessed 15 October 2012 at http://golfweek.com/news/2012/feb/28/polo-golfs-sponsorships-investment-authenticity/?print.

# Index